Computational Biology

Computational Biology

Edited by **Daniel McGuire**

SYRAWOOD
PUBLISHING HOUSE
New York

Published by Syrawood Publishing House,
750 Third Avenue, 9th Floor,
New York, NY 10017, USA
www.syrawoodpublishinghouse.com

Computational Biology
Edited by Daniel McGuire

International Standard Book Number: 978-1-68286-171-4 (Hardback)

Printed in the United States of America.

Contents

             Permissions

             List of Contributors

Preface

Computational biology is an emerging discipline dealing with applications of computational and data-analysis techniques to study biological systems. It is an interdisciplinary field which includes theories and concepts of molecular genetics, applied mathematics, statistics and computer science. The book presents researches and studies performed by experts across the globe. Diverse approaches, evaluations, methodologies and advancements in modeling biological systems, bioinformatics and genetics have been included in this book. It will prove to be immensely beneficial to students and researchers involved in this field.

This book is a result of research of several months to collate the most relevant data in the field.

When I was approached with the idea of this book and the proposal to edit it, I was overwhelmed. It gave me an opportunity to reach out to all those who share a common interest with me in this field. I had 3 main parameters for editing this text:

1. Accuracy – The data and information provided in this book should be up-to-date and valuable to the readers.
2. Structure – The data must be presented in a structured format for easy understanding and better grasping of the readers
3. Universal Approach – This book not only targets students but also experts and innovators in the field, thus my aim was to present topics which are of use to all

Thus, it took me a couple of months to finish the editing of this book.

I would like to make a special mention of my publisher who considered me worthy of this opportunity and also supported me throughout the editing process. I would also like to thank the editing team at the back-end who extended their help whenever required.

Editor

Development of genodynamic metrics for exploring the biophysics of DNA polymorphisms

James Lindesay[1], Tshela E Mason[2], William Hercules[1] and Georgia M Dunston[2,3]

[1]Computational Physics Laboratory, Department of Physics and Astronomy, Howard University, Washington, DC, 20059, U.S.
[2]National Human Genome Center, Howard University, Washington, DC, 20060, U.S.
[3]Department of Microbiology, Howard University, Washington, DC, 20059, U.S.

Single nucleotide polymorphisms (SNPs) represent an important type of dynamic sites within the human genome. These common variants often locally correlate within more complex multi-SNP haploblocks that are maintained throughout generations in a stable population. Information encoded in the structure of SNPs and SNP haploblock variation can be characterized through a normalized information content metric. Genodynamics is being developed as the analogous "thermodynamics" characterizing the state variables for genomic populations that are stable under stochastic environmental stresses. Since living systems have not been found to develop in the absence of environmental influences, this paper describes the analogous genomic free energy metrics in a given environment. SNP haploblocks were constructed by Haploview v4.2 for five chromosomes from phase III HapMap data, and the genomic state variables for each chromosome were calculated. An *in silico* analysis was performed on SNP haploblocks with the lowest genomic energy measures. Highly favorable genomic energy measures were found to correlate with highly conserved SNP haploblocks. Moreover, the most conserved haploblocks were associated with an evolutionarily conserved regulatory element and domain.

Key words: Information theory, entropy, genomic variation, biological information, genodynamics.

INTRODUCTION

The human genome consists of 3 billion nucleotides, most of which are fixed alleles. A significant number of sites (about 0.1%) consist of single nucleotide polymer-phisms (SNPs) non-randomly distributed across the human genome. SNPs are (usually) bi-allelic dynamic sites on the human genome whose allelic distribution reflects the homeostasis of a population within a given environment (Dunston et al., 2014). Here, environment will refer not only to geographic or geophysical parameters, but also to the complete interface of the population to biologic and evolutionary stresses. The defining charac-teristics of a population are directly reflected within genomic information measures that are maintained throughout generations. Populations are here defined by the maintained order and diversity of the whole genome in its environment.

In developing metrics for the interaction of the human genome with its environment, the genomic environment is the stochastic bath driving variations within a locally viable population. SNPs are dynamic sites that are often highly correlated into SNP haplotypes maintained with fixed frequencies within a given stable population. Combinations of SNPs that are very highly correlated within a population are said to be in linkage disequilibrium (LD). It should be noted that certain SNP allelic combinations never appear within the population. Therefore only certain SNP haplotypes are biologically viable and generationally maintained.

The dynamically independent statistical micro-states are SNP haplotypes together with SNP sites that are not in LD with any other SNPs. The linkage of several SNPs as conserved units that are passed between generations represents a type of statistical phase transition in forming complex dynamic units for a population within a given environment. It is therefore very useful to develop information metrics for SNP microstates that can quantify viable sequence variation in the human genome.

What is genodynamics?

Genodynamics explores nucleotide structure-function relationships of common sequence variation and population genetics, grounded in first principles of thermodynamics and statistical physics (Lindesay et al., 2012). Our use of the term "genodynamics" is conceptually unrelated to and derived totally independent of any prior use of this term in the published literature. Using genodynamics, we study the informatics of SNPs as dynamic sites in the genome. Viewing structural configurations of SNPs as complex dynamical systems, we earlier developed and utilized the normalized information content (NIC) as a biophysical metric for interrogating the information content (IC) present in SNP haploblocks. SNP haploblocks are defined by the location of the distribution of SNP haplotypes in the genome. The NIC metric, derived from Boltzman's canonical ensemble and used in information theory, facilitates translation of biochemical DNA sequence variation into a biophysical metric for examining 'genome-environment interactions' at the nucleotide level. From this biophysical vantage point, the genome is perceived as a dynamic information system defined by patterns of SNP and SNP haploblock variation that correlate with genomic energy units (GEUs), herein introduced and developed. The quantification of structural configurations encoded in SNP microstates using GEUs provides an additional biophysical metric for interrogating and translating the biology of common sequence variation.

MATERIALS AND METHODS

Entropy and information

Information can be quantified in terms of the maintained order of a given system. In the physical sciences, the concept of *entropy* quantifies the dis-order of a physical system (Susskind and Lindesay, 2005). Therefore, entropy can serve as an additive measure of genodynamic variation within a population. This is done by taking the logarithm of multiplicative independent probabilities p_h, which define the *surprisals* $\log_2 p_h$. The specific (or per capita) entropy of a SNP haploblock consisting of a set of strongly depen-dent bi-allelic SNPs is taken to be the statistical average of this additive measure:

$$s^{(H)} \equiv -\sum_{h}^{2^{n^{(H)}}} p_h^{(H)} \log_2 p_h^{(H)} \qquad (1)$$

where $n^{(H)}$ is the number of bi-allelic SNP locations in haploblock H, and $p_h^{(H)}$ represents the probability (frequency) that haplotype h occurs in the population. This measure of maintained (dis)order takes the value of zero for a completely homogeneous population with only one haplotype (since for $p_h^{(H)} = 1$, $\log_2 p_h^{(H)} = 0$) while it takes the value $s_{\max}^{(H)} = n^{(H)}$ for a completely stochastic distribution of all SNP alleles with all mathematically possible SNP haploblocks occurring with equal likelihood

$$p_h^{(H)} = \left(\frac{1}{2}\right)^{n^{(H)}}.$$

For bi-allelic SNPs that are not in LD, there are only 2 possible states at that location. Therefore, the specific entropy of the SNP location *(S)* takes the form:

$$s^{(S)} \equiv -\sum_{a=1}^{2} p_a^{(S)} \log_2 p_a^{(S)} \qquad (2)$$

where $p_a^{(S)}$ represents the probability (frequency) that allele a occurs in the population. As defined here, the entropy has no dimensional units. The total specific entropy of the genome in the specified environment is given by the sum over all genetically viable blocks, including correlated SNPs in the haploblocks, along with individual SNPs between the haploblocks that are not in LD,

$$s_{Genome} = \sum_{H} s^{(H)} + \sum_{S} s^{(S)} \qquad (3)$$

This insures that all dynamic SNP degrees of freedom are included in calculating the genomic entropy. Because this entropy measure is additive, it also quantifies the entropy within any region of the genome. The overall entropy of a population distribution is proportional to the size of the population $N_{Population}$, that is,

$$S_{Genome} = N_{Population}\, s_{Genome},$$ making entropy an extensive state variable.

Since entropy is a measure of the disorder of a distribution, a system with maximum disorder is one of maximum entropy. In contrast, the information content of a distribution is measured by the degree of order that the distribution has relative to a completely disordered one, that is, the difference between the entropy of the distribution and that of a completely disordered distribution

$IC = S_{max} - S$. Such an information measure is likewise additive due to the additive nature of the entropy (Lindesay, 2013).

In our previous work (Lindesay et al., 2012), a normalized information metric was developed as a means of comparison of the information contained within specific regions of the genome, as well as between various populations. This NIC value ranges between 0 and 1, where a value of zero indicates a completely random allelic distribution, while a value of unity represents a homogeneous allelic distribution without variation. The NIC for a given SNP haploblock (H) is defined by:

$$NIC^{(H)} \equiv \frac{s_{max}^{(H)} - s^{(H)}}{s_{max}^{(H)}} = \frac{n^{(H)} - s^{(H)}}{n^{(H)}} \tag{4}$$

One should note that unlike the information content, NIC is not an additive measure for multi-SNP haploblocks. The information measure for the whole genome in an environment must be calculated using the total number of SNP locations in the genome, as well as the total specific entropy of the genome.

Statistical energetics

The statistical "genomic energy" of a population in a given environment is expected to be an additive (extensive) state variable that depends upon the entropy, the populations of various allelic constituencies, and possibly the "genomic volume" of the environment, if population pressures have a significant effect on the environment. The functional dependence of the contribution of haploblock H to the average genomic energy U can be expressed using the differential expression:

$$dU^{(H)} \equiv T_E\, dS^{(H)} + \sum_h \mu_h^{(H)} dN_h^{(H)} - \Pi_E^{(H)} dV^{(H)} \tag{5}$$

where T_E represents an environmental potential (which is conjugate to the entropy state variable), $\mu_h^{(H)}$ represents the haplotype potential of haplotype h in SNP haploblock H,

$N_h^{(H)} = p_h^{(H)} N_{Population}$ represents the population of haplotype

h, and $\Pi_E^{(H)}$ represents any "pressure" by the haploblock on the environment that would result in expansion of the genomic "volume" $V^{(H)}$. In all subsequent expressions, any genomic effects that would modify the genomic volume will be neglected $\Pi_E^{(H)} dV^{(H)} = 0$.

As is the case for thermodynamics and statistical physics, it is quite convenient to define an additive free energy state variable that is most naturally expressed as a function of the potential of the environmental bath T_E and the populations, through the Legendre transformation

$$F^{(H)} \equiv U^{(H)} - T_E S^{(H)} \quad, \quad dF^{(H)} = -S^{(H)} dT_E + \sum_h \mu_h^{(H)} dN_h^{(H)} \tag{6}$$

A focus on the free energy as the fundamental dynamic state variable has the advantage of inherently including environmental-genomic interchanges as necessary considerations in describing the dynamics. It is a particularly convenient parameter for describing dynamics in a fixed environmental bath for which $dT_E = $

0. As one recognizes that living cells have evolved their cellular functions within the warm, wet physiologic environment, one can safely conclude that a homeostatic living population distribution has evolved directly in association with the ecosystem within which it is being characterized. Thus, we assert that the evolution of living populations cannot be separated from their interchanges with the environment. In a statistical environment that is stochastically varying, it is the genomic free energy rather than the genomic energy that is minimized. The genomic free energy is a state variable that balances between conservation and variation of SNP haplotypes within an environment. Minimizing the genomic free energy optimizes the population's survivability under environmental stresses, establishing the balance between conservation and variation in the dynamics of the population distribution.

For the genome, only the site locations and bi-allelic nature of the specific SNPs are conserved parameters. In addition, phase transitions involving the stability of SNP haploblock structures are common between differing populations, resulting in non-conservation of the number and SNP composition of the haploblocks. This is in marked contrast with the standard micro-units in statistical physics, whose universal energy states are only weakly dependent upon the environment, and have well defined conservation properties with regards to the creation of new states (or changing dynamic degrees of freedom). Therefore, rather than seeking universal energy measures that are independent of the genomic environment, the emphasis here will be based on establishing convenient genomic measures of the dynamics that are inseparably coupled with environmental parameters. Since the allelic potentials, given by

$$\mu_h^{(H)} = \left(\frac{\partial F^{(H)}}{\partial N_h^{(H)}} \right)_{T_E}$$, are the parameters

in the environmental bath that dynamically couple to the SNP haplotype unit h, the formulation will be developed in a manner that most directly interprets these genomic energy measures.

Using the differential form for the haploblock free energy

$$dF^{(H)} = -S^{(H)} dT_E + \sum_h \mu_h^{(H)} dN_h^{(H)}$$ from (Equation 6), we

can use the expression of the population with haplotype h given by

$$N_h^{(H)} = p_h^{(H)} N_{Population}$$ to expand the differential

$$dN_h^{(H)} = dp_h^{(H)} N_{Population} + p_h^{(H)} dN_{Population} .$$

Re-writing the variation of the haploblock free energy in terms of the population gives:

$$dF^{(H)} = \left(-s^{(H)} dT_E + \sum_h \mu_h^{(H)} dp_h^{(H)} \right) N_{Population} + \left(\sum_h \mu_h^{(H)} p_h^{(H)} \right) dN_{Population} \tag{7}$$

Population stability

Values for all of these additive genomic state variables can be likewise assigned to those SNPs that are not in linkage disequilibrium by simply replacing the particular haploblock index *(H)* in any of the previous formulas with the SNP location *(S)*. The total genomic free energy will be a sum over all SNP haploblocks and non-linked SNPs given by:

$$F_{Genome} = \sum_H F^{(H)} + \sum_S F^{(S)} \tag{8}$$

We further examined the condition that a stable population is defined by the genomic data. Our condition will require that the genomic free energy be a minimum under changes in the population within the local environment when the population is stable, that is, $\left(\dfrac{\partial F_{Genome}}{\partial N_{Population}} \right) = 0$.

The average allelic potential within a SNP haploblock

$\sum_h \mu_h^{(H)} p_h^{(H)} = \left\langle \mu^{(H)} \right\rangle$ will be referred to as the block potential

for haploblock *(H)*, while the average allelic potential at a non-linked

SNP location $\sum_a \mu_a^{(S)} p_a^{(S)} = \left\langle \mu^{(S)} \right\rangle$ will be referred to as the

SNP potential for location *(S)*.

From Equation 7 for the genomic free energy in terms of block potentials and SNP potentials holding the environmental potential and frequencies fixed, the population is seen to be stable if the overall genomic free energy satisfies:

$$\left(\frac{\partial F_{Genome}}{\partial N_{Population}} \right) = 0 = \sum_H \sum_h \mu_h^{(H)} p_h^{(H)} + \sum_S \sum_a \mu_a^{(S)} p_a^{(S)} = \sum_H \left\langle \mu^{(H)} \right\rangle + \sum_S \left\langle \mu^{(S)} \right\rangle \equiv \mu_{Geno} \tag{9}$$

where *a* shows the particular allele at SNP location (S).

Our population stability condition incorporates Hardy-Weinberg equilibrium (Hardy, 1908; Weinberg, 1908) in population genetics. Hardy-Weinberg equilibrium asserts that in order for the genomic distributions to meaningfully represent a stable population, the various frequencies of haplotypes and alleles should be stable. Since the frequencies directly determine the block and SNP potentials, a requirement that these environmentally dependent potentials remain fixed and sum to zero satisfies Hardy-Weinberg equilibrium. Such stable populations maintain the distribution of SNPs throughout the generations within the given environment. The genomic average allelic potential μ_{Genome}, which is seen to be the sum over all block potentials and SNP potentials, is seen to vanish if the population does not increase or decrease. This means that a stable population is balanced with regards to its overall sum over allelic potentials, $\mu_{Genome}=0$. The genomic free energy is lowered by a population with negative overall genomic potential $\mu_{Genome}<0$ if its size increases, while if $\mu_{Genome}>0$ the genomic free energy is lowered if the population decreases.

As is the case of thermodynamics, the additive allelic potentials $\mu_h^{(H)}$ are expected to scale relative to the environmental parameter T_E, and allelic potential differences should directly reflect in the ratio of the frequencies of occurrence of those haplotypes within the population. A functional form that has these properties is given by:

$$\frac{\mu_{h2}^{(H)} - \mu_{h1}^{(H)}}{T_E} = -\log_2 \frac{p_{h2}^{(H)}}{p_{h1}^{(H)}} \tag{10}$$

The genomic energy labeled $\widetilde{\mu}$ will be defined as the unique allelic

potential that will insure that a single (bi-allelic) SNP will be in its state of highest variation $\widetilde{p} = \dfrac{1}{2}$ within the given species. Similarly, a haploblock with $n^{(H)}$ SNPs in its state of highest variation with all mathematically possible haplotypes occurring with frequencies

$$p_h^{(H)} = \left(\frac{1}{2} \right)^{n^{(H)}}$$ will have a block potential of

$n^{(H)} \widetilde{\mu}$. The unit $\widetilde{\mu}$ will be universal across all populations of a given species, but likely differs between species. Solving the previous equation, the allelic potential of the haplotype *h* or allele *a* in an environmental bath characterized by environmental potential T_E can be expressed as:

$$\mu_h^{(H)} = \left(\widetilde{\mu} - T_E \right) n^{(H)} - T_E \log_2 p_h^{(H)}$$
$$\mu_a^{(S)} = \left(\widetilde{\mu} - T_E \right) - T_E \log_2 p_a^{(S)} \tag{11}$$

where the allelic potential for a single non-linked SNP location *(S)* has $n^{(S)} = 1$. Using our identifications, a lower allelic potential is then associated with a higher conservation of the SNP haplotype within the population, as high entropy is associated with large variation within the population. The ability to assign a well defined genomic energy measure for an individual haplotype once the environmental potential T_E is known allows this formulation to establish biophysical measures beyond statistical statements about the population as a whole.

Haplotypes and alleles with high genomic energy are highly unfavorable in the given environment. The value of the allelic potential $\mu_a^{(S)}$ that fixes a single non-linked SNP location (S) into a given allele ($p_a^{(S)} \to 1$) will be defined to be the fixing potential in the given environment. If the allele has this potential, it is homogeneous throughout the population. This value is directly related to the environmental potential through:

$$\mu_{Fixing} = \widetilde{\mu} - T_E \tag{12}$$

Thus, the allelic potential of any single SNP location cannot be determined to be less than the fixing potential through measurements in a single environment.

The population stability condition $\mu_{Genome} = \sum_H \left\langle \mu^{(H)} \right\rangle + \sum_S \left\langle \mu^{(S)} \right\rangle = 0$ can be used to

determine the environmental potential. By substituting the forms of the allelic potentials $\mu_h^{(H)}$ and $\mu_a^{(S)}$ expressed in terms of the probabilities into the population stability condition, an explicit expression of the environmental potential can be obtained:

$$T_E = \frac{\widetilde{\mu} \, n_{SNPs}}{n_{SNPs} - s_{Genome}} = \frac{\widetilde{\mu}}{NIC_{Genome}} \tag{13}$$

where $n_{SNPs} \equiv \sum_H n^{(H)} + \sum_S n^{(S)}$ is the total number of SNP locations on the genome. The average allelic potential for a given SNP haploblock, which has been defined as the block potential of that haploblock, then satisfies:

$$\left\langle \mu^{(H)} \right\rangle = \left(1 - \frac{NIC^{(H)}}{NIC_{Genome}} \right) n^{(H)} \widetilde{\mu} \qquad (14)$$

which has been obtained by simply taking the statistical average of the allelic potentials in (Equation 11), and substituting the expression for the environmental potential in terms of the genomic normalized information content.

These measures of genomic potentials have several convenient features:

1. The environmental potential T_E is inversely proportional to the IC of the whole genome. Low IC results from a high environmental potential, while a completely conserved genome has the lowest possible environmental potential, which we can define to have the value of one genomic energy unit $\widetilde{\mu}$ =1 GEU. A population with a completely disordered genomic distribution would inhabit an environment with infinite environmental potential.
2. SNP haploblocks that are highly conserved relative to the whole genome will have negative block potentials, while those that are highly varying will have positive block potentials. The block potentials typically lie within the range specified by $n^{(H)} \mu_{Fixing} \leq \left\langle \mu^{(H)} \right\rangle \leq n^{(H)} \widetilde{\mu}$ (although the lower bound is not rigorously required).
3. The number of highly correlated SNPs within the haploblock $n^{(H)}$ amplifies SNP haploblock allelic potentials.

One should note that while the environmental potential T_E, the block potentials $\left\langle \mu^{(H)} \right\rangle$ and the SNP potentials $\left\langle \mu^{(S)} \right\rangle$ can only be defined for a population, the individual allelic potentials $\mu_h^{(H)}$ and $\mu_a^{(S)}$ define an overall allelic potential for each individual in the population:

$$\mu_{individual} = \sum_H \mu_h^{(H)} + \sum_S \mu_a^{(S)} \qquad (15)$$

where the SNP haplotypes h and alleles a are unique to the individual. An individual's overall allelic potential is not a universal parameter, but rather depends strongly upon the environment. Thus, the overall allelic potential of an individual is not an essentially fixed microphysical genomic energy state, in contrast to the energetics of particles in statistical physics. An environment within which an individual haplotype or allele has a negative allelic potential tends to conserve that characteristic, while a haplotype or allele that has a positive allelic potential provides diversity and viable genomic variation within that environment. The value of the allelic potential gives a direct measure of the dynamic (un)favorability of a haplotype as a function of the environment.

Analysis of the block potentials associated with five chromosomes in the human genome

To demonstrate the usefulness of the previously defined genomic

state variables, the parameters will be calculated using genomic data for stable populations. We choose to utilize genotype data provided by the HapMap Project on the Yoruba in Ibadan, Nigeria (YRI) and the Utah residents with ancestry from Northern and Western Europe (CEU). Because of the time involved in the calculations, we have chosen representative large, medium and small chromosomes (1, 6, 11, 19, and 22) within the genome to examine the uniformity of the genomic potentials, and comparisons between populations.

Our formulation requires that the SNP haploblock structure that codifies the LD between local SNPs be established for a given population. For this purpose, we used Haploview, which is a software package in the public domain that is in general use. SNP haploblocks were constructed for the representative chromosomes using the confidence interval algorithm developed by Gabriel et al. (2002) in Haploview v 4.2 from HapMap phase III data. Haploview uses a two marker expectation-maximization algorithm with a partition-ligation approach that creates highly accurate population frequency estimates of the phased haplotypes based on the maximum-likelihood as determined from the unphased input (Barrett et al., 2005). Once the block structure of the population has been constructed, we have developed software that takes that data and calculates the genomic state variables for each of the chromosomes. This data was then graphed for analysis. In order to demonstrate the usefulness of the genomic state variables, rather than overwhelm the reader with the abundance of data contained within all the chromosomes that have been examined, the parameters are here demonstrated for chromosome 6 of both the examined populations. Additionally, an in silico analysis was performed on SNP haploblocks with the lowest genomic energy measures on chromosome 6 scanning for associated regulatory elements, signatures of positive selection, protein domains, molecular functions and biological processes using publically available bioinformatics tools (Boyle et al., 2013; Brown et al., 2013; Friedman et al., 2014; Gagen et al., 2005 ;Genome Bioinformatics Group of UC Santa Cruz, 2013; Greer et al., 2014; Lee and Shatkay, 2013; Sandelin et al., 2013; Sherry et al., 2012; Sigrist et al., 2013; Thorisson et al., 2012; Wu et al., 2013; Zhang et al., 2013).

It will be assumed that the environmental potential T_E that would be calculated from the NIC of the whole genome does not differ significantly from that calculated using the five chromosomes. This parameter takes the value $T_{E,(YRI)}$=1.26 GEUs for the YRI population, and $T_{E,(CEU)}$=1.12 GEUs for the CEU population.

RESULTS

The distributions of the NIC values across the genomes of the YRI and CEU populations are demonstrated in Figure 1. The overall distributions of NIC values for these two populations have a similar chromosomal distribution pattern despite the NIC values for the CEU population being higher than those for the YRI. In the CEU population, the NIC values for the chromosomes studied are as follows: $NIC_1 \cong 0.90$, $NIC_6 \cong 0.90$, $NIC_{11} \cong 0.89$, $NIC_{19} \cong 0.85$ and $NIC_{22} \cong 0.87$; while the NIC values for the YRI population are: $NIC_1 \cong 0.79$, $NIC_6 \cong 0.80$, $NIC_{11} \cong 0.79$, $NIC_{19} \cong 0.74$ and $NIC_{22} \cong 0.76$.

The genomic energy spectra for chromosome 6 of the YRI and CEU populations are demonstrated in Figure 2. In the YRI population, there were 6,810 SNP haploblocks with positive potentials and 6,738 with negative potentials. In comparison, the CEU population had 5,160

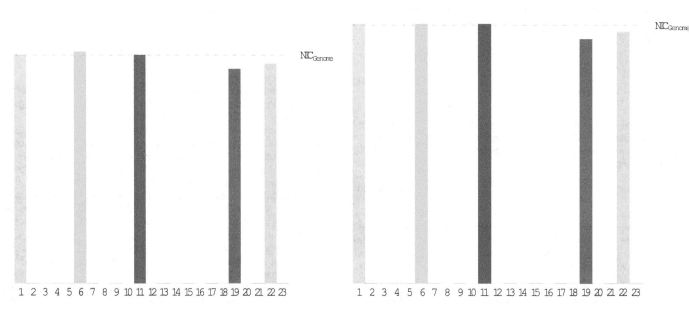

Figure 1. Analysis of NIC values for chromosomes 1, 6, 11, 19 and 22 in the YRI and CEU populations.

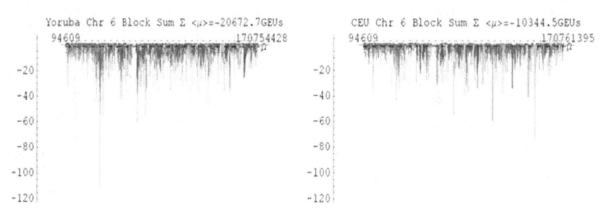

Figure 2. Analysis of the genomic energy measurements for chromosome 6 in the YRI and CEU populations.

SNP haploblocks with positive potentials and 3,600 with negative potentials. No highly varying SNP haploblock has a block potential significantly larger than the environmental potential T_E.

The block potential as a function of the number of SNP locations in the haploblock for each population was examined, and this is illustrated in Figure 3. A set of good fits for the block potentials for large haploblocks are given by:

$$\mu_{YRI}^{(H)} \cong \left(3.84 - 0.26 n^{(H)}\right) GEUs$$
$$\mu_{CEU}^{(H)} \cong \left(2.81 - 0.11 n^{(H)}\right) GEUs$$

where again, $n^{(H)}$ is the number of SNP locations in haploblock H. This indicates that those SNP haploblocks

that are highly conserved are seen to have bloc potentials that approach the fixing potential μ_{fixing} for th given specific environment times the number of SNF locations in the block.

The number of SNP haploblocks within given interval of NIC as a measure of the proportion of haploblocks tha maintain a specific degree of variation were plotted, an bar graphs of these proportions are demonstrated i Figure 4. The distribution for the CEU population i shifted relative to that of the YRI population, so that ther are an increased number of SNP haploblocks with highe NIC values. Also, it was noticed that there are no SNP haploblocks with a NIC value lower than ~0.2.

The block spectrum of SNP haploblocks in the MH(region for the populations of interest was examined. Th genomic energies for the YRI population ar

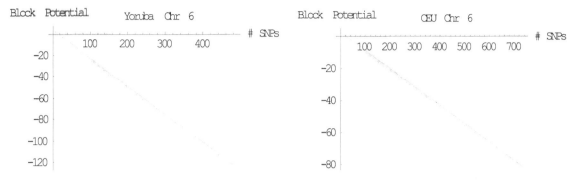

Figure 3. Comparison of the genomic energy spectra for chromosome 6 in the YRI and CEU populations.

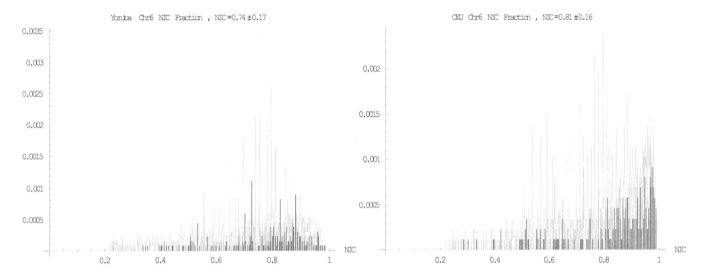

Figure 4. Comparison of the informatics of chromosome 6 in the YRI and CEU populations. The NIC value for the YRI population is 0.74±0.17 and 0.81±16 for the CEU population.

$\sum_{H} \mu^{(H)} \cong -2293\,GEUs$ as compared to CEU whose genomic energies are $\sum_{H} \mu^{(H)} \cong -751\,GEUs$. The most highly conserved haploblock found within any of the chromosomes thus far examined is Block 3013 on chromosome 6 in this region of the YRI population. It is worth noting that the most highly conserved haploblock in the CEU population, Block 7016, is also located on chromosome 6 however it is not in the MHC region.

In silico analysis of blocks 3013 in the YRI population and 7016 in the CEU population

Block 3013 is located between 6p22 and 6p21.3 bands (29,960,986-30,043,628) on chromosome 6 (Figure 6a). It has 441 SNP locations, with 226 of them being dynamic. It contributed a highly favorable averaged block potential of -112 GEUs to the overall genomic energy and had a NIC value of 0.991. Block 3013 has 253 SNPs in

genes and 188 SNPs in non-genic regions. This block included six genes: (1) Zinc ribbon domain 1 (ZNRD1); (2) ZNRD1-antisense RNA1 (ZNRD1-AS1); (3) Human leukocyte antigen (HLA) complex group 8 (HCG8); (4) Protein phosphatase 1 regulatory inhibitor subunit 11 (PPP1R11); (5) HLA-J and (6) Ring finger protein 39 (RNF39) as shown in Figure 6a.

ZNRD1, PPP1R11 and RNF39 are genes with functional proteins, whereas HCG8 and ZNRD1-AS1 are both non-coding RNAs (ncRNAs). HLA-J is a transcribed pseudogene. ZNRD1, PPP1R11, and RNF39 are highly conserved across species ranging from chimpanzee to zebrafish. These genes also display signatures of positive selection, but only in populations of European descent. Several putative and confirmed transcription factor binding sites (TFBS) are in Block 3013. Also, several broadly conserved microRNAs (miRNAs) are in Block 3013. It is worth noting that the ncRNA, ZNRD1-AS1, is a natural antisense transcript (NAT) that regulates the expression of ZNRD1.

Block 7016 is located on the 6q24 band (145,851,676-

Table 1. Protein domains associated with functional genes located in block 3013 (YRI) and block 7016 (CEU). The protein sequences were scanned using PROSITE, a database of protein domains, families and functional sites. CDART, a domain architecture retrieval tool, was used to identify evolutionarily conserved domains which are in lowercase; while those in boldface are common in both blocks.

Protein domains	ZNRD1	PPP1R11	RNF39	EPM2A	FBXO30	SHPRH
carbohydrate binding module family 20 (CBM)				x		
Carbohydrate-binding-like fold				X		
Dual Specificity Phosphatase, Catalytic Domain				X		
protein-tyrosine/dual specificity phosphatase				x		
c-terminal helicase						x
Helicase, superfamily ½, ATP-binding domain						X
linker histone H1/H5, domain H15						x
P-loop containing nucleoside triphosphate hydrolase						X
SNF2-related Domain						X
WW Domain						X
zinc finger	x		x		x	x
f-box domain, cyclin-like					x	
TRAF-like domain					X	
b30.2/spry			x			
Butyrophilin-like			X			
Concanavalin A-like			X			
SPRY-associated			X			
SPla/RY anodine receptor SPRY			X			
protein phosphatase inhibitor		x				

146,351,676) on chromosome 6 (Figure 6b). This block contributed a highly favorable averaged block potential of -73.85 GEUs to the overall genomic energy and had a NIC value of 0.995. Block 7016 contains 666 SNPs, with 353 of them being dynamic. This block has 399 SNPs in genes and 267 SNPs in non-genic regions. It included four genes: (1) Epilepsy, progressive myoclonus type 2, Laforin disease [laforin] (EPM2A); (2) Uncharacterized protein (RP11-54515.3); (3) SNF2 histone linker PHD RING helicase E3 ubiquitin protein ligase (SHPRH) and (4) F-box protein 30 (FBXO30) as shown in Figure 6b.

EPM2A, SHPRH and FBXO30 are genes with functional proteins whereas RP11-54515.3 is a ncRNA. The protein coding genes located in this block are also highly conserved across species ranging from chimpanzee to *Arabidopsis thaliana*. Even though the protein coding genes in this block are highly conserved across species, there were no signatures of positive selection associated with any of the genes in this block. There are several putative and confirmed TFBS associated with Block 7016. Like Block 3013, Block 7016 also has several broadly conserved miRNAs. The ncRNA, RP11-54515.3, is also a NAT which regulates the expression of SHPRH and FBXO30.

Listed in Table 1 are the protein domains associated with the genes in Blocks 3013 and 7016, while Table 2 outlines the molecular functions associated with these genes. Table 3 depicts the biological processes associated with the genes in these blocks. With regard to their protein domains, both blocks contain genes with evolutionarily conserved domains which are in lowercase in Table 1. Also, in boldface in Table 1 are the protein domains that both blocks have in common. In Table 2, the molecular functions that are associated with one or more evolutionarily conserved protein domains are in lowercase while those molecular functions that both blocks have in common are in boldface. With regard to their biological processes, there were no commonalities between the two blocks. However, those processes associated with one or more evolutionarily conserved protein domains found in Blocks 3013 and 7016 are in lowercase. It is worth noting that the ncRNAs and pseudogene were excluded from this analysis due to the fact that they are non-coding genes and would lack said domains, functions and processes.

DISCUSSION

We have developed genomic energy measures for the human genome that relate the distribution of alleles within a stable population to state variables associated with the environment within which that population resides. The state variables defined by common variations utilize the entropy of the statistical distribution of alleles to establish normalized information measures for persistent dynamic units within arbitrary regions of the genome, as well as for the genome as a whole. For our initial analysis, YRI and

Table 2. Molecular functions associated with the genes in block 3013 (YRI) and block 7016 (CEU). The molecular functions were determined by searching BioGPS, a gene annotation portal. Functions associated with one or more of the evolutionarily conserved protein domains are in lowercase, while those in boldface are common in both blocks.

Molecular functions	ZNRD1	PPP1R11	RNF39	EPM2A	FBXO30	SHPRH
Protein Binding				X		
protein ser/thr phosphatase activity				x		
protein try phosphatase activity				x		
protein ser/thr/tyr phosphatase activity				x		
starch binding				x		
ATP Binding						X
dna binding						x
helicase activity						x
ligase activity						x
zinc ion binding	**x**		**x**		**x**	**x**
ubiquitin-protein ligase activity					x	
DNA-directed RNA Polymerase Activity	X					
Nucleic Acid Binding	X					
protein phosphatase inhibitor activity		x				

Table 3. Biological processes associated with the genes in blocks 3013 (YRI) and 7016(CEU). The biological processes were determined using the web-based gene annotation tool, BioGPS. Those processes that are associated with one or more of the evolutionarily conserved protein domain are in lowercase.

Biological processes	ZNRD1	PPP1R11	RNF39	EPM2A	FBXO30	SHPRH
Behavior				X		
glycogen metabolic process				x		
Nervous System Development				X		
peptidyl-tyrosine dephosphorylation				x		
protein dephosphorylation				x		
DNA Repair						X
nucleosome assembly						x
protein ubiquitination						x
Nucleobase-Containing Compound Metabolic Process	X					
DNA-Dependent Transcription	X					

CEU were chosen as representative populations in or very near homeostasis with their respective environments. Moreover, these populations have significant differences in the degree of variation in SNP allele and haplotype frequencies. As demonstrated in Figure 1, the YRI population has overall greater variation, while the CEU population exhibits more conservation, as quantified by its higher overall NIC. In both populations, it is clear that each of the five chromosomes examined in this study has a NIC value within 10% of the composite NIC value for that population. Also, the larger chromosomes have NIC values that seem to be quite representative of the composite NIC value for that population, while the smaller chromosomes seem to maintain slightly higher variation. Moreover, the relative distribution of conservation amongst the chromosomes seems to take the same shape between

the two populations. Whether these features are fundamental properties of the genome remains an unsettled question for further studies. We will first expand our exploration to include all chromosomes for the selected populations; then include all populations we expect to be in environmental homeostasis. The formulation should be applicable to all populations in quasi-homeostasis consistent with publically available genomic distribution data.

We further made comparisons of genomic energy measures between the individual SNP haploblocks within chromosome 6 which is illustrated in Figure 2. We developed a genomic energy spectrum by plotting the block potential of each haploblock in GEUs as a function of its location on the chromosome. Since the block potential is an average of the allelic potentials of the various

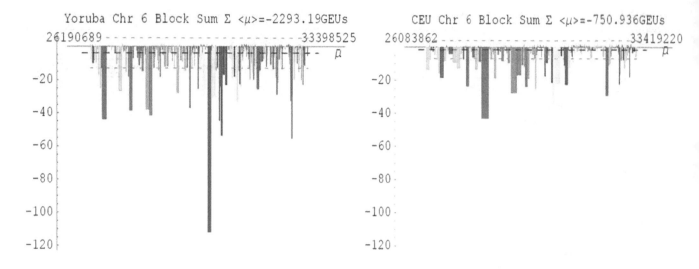

Figure 5. Comparison of the major histocompatibility complex (MHC) region on chromosome 6 for the YRI and CEU populations.

haplotypes that make up the haploblock, such genomic energy spectra describe the population as a whole. Given that their sum must vanish, it was initially expected that the spectrum would display an even distribution of positive and negative potentials. However, it is clear that although those haploblocks contributing positive block potential are uniformly distributed, those haploblocks contributing negative block potentials are far fewer and more conserved, displaying an inverted Manhattan-plot profile.

There is another interesting characteristic of the block potentials that was seen across all the chromosomes examined. This feature was discovered upon exploring the dependency of the block potentials upon the number of SNP locations within those haploblocks (Figure 3). Although the block potential per SNP varied somewhat for haploblocks containing fewer than ~50 SNPs, the block potential per SNP for larger haploblocks is constant within a given population, regardless of the chromosome examined. The slope of this linear relationship is the fixing potential in the given environment, suggesting that larger haploblocks have been "optimally" shaped by the environment. This is sensible when recognizing that as block size increases, relatively fewer variations remain biologically viable.

It was instructive to directly compare the informatics of chromosome 6 in the two populations. The NIC takes values between zero and one, where a value of zero indicates maximal variation in SNP haplotypes, while a value of one indicates complete sequence homogeneity of the population. We plotted the number of SNP haploblocks within given intervals of NIC as a measure of the proportion of haploblocks that maintain a specific degree of variation (Figure 4). It is clear that the distribution of the NIC values for the CEU population is shifted towards one relative to that of the YRI population. Our prior studies (Lindesay et al., 2012) demonstrated

that those SNP haploblocks with low NIC were associated with innate immune regulation and functions that require rapid response to environmental stresses. It is also worth noting that neither population has haploblocks with NIC values lower than ~0.2. This indicates that many mathematically possible variations of alleles within the haploblocks are not viable within these stable human populations.

To further examine the biophysical interpretations of genomic energies, we considered the block spectrum of SNP haploblocks in the MHC region for the populations of interest. A striking feature of comparison between the spectra is that despite the overall higher diversity in the YRI population as quantified in its considerably lower NIC when compared to the CEU population, the YRI population had genomic energies that were considerably

more conserved $\sum_{H} \mu^{(H)} \cong -2293\,GEUs$ as compared

to those of the CEU population $\sum_{H} \mu^{(H)} \cong -751\,GEUs$.

This is also apparent from the lower value for the average block potential demonstrated by the middle dashed lines in Figure 5. It is intriguing to find that despite the relatively large difference between YRI and CEU in their composite NIC values (~13%), the NIC values of their respective MHC regions were within 2%, indicating comparable normalized information content (NIC). This results in considerably lower GEUs for alleles in the MHC region of the YRI as compared to the CEU population (~300%). Within a given environment, the MHC region seems to adjust its GEUs to conserve its NIC.

Given that this region is important for encoding immune

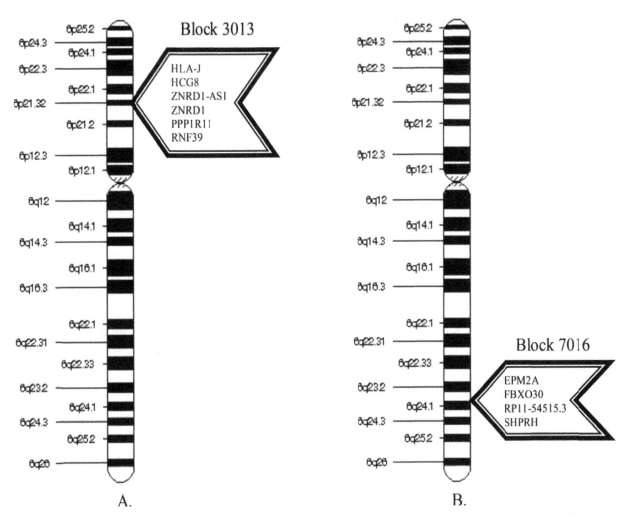

Figures 6a and 6b. The ideogram on the left is of chromosome 6 illustrating the location of Block 3013 in the YRI population, while the ideogram on the right illustrates the location of Block 7016 in the CEU population on chromosome 6.

responses, it is expected that it would be particularly sensitive to environmental influences. Surprisingly, the most highly conserved haploblock found within any of the chromosomes thus far examined is the Block 3013 on chromosome 6 in the MHC region of the YRI population, while the most highly conserved haploblock in the CEU population is also on chromosome 6, Block 7016, though this block is not located in the MHC region. Both blocks have NIC values approaching one (complete sequence homogeneity of the population) and the protein coding genes located in these blocks are highly conserved across species, implying that these genes may play a fundamental role in the biological processes necessary for life. The protein coding genes ZNRD1, RNF39 and PPP1R11, along with the ncRNA ZNRD1-AS1, have been associated with disease states that are related to autoimmunity, immunity, and infection; while EPM2A and SHPRH have been associated with glycogen metabolism, cancer, and chemical dependency (Hindorff et al., 2013; Becker et al., 2013). In addition to this, a conserved

regulatory element, NAT, was also found in these two blocks. NATs are an evolutionarily conserved group of ncRNAs that have been shown to mediate a number of cellular processes ranging from epigenetic modifications to regulation of transcription and post-transcription of protein coding genes in a multitude of species (Scherbakov and Garber, 2000; Havilio et al., 2005; David et al., 2006; Wang et al., 2005; Jen et al., 2005; Chen et al., 2004; Yelin et al., 2003; Zhang et al., 2006; Kiyosawa et al., 2003; Wang et al., 2008; Li et al., 2006, 2008; Sun et al., 2006; Chan et al., 2006; Rosok and Sioud, 2005; Imamura et al., 2004; Sleutels et al., 2000; Lee et al., 1999; Khochbin et al., 1992; Krystal et al., 1990; Munroe and Lazar, 1991; Enerly et al., 2005; Mihola et al., 2007; Volk et al., 1989; Kiyosawa et al., 2005; Kumar and Carmichael, 1997; Rossignol et al., 2002; Lapidot and Pilpel, 2006). St. Laurent and Wahlestadt (2007) have proposed that throughout evolutionary history, ncRNAs have experienced dramatic expansions that were in concert with increased organismal complexity. Pang et al. (2006) have shown that between mouse and human the sequence homology of the NATs (less than 70%) is equivalent to the sequence homology present in introns. This relaxation of evolutionary constraint may allow NATs to evolve at a faster rate as compared to other ncRNAs (Qu and Adelson, 2012). Studies suggest that the transition from unicellular organisms to multicellular organisms may have been possible due to the pervasive incorporation of ncRNAs into the genomes of early multicellular organisms (Gagen et al., 2005; Taft et al., 2007; Mattick, 2004, 2007). Georges St. Laurent et al. (2007) regard ncRNAs as "molecular information processors" that enhance the performance of cellular processes by integrating high density information between functional networks thereby facilitating the refined incorporation and collaborative action of many different molecular machines. For every species that has been sequenced to date, there is a correlation between organismal complexity and the number of ncRNAs (Taft et al., 2007), which has led to the view that ncRNAs are central to the information processing of complex organisms (Mattick, 2007; St. Laurent and Wahlestadt, 2007).

Moreover, we observed that Blocks 3013 (YRI) and 7016 (CEU) had genes that bind zinc ions and contain zinc finger (ZNF) domains. Zinc is a heavy metal that is an essential structural component of many proteins which include intracellular signaling enzymes and transcription factors (Vallee and Auld, 1993; Prasad, 1995). Zinc and ZNF domains play an important role in a number of biological functions, including wound healing, cellular communication, immune function, cell division, nucleic acid metabolism, cell replication, synaptic plasticity and protein synthesis (Classen et al., 2011; Sandstead, 1994; McCarthy et al., 1992; Solomons, 1998; Prasad, 1995; Fabris and Mocchegiani, 1995; Bitanihirwe and Cunningham, 2009; Murakami and Hirano, 2008). Zinc can be found in the brain, muscle, bone, kidney and liver (Wapnir, 1990; Pfeiffer and Braverman, 1982). The earliest use of zinc appears ~3.5 billion years ago (bya) and is believed to have been utilized as a messenger in nerve signaling, while the ZNF motif was associated with hormonal signaling (Williams, 2012). Likewise, it was noted that during times of rapid evolution, as seen in the Cambrian Explosion ~0.54 bya, dramatic expansion of ZNF domains occurred in response to the changing chemical composition of the sea shown by geochemical evidence of the accelerated rise of oxygen in the atmosphere, the increase in sulphate in the sea and the sedimentation of trace elements including zinc (Williams, 2012). This illustrates how life has adapted to its ever changing environment. In addition, the increase in the zinc content of proteins has been associated with the evolution of cellular complexity (Frausto da Silva and Williams, 2001; Williams and Frausto da Silva, 2006; Dupont et al., 2010; Zhang and Gladyshev, 2009).

In summary, the use of genomic energy units (GEUs) as a biophysical metric in SNP haploblock analysis has provided insights into the inherent structure and conservation of information in the human genome. We have demonstrated that highly favorable allelic potentials correlate with highly conserved genomic information units, in this case SNP haploblocks. Furthermore, the protein coding genes associated with the haploblocks of lowest block potential have strong homology across species underlining their fundamental role in the biological processes necessary for life. In addition to this, a conserved regulatory element and an evolutionarily conserved protein domain were also found in these blocks.

The development of genomic energy measures for the human genome relates the distribution of allele frequencies within a stable population to state variables associated with the environment within which that population resides. The state variables defined by the frequencies of common variants utilize the entropy of the statistical distribution of alleles to establish normalized information measures. Moreover, 'genodynamics' introduces more robust metrics for defining populations based on the genotypes of all individuals in the population as opposed to many current metrics based on the most frequent or common genotype in the population.

The NIC of the whole genome was found to determine an overall environmental potential that is a state variable which parameterizes the extent to which the environment drives variation and diversity within the population. Once this environmental potential (which is canonically conjugate to the entropy) has been determined, the genomic energies of individual alleles (nucleotides) and sets of alleles (haplotypes), as well as statistically averaged genomic energies for each persistent dynamic unit (haploblocks), can be directly calculated.

The assignment of genomic energies to alleles within a given environment allows the parameterization of specific environmental influences upon shared alleles across populations in varying environments. We are examining simple allelic dependencies on environmental parameters for future presentation.

Conflict of Interests

The authors have not declared any conflict of interests.

ACKNOWLEDGEMENTS

The authors wish to express appreciation for the continuing support of the National Human Genome Center, and the Computational Physics Laboratory, at Howard University. This research was supported in part by NIH Grant NCRR 2 G12 RR003048 from the RCMI Program, Division of Research Infrastructure. We also acknowledge Zahra Dawson for developing computer programs for calculating biophysical metrics from Haploview raw data.

Abbreviations: SNPs, Single nucleotide polymorphisms; **LD,** linkage disequilibrium; **NIC,** normalized information content; **IC,** information content; **T_E,** environmental potential; **GEUs,** genomic energy units; **YRI,** Yoruba in Ibadan, Nigeria; **CEU,** Utah residents with ancestry from Northern and Western Europe; **MHC,** major histocompatibility complex; **ZNRD1,** zinc ribbon domain 1; **ZNRD1-AS1,** ZNRD1-antisense RNA1; **HLA,** human leukocyte antigen; **HCG8,** human leukocyte antigen complex group 8; **PPP1R11,** protein phosphatase 1 regulatory inhibitor subunit 11; **HLA-J,** human leukocyte antigen J; **RNF39,** ring finger protein 39; **ncRNAs,** non-coding RNAs; **TFBS,** transcription factor binding sites; **miRNAs,** microRNAs; **NAT,** natural antisense transcript; **EPM2A,** epilepsy, progressive myoclonus type 2, Laforin disease [laforin]; **RP11-54515.3,** uncharacterized protein; **SNF2,** sucrose nonfermentable 2; **PHD,** plant homeo domain; **RING,** really interesting new gene; **E3,** ubiquitin ligase; **SHPRH,** SNF2 histone linker PHD RING helicase E3 ubiquitin protein ligase; **FBXO30,** F-box protein 30; **ZNF,** zinc finger; **bya,** billion years ago.

Bioinformatics Tools utilized for this manuscript:
GAD, Regulome dB, GENE, CDART, GWAS catalog, F-SNP, dbSNP, PROSITE, HapMap, BioGPS, NATs DB, TargetScan Human, ConSite, USCS Genome Browser

REFERENCES

Barrett JC, Fry B, Maller J, Daly MJ (2005). Haploview: analysis and visualization of LD and haplotype maps. Bioinformatics 21:263-265.

Becker KG, Barnes KC, Bright TJ, Wang SA (2013). Genetic Association Database Available at http://geneticassociationdb.nih.gov/. Accessed June 2013.

Bitanihirwe BK, Cunningham MG (2009). Zinc: the brain's dark horse. Synapse 63: 1029.

Boyle AP, Hong EL, Hariharan M, Cheng Y, Schaub MA, Kasowski M, Karczewski KJ, Park J, Hitz BC, Weng S, Cherry JM, Synder M (2013). Regulome DB: Annotation of functional variation in personal genomes. Available at: http://www.regulomedb.org/. Accessed June 2013.

Brown G, Wallin C, Tatusova T, Pruitt K, Maglott D (2013). Gene: Integrated Access to Genes of Genomes in Reference Sequence Collection. Available at: http://www.ncbi.nlm.nih.gov/gene.Accessed June 2013.

Chen J, Sun M, Kent WJ, Huan X, Xie H, Wang W, Zhou G, Shi RZ, Rowley JD (2004). Over 20% of human transcripts might form sense-antisense pairs. Nucleic Acids Res. 32: 4812-4820.

Classen HG, Grober U, Low, D, Schmidt J, Stracke H (2011). Zinc deficiency: symptoms, causes, diagnosis and therapy. Med. Monatsschr. Pharm. 34:87-95.

David L, Huber W, Granovskaia M, Toedling J, Palm CJ, Bofkin L, Jones T, Davis RW, Steinmetz LM (2006). A high-resolution map of transcription in the yeast genome. Proc. Natl. Acad. Sci. USA 103: 5320-5325.

Dunston G, Mason TE, Hercules W, Lindesay J (2014). Single Nucleotide Polymorphisms: A Window into the Informatics of the Living Genome. Adv. Biosci. Biotechnol. 5:623-626.

Dupont CL, Butcher A, Valas RE, Bourne PE, Caetano-Anolles G (2010). History of biological metal utilization inferred through phylogenomics analysis of protein structures. Proc. Natl. Acad. Sci. USA 107:10567-10572.

Enerly E, Sheng Z, Li KB (2005). Natural antisense as potential regulator of alternative initiation, splicing and termination. *In Silico* Biol. 5: 367-377.

Fabris N, Mocchegiani E (1995). Zinc, human diseases and aging. Aging 7:77-93.

Frausto da Silva JJR, Williams RJP (2001). The Biological Chemistry of the Elements. Oxford University Press, Oxford.

Friedman RC, Farh KK, Burge CB, Bartel DP (2014). TargetScan Human: Prediction of microRNA targets. Available at: http://www.targetscan.org/vert_61/. Accessed July 2014.

Gabriel SB, Schaffner SF, Nguyen H, Moore JM, Roy J, Blumenstiel B, Higgins J, DeFelice M, Lochner A, Faggart M, Liu-Cordero SN, Rotimi C, Adeyemo A, Copper R, Ward R, Lander ES, Daly MJ, Altshuler D (2002). The Structure of Haplotype Blocks in the Human Genome. Science 296:2225-2229.

Gagen MJ and Mattick JS (2005). Accelerating, hyperaccelerating, and decelerating networks. Phys. Rev. E. Nonlin. Soft Mattter Phys. 72:016123.

Genome Bioinformatics Group of UC Santa Cruz (2013). UCSC Genome Browser. Available at: https://genome.ucsc.edu/. Accessed June 2013.

Greer L, Domrachev M, Lipman DJ, Bryant SH (2014). Conserved Domain Architecture Retrieval Tool. Available at: http://www.ncbi.nlm.nih.gov/Structure/lexington/lexington.cgi. Accessed July 2014.

Hardy GH (1908). Mendelian proportions in a mixed population. Science 28:49-50.

Havilio M, Levanon EY, Lerman G, Kupiec M, Eisenberg E (2005). Evidence for abundant transcription of non-coding regions in the Saccharomyces cerevisiae genome. BMC Genomics 6: 93.

Hindorff LA, MacArthur J (European Bioinformatics Institute), Morales J (European Bioinformatics Institute), Junkins HA, Hall PN, Klemm AK, Manolio TA (2013). A Catalog of Published Genome-Wide Association Studies. Available at: www.genome.gov/gwastudies. Accessed June 2013.

Imamura T, Yamamoto S, Ohgane J, Hattori N, Tanaka S, Shiota K (2004). Non-coding RNA directed DNA demethylation of Sphk1 CpG island. Biochem. Biophys. Res. Commun. 3: 593-600.

Jen CH, Michalopoulos I, Westhead DR, Meyer P (2005). Natural antisense transcripts with coding capacity in Arabidopsis may have a regulatory role that is not kinked to double-stranded RNA degradation. Genome Biol. 6:R51.

Khochbin S, Brocard MP, Grunwald D, Lawrence JJ (1992). Antisense RNA and p53 regulation in induced murine cell differentiation. Ann. NY Acad. Sci. 660:77-87.

Kiyosawa H, Mise N, Iwase S, Hayashizaki Y, Abe K (2005). Disclosing hidden transcripts: mouse natural sense-antisense transcripts tend to be poly(A) negative and nuclear localized. Genome Res. 15:463-474.

Kiyosawa H, Yamanaka I, Osato N, Kondo S, Hayashizaki Y, RIKEN GER Group, GSL Members (2003). Antisense transcripts with FANTOM2 clone set and their implications for gene regulation. Genome Res. 13: 1324-1334.

Krystal GW, Armstrong BW, Battey JF (1990). N-myc mRNA forms an RNA-RNA duplex with endogenous antisense transcripts. Mol. Cell Biol. 10:4180-4191.

Kumar M, Carmichael GG (1997). Nuclear antisense RNA induces extensive adenosine modification and nuclear retention of target transcripts. Proc. Natl. Acad. Sci. USA 94: 3542-3547.

Lapidot M, Pilpel Y (2006). Genome-wide natural antisense transcription: coupling its regulation to its different regulatory mechanisms. EMBO reports 7: 1216-1222.

Lee JT, Davidow LS and Warshawsky D (1999). Tsix, a gene antisense to Xist at the X-inactivation centre. Nat. Genet. 21: 400-404.

Lee PH and Shatkay H. F-SNP: Computationally predicted functional SNPs for disease association studies. Available at: http://compbio.cs.queensu.ca/F-SNP/. Accessed June 2013.

Li JT, Zhang Y, Kong L, Liu QR, Wei L (2008). Trans-natural antisense transcripts including noncoding RNAs in 10 species: implications for expression regulation. Nucleic Acids Res. 35:4833-4844.

Li YY, Qin L, Guo ZM, Liu L, Xu H, Hao P, Su J, Shi Y, He WZ, Li YX (2006). In silico discovery of human natural antisense transcripts. BMC Bioinformatics 7: 18.

Lindesay J (2013). Foundations of Quantum Gravity. Cambridge University Press, Cambridge.

Lindesay J, Mason TE, Ricks-Santi L, Hercules WM, Kurian P, Dunston GM (2012). A New Biophysical Metric for Interrogating the Information Content in Human Genome Sequence Variation: Proof of Concept. J. Comput. Biol. Bioinform. Res. 4:15-22.

Mattick JS (2004). RNA regulation: a new genetics? Nat. Rev. Genet. 5:316-323.

Mattick JS (2007). A new paradigm for developmental biology. J. Exp. Biol. 210:1526-1547.

McCarthy TT, Zeelie JJ, Krause DJ (1992). The antimicrobial action of zinc ion/antioxidant combinations. Clin. Pharmacol. Ther. 17: 5.

Mihola O, Forejt J, Trachtulec Z (2007). Conserved alternative and antisense transcripts at the programmed cell death 2 locus. BMC Genomics 8:20.

Munroe SH, Lazar MA (1991). Inhibition of c-erbA mRNA splicing by a naturally occurring antisense RNA. J. Biol. Chem. 266: 22083-22086.

Murakami M, Hirano T (2008). Intracellular zinc homeostasis and zinc signaling. Cancer Sci. 99:1515-1522.

Chan WY, Wu SM, Ruzczyk L, Law E, Lee TL, Baxendale V, Lap-Ying Pang A, Rennert OM (2006). The complexity of antisense transcription revealed by the study of developing male germ cells. Genomics 87:681-692.

Pang KC, Frith MC, Mattick JS (2006). Rapid evolution of non-coding RNAs: lack of conservation does not mean lack of function. Trends Genet. 22:1-5.

Pfeiffer CC, Braverman ER (1982). Zinc, the brain and behavior. Biol. Psychiatry 17:513-532.

Prasad AS (1995). Zinc: an overview. Nutrition 11:93-99.

Qu Z, Adelson DL (2012). Evolutionary conservation and functional roles of ncRNA. Front. Genet. 3:1-11.

Rosok O, Sioud M (2005). Systematic search for natural antisense transcripts in eukaryotes (review). Int. J. Mol. Med. 15: 197-203.

Rossignol F, Vache C, Clottes E (2002). Natural antisense transcripts of hypoxia-inducible factor I alpha are detected in different normal and tumour human tissues. Gene 299:135-140.

Sandelin A, Wasserman WW, Lenhard B (2013). ConSite: web-based prediction of regulatory elements using cross species comparison. Available at: https://genome.ucsc.edu/. Accessed June 2013.

Sandstead HH (1994). Understanding zinc: recent observations and interpretations. J. Lab. Clin. Med. 124: 322-327.

Scherbakov DV, Garber MB (2000). Overlapping Genes in Bacterial and Phage Genomes. Mol. Biol. 34:485-495.

Sherry ST, Ward, MH, Kholdov M, Baker J, Phan L, Smigielski EM, Sirotkin K (2012). dbSNP: the NCBI database of genetic variation. Available at: http://www.ncbi.nlm.nih.gov/SNP/. Accessed December 2012.

Sigrist CJA, de Castro E, Cerutti L, Cuche BA, Huo N, Bridge A , Bouagueleret L, Xenarios I (2013). PROSITE: Database of protein domains, families and functional sites. Available at: http://prosite.expasy.org/. Accessed June 2013.

Sleutels F, Barlow DP, Lyle R (2000). The uniqueness of the imprinting mechanism. Curr. Opin. Genet. Dev.10:299-233.

Solomons NW (1998). Mild human zinc deficiency produces an imbalance between cell-mediated and humoral immunity. Nutr. Rev. 56:27-28.

Sun M, Hurst LD, Carmichael GG, Chen J (2006). Evidence for variation in abundance of antisense transcripts between multicellular animals but no relationship between antisense transcriptional organismic complexity. Genome Res. 16:922-933.

Susskind L, Lindesay J (2005). An Introduction to Black Holes, Information and the String Theory Revolution. World Scientific Publishing Company, Hackensack.

Taft RJ, Pheasant M, Mattick JS (2007). The relationship between non-protein-coding DNA and eukaryotic complexity. Bioessays 29:288-299.

Thorisson GA, Smith AV, Krishnan L, Stein LD (2012). The International HapMap Project Website. Available at: http://hapmap.ncbi.nlm.nih.gov/. Accessed December 2012.

Vallee BL, Auld DS (1993). Cocatalytic zinc motifs in enzyme catalysis. Proc. Natl. Acad. Sci. USA 90:2715-2718.

Volk R, Koster M, Poting A, Hartmann L, Knochel W (1989). An antisense transcript from the Xenopus laevis bFGF gene coding for an evolutionarily conserved 24kd protein. Embo. J. 8:2983-2988.

Wang A, Yasue H, Li L, Takashima M, deLeon FA, Liu WS (2008). Molecular characterization of the bovine chromodomain Y-like genes. Anim. Genet. 39:207-216.

Wang XJ, Gaasterland T, Chua NH (2005). Genome-wide prediction and identification of cis-natural antisense transcripts in Arabidopsis thaliana. Genome Biol. 6:R30.

Wapnir RA (1990). Protein Nutrition and Mineral Absorption. CRC Press, Boca Raton.

Weinberg W (1908). Über den Nachweis der Vererbung beim Menschen. Jahresh. Ver. Vaterl. Naturkd. Württemb. 64: 369–382.

Williams RJP (2012). Zinc in evolution. J. Inorg. Biochem. 111:104-109.

Williams RJP, Frausto da Silva JJR (2006). The Chemistry of Evolution. Elsevier, Amsterdam.

Wu C, Orozco C, Boyer J, Leglise M, Goodale J, Batalov S, Hodge CL, Haase J, Janes J, Huss JW 3rd, Su AI (2013). BioGPS: An extensible and customizable portal for querying and organzing gene annotation resources. Available at: http://biogps.org/. Accessed June 2013.

Yelin R, Dahary D, Sorek R, Levanon EY, Goldstein O, Shoshan A, Diber A, Biton S, Tamir Y, Khosravi R, Nemzer S, Pinner E, walach S, Bernstein J, Savisky K, Rotman G (2003). Widespread occurrence of antisense transcription in the human genome. Nat. Biotechol. 21:379-386.

Zhang Y and Gladyshev VN (2009). Comparative Genomics of Trace Elements: Emerging Dynamic View of Trace Element Utilization and Function. Chem. Rev. 109:4828-4861.

Zhang Y, Li JT, Kong L, Gao G, Liu QR, Wei L (2013). NATs DB: Natural Antisense Transcripts Database. Available at http://natsdb.cbi.pku.edu.cn/. Accessed June 2013.

Zhang Y, Liu XS, Liu QR, Wei L (2006). Genome-wide in silico identification and analysis of cis natural antisense transcripts (cis-NATs) in ten species. Nucleic Acids Res. 34:3465-3475.

2

ClustPK: A windows-based cluster analysis tool

Masood ur Rehman Kayani, Umair Shahzad Alam, Farida Anjum and Asif Mir*

Department of Biosciences,COMSATS Institute of Information Technology,Bio-Physics Block, Chak Shahzad Campus,Islamabad-44000, Pakistan.

There is a great need to develop analytical methodologies to analyze and exploit the information contained in gene expression data obtained from microarray-based experiments. Because of large number of genes and complexity of biological networks, clustering is a useful exploratory technique for analysis of such data. Different data analysis techniques and algorithms have been developed which are used to cluster the gene expression data. Various tools have been developed that implement these algorithms. Clusters of co-expressed genes provide useful basis for further investigation of gene function, regulation and their possible involvement in causing different diseases. ClustPK has been developed using C# .NET and implementing *k-means* and PCA algorithms. Analysis of microarray data using the already existing tools is difficult and the results are also hard to be analyzed. While, ClustPK is an easy-to-use and user friendly tool that provides the easy visualization and analysis of the results obtained from either *k-means* or PCA.

Key words: Microarray, gene expression, data sets, cluster analysis, k-means, principle component analysis.

INTRODUCTION

Genes are responsible for the functionality of various cellular components and are also important for the phenotype of an organism. Expression of genes under different conditions has a different effect on cell proliferation, differentiation and on various other cellular processes (Leung and Cavalieri, 2003; Ahmed, 2002). Traditional methods of analyzing the gene expression are either too time consuming, difficult to automate or analyze one mRNA at a time. Multiple mRNAs can be analyzed by using the newly developed techniques such as microarrays (Ahmed, 2002; Jiang et al., 2004).

Microarray technology is very powerful and comes with enormous benefits. Use of this technology can provide an opportunity to identify new drug targets and finding out what effects are produced by a drug on the expression of a gene (Brazma et al., 2001; Eisen et al., 1998). It has also been used for the prediction of function of various genes that may be involved in causing diseases under certain conditions (Burgess, 2001; Garaziar et al., 2006).

Microarray has also been used for expression profiling of immune cells (Ambrosio et al., 2005; Subaramanya et al., 2003).

After performing a microarray experiment, data analysis is required for the interpretation of results. This analysis involves multiple steps including acquiring image of the microarray, image analysis, data preprocessing and normalization (Brazma et al., 2001). The processed data is represented as a gene expression matrix with rows representing the genes included in the experiment and columns representing the conditions under which genes were studied. This matrix can be manipulated for cluster analysis (Brazma et al., 2001). Cluster analysis is a technique that clusters genes into different groups on the basis of similarities in their expression under different conditions. Genes present in one group have high similarity with each other and highly dissimilar with genes present in a different group. Computational tools that are based on clustering algorithms (including *k-means*, Principle Component Analysis, Hierarchical Clustering and Biclustering) are required to achieve the clustering of genes (Jiang et al., 2004).Various tools have been developed for performing the cluster analysis using different algorithms. Most of the existing softwares do not provide an easy interface for their usage and the analysis of a dataset as well. For overcoming these limitations, ClustPK has been developed.

---

*Corresponding author. E-mail: asif_mir@comsats.edu.pk.

Abbreviations: C#; C Sharp, **PC;** Principle Component, **PCA;** Principle Component Analysis.

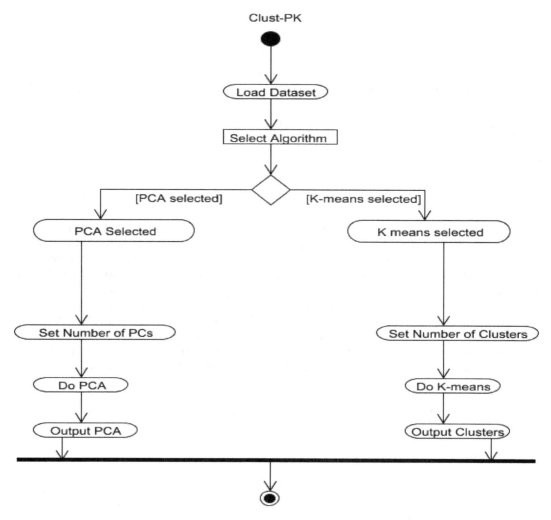

Figure 1. Activity Diagram of ClustPK. A user begins by uploading the dataset to ClustPK and then proceeds with the selection of an appropriate algorithm. In case *k-means* is selected, he/she will be prompted to input the number of clusters that is, *k* then *k-means* is performed and finally clusters are output. In case PCA is selected, he/she will be asked to enter the number of PCs after which PCA will be performed and finally output will be provided.

Program description

ClustPK has been developed using C# .NET (C-sharp dot net) and has an implementation of the following two clustering algorithms:1. *k-means* that groups the given genes into *k* number of clusters.Here *k* is a positive integer value that should be at least 2 and less than the total number of genes in an experiment. This number is selected by the user and must be input before performing *k-means*. 2. Principle Component Analysis (PCA) is a data-dimension reduction technique and identifies patterns in a given dataset and expresses them in a way that highlights their similarities and differences. Figure 1 is the activity diagram of ClustPK and shows different steps required to perform clustering using ClustPK.

Program interface

Heat map

Heat map (Figure 2) is generated immediately after the user inputs

a valid dataset to ClustPK. Heat map is a graphical representation of the expression values present in the dataset. Different expression values are represented by different colors.

Expression view

Expression view shows a graphical representation of the results after the input of a valid dataset and performing clustering using any of the two algorithms. ClustPK displays the results as a bargraph for *k-means* (Figure 3A) and for PCA, a scatter plot is displayed (Figure 3B).

Analysis view

For further analysis of a single cluster/PC, user can select that cluster/PC from the analysis menu. For *k-means*, a list of genes and a graph (showing the range of expression values in selected cluster) appears in the Analysis view (Figure 3C). For PCA, a list of final values obtained after performing statistical and linear

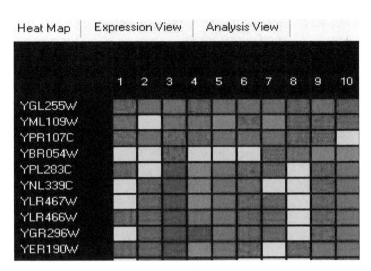

Figure 2. Heat map of the loaded dataset. Differences in expression values are indicated by different colors.

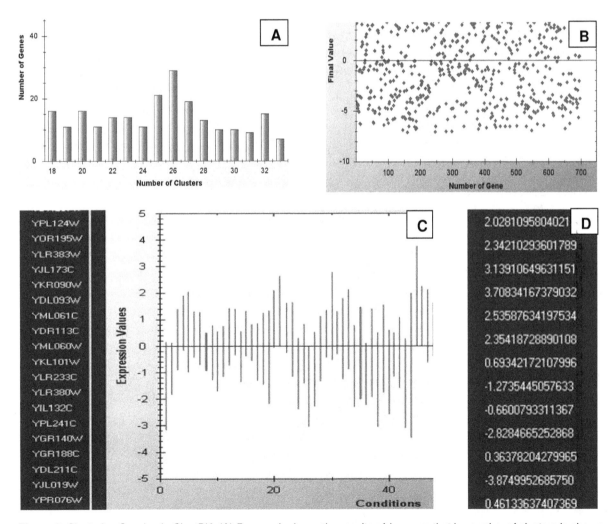

Figure 3. Clustering Session in ClustPK. (A) Bar graph shows the results of *k-means* that is, number of clusters is shown on x-axis while number of genes in a cluster is shown on y-axis by height of bar. (B) Scatter plot of PCA. (C) Analysis view of a cluster that is, for a selected cluster in *k-means*, genes included that cluster and their expression value ranges are plotted. (D) Analysis view of a PC shows the final transformed data values in algebraic calculations is shown in the analysis view (Figure 3D).

Saving project

During each session of *k-means* or PCA, ClustPK generates different intermediate files. For *k-means*, files for the 1-0 matrix, Euclidean distance and Gene ID are generated. For PCA, these files include the files for covariance matrix, Eigen vector, Feature Vector and Final transformed data. The graphs generated in a session can also be saved and printed.

DISCUSSION

Microarray analysis is widely used for studying gene expression data. Clustering is used for grouping the given objects into distinct groups so that the objects within one group have high similarity and objects in separate groups are more dissimilar. An object refers to a gene or an experimental condition.

algebraic calculations is shown in the analysis view (Figure 3D).Clustering techniques are applied on the microarray datasets using different available software tools. ClustPK applies two clustering algorithms that is, *k-means* and PCA on the microarray gene expression datasets. *k-means* clusters the objects into a predefined number of clusters that is, *k*. Principle Component Analysis (PCA) is used to reduce the dimensions of a given dataset and can also be used for clustering microarray gene expression dataset. ClustPK, a user friendly tool, provides the utility to visualize and analyze the results of *k-means* or PCA. The results are visualized as a fully zoom-able and pan-able graph. Designed tool provides a gene list for a selected cluster and the final transformed values along with their respective gene ID for a selected PC as analysis of results.

ClustPK can be used to analyze only one type of microarray dataset that is, the dataset in a text format only. Future developments of ClustPK include: (1) analysis of more than one format of microarray datasets that is, CEL, GPR, CHP formats, (2) clustering of microarray datasets using biological networks that is, metabolic network, gene networks or any other type of network and (3) annotation of clusters.

System Requirements and Availability

ClustPK has been developed using C# language and based on the .NET technology. The main requirements for running this software include:

a) Windows XP/ Windows Vista.
b) .NET framework 2.0 or higher.
c) 512 MB of RAM (minimum).

For installation of .NET framework, windows installer 3.0 or later is required. Windows installer and .NET framework can be downloaded from Microsoft's website. ClustPK is freely-available software and can be downloaded from our web site (http://www.bioinformaticshub.com/softwares/ClustPK.rar).

REFERENCES

Ahmed EF (2002). Molecular techniques for studying gene expression in carcinogenesis. J. Env. Sci. Health 20: 77-116.

Ambrosio DC, Gatta L, Bonin S (2005). The future of microarray technology: networking the genome search. *Allergy* 60: 1219-1226.

Brazma A, Hingamp P, Quakenbush J, Sherlock G, Spellman P, Stoeckert C, Aach J, Ansorge W, Ball AC, Causton CH, Gaasterland T, Glenisson P, Holstege CPF, Kim FI, Markowitz V, Matese CJ, Parkinson H, Robinson A, Sarkans U, Schulze-Kremer S, Stewart J, Taylor R, Vilo J, Vingron M (2001). Minimum information about a microarray experiment (MIAMI)-toward standards for microarray data. Nature Genetics 29: 365-371.

Burgess KJ. Special Technical Review (2001). Gene expression studies using microarrays. Clin. Exper. Pharmacol, Physiol. 28: 321-332.

Eisen MB, Spellman PT, Brown P, Botstein D (1998). Cluster analysis and display of genome-wide expression patterns. Proc. Natl. Acad. Sci. 95: 14863-14868.

Garaziar J, Rementeria A, Porwollik S (2006). DNA microarray technology: a new tool for the epidemiological typing of bacteria pathogens. *FEMS* Immun. Med. Microbiol. 47: 178-189.

Jiang D, Tang C, Zhang A (2004). Cluster Analysis for Gene Expression Data: A Survey. *IEEE* Transactions on Knowledge and Data Engineering 16: 1370-1386.

Leung FY, Cavalieri D (2003). Fundamentals of cDNA microarray data analysis. Trends in Genetics 19 : 649-659.

Subaramanya DR, Lucchese G, Kanduc D, Sinha AA (2003). Clinical applications of DNA microarray analysis. J. Exp. Therap. Oncol. 3 297-304.

3

Theoretical analysis indicating that human genome is not a blueprint and that human oocytes have the instructions

Koichi Itoh

The Institute for Theoretical Molecular Biology, 21-13, Rokurokuso-cho, Ashiya, Hyogo, Japan 659-0011.
E-mail: koichiitoh@yahoo.co.jp, itoh@i-tmb.com.

Is human genome really a blueprint? If it is not a blueprint, how are human bodies constructed? This paper solves this hypothetical proposition. Firstly, it indicates 8 examples of important biological pathways and factors among house-keeping genes and proved that human genome is not a blueprint, but a storage of genes. Secondly, it proved that human oocytes have the instructions for development and differentiation. In this case, the study used opened public database for expression profile of human oocytes. It selected 12700 genes, which are expressed in human oocytes. Among 12700 genes, more than 800 genes which are related to development and differentiation are expressed. Here, the study shows that human genome is not a blueprint and human oocytes have the instructions.

Key words: Blueprint, gene expression, human genome, human oocytes, theoretical biology.

INTRODUCTION

Human genome has been thought to be a blueprint, but what type of blueprint has been a mystery. Human genome project was over in 2003, and seven years had already passed, but the number of human genes is still unknown. Analysis of human genomes has been continuously done, but the discussion that entails human genome as a blueprint has not been done. Far from that, any traces of a blueprint are not found in human genomes. This may be an evidence that human genome is not a blueprint.

The Watson-Click's DNA double helix is very beautiful; hence, life-scientists have imprinted that a human genome is a blueprint. If we hypothesize that a human genome is a blueprint, what types of absurdity would emerge? And if a human genome is not a blueprint, what must be needed to construct human bodies? To solve these hypothetical propositions are the aim of this document. In the case of unicellular organisms, such as *E. coli*, their genomes may play a role for blueprints.

However, biological mechanisms of multicellular organisms such as *Homo sapiens*, are much complex and it is difficult to contain all information as a blueprint in their genomes. Therefore, a human genome plays a role for storage of genes and the study thinks that human oocytes have the instructions. However, a fertilized egg selects necessary genes from that storage and expresses genes for development and differentiation.

MATERIALS AND METHODS

Table 1 was made from NCBI database (http://www.ncbi.nlm.nih.gov/) and KEGG (http://www.kegg.jp/ja/). One hundred and ninety six key words in Supplemental Table 1 were selected from reference 3 to 7. Supplemental Table 2 was made from supplementary data 1, 2 and 3, which were originally located in http://www.canr.msu.edu/dept/ans/community/people/cibelli_jose.html (Kocabas 2006) and were later re-located by the study to http://www.i-tmb.com/text.html. Supplementary data 1 contains up-regulated genes in human oocytes, supplementary data 2 contains down-regulated genes in human oocytes and supplementary data 3 contains uniquely expressed genes in human oocytes. The study combined supplementary data 1, 2 and 3 and eliminated duplicated genes.

Finally, it got 12764 genes, which were expressed in human oocytes (Supplemental Table II). It surveyed 12764 genes with 196 key words and selected 823 genes which are thought to be important in the development and differentiation in GenBank release 175.0 (Supplemental Table III). Table 2 shows the number of important genes for development and differentiation. Supplemental Tables I, II and III are located in http://www.i-tmb.com/.

Table 1. Loci of genes for major biological pathway.

I. Glycolysis

Gene Name	Locus
Glucokinase (Hekisokinase 4)	7p15-p13
Phosphoglucose isomerase	19q13.1
Phosphofructokinase, liver type	21q22.3
Phosphofructokinase, muscle type	12q13.3
Phosphofructokinase, platelet type	10p15.3-p15.2
Aldolase A	16p11.2
Aldolase B	9q22.3
Aldolase C	17cen-q12
Glyceraldehyde 3-phosphate dehydrogenase	12p13.31-p13.1
Phosphoglycerate kinase 1	Xq13
Phosphoglycerate mutase 2 (muscle)	7p13-p12
Phosphoglycerate mutase 1 (brain)	10q25.3
Enolase 1, (alpha)	1p36.3-p36.2
Enolase 2 (gamma, neuronal)	12p13
Enolase 3 (beta, muscle)	17pter-p11
Pyruvate kinase, muscle	15q22
Pyruvate kinase, liver and RBC	1q21

II. TCA cycle

Gene name	Locus
Aconitase	22q11.21-q13.31
Isocitrate dehydrogenase	15q26.1
2-oxoglutarate dehydrogenase E1 component	7p14-p13
2-oxoglutarate dehydrogenase E2 component (dihydrolipoamide succinyltransferase)	14q24.3
Succinyl-CoA synthetase alpha subunit	2p11.2
Succinate dehydrogenase	5p15
Fumarase	1q42.1

VI. Purine biosynthesis

Gene name	Locus
Amidophosphoribosyltransferase	4q12
Phosphoribosylamine glycine ligase	21q22.1; 21q22.11
Phosphoribosylglycinamide formyltransferase	21q22.1; 21q22.11
Phosphoribosylformylglycinamidine synthase	17p13.1
Phosphoribosylformylglycinamidine cyclo-ligase	21q22.1; 21q22.11
Phosphoribosylaminoimidazole carboxylase	4q12
Phosphoribosylaminoimidazole-succinocarboxamide synthase	4q12
Adenylosuccinate lyase	22q13.1; 22q13.2
Phosphoribosyl aminoimidazole carboxamide formyltransferase	2q35
IMP cyclohydrolase	2q35
adenylosuccinate synthase	14q32.33
IMP dehydrogenase	7q31.3-q32
GMP synthase	3q24

VII. Primidine biosynthesis

Gene name	Locus
Carbamoyl-phosphate synthase	2p22-p21
Aspartate carbamoyltransferase	2p22-p21
Dihydroorotase	2p22-p21
Dihydroorotate dehydrogenase	16q22
Orotate phosphoribosyltransferase	3q13
Orotidine-5'-phosphate decarboxylase	3q13
CTP synthase	1p34.1
Thymidylate synthase	18p11.32

VIII. Basal transcription factors

Gene name	Locus
TATA-box-binding protein	14q22.3

Table 1. Contd.

Gene name	Locus		Locus
Malate dehydrogenase	7cen-q22	Transcription initiation factor TFIID subunit D1	9p21.1
Citrate synthase	12q13.2-q13.3	Transcription initiation factor TFIID subunit D2	8q24.12
III. Pentose phosphate pathway		Transcription initiation factor TFIID subunit D3	20q13.33
Gene name	**Locus**	Transcription initiation factor TFIID subunit D4	1q42.13
Glucose-6-phosphate dehydrogenase	Xq28	Transcription initiation factor TFIID subunit D5	11q12.3
6-phosphogluconolactonase	19p13.2	Transcription initiation factor TFIID subunit D6	Xq22.1
6-phasphogluconate dehydrogenese	1p36.3-p36.13	Transcription initiation factor TFIID subunit D7	Xq13.1-q21.1
Ribrose 5-phosphate ketoisomerase	2p11.2	Transcription initiation factor TFIID subunit D8	11p15.3
Transketolase	3p14.3	Transcription initiation factor TFIID subunit D9	5p15.1
Transaldolase	11p15.5-p15.4	Transcription initiation factor TFIID subunit D10	1p35.3
		Transcription initiation factor TFIID subunit D11	1p13.3
IV. Urea cycle		Transcription initiation factor TFIIB	1p22-p21
Gene name	**Locus**	Transcription initiation factor TFIIA large subunit	2p16.3
Carbamoyl phoshpate synthase I	2q35	Transcription initiation factor TFIIA small subunit	15q22.2
Ornithine transcarbamylase	Xp21.1	Transcription initiation factor TFII-I	7q11.23
Argininosuccinic acid synthase	9q34.1	Transcription initiation factor TFIIF alpha subunit	19p13.3
Argininosuccinase	7cen-q11.2	Transcription initiation factor TFIIF beta subunit	13q14
Arginase	6q23	Transcription initiation factor TFIIE alpha subunit	3q21-q24
		Transcription initiation factor TFIIE beta subunit	8p21-p12
V. Fatty acid metabolism		Transcription initiation factor TFIIH subunit H1	11p15.1-p14
Gene Name	**Locus**	Transcription initiation factor TFIIH subunit H2	5q12.2-q13.3
Long-chain acyl-CoA synthetase	4q34-q35	Transcription initiation factor TFIIH subunit H3	12q24.31
Acyl-CoA dehydrogenase	1p31	Transcription initiation factor TFIIH subunit H4	6p21.3
Acyl-CoA oxidase	17q24-q25.1		
Enoyl-CoA hydratase	10q26.2-q26.3		
3-hydroxyacyl-CoA dehydrogenase	3q26.3-q28		
Long-chain 3-hydroxyacyl-CoA dehydrogenase	2p23		
Acetyl-CoA acyltransferase	18q21.1		

Table 2. Genes for development and differentiation in human oocytes.

Gene group	Number of genes	Gene group	Number of genes
Activin	6	lim	28
AKT	3	lin	4
Armadillo	10	MAP	36
ATM	1	Meltrin	1
BCL	25	Mindbomb	1
BDNF	1	Mix	1
Beta-catenin	1	Myf	1
BMP	12	Nanos	1
Cadherin	4	NCAM1	1
Caspase	15	NENF	1
Catenin	4	Netrin	1
Caudal	1	Neuregulin	2
Ced	7	Neuropilin	3
Chordin	4	NF-kappa-B	3
CNTF	1	Nodal	2
Dachshund	2	NOTCH	4
Deformed	1	Numb	1
Delta	2	Odd-skipped	1
Dickkopf	2	Orthodenticle	2
Dishevelled	2	paired	1
Distal-less	2	par	4
E-cadherin	1	PAX	4
EGF	1	Plexin	7
Ephrin	7	Polycomb	8
Even-skipped	1	Pumilio	2
F-box	3	Ras	13
FGF	10	Rhomboid	4
follistatin	3	Robo	4
FOX	17	Runt	4
Frizzled	8	Semaphorin	9
GATA	7	Sex comb	6
GDF	2	SMAD	10
Geminin	1	snail	1
Gfap	1	SOX	10
Giant	1	STAT	1
Hairy	6	T-box	5
Hedgehog	2	TCF3	1
Helix-loop-helix	9	TGF	8
HGF	1	Trk	1
hmg	20	Twist	3
HOX	38	VEGF	1
I-kappa-B	3	Vimentin	1
Insulin	6	WNT	6
Integrin	15	WT1	1
JAK	3	XIST	1
Kruppel	14	Zinc finger	234

RESULTS AND DISCUSSION

Human genome is not a blueprint

At first, the definition of a blueprint must be determined. According to a dictionary, a blueprint for something is a plan or set of proposals that shows how it is expected to work. The study scrutinized loci of genes for 8 important biological pathways and factors, and their loci were scattered all over the human genome at random (Table 1). The study thinks that a blueprint must have regularity, periodism, harmony, some types of patterns and consistency or beauty which a blueprint itself has, but there was no existence of such things.

On the contrary, more than half of the human genome sequence consists of lines, sines, retroviral-like elements, DNA-only transposon fossils, *Alu* sequences and pseudogenes (Alberts, 2008). The loci of genes for 8 pathways and factors scattered all over the human genome, shows that there is no existence of any operons such as bacterial genomes. Some reports exist that genes clustered in one-dimensional, construct a cluster in three-dimensional, but there are no reports that scattered genes in one-dimensional construct a cluster in three-dimensional (Schneider and Grosschedl 2007).

In mathematics, one opposite example is enough for proof, but biology has some exceptions. However, genes in Table 1 are biologically important genes, and if a human genome is a blueprint, 8 exceptions must not be permitted. Here, the study logically shows that a human genome is not a blueprint. Hence, how are human bodies constructed from a human genome, which is a storage of genes?

Human oocytes have the instructions

Before fertilization, human oocytes express genes. If a human genome is a storage of genes, mRNAs which are important for development and differentiation must be expressed in human oocytes and translated into proteins as soon as fertilization begins. Therefore, the study surveyed public databases and found an expression profile in human oocytes. In that profile, there are 12700 genes, and among these genes, more than 800 genes which are related to development and differentiation were found.

In general, many sample data must be necessary for comparison of gene expression levels in statistical analysis; but in this case, the study does not need statistical analysis, because the importance is seen only in cases where certain types of genes are expressed in human oocytes.

The study thinks that human oocytes play a major role because of the amount of genes related to development and differentiation. Moreover, essential genes for human development and differentiation such as *Oct3* and *Oct4* are not found in Table 2, but the study does not think that this is critical. It thinks that mRNAs of *Oct3* and *Oct4* did not hybridize on the microarray chips, because the genes which must be expressed must be expressed in human oocytes and as such, because of RNA interference, some mRNA might be broken. However, the amount of genes in human oocytes related in development and differentiation indicates that human oocytes have the instructions.

Definition of instruction must be done, in that instructions are clear and detailed information on how to do something. In this point, the study thinks that human oocytes have the simple instructions. If human oocytes do not have the simple instructions, where is the blueprint or the instructions? The study already indicates that a human genome is not a blueprint; hence, it is logical that human oocytes have the simple instructions because a human body starts building from only one cell to a fertilized egg.

If other cells except for human oocytes give proteins or mRNAs from outside of human oocytes, nurse cells or stromal cells might be candidates for the simple instructions; but it is not realistic that those cells give most of their biologically important proteins or mRNAs into fertilized eggs. Therefore, the study logically proved that human oocytes have the simple instructions. Important genes for the instruction in human oocytes (Gilbert, 2006; Moody, 2007; Schoenwolf, 2009; Slack, 2006; Wolpert, 2007)

The homeodomain is an approximately 60 amino acid sequence containing many basic residues, and forms a helix-turn-helix structure that binds specific sites in DNA. The homeodomain sequence itself is coded by a corresponding homeobox (HOX) in the gene. The homeobox was given its name because it was initially discovered in homeotic genes. However, there are many transcription factors that contain a homeodomain as their DNA-binding domain and although they are often involved in development, possession of a homeodomain does not guarantee a role in development, nor are mutants of homeobox genes necessarily homeotic. A very large number of homeodomain proteins have important functions, for example, engrailed in *Drosophila* segmentation, goosecoid in the vertebrate organizer and Cdx proteins in anteroposterior patterning. An important subset is the HOX proteins which have a special role in the control of anteroposterior pattern in animals. Homeobox genes are found in animals, plants and fungi, but the Hox subsets are only found in animals.

The LIM domain is a cysteine-rich zinc-binding region responsible for protein-protein interactions, but is not itself a DNA-binding domain. LIM-homeoproteins possess two LIM domains together with the DNA-binding homeodomain. Examples are Lim-1 in the organizer, Islet-1 in motorneurons, Lhx factors in the limb bud and Apterous in the *Drosophila* wing. PAXs are characterized by a DNA-binding region called a paired domain with 6 alpha-helical segments and the name is derived from the paired protein in Drosophila. A lot of Pax proteins also contain homeodomain, examples of which are: Pax6 in the eye and Pax3 in the developing somite. Zinc-finger protein is a large and diverse group of proteins in which the DNA-binding region contains projections ("fingers") with Cys and/or its residues folding around a zinc atom. Some examples are the GATA factors, which are important in blood and gut, Krupple in the early *Drosophila* embryo and WT-1 in the kidney. Basic helix-loop-helix (bHLH) protein transcription factors are active as heterodimers. They contain a basic DNA-binding region and a hydrophobic helix-loop-helix region responsible for protein dimerization.

One member of the dimer is found in all tissues of the organism and the other member is tissue specific. There are also proteins containing the HLH, but not the basic part of the sequence. These form inactive dimmers with other bHLH proteins and so inhibit their activity. Examples of bHLH proteins include E12 and E47 which are ubiquitous in vertebrates, the myogenic factor MyoD and the hairy *Drosophila* pair-rule protein. An inhibitor with no basic region is Id, which is an inhibitor of myogenesis. FOX have a 100 amino acid winged helix domain which forms another type of DNA-binding region and known as "FOX" proteins. Examples are forkhead in *Drosophila* embryonic termini and Fox2A in the vertebrate main axis and gut. T-box factors have a DNA-binding domain similar to the prototype gene product known as "T" in the mouse and as brachyury in other animals. They include the endodermal VegT and the limb identity factors Tbx4 and Tbx5. High mobility group (HGM)-box factors differ from most others because they do not have a specific activation or repression domain, instead they work by bending the DNA to bring other regulatory sites into contact with the transcription complex. Examples are SRY, the testis-determining factor, Sox9, a "master switch" for cartilage differentiation and the TCF and LEF factors whose activity is regulated by the Wnt pathway.

Transforming growth factor (TGF) beta was originally discovered as a mitogen secreted by "transformed" (cancer-like) cells. It has turned out to be the prototype for a large and diverse superfamily of signaling molecules, all of which share a number of basic structural characteristics. The matured factors are disulfide-bonded dimers of approximately 25 kDa. They are synthesized as longer pro-forms which need to be protrolytically cleaved to the matured form in order for biological activity to be shown. The TGF-beta themselves are, in fact, often inhibitory to cell division and promote the secretion of extracellular matrix materials. They are involved mainly in the organogenesis stages of development. The activin-like factors include the nodal-related family, which are all involved in induction and patterning of the mesoderm in vertebrate embryos. The bone morphogenetic proteins (BMPs) were discovered as factors promoting ectopic formation of cartilage and bone in rodents. They are involved in skeletal development and also in the specification of the early body plan.

There are a number of receptors for the TGF-beta superfamily. Their specificity for different factors is complex and overlapping, but in general, different subsets of receptors bind to the TGF-beta themselves, the activin-like factors and the BMPs. In all cases, the ligand binds first to a type II receptor and enables it form a complex with a type I receptor. The type I receptor is a Ser-Thr kinase, which becomes activated in the ternary complex. Activation causes phosphorylation of smad proteins in the cytoplasm. Smads 1, 5 and 8 are targets for BMP receptors, smads 2 and 3 for activin receptors, smad 4 is required by both pathways and smad 6 is inhibitory to both by displacing the binding of smad 4. Phosphorylation causes the smads to migrate to the nucleus where they function as transcription factors, regulating target genes. The hedgehogs were first identified because mutations of the gene in *Drosophila* disrupted the segmentation pattern and made the larvae look like hedgehogs.

Sonic hedgehog is very important for the dorsoventral patterning of the neural tube and for the anteroposterior patterning of the limbs. It should be noted that Indian hedgehog is important in skeletal development and the full-length hedgehog polypeptide is an autoprotease that cleaves itself into an active N-terminal and an inactive C-terminal part. The N-terminal fragment is normally modified by covalent addition of a fatty acyl chain and of cholesterol, which are needed for full activity. The hedgehog receptor is called patched, again named after the phenotype of the gene mutation in *Drosophila*. This is of the G-protein-linked class. It is constitutively active and is repressed by ligand binding. When active, it represses the activity of another cell membrane protein that is smoothened, and which in turn represses the proteolytic cleavage of Gli-type transcription factors. Full-length Gli factors are transcriptional activators that can move to the nucleus and turn on target genes, but the constitutive removal of the C-terminal region makes them into repressors. In the absence of hedgehog, patched is active, smoothened is inactive and Gli is inactive.

In the presence of hedgehog, patched is inhibited, smoothened is active and Gli is active. Activation of protein kinase A also represses Gli and hence antagonizes hedgehog signaling. The founder member of the Wnt family was discovered through two routes, as an oncogene in mice and as the wingless mutation in *Drosophila*. Wnt factors are single-chain polypeptides containing a covalently linked fatty acyl group which is essential for activity and renders them insoluble in water. The Wnt receptors are called frizzled after another *Drosophila* mutation. There are several classes of receptor for different ligand types and they do not necessarily cross-react. Wnt 1, 3A or 8 will activate frizzles that cause the repression of a kinase, glycogen synthase kinase 3 (gsk3) via a multifunctional protein that is dishevelled. When active, gsk3 phosphorylates beta-catenin, which is an important molecule is involved both in cell adhesion and gene regulation. When gsk3 is repressed, beta-catenin remains unphosphorylated and in this state, it can be combined with a transcription factor, Tcf-1, and conveyed into the nucleus. This pathway is important in numerous developmental contexts, including early dorsoventral patterning in Xenopus, segmentation in a Drosophila and kidney development.

Other Wnts, including Wnts 4,5 and 11,bind to a different subset of frizzled that activate two other signal transduction pathways. In the planar cell polarity pathway, a domain of the dishevelled protein interacts with small GTPases and the cytoskeleton to bring about a polarization of the cell. In the Wnt-Ca pathway, phospholipase C becomes activated by a frizzled. This then acts to generate diacylglycerol and inositol 1, 4 and 5 triphosphate, with consequent elevation of cytoplasmic calcium, as described above under G-protein-coupled receptors. For the Delta-Notch system, both the ligand (Delta and Jagged) and receptor (Notch) are integral membrane proteins. Their interaction can therefore only take place if the cells making them are in contact. As for the ephrin-Eph system, binding of ligand to Notch causes cleavage of the cytoplasmic portion of Notch by an intramembranous protease, gamma-secretase, and this causes a release into the cytoplasm of the transcription factor, CSL-kappa. This migrates to the nucleus and activates the target genes. The gamma-secretase is the same protease that generates the peptide whose accumulation in the brain leads to Alzheimer's disease. Notch can carry O-linked tetrasaccharides and the presence of this carbohydrate chain can affect its specificity, thereby increasing sensitivity to Delta and reducing sensitivity to Jagged. Control is often exercised through the activity of the glycosyl transferase fringe, which adds GlcNAc to the O-linked fucose.

The Delta-Notch system is important in numerous developmental situations, including neurogenesis, somitogenesis and imaginal disc development. Cadherins are families of single-pass transmembrane glycoproteins which can adhere tightly to similar molecules on other cells in the presence of calcium. Cadherins are the main factors attaching embryonic cells together, which is why embryonic tissues can often disaggregate simply by a removal of calcium. The cytoplasmic tail of cadherins is anchored to actin bundles in the cytoskeleton by complex inclusion proteins called catenins. One of these, beta-catenin, is also a component of the Wnt signaling pathway, providing a potential link named for the tissues in which they were originally found, so that E-cadherin occurs mainly in epithelia and N-cadherin mainly in neural tissue.

The integrins are cell-surface glycoproteins that interact mainly with components of the extracellular matrix. They are heterodimers of alpha- and beta- subunits and require either magnesium or calcium for binding. There are numerous different alpha and beta chain types and so there is a very large number of potential heterodimers.

Integrins are attached by cytoplasmic domains to microfilament bundles, so, like cadherins, they provide a link between the outside world and the cytoskeleton. They are also thought on occasion to be responsible for the activation of signal transduction pathways and new gene transcription following exposure to particular extra cellular components.

After the birth of molecular biology, life-scientists proved only two things, in the study's opinion. Firstly, there is high possibility that genes or proteins which have similar nucleic acid or amino acid sequences have similar 3-demensional structures and functions. Secondly, genes or proteins have many functions because of the timing of working, permutation and combination. However, the number of human genes might be 40000 at most. In the first place, only 40000 genes cannot control complex biological mechanisms. Therefore, the study thinks that limited number of genes and proteins change the timing of working, permutation and combination and control the diverse biological mechanisms in human bodies. Genomes of viruses or bacteria might have the possibility that those genomes play a role for blueprints, but it will become impossible that human genome play a role for a blueprint.

Hence, the study thinks that human genome begins to exist as storage of genes and human oocytes express essential genes for development and differentiation as the simple instructions. After fertilization, a fertilized egg differentiates according to the micro-environment that surrounds the fertilized egg. Therefore, human oocytes express genes for adhesion molecules such as integrins, cadherins and so on. From now on, a lot of evidence will be piled up to support the study's hypothesis.

Finally, the study foresees that once organogenesis begins, tissue differentiation proceeds autonomously and human bodies are built. This is, thought as theoretical molecular biology and 'Itoh hypothesis'.

REFERENCES

Alberts B, Johnson A, Walter P, Lewis J, Raff M, Roberts K (2008). Molecular Biology of the Cell, 5th edition, Garland Science, Mortimer Street, London, pp. 1-1601.

Gilbert SF (2006). Developmental Biology, 8th edition, Sinauer Association Inc. Sunderland, MA, pp. 3-751.

Kocabas AM, Crosby J, Ross PJ (2006). The transcriptome of human oocytes, Proc. Natl Acad. Sci. USA. 103: 14027-14032.

Moody SA (2007). Principles of Developmental Genetics. Academic Press, New York, pp. 2-1022.

Schneider R, Grosschedl R (2007). Dynamics and interplay of nuclear architecture, genome organization, and gene expression. Genes Dev., 21: 3027-3043.

Schoenwolf GC, Bleyl SB, Brauer PR (2009). Larsen's Human Embryology, 4th edition, Churchill Livingstone, New York, pp. 1-644.

Slack JMW (2006). Essential Developmental Biology 2nd edition, Blackwell Publishing, West Sussex, UK, pp. 3-336.

Wolpert L (2007). Principles of Development, 3rd edition. Oxford University Press, pp. 1-522.

4

Prediction of 3D structure of P2RY5 gene and its mutants via comparative homology modelling

Samina Bilal[1], Hina Iqbal[1], Farida Anjum[2] and Asif Mir[1]*

[1]Department of Biosciences, Comsats Institute of Information Technology, Bio-Physics Block, Chak Shahzad Campus, Islamabad-44000, Pakistan.
[2]Pakistan Council for Science and Technology, Islamabad-44000, Pakistan.

3-D Structure of proteins gives valuable insights into the molecular organization, function, docking simulations and also effective drug designing experiments. Autosomal recessive hypotrichosis is a genetic hair disorder that is though not life threatening but it can lead to abhorrent effect on person's psyche. In the lack of an experimentally determined structure, comparative or homology modeling can provide valuable 3D models. Most recently, mutations in the P2RY5 gene have been identified as a cause of Autosomal recessive hypotrichosis in families of different origin. Current study encompasses broad analysis of alterations brings by mutations in P2RY5 gene through Bioinformatics tools and determination of 3D structure of P2RY5 gene product using comparative modeling approach.

Key words: Comparative homology modeling, P2RY5, ramachandran plot, 3D model, protein modeling, bioinformatics, LAH3.

INTRODUCTION

Autosomal recessive hypotrichosis is a rare form of hair loss characterized by sparse hair on scalp, sparse to absent eyebrows and eyelashes, and sparse axillary and body hair. Affected adult male individuals have normal beard hair (Ali et al., 2007). Three clinically similar form of hereditary hypotrichosis, LAH1, LAH2 and LAH3, segregating in autosomal recessive fashion have be mapped on chromosomes 18 q12.1, 3q27.3 and 13q14.11-q21.32, respectively (Wali et al., 2007). LAH3 is caused by mutations in P2RY5 gene. Total 7 mutations have been reported in P2RY5. 4 missense mutations are c.436G>A, c.8G>C, c.565G>A, c.188A>T and 3 frame shift reported mutations are c.36insA, c.160insA, c.69insCATG. (Zahid et al., 2008) The protein encoded by this gene belongs to the family of G-protein coupled receptors. The P2RY5 gene encodes 344 amino acids of P2Y5 protein (Herzog et al., 1996). This contains four potential extracellular domains, four cytoplasmic domains and seven predicted hydrophobic transmembrane regions (Laskowski et al., 1993).

Strategies that have been currently used to predict 3D structures are X-ray Crystallography and Nuclear mag-netic resonance spectroscopy but these methods are costly, protracted, time taking and have certain protein size constraints. Due to these reasons proteins structure information is still limited. Bioinformatics computational methods and molecular dynamic simulations are the solution to this problem and serve as alternative tool for protein structure prediction (Liang et al., 2005). To understand alterations brought out by mutations, affect of mutations at molecular level has to be highlighted. In order to have a therapy for LAH3, affect of mutations on physiochemical properties, domains, post-translational modifications 2D and 3D structure of P2RY5 must be predicted.

Comparative modeling is a useful technique in bio-informatics because this process constructs three dimensional models that are related to known structures (template) (Sali et al., 1993; Marti et al., 2000). Thus this approach is relevant to structural based functional annotation. As a result, it enhances impact of structure and function on biology and medicine.

MATERIALS AND METHODS

Retrieval of target sequence

The amino acid sequence of P2RY5 was obtained from sequence database at NCBI (Lund et al., 2002). It contains 344 amino acid

---

Table 1. Percentage similarity between target and template sequence.

Model Number	Tool used	Template	Similarity	No. of residues modeled
1	Modeller	2ZIY	29%	344
2		3EML	25%	344
3	Swiss pdb Viewer	2ZIY	29%	344
4	SWISS-MODEL	2Z73A	17.6%	288
5	3Djigsaw	------	------	292
6	CPHmodels	2RH1	24.9%	197
7	ESyPred3D	1JFP	18.1%	311

sequences. It was ensured that the three-dimensional structure of the gene was not available in Protein Data Bank (Lambert et al., 2002), therefore the present work of predicting the 3D model of the P2RY5 was planned out. Reported mutations were retrieved from Literature.

Template selection

Template was searched by BLASTP, scanning the non redundant gene sequence database at NCBI. Two templates were selected based on the significant e-value and alignment among the searched templates. Web based tools that is SWISS-MODEL (Combet et al., 2002), 3Djigsaw (Bates et al., 1999), CPHmodels (Laskowski et al., 1993), (Lambert et al., 2002) Geno3d (Hooft et al., 1996) obtained templates automatically without any user intervention. All the obtained templates using these tools are listed in Table 1.

Sequence alignment

The target and template sequences were aligned using the align2d command of MODELLER (Sali et al., 1993) which uses global dynamic programming, with linear gap penalty function for aligning the two profiles. ESyPred3D use neural network method for increasing the alignment performance between the query and template sequence. Geno3D further validates the alignment by secondary structure agreement between target and template. CPHmodel uses profile-profile alignment between target and template.

Model building

A three dimensional structure was developed from sequence alignment between P2RY5 and template using MODELLER8v1. It constructs model by satisfaction of spatial restraints. Distance and dihedral angle restraints on target sequence were derived from alignment with template structure. Stereochemical restraints such as bond angles and bond lengths were extracted from CHARM22 molecular mechanics force field. CHARMM energy functions were combined to obtain objective function. Final model was obtained by optimization of objective function using conjugate gradients and molecular dynamics with simulated annealing.

SWISS-MODEL, 3Djigsaw, CPHmodels, ESyPred3D, Geno3d automatically build model by using their own set of modeling algorithms. Swiss PdbViewer 3.7 follows homology modeling approach. It first takes template and then by superimposing both structures builds structure through modeling server CPHmodel uses segmod program from the GeneMine package. It further refines the model using encad program from the GeneMine package. ESyPred3D uses MODELLER and Geno3d uses distance geome-

try approach for model building.

Energy minimization

The constructed models were subjected to energy minimization by steepest descent, using GROMOS96 force field, implementation of Swiss-pdb Viewer.

Evaluation of models

Accuracy of the predicted models was subjected through a series of tests. Stereochemical properties were evaluated through Procheck (Laskowski et al., 1993). Backbone conformation was evaluated by investigating PSi/Phi Ramachandran plot using Procheck and RAMPAGE (Laskowski et al., 1993; Lovell et al., 2002). Packing quality and RMS of model was evaluated using Whatif packing quality control and protein analysis (Hooft et al., 1996).

RESULTS

Domains prediction tools, that is SMART acknowledged a number of regions in P2RY5 gene which includes intrinsic disorder (1 - 12), Pfam:7tm_1 (34 - 291), intrinsic disorder (327 - 344) (Herzog et al., 1996). It contains an important family i-e G-protein coupled receptors family, an extensive group of hormones, neurotransmitters, odorants and light receptors which transduce extracelular signals by interaction with guanine nucleotide-binding (G) proteins and many sites that are important for various biological processes. These are: N-glycosylation site, Protein kinase C phosphorylation site, N-myristoylation site, Tyrosine kinase phosphorylation site (Sali and Blundell, 1993; Marti-Renom et al., 2000). Different mutations have been reported in P2RY5 gene that includes 4 Missense mutations and 3 Frame shift mutations (http://www.ncbi.nlm.nih.gov/sites/entrez?dopt=GenPept&cmd=Retrieve&db=protein&list_uids=17466994). Thus this protein is desired to be functionally silent and manipulated. Towards this conclusion, it is useful to know its three - dimensional structure (http://www.rcsb.org/pdb/results/results.do?outformat).

Amino acid sequence of P2RY5 was obtained through NCBI, sequence database. Templates using blastp at NCBI were obtained with high resolution X-ray diffraction templates that are 2ZIY and 3EML (Table 1). Sequence

Table 2. Ramachandran plot values obtained through PROCHECK.

Model Number	Ramachnadran plot values			
	Core	Allowed	Generously	Disallowed
1	91.0%	7.8%	0.9%	0.3%
2	91.6%	6.5%	0.3%	1.6%
3	73.6%	23.6%	2.2%	0.6%
4	85.4%	12.4%	1.9%	0.4%
5	80.4%	15.1%	4.1%	0.4%
6	85.6%	11.7%	1.1%	1.7%
7	64.0%	24.9%	6.6%	4.5%

Table 3. Ramachandran plot values obtained through RAMPAGE.

Model Number	Ramachandran plot values		
	No of residues in favoured region	No of residues in allowed region	No of residues in outlier region
1	93.9%	5.6%	0.6%
2	95.6%	3.2%	1.2%
3	73.4%	20.5%	6.1%
4	91.2%	5.6%	3.2%
5	82.8%	12.1%	5.2%
6	91.3%	5.1%	3.6%
7	73.8%	17.2%	9.1%

identity is good determinant for the quality of the model. Among the different alignments, the more related alignment is of models obtained through MODELLER and Swiss pdb Viewer. More then one tools used the 2ZIY template.

Values for the Ramachandran plot obtained through Procheck are shown in Table 2. The plot is subdivided into favored, allowed, generously allowed and disallowed regions. The models obtained through MODELLER and EsyPred3d showed better Ramachandran plot values, as denser core region (>90%) accounts for better structure.

Rampage assessment is given in Table 3. Rampage derives Phi/Psi plots for Gly, Pro, Pre-Pro and other residues. The plot was divided into three regions that is, favored, allowed and outlier regions. The result for models obtained through MODELLER and Esypred were significant, as denser number of residues in favored region(>90%) is the measure of good quality of a model, but Esypred created the model for 311 residues while MODELLER created the model for all 344 residues.

These results demonstrate that prediction of the best possible target would be a difficult task because the target performing well in one case was not found good in other cases. Swiss Model and CPHmodels show good stereochemistry but they don't have good sequence identity and modeled 288 and 197 residues respectively. Swiss pdb Viewer show some better sequence identity but don't show good stereochemistry.

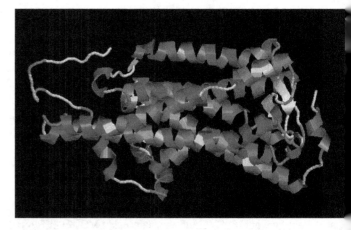

Figure 1. Three dimensional structure of normal P2RY5 gene in Rasmol version 2.7.5. Display: Cartoons, Colours: Structure

For all the targets described herein, the structure obtained through MODELLER, using 2ZIY template was found to be satisfactory based on the above results. This model is shown in Figure 1. Ramachandran plot analysis through Procheck showed that 93.9% residues are within the favored region (Figure 2). RMS and packing quality was evaluated through Whatif and found satisfactory for this model. After generating the normal model for P2RY5, the mutated structure models were built using the repor-

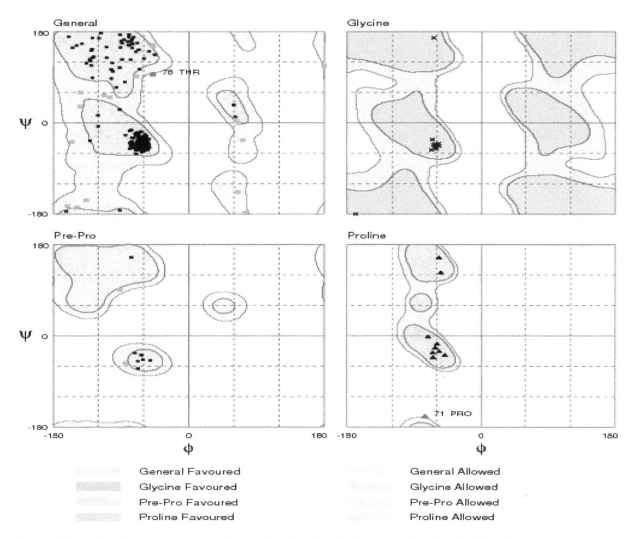

Figure 2. Ramachandran plot values showing number of residues in favoured, allowed and outlier region.

```
MVSVNSSHCF YNDSFKYTLY GCMFSMVFVL GLISNCVAIY IFICVLKVRN ETTTYMINLA
MSDLLFVFTL PFRIFYFTTR NWPFGDLLCK ISVMLFYTNM YGSILFLTCI SVDRFLAIVY
PFKSKTLRTK RNAKIVCTGV WLTVIGGSAP AVFVQSTHSQ GNNASEACFE NFPEATWKTY
LSRIVIFIEI VGFFIPLILN VTCSSMVLKT LTKPVTLSRS KINKTKVLKM IFVHLIIFCF
CFVPYNINLI LYSLVRTQTF VNCSVVAAVR TMYPITLCIA VSNCCFDPIV YYFTSDTIQN
SIKMKNWSVR RSDFRFSEVH GAENFIQHNL QTLKSKIFDN ESAA
```

Figure 3. The protein encoded by P2RY5 gene belongs to the family of G-protein coupled receptors, which are preferentially activated by adenosine and uridine nucleotides. It contains seven transmembrane Domains scattered at different locations (20 - 42, 55 - 77, 135 - 154, 179 - 201, 272 - 294, and 230 - 252). Highlighted areas present the physical locations of these domains in the amino acid sequence. (Data obtained from Human Protein Reference Database).

ted mutations (Figure 3). Alterations brings by different mutations have diverse effect on the different level of protein structures which cause the malfunctioning of specific protein to cause relevant disease. For exam-ple, In P2RY5 glutamic acid participates in formation of alpha helix, but due to mutation (p.E189 K) replaced amino acid is also making alpha helix but at position number 172 phenyl alanine that was making an alpha helix is now part of random coil. Random coil is not considered as true secondary structure so; phenyl alanine is no longer participating in secondary structure. P2Y5 is a member of GPCR. Through interaction with Guanine binding proteins, these receptors transduce extra cellular signals. P2RY5 is a member of purine and pyrimidine nucleotides receptors family. Alpha helices are crucial for binding of particular protein with nucleotides. This mutated structure

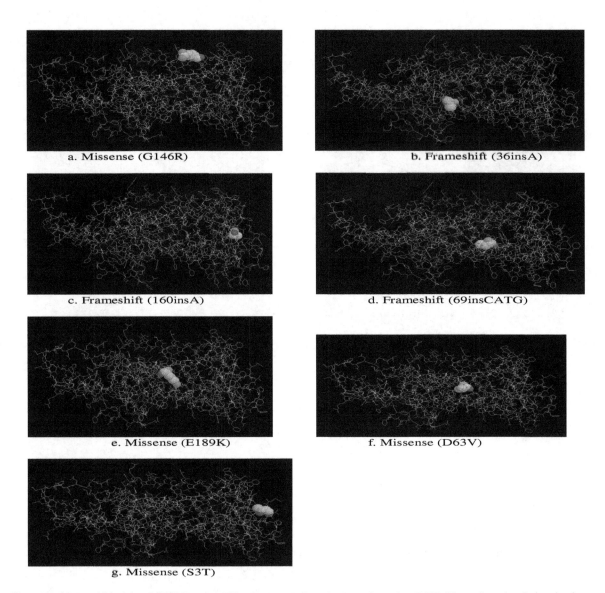

a. Missense (G146R)

b. Frameshift (36insA)

c. Frameshift (160insA)

d. Frameshift (69insCATG)

e. Missense (E189K)

f. Missense (D63V)

g. Missense (S3T)

Figure 4. Mutated Models of P2RY5 gene with report mutations in rasmol version 2.7.5. Normal portion is in wire frame view while mutated region is displayed in spacefill view. Mutated Models ie. a-f indicates mutation lies in the Transmembrane domains while in model g its lie in intrinsic region of P2RY5.

might have reduced binding with Guanine binding proteins which leads to reduction in amino acid is also making extended strand but at position number 4 valine, which was making random coil is now making an extended strand. Random coil is not considered as true secondary structure so; valine is now participating in secondary structure. Valine that is now a part of extended strand might be forming hydrogen bond with some distant residue. This additional residue in extended strand might leads to changed tertiary structure.

Post-translational modification like p.G146R mutation, results in conversion of glycine at position number 146 to arginine. Glycine at position number 146 in P2RY5 is a part random coil but due to mutation, replaced amino acid is now participating in extended strand formation. Arginine that is now a part of extended strand might be forming hydrogen bond with some distant residue. This

additional residue in extended strand might leads to changed tertiary structure.

DISCUSSION

Different mutations interrupt normal functioning of protein through changing their structure at different levels.

Change in structure can affect isoelectric point of protein (change the protein interaction), addition of domain (interrupt normal protein function) and alteration in phosphorylation pattern of proteins. Our modeling suggests six identified mutations are located in trans membrane domain. Three Missense mutaion (G146R, E189K, D63V) and three frameshift mutations (36 insA, 160 insA, 69 insCATG) located in these domains (Figure 4). Presence of most of the mutation in the region o

transmembrane suggests that it has pivotal role in the mechanism of normal hair growth. Any disturbance in this region by genetic mutation cause autosomal recessive hypotrichosis (LAH3). Disruption of P2RY5 change the structure of protein which is unable to perform the normal functional pathway of signalling and result in the disease. Mutated models can be confirmed
by experiments of extraction of proteins using genetically modified mouse for specific mutation.

REFERENCES

Ali G, Chishti MS, Raza SI, John P, Ahmed W (2007). A mutation in the lipase H (LIHP) gene underlie autosomal recessive hypotrichosis. Hum Genet 121: 319-325

Arnold K, Bordoli L, Kopp J, Schwede T. (2006). The SWISS-MODEL Workspace: A web-based environment for protein structure homology modelling. Bioinformatics 22:195-201.

Bates PA, Sternberg MJE (1999) Model Building by Comparison at CASP3: Using Expert Knowledge and Computer Automation. Proteins: Structure, Function and Genetics, Suppl. 3:47-54.

Combet C, Jambon M, Deléage G, Geourjon C (2002). Geno3D: Automatic comparative molecular modeling of protein. Bioinformatics

Herzog H, Darby K, Hort YJ, Shine J (1996). intron 17 of the human retinoblastoma susceptibility gene encodes an actively transcribed G protein-coupled receptor gene. Genome Res. 6:858-861

Hooft, RWW, Vriend G, Sander C, Abola EE 1996. Errors in protein structures. Nature 381:272-272. (Server: http://swift.cmbi.kun.nl/WIWWWI/)

Lambert C, Leonard N, De Bolle X, Depiereux E (2002). ESyPred3D: Prediction of proteins 3D structure. Bioinformatics 18(9):1250-1256.

Jorg S, Frank M, Peer B, Chris PP (1998). SMART, a simple modular architecture research tool: Identification of signaling domains. Proc. Natl. Acad. Sci. 95: 5857–5864.

Laskowski RA, MacArthur MW, Moss DS, Thornton JM (1993). PROCHECK: a program to check the stereochemical quality of protein structures. J. Appl. Cryst. 26: 283-291.

Liang L, Ping H (2005). Recent developments in structural proteomics for protein structure determination. Proteomics 5: 2056–2068.

Lovell SC,. Davis I.W. Arendall III WB,. de Bakker PIW, Word JM, Prisant MG, Richardson JS, Richardson DC (2002) Structure validation by Calpha geometry: phi,psi and Cbeta deviation. Proteins: Structure, Function Genet. 50: 437-450.

Lund O, Nielsen M, Lundegaard C, Worning P (2002). X3M a Computer Program to Extract 3D Models. CASP5 conference A102.

Marti-Renom MA, Stuart AC, Fiser A, Sanchez R, Melo F, Sali A (2000). Comparative protein structure modeling of genes and genomes. Annu. Rev. Biophys. Biomol. Struct. 29:291-325.

National Center for Biotechnology Information: http://www.ncbi.nlm.nih.gov/

Protein Data Bank: http://www.rcsb.org/pdb/ Sali A, Blundell TL.(1993). Comparative protein modeling by satisfaction of spatial restraints. J. Mol. Biol. 234:779-815.

Wali A, Chishti MS, Ayub M, Yasinzai M, Kafaitullah, Ali G, John P, Ahmad W (2007). Novel Mutations in G protein-coupled receptor gene (P2RY5) in families with autosomal recessive hypotrichosis (LAH3) Clin Genet. 72:23-9

Zahid A, Jelani M, Gul N, Tariq M, Wasif N, Naqvi K, Ayub M, Yasinzai M, Amin-ud-din M, Wali A, Ali G, Salman M C, Ahmad W. (2008). Novel mutations in G protein-coupled receptor gene (P2RY5) in families with autosomal recessive hypotrichosis (LAH3). Hum. Genet. 123: 515-519.

5

Nuclear mitochondrial DNA pseudogenes in the genome of the silkworm, *Bombyx mori*

Guangli Cao[1,2], Renyu Xue[1,2], Yuexiong Zhu[1], Yuhong Wei[1] and Chengliang Gong[1,2*]

[1]School of Biology and Basic Medical Science, Medical college of Soochow University, Suzhou, 215123, China.
[2]National Engineering Laboratory for Modern Silk, Soochow University, Suzhou, 215123, China.

To understand the types of mitochondrial deoxyribonucleic acid (mtDNA) pseudogenes in the genome of the silkworm *Bombyx mori* L. (Lepidoptera: Bombycidae) and to determine the origin of the *B. mori*, the mtDNA of the wild silkworm, *Bombyx mandarina* Morre was sequenced. Several fragments from the *B. mori* genome database were obtained with varying degrees of homology to *B. mandarina* mtDNA by sequence alignment between the *B. mori* genome and *B. mandarina* mtDNAs. The results showed that in the *B. mori* genome database there are not only mtDNA (Dazao strain) sequence but also pseudogenes derived from *B. mandarina* mtDNA. There is a potential reverse repeated sequence at the terminal sequence of the pseudogenes, and there are random point mutations and insertion mutations in the pseudogenes sequences. One *B. mandarina* mtDNA could be repeatedly inserted into different positions within the nuclear genome. Evolutionary analysis indicates that the transfer of mtDNA pseudogenes might have occurred at different points during evolution, some sequences might be transferred after Lepidoptera had formed, and possibly before the families of Lepidoptera were formed. *B. mori* probably originated from *B. mandarina* of China.

Key words: *Bombyx mori*, *Bombyx mandarina*, nDNA, mtDNA, nuclear mitochondrial DNA pseudogenes.

INTRODUCTION

The mitochondria of the eukaryotic cells are important organelles. The genome of mitochondrial deoxyribonucleic acid (mtDNA) contains mitochondrial tRNA genes, rRNA genes and cytochrome genes and thus is able to synthesize the specific protein of itself, but the mitochondrial genome is regulated by the nuclear genes, including mitochondrial genome transcription and translation process, especially for the greater impact on the regulation of transcriptional level. The evidence has been found that there are similar mitochondrial genes sequences in nuclear Deoxyribonucleic acid (nDNA). These sequences that exist in the pseudogene form were named nuclear mitochondrial pseudogenes (*numt*, nuclear mitochondrial DNA segments). The *numts* are nonfunctional copies of mtDNA in the nucleus that have been found in major clades of eukaryotic organisms

(Zhang and Hewitt, 1996; Bensasson et al., 2001a; Song et al., 2008). Experiments show that mtDNA was reverse-transcribed from the mitochondrial RNA in the cytoplasm, through the nuclear pore of the nuclear membrane and randomly integrated into the nDNA by DNA ligase (Woischnik and Moraes, 2002; Nugent and Palmer, 1991). These *numts* copies may be very long, but their richness varied in different species and they and their corresponding mtDNA have strong homology. mtDNA and similarities in the sequence of the nuclear genome shows there has been an exchange of genetic material between nucleus and cytoplasm during the evolution of the cell.

The high mutation rates of mtDNA can produce intraspecific polymorphism and deep interspecific divergence in relatively short evolutionary times (Avise et al., 1987). This makes mtDNA particularly informative for the determination of genetic population structure and inference of population history within species as well as for deducing phylogenetic relationships between closely related species (Hlaing et al., 2009). The use of mtDNA sequences has been proposed for several DNA

*Corresponding author. E-mail: gongcl@suda.edu.cn.

barcoding initiatives for taxonomic identification and biodiversity assessment (Song et al., 2008; Hebert et al., 2003). However, such studies can generate misleading results if the species concerned contain *numts* as these may amplify in addition to, or even instead of, the authentic target mtDNA. The evolutionary rate of the *numt* sequences is very low, *numts* result from the translocation of mitochondrial sequences from the mitochondrial genome into the nuclear genome and, once integrated, these non-functional sequences accumulate mutations freely (Hlaing et al., 2009). Because the *numt* still can represent the original form of mtDNA sequence to a certain extent, it is possible to determine the early evolutionary relationships between species (Zhang and Hewitt, 1996; Sorenson and Quinn, 1998; Perna and Kocher, 1996).

There are seven complete mtDNA genome of Bombycidae strains (or varieties) have been sequenced, including *B. mori* variety C-108 and Xiafang (Chinese), Aojuku (Japanese), Backokjam (South Korea), *B. mandarina* strain Ankang and Qingzhou (Chinese), and Tsukuba (Japanese). These data provides the basis for an evolutionary analysis. *Bombyx mori* is used as a model organism for Lepidopteran insects (Goldsmith, 1995; Goldsmith et al., 2005), and the draft sequence for the genome of *B. mori* provided a good platform for the study of the biological information of Lepidoptera (Xia et al., 2004; Mita et al., 2004).

There is a lot of evidence to support the origin of the *B. mori* in China. There are many theories for the geographical origin of silkworms and differentiation of voltinism. The "multi centers" and "mono center" hypotheses of *B. mori* origin are examples. In recent years, molecular biology research provided strong evidence at the molecular level for the origin of silkworms in China, and the evidence from molecular biology also support the "multi-center" hypotheses of silkworm origin (Zhang and Lü, 2005). The origin and differentiation of *B. mori* is related to the major issues, such as silkworm genetics, breeding, character formation, and other subjects, therefore also the need for more direct or indirect evidence to understand the problem. There are numerous reports of the analysis of molecular evolution of silkworms using mtDNA protein coding genes or rRNA genes (Chen et al., 2007), but so far there are no reports of the analysis of silkworm evolution using the *numt* of nDNA sequence. This paper uses sequence searching to compare and analyze the *B. mori* genome *numt* (*Bombyx mori numt*, *Bmnumt*) based on the complete mtDNA sequence of *B. mandarina* (Qinzhou) that was sequenced, to provide new evidence of molecular evolution of *B. mori*.

MATERIALS AND METHODS

Insect, mitochondrial DNA extraction and sequencing

Bombyx mandarina strain Qingzhou was collected from Qingzhou in the Shandong Province of China. Mitochondrial DNA was extracted from larval insects using a standard phenol/chloroform method for genomic DNA extraction (Sambrook and Russell, 2001).

Restriction enzymes *Pst*I (use for identification of TA clone), PCR reagents, T-vector, the T4 DNA ligase and the gel DNA purification kit were purchased from the Sangon (Shanghai Sangon Biological Engineering Technology and Services Co., Ltd, Shanghai, China) and TaKaRa (Dalian, China) or Bio Flux (Hangzhou, China). The full mitogenome of *B. mandarina* strain Qingzhou was amplified in 15 overlapping fragments by PCR using insect-specific designed primers (Hu et al., 2009). The mtDNA fragments were amplified using a standard PCR method. After purification with the gel DNA purification kit, each fragment was cloned into the T-vector and sequenced (Sangon, Shanghai, China). The mitochondrial genome sequence of *B. mandarina* strain Qingzhou was deposited in the GenBank database under the accession no. FJ384796.

Sequence analysis

Sequence analysis was performed as follows. Initially, the mtDNA sequence and *numt* sequence were identified using the NCBI internet blast (Altschul et al., 1990) search function. The probe sequence was used complete mtDNA sequences, including four *B. mori* strains (Xiafang, AY048187; Aojuku, AB083339; C-108, AB070264; Backokjam, AF149768), three *B. mandarina* strains (Tsukuba, AB070263; Ankang, AY301620; Qingzhou, FJ384796), and other insects (*Drosophila melanogaster*, AJ400907; *Adoxophyes honmai*, DQ073916; *Locusta migratoria*, NC_011119; *Tribolium castaneum*, AJ312413), respectively. After selected blast analysis the "highly similar sequences, megablast" and "somewhat similar sequences, blastn" were chosen for comparison with the *B. mori* genome (Dazao strain) database "wgs" (whole – genome shotgun reads). Suspected mtDNA sequence of the Dazao strain, and suspected *numt* sequences (*Bmnumt*) were obtained. The sequences were aligned with Clustal X (Thompson et al., 1997).

Phylogenetic analysis

The *numt* sequences and homologous regions in different *B. mori* mitogenome sequences were aligned with Clustal X (Thompson et al., 1997). A phylogenetic analysis was performed based on the concatenated nucleotide sequences of the *Bmnumt* using the neighbor joining (NJ), minimum evolution (ME), maximum parsimony, and UPGMA programs of the MEGA3 software package (Kumar et al., 2004; Pan et al., 2008), with a bootstrap of 500 replicates. Pairwise genetic distances were calculated with MEGA3 using the Kimura two-parameter model for nucleotide substitution (Kumar et al., 2004).

Based on the supposition that the different strains of *B. mandarina* arose through geographic isolation and the generally accepted belief that the Japanese islands were separated from the Asian continent 0.02 Mya, the MEGA3 program was used to set the divergence time to understand the divergence time during origin of *B. mori*. The molecular clock was based on a substitution rate of $(7.8$ to $10.2) \times 10^{-9}$ per site per year (Zakharov et al., 2004) in the $COI + COII$ mitochondrial genes of *Papilio* sp. (Lepidoptera: Papilionidae). The mutation rate of mtDNA is calculated to be about ten times greater than that of nuclear DNA (including *numts*), possibly due to a paucity of DNA repair mechanisms (Haag-Liautard et al., 2008; Brown et al., 1979). The molecular dating for the *Bmnumt* origin was estimated from the overall genetic distance between *numt* and mtDNA, applying the equation of Li et al. (1981) whereby the fraction of sequence divergence is: $\delta = (\mu_1 + \mu_2)\, t$ (Li et al., 1981; Kim et al., 2006), where $\mu_1 = (7.8$ to $10.2) \times 10^{-9}$ substitutions/sites/year and $\mu_2 = (7.8$ to $10.2) \times 10^{-10}$ substitutions/sites/year for nuclear pseudogene distance and t is the time elapsed. Either, estimates of the divergence time (*T*) between the domesticated silkworm, *B. mori*, and its closely related species were derived from the molecular clock (*r*) and genetic distance (*K*) using the simple equation *T* = *K*/2*r* (Fu and Li, 1997).

RESULTS

Genome organization of the mitogenome of *B. mandarina* strain Qingzhou

The complete mitogenome of *B. mandarina* strain Qingzhou is 15,717 bp, similar to other sequenced lepidopteran mitogenomes, and presents the typical gene content observed in metazoan mitogenomes. It has 13 protein-coding genes, 22 tRNA genes, and 2 rRNA genes, and a major noncoding region known as the "A + T-rich region", as has been detected in other insects. The gene order and orientation of the *B. mandarina* strain Qingzhou mitogenome are identical to those of the other completely sequenced lepidopteran mitogenomes (Hu et al., 2009).

The information of mtDNA sequence in the database of the *B. mori* genome

The *B. mori* genomic sequence database was searched with the MEGA blast program online. The probe sequence used complete mtDNA sequence of the *B. mori* strains and *B. mandarina* strain, respectively, for comparison with the *B. mori* genome database "wgs", and suspected mtDNA (Dazao) sequence was obtained (Table 1).

The *Bmnumt* sequence is highly homologous with the mtDNA sequence

The *B. mori* genomic sequence database was searched with the MEGA blast program online. The probe sequence selected was the complete mtDNA sequence of the *B. mandarina* strain Qingzhou and used the process "highly similar sequences, megablast" for comparison with the *B. mori* genome database "wgs" to obtain suspected *Bmnumt* sequence. The other analysis parameters of blast were default. The results show that there were high identities nDNA fragments (*Bmnumt*-H) in the *B. mori* genome sequence when be compared with the *B. mandarina* mtDNA genome sequence, more than 30 DNA fragments (*Bmnumt*) of 78 to 252 bp in length, with identities of 84 to 98% to the *B. mandarina* mitochondrial DNA, were found in the nuclear genome of *B. mori*, and can be summarized into 14 nonredundant *Bmnumt*-H (Table 2).

Most *Bmnumt*-H fragment was structural gene for the mtDNA, included *CO I*, *CO II*, *ATPase6*, *ND3*, *ND6*, *Cytb*, *ND1*, tRNA and 16S rRNA gene fragments. The homologous fragment of mtDNA non-coding sequences were in the nDNA. The (AT)n sequence in the mtDNA

was inter tRNA[Ala] and tRNA[Arg] gene, this sequence of homologous fragment was repeated many times in *B. mori* nDNA. Because these repeats sequences were too short in the nDNA, and did not have another coding sequence of mtDNA, it was therefore not analyzed. The same homologous fragments may appear in a different region of the nuclear genome. For example, the same sequence of an *ATPase6* gene fragment occurs in sequences BABH01027843 and BABH01031741 that are nonredundant sequences. This provides evidence that the exchange of genetic material occurred between the mitochondrial DNA and nuclear DNA during the course of evolution. Two *Bmnumt*-H fragments (2646 to 2554 and 2552 to 2512) of the sequences BABH01027843 were closely linked, and corresponding to the mtDNA in *B. mori* and *B. mandarina* were two fragments of *ATPase6* gene. This shows that evolution was more likely to occur initially by mtDNA fragments transferred to the nDNA, and then the middle region had a 62 bp deletion mutation in the evolutionary process. Blast analysis showed that all of these *Bmnumt*-H fragments were not found.

The sequence BABH01001168 contain two homologous fragments of mtDNA sequence (13365 to 13442 and 13596 to 13689), separated by 153 bp, while the intervening sequences in nDNA of *B. mori* was a large number of repeat sequences, and two *Bmnumt*-H fragments were homologous to one region of the *B. mori* and *B. mandarina* mtDNA sequences, such as the homologous region 5765 to 5844 and 5837 to 5928 in the mtDNA of the *B. mandarina* strain Qingzhou. Analysis of sequence showed that in *B. mandarina* the transfer of mtDNA to nDNA occurred and then the middle region of the nDNA was inserted in the repeat sequences during the evolutionary process. The repeat sequences may be inserted as a transposon sequence, which ends with the reverse repeat sequence aTgtaCAcacAAAAAA (13443 to 13458) and TTTTTTaatTGatgAg (13580 to 13595), and contains duplication of mtDNA target sequence TTTAATTT (13596 to 13603), while one target sequence of duplication had been deleted by mutation to TTTATTT (13436 to 13442), the mutations may result in relative stability in the region of the genome.

By selecting 50 nt (+1 to +50) of the 5' end of *Bmnumt*-H sequence and 50 nt (-1 to -50) of the upper sequence of *Bmnumt*-H, also obtained 100 nt of the 3' end of *Bmnumt*-H complementary sequence. The results of homology comparisons show that the *Bmnumt*-H terminal has a consensus sequence in the +5 area $T_{13}A_{14}T_{13}A_{16}G_{13}A_{17}$, while conservation was not high, but different with *numt* results from other species (Blanchard and Schmidt, 1996; Zischler, 2000). The 5' end sequences and 3' end sequence comparisons did include the consensus repeat sequence of the nDNA target.

The evolution analysis of the *Bmnumt*-H sequences

The homology region sequence of mtDNA obtained was

Table 1. Lists only those sequences corresponding to the homologous region of mtDNA of *B. mandarina* Qingzhou strains or *B. mori* Xiafang strains[a]

GenBank Accession No.	bp	Homologous region			Contains genes
		nDNA	Qingzhou	Xiafang	
AADK01034881	2 968	1-2 944	1 316-4 260	1 279-4 222	< ND2, tRNA^{Trp}, tRNA^{Cys}, tRNA^{Tyr}, COI, tRNA^{Leu}, COII, tRNA^{Lys}, tRNA^{Asp}, ATP8, ATP6 >
BABH01045921	2 898	2 898-1	1 382-4 281	1 345-4 243	< tRNA^{Cys}, tRNA^{Tyr}, COI, tRNA^{Leu}, COII, tRNA^{Lys}, tRNA^{Asp}, ATPase8, ATPase6 >
BABH01050552	951	3-951	1 920-2 869	1 882-2 831	< COI >
AADK01054955	994	974-16	4 477-5 434	4 439-5 398	< ATPase6, COIII >
BABH01045920	665	665-1	4 729-5 392	4 691-5 356	< ATPase6, COIII >
BABH01049001	1 125	549-9	5 414-5 953	5 378-5 917	< COIII, tRNA^{Gly}, ND3 >
		545-1 125	6 616-7 196	6 554-7 134	< ND5 >
BAAB01163697	1 116	562-1	6 616-7 177	6 554-7 115	< ND5 >
		558-1 098	5 414-5 953	5 378-5 917	< COIII, tRNA^{Gly}, ND3 >
AADK01061636	768	29-644	5 616-6 251	5 580-6 192	< tRNA^{Gly}, ND3, tRNA^{Ala}, tRNA^{Arg}, tRNA^{Asn} >
BABH01068416	647	3-647	6 013-6 684	5 973-6 622	tRNA^{Ala}, tRNA^{Arg}, tRNA^{Asn}, tRNA^{Ser}, tRNA^{Glu}, tRNA^{Phe}, ND5 >
		17-647			
AADK01047228	1 387	1 186-29	7 078-8 229	7 016-8 167	< ND5 >
BABH01058819	715	1-713	7 657-8 369	7 595-8 307	< ND5, tRNA^{His} >
AADK01058254	854	845-33	8 621-9 438	8 560-8 560	< ND4 >
BABH01045778	2 006	1-2005	9 454-1 1481	9 393-1 1401	< ND4, ND4L, tRNA^{Thr}, tRNA^{Pro}, ND6, Cytb >
BAAB01148239	933	933-1	10 399-11 351	10 336-11 271	< ND6, Cytb >
AADK01051126	1 183	51-1 138	10 507-11 637	10 443-11 557	< ND6, Cytb >
		50-1 138			
BABH01069147	642	4-629	10 842-11 469	10 762-11 389	< Cytb >
AADK01040309	2 124	41-2 075	11 714-13 750	11 634-13 667	< Cytb, tRNA^{Ser}, ND1, tRNA^{Leu}, 16S rRNA >
BABH01045779	1 963	1-1 963	11 726-13 689	11 646-13 609	< Cytb, tRNA^{Ser}, ND1, tRNA^{Leu}, 16S rRNA >

a): The symbols " < >" means the gene sequence is incomplete and lacks sequence in front (<) or behind (>) the symbol.

compared with the 14 Bmnumt-H sequences and different mtDNA sequences of *B. mori* (Table 3). A phylogenetic analysis was performed based on the concatenated nucleotide sequences of 14 Bmnumt-H using the NJ, ME, maximum parsimony, and UPGMA programs of the MEGA 3 software package, and phylogenetic trees identical or similar in topological structure were obtained.

Table 2. The highly similar genome sequence with mtDNA fragments[a].

GenBank Accession No.	Homologous region of nDNA	Homologous region of mtDNA	Identities (%)	The sequence of mtDNA contains genes
BABH01027970	1 9113–1 8970	1 469–1 618	127/151 (84)	< tRNA^{Tyr}-COI >
BABH01026725	8 372–8 257	3 413–3 526	107/116 (92)	< COII >
BABH01027843	2 646–2 554	4 143–4 235	85/93 (91)	< ATPase6 >
	2 552–2 512	4 296–4 336	37/41 (90)	< ATPase6 >
BABH01031741	8 779–8 554	4 197–4 423	218/228 (95)	< ATPase6 >
BABH01001168	13 365–13 442	5 765–5 844	77/80 (96)	< ND3 >
	13 596–13 689	5 837–5 928	88/96 (91)	< ND3 >
BABH01021008	11 183–11 325	8 003–8 138	125/143 (87)	< ND5 >
BABH01000761	4 815–4 654	10 037–10 202	148/168 (88)	< tRNA^{Thr}-tRNA^{Pro}-ND6 >
BABH01026106	1 062–1 313	11 248–11 498	234/253 (92)	< Cytb >
BABH01013865	11 308–11 510	11 887–12 087	189/204 (92)	< Cytb-tRNA^{Ser}-ND1 >
BABH01017043	1 312–1 467	12 125–12 279	153/156 (98)	< ND1 >
BABH01041409	4 889–5 170	12 869–13 158	258/293 (88)	< ND1-tRNA^{Leu}-16S rRNA >
BABH01031124	6 700–6 806	15 322–15 430	103/110 (93)	< A+T rich region >

a): The symbol "<" or ">" representing the gene sequence is incomplete and lack of sequence in front (<) or behind (>) the symbol.

Table 3. Homologous region of mtDNA and Bmnumt-H

Bmnumt Accession No.	mtDNA (Dazao) Accession No	region	Xiafang AY048187	Aojuku AB083339	C-108 AB070264	Backokjam AF149768	Ankang AY301620	Tsukuba AB070263
BABH01027970	BABH01045921	2 812–2 664	1 432–1 580	11 764 – 11 912	11 787–1 1935	11 774–11 922	11 813–11 963	12 059–12 209
BABH01026725	BABH01045921	868–756	3 375–3 488	13 708–13 820	13 731–13 843	13 718–13 830	13 759–13 871	14 004–14 117
BABH01027843	BABH01045921 [a]	139–47	4 106–4 197	14 437–14 529	14 460–14 552	14 447–14 539	14 488–14 580	14 734–14 826
	—		4 258–4 298	14 590–14 630	14 613–14 653	14 600–14 640	14 641–14 681	14 888–14 927
BABH01031741	BABH01045921	84–1 >[b]	4 160–4 385	14 492–14 717	14 515–14 740	14 502–14 727	14 543–14 768	14 788–15 014
BABH01001168	BAAB01163697	910–988	5 729–5 808	427–505	429–507	429–507	431–510	428–507
		981–1 073	5 801–5 892	498–589	500–591	500–591	503–596	500–591

BABH01021008	AADK01047228	254–119	7 941–8 076	2 611–2 746	2 637–2 772	2 617–2 752	2 648–2 783	2 642–2 777
BABH01000761	BABH01045778	584–749	9 976–10 141	4 645–4 810	4 669–4 834	4 652–4 817	4 683–4 848	4 674–4 839
BABH01026106	AADK01051126	771–1021	1 1168–11418	5 837–6 087	5 862–6 112	5 846–6 096	5 884–6 133	5 875–6 124
BABH01013865	BABH01045779	162–362	11 807–12 007	6 476–6 676	6 501–6 701	6 485–6 685	6 523–6 725	6 514–6 716
BABH01017043	BABH01045779	400–554	12 045–12 199	6 714–6 868	6 738–6 892	6 723–6 877	6 763–6 917	6 754–6 908
BABH01041409	BABH01045779	1 144–1 433	12 789–13 078	7 458–7 747	7 482–7 770	7 467–7 756	7 506–7 799	7 497–7 790
BABH01031124	—	15 227–15 335	9 898–10 006	9 921–10 029	9 904–10 012	9 941–10 051	9 941–10 049	

a): The sequence BABH01031124 (6 700–6 806) and BABH01027843 (2 552–2 512) of Bmnumt-H were lack of the corresponding sequence of mtDNA (Dazao) (with "–" indicates, see Table 5 and Table 9) b): The sequence BABH01045921 (84–1) of mtDNA (Dazao) corresponding sequence BABH01031741 (8 779–8 554) of Bmnumt-H was incomplete (with "84–1 >" indicates).

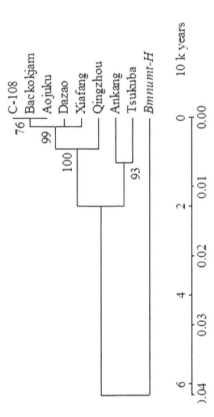

Figure 1. NJ-TREE according to mtDNA and *Bmnumt*-H homologous sequence. The phylogenetic analysis was performed based on the concatenated nucleotide sequences of the *Bmnumt*-H (***Bmnumt*** sequence) using the neighbor joining (NJ) programs of the MEGA3 software. The divergence of the different geographic varieties of the *B. mandarina* has been inferred to have occurred 0.02 Mya (20 k years).

The phylogenetic tree shown in Figure 1 was constructed with the NJ program. It indicates that the *Bmnumts*-H resulted from the transfer of *B. mandarina* mtDNA fragments to the nuclear genome before domesticated *B. mori* diverged from *B. mandarina*. Based on the supposition that the different strains of *B. mandarina* arose through geographic isolation and the generally accepted belief that the Japanese islands were separated from the Asian continent 0.02 Mya, the divergence of the different geographic varieties of *B. mandarina* has been inferred to have occurred 0.02 Mya. So, with the MEGA 3 software package, it can be calculated that the domesticated *B. mori* separated from *B. mandarina* about 7,000 years ago (7,057 years), which is consistent with archeological findings (Hemudu Relics Archaeological Team, 1980).

Table 4. The somewhat similar genome sequence with mtDNA fragments [a].

GenBank Accession No.	Homologous region of nDNA	Homologous region of mtDNA	Identities (%)	The sequence of mtDNA contains genes
BABH01034256	24 483–2 4572	35–121	79/91 (86)	< A+T rich region-tRNA^{Met} >
BABH01037485	407–544	282–418	120/138 (87)	< tRNA^{Gln}-ND2 >
BAAB01195380	934–814	405–525	109/121 (90)	< ND2 >
BABH01014043	19 606–19 825	405–626	192/222 (86)	< ND2 >
BABH01035568	4 899–4 713	541–723	152/187 (81)	< ND2 >
BABH01078039	21–584	4 804–5 367	466/565 (82)	< COIII >
AADK01004266	9 609–9 514	5 978–6 075	74/98 (75)	< ND3-tRNA^{Ala} >
BABH01009450	62 792–62 852	6 250–6 309	55/62 (88)	< tRNA^{Arg}-tRNA^{Asn} >
BABH01022999	35 029–35 148	7 820–7 941	96/126 (76)	< ND5 >
BABH01032998	20 118–20 259	8 105–8 252	127/148 (85)	< ND5 >
BABH01041352	25 083–24 945	9 421–9 558	109/141 (77)	< ND4 >
BABH01026242	56 935–57 117	9 951–10 145	145/199 (72)	< ND4L-tRNA^{Thr}-tRNA^{Pro} >
AADK01009125	4 485–4 672	10 318–10 504	168/188 (89.4)	< ND6 >
BABH01031256	19 360–19 284	10 973–11 047	66/77 (85)	< Cytb >
BABH01018554	5 567–5 648	11 223–11 305	75/83 (90)	< Cytb >
BABH01018464	10 951–10 907	13 542–13 586	41/45 (91)	< 16S rRNA >
BABH01019526	16 978–17 104	2 400–2 530	95/134 (70)	< COI >

a): The symbol "<" or ">" representing the gene sequence is incomplete and lack of sequence in front (<) or behind (>) the symbol.

The *Bmnumt* sequence has low homology with the mtDNA sequence

The results of the blast (blastn) searches demonstrate the presence of "somewhat similar sequences" in the genome of *B. mori*. There were relatively low homology sequences (*Bmnumt*-L) in the nuclear genome of *B. mori*, in addition to the analysis of the *Bmnumt*-H sequence. These *Bmnumt*-L fragments of 45 to 564 bp in length, with identities of 70 to 91% to the *B. mandarina* mitochondrial DNA, can be summarized into 17 nonredundant *Bmnumt*-L (Table 4). Because blast parameters selected was "somewhat similar sequences blastn", the *Bmnumt*-L sequences obtained may be mtDNA fragments that were transferred to the nDNA in earlier periods of evolution, therefore, these *Bmnumt*-L sequences were examined in a separate correlation analysis.

The evolutionary analysis of the *Bmnumt*-L sequences

The homologous region of mtDNA obtained by comparison with the 17 *Bmnumt*-L sequences and different mtDNA sequences of *B. mori* (Table 5). A phylogenetic analysis was performed based on the concatenated nucleotide sequences of the 17 *Bmnumt*-L using the minimum evolution (ME) program of the MEGA 3 software package (Figure 2). This result was similar to

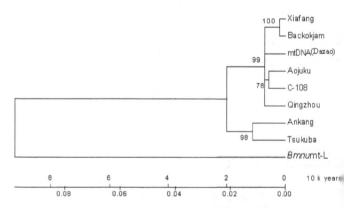

Figure 2. ME-TREE according to mtDNA and *Bmnumt*-L homologous sequence. The phylogenetic analysis was performed based on the concatenated nucleotide sequences of the *Bmnumt*-L (*Bmnumt* sequence was low homologous with the *Bombyx* mtDNA sequence) using the minimum evolution (ME) programs of the MEGA3 software. The divergence of the different geographic varieties of the *B. mandarina* has been inferred to have occurred 0.02 Mya (20 k years).

the results of *Bmnumt*-H analysis. It can be calculated that domesticated *B. mori* separated from *B. mandarina* about 7,000 years ago (7,146 years). However, *B. mori* strain Dazao demonstrated more differences with other silkworms because the mtDNA (Dazao) sequence from the "wgs" database was incomplete.

Table 5. Homologous region of mtDNA and *Bmnumt*-L.

Bmnumt	mtDNA (Dazao)		Xiafang	Aojuku	C-108	Backokjam	Ankang	Tsukuba
Accession No.	Accession No	region	AY048187	AB083339	AB070264	AF149768	AY301620	AB070263
BABH01034256	—	—	1–87	10 330–10 416	10 353–10 439	10 339–10 425	10 378–10 464	10 625–10 711
BABH01037485	—	—	245–381	10 577–10 713	10 600–10 736	10 587–10 723	10 626–10 762	10 872–11 008
BAAB01195380	—	—	368–488	10 700–10 820	10 723–10 843	10 710–10 830	10 749–10 869	10 995–11 115
BABH01014043	—	—	368–589	10 700–10 921	10 723–10 944	10 710–10 931	10 749–10 970	10 995–11 216
BABH01035568	—	—	504–686	10 836–11 018	10 859–11 041	10 846–11 028	10 885–11 067	11 131–11 313
BABH01019526	BABH01050552	482–612	2362–2492	12 694–12 824	12 717–12 847	12 704–12 834	12 745–12 875	12991–13 121
BABH01078039	AADK01054955	643–80	4 768–5 331	15100–15635, 1–28	15123–15656, 1–30	15110–15643, 1–30	15149–15682, 1–30	15395–15928, 1–30
AADK01004266	AADK01061636	395–488	5 942–6 042	600–705	641–732	641–735	644–734	641–731
BABH01009450	BABH01068416	218–276	6 191–6 250	862–921	888–947	868–927	908–967	901–960
BABH01022999	BABH01058819	164–285	7 758–7 879	2 428–2 549	2 454–2 575	2 434–2 555	2 465–2 586	2 459–2 580
BABH01032998	BABH01058819	449–596	8 043–8 190	2 713–2 860	2 739–2 886	2 719–2 866	2 750–2 896	2 744–2 891
BABH01041352	BABH01045778	<1–105	9 360–9 497	4 029–4 166	4 053–4 190	4 036–4 173	4 067–4 204	4 058–4 195
BABH01026242	BABH01045778	498–692	9 890–10 084	4 559–4 753	4 583–4 777	4 566–4 760	4 597–4 791	4 588–4 782
AADK01009125	BABH01045778	863–10 50	10 255–10 442	4 924–5 111	4 948–5 135	4 931–5 118	4 964–5 151	4 955–5 142
BABH01031256	AADK01051126	496–570	10 893–10 967	5 562–5 636	5 587–5 661	5 571–5 645	5 609–5 683	5 600–5 674
BABH01018554	BABH01069147	384–466	11 143–11 225	5 812–5 894	5 837–5 919	5 821–5 903	5 859–5 941	5 850–5 932
BABH01018464	AADK01040309	1 868–1 912	13 462–13 506	8 130–8 174	8 153–8 197	8 139–8 183	8 183–8 227	8 171–8 215

The origin analysis of the *Bmnumt* sequence

The sequence BABH01078039 with identities of 81.9% to the homologous region of sequence AADK01054955 of mtDNA (Dazao), and no EST evidence, indicates that this sequence (*Bmnumt*564) was *Bmnumt*-L in *B. mori* nDNA (Table 4). The *Bmnumt*564 contained 101 mutation sites compared to the homologous region (564 bp) of the *COIII* gene of *B. mandarina* strain Qingzhou mtDNA, which has 23 mutations in the first base of the genetic code, 13 mutations in the second base, 65 mutations in the third base, with a total of 32 missense mutations. Substitution mutations including 33 transitions and 68 transversions, transversion was significantly higher than transition. The *Bmnumt* sequence was the longest *Bmnumt* sequence in *B. mori* genome sequence. Because of the limited genome sequence information, the actual length and characteristics at both ends of nDNA sequence could not be determined.

Because *Bmnumt*564 was a longer sequence, it is possible to analyze the origin of the *Bmnumt B. mori* genome sequence. The Blast results show that the mtDNA of *Adoxophyes honmai* (GenBank accession number: DQ073916) has high identity 88% to the *Bmnumt*564 sequence. Its difficult to understand why the mRNA sequence of unknown function in *Picea sitchensis* (GenBank accession number: EF082272) has the highest identity 98% to the *Bmnumt*564 sequence. A representative of the mtDNA sequence of insects was chosen in each order to obtain the homologous sequence of *Bmnumt*564 for evolutionary analysis. Table 6 shows the source of insect mtDNA sequences data and the classification of insects.

The evolutionary analysis of homologous sequences (non-coding sequences) was done using the MEGA3 software ME program. The results (Figure 3) show that the *Bmnumt*564 fragments could have occurred when *B. mori* and *B. mandarina* separated, and may have occurred after insects differentiated into different orders. Because *numt* had a different evolution rates with mtDNA, and the transfer of mtDNA to nDNA formed *numt* could have occurred at different evolutionary stages, Figure 3 can only reflect the

Table 6. The source of insect mtDNA sequences data.

GenBank Accession No.	Species	Order	Family
AY956355	*Petrobius brevistylis*	Archaeognatha	Machilidae
AB126004	*Periplaneta fuliginosa*	Blattoidea	Blattidae
AJ312413	*T. castaneum*	Coleoptera	Tenebrionidae
AF272824	*Tetrodontophora bielanensis*	Collembola	Onychiuridae
AJ400907	*D. melanogaster*	Diptera	Drosophilidae
DQ241796	*Grylloblatta sculleni*	Grylloblattodea	Grylloblattidae
AY521259	*Bemisia tabaci*	Hemiptera	Aleyrodidae
L06178	*Apis mellifera ligustica*	Hymenoptera	Apidae
DQ073916	*A. honmai*	Lepidoptera	Tortricidae
AY242996	*Antheraea pernyi*	Lepidoptera	Saturniidae
DQ241797	*Tamolanica tamolana*	Mantodea	Mantidae
DQ241798	*Sclerophasma paresisensis*	Mantophasmatodea	Mantophasmatidae
AB126005	*Orthetrum triangulare*	Odonata	Libellulidae
X80245	*Locusta migratoria*	Orthoptera	Acrididae
DQ241799	*Timema californicum*	Phasmatodea	Timematidae
AY968672	*Campanulotes bidentatus*	Phthiraptera	Philopteridae
AF335994	*Lepidopsocid RS-2001*	Psocoptera	Lepidopsocidae
AF335993	*Thrips imaginis*	Thysanoptera	Thripidae
AY639935	*T. domestica*	Thysanura	Lepismatidae

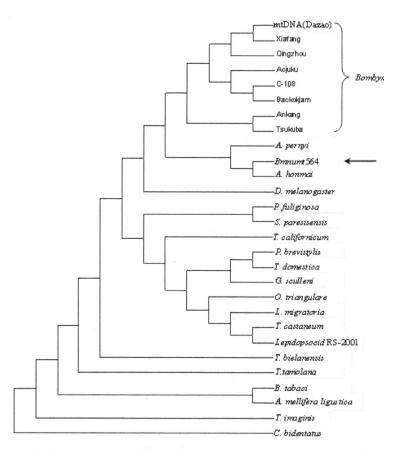

Figure 3. ME-TREE according to *Bmnumt*564 homologous sequence of insect. To choose the mtDNA sequence of insect that representative in each of the order on classification. The evolution analysis using MEGA3 software ME program (non-coding sequences, 500 bootstrap). The arrow was the *Bmnumt*564.

Table 7. The origin of Lepidoptera mtDNA sequences data.

GenBank accession No.	Science name of species	Family
FJ384796	*Bombyx mandarina* (strain Qingzhou)	Bombycidae
AB070264	*Bombyx mori* (strain C-108)	Bombycidae
AB083339	*Bombyx mori* (strain:Aojuku)	Bombycidae
AY048187	*Bombyx mori* (strain Xiafang)	Bombycidae
AF149768	*Bombyx mori* (strain Backokjam)	Bombycidae
AY301620	*Bombyx mandarina* (strain Ankang)	Bombycidae
AB070263	*Bombyx mandarina* (strain Tsukuba)	Bombycidae
AY242996	*Antheraea pernyi*	Saturniidae
FJ685653	*Eriogyna pyretorum*	Saturniidae
AF442957	*Ostrinia nubilalis*	Crambidae
AF467260	*Ostrinia furnacalis*	Crambidae
DQ073916	*A. honmai*	Tortricidae
DQ102703	*Coreana raphaelis*	Lycaenidae
EU286785	*Manduca sexta*	Sphingidae
AB277671	*Eurema hecabe*	Pieridae
AB277672	*Eurema blanda*	Pieridae
EF206706	*Spodoptera exigua*	Noctuidae
EF621724	*Papilio xuthus*	Papilionidae
EU597124	*Artogeia melete*	Pieridae
EF622227	*Caligula boisduvalii*	Saturniidae
AM946601	*Ochrogaster lunifer*	Notodontidae
EU726630	*Antheraea yamamai*	Saturniidae
EU569764	*Phthonandria atrilineata*	Geometridae
AJ400907	*D. melanogaster*	Diptera: Drosophilidae

relative evolutionary periods of the *Bmnumt564* fragment sequence.

The *Bmnumt564* fragment from the homology comparison shows that this *Bmnumt* fragment may have occurred after formation of the Lepidoptera, therefore, with a view to understand the conservation of *Bmnumt564* fragments in the mtDNA sequence of Lepidoptera, further mtDNA sequences of Lepidoptera were retrieved from GenBank to obtain the homologous sequence of *Bmnumt564* for comparison with that of *Bmnumt564* (Table 7). The *Drosophila melanogaster* sequences were retrieved from GenBank for comparison with that of *Bmnumt564*. The evolutionary analysis of homologous sequences (non-coding sequences) was done using the MEGA3 software ME program. The result (Figure 4) show that the *Bmnumt564* fragments may have occurred before the Lepidoptera differentiated into different families.

The evolutionary analysis of the somewhat similar genome sequence with other insects mtDNA sequences (*Bmnumt-O*)

The probe sequence used was complete mtDNA sequences of other insects (*D. melanogaster*, *A. honmai*,

L. migratoria, *T. castaneum*), and the selected process was "somewhat similar sequences, blastn" when compared with the *B. mori* genome database. There were relatively low homology sequences (*Bmnumt-O*) found in the nuclear genome of *B. mori*, in addition to the analysis of the *Bmnumt-H* and *Bmnumt-O* sequences. These *Bmnumt-O* fragments of 36 to 193 bp in length, with identities of 62.1 to 98% to the *B. mandarina* mtDNA (Qingzhou), can be summarized into 13 nonredundant *Bmnumt-L* (Table 8). The *Bmnumt-O* sequences may be the "molecular fossil". There were other shorter homologous fragments (50 to 90 bp), and these fragments were not conserved in the mtDNA of *B. mori*, and it is difficult to explain whether these fragments were transfered from the mtDNA or which the fragments of mtDNA had been transfered, therefore, these fragments could not be analyzed and included in the Bmnumt-O.

The homologous sequence of mtDNA obtained by comparison with the 13 *Bmnumt-O* sequences and different mtDNA sequences of *B. mori* (Table 9). A phylogenetic analysis was performed based on the concatenated nucleotide sequences of 13 *Bmnumt-O* using the ME program of the MEGA 3 software package (Figure 5). This result was similar to the results of *Bmnumt-H* analysis (Figure 1) and *Bmnumt-L* (Figure 2). However, these *Bmnumt-O* sequences were more

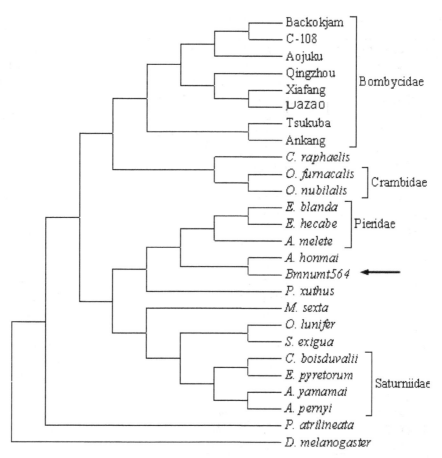

Figure 4. ME-TREE according to *Bmnumt*564 homologous sequence of Lepidoptera. To options mtDNA sequence of Lepidoptera were retrieved from GenBank to obtain the homology region sequence of *Bmnumt*564 for comparison with that of *Bmnumt*564. The *Bmnumt*564 homology region sequence of *D. melanogaster* (Diptera: Drosophilidae) mtDNA sequence were retrieved for outgroups. The evolution analysis using MEGA3 software ME program (non-coding sequences, 500 bootstrap). The arrow was the *Bmnumt*564.

Table 8. The somewhat similar genome sequence with other mtDNA fragments [a).

GenBank Accession No.	Homologous region of nDNA	Homologous region of mtDNA	bp	The sequence of mtDNA contains genes
BAAB01212268	5–74	558–626	70	< ND2 >
BABH01003279	10 248–10 292	1 531–1 576	46	< CO I >
BABH01006274	10 598–10 542	5 698–5 755	57	< ND3 >
BABH01017611	4 474–4 282	6 645–6 830	193	< ND5 >
BABH01019913	1 867–1 820	8 667–8 718	48	< ND4 >
BABH01012405	4 648–4 570	9 130–9 216	79	< ND4 >
BAAB01023567	74–4	10 037–10 107	71	< tRNA^{Thr}–tRNA^{Pro} >
BABH01017047	10 382–10 433	10 133–10 186	52	< tRNA^{Pro}–ND6 >
AADK01028330	3 463–3 540	10 973–11 054	78	< Cytb >
BABH01033821	3 986–4 021	11 034–11 069	36	< Cytb >
BAAB01133008	7–57	12 037–12 087	51	< ND1 >
AADK01000378	32 802–32 968	13 894–14 074	167	< 16S RNA >
BABH01013212	30 399 –30 360	14 072–14 111	40	< 16S RNA >

a): The symbol "<" or ">" representing the gene sequence is incomplete and lack of sequence in front (<) or behind (>) the symbol.

ancient than the above Bmnumt-H and Bmnumt-L sequences.

Evolutionary age estimates

Applying the equation of Li et al. (1981) whereby the fraction of sequence divergence is: $\delta = (\mu_1 + \mu_2) t$ (Li et al., 1981; Zakharov et al., 2004), the molecular clock was based on a substitution rate of $(7.8 \text{ to } 10.2) \times 10^{-9}$ per site per year (Zakharov et al., 2004). The Bmnumt564 compared with homologous sequences of the B. mandarina (Qingzhou) mtDNA, 564 bp fragment contains 101 substitution mutations. According to MEGA3 the substitution rate of Bmnumt564 was obtained and mtDNA of related species (Table 10), thus the divergence times of the Bmnumt564 transfered from mtDNA to nDNA has been inferred to have occurred approximately 21.02 ± 7.93 to 27.48 to 10.37 Mya. By origin analysis of the Bmnumt564 fragment found that the Bmnumt564 transferred from mtDNA to nDNA has been inferred to have occurred after the insects differentiated into different orders and before the Lepidoptera differentiated into different families (Figures 3 and 4). Some studies showed that the B. mandarina (strain Ankang) and B. mandarina (strain Tsukuba) diverged 1.11 ± 0.16 to 1.45 ± 0.21 Mya (Pan et al., 2008), and B. mori and fruit fly diverged about 260 Mya ago (Purugganan, 1998), The Bmnumt564 divergence times is not in contradiction with these comparisons. Using MEGA3 to obtain the substitution rate of Bmnumt-H, Bmnumt-L, and Bmnumt-O (Table 11), based on this molecular clock, divergence times were calculated between B. mandarina (Qingzhou) and the related Bmnumt. The earliest divergence time estimates for B. mandarina – Bmnumt-H, B. mandarina – Bmnumt-L and B. mandarina – Bmnumt-O were 3.20 ± 18.54 to 4.18 ± 24.24 Mya, 68.35 ± 0.62 to 89.38 ± 0.82 Mya and 50.40 ± 1.69 to 65.91 ± 2.21 Mya, respectively.

DISCUSSION

Although taxonomically widespread, there is substantial variation among species in numt copy number (Richly and Leister, 2004). The numts exhibit different degrees of homology to their mitochondrial counterparts; are variable in size; evenly distributed within and among chromosomes, and, in some cases, are highly rearranged and or fragmented (Zhang and Hewitt, 1996; Woischnik and Moraes, 2002; Richly and Leister, 2004; Ricchetti et al., 1999). Even within insects, numt copy number varies greatly with high numbers in Tribolium flour beetles, honeybee and the brown mountain grasshopper (Pamilo et al., 2007; Bensasson et al., 2001b), but few or none in Drosophila and Anopheles mosquitoes (Richly and Leister 2004). Bmnumts analysis found that B. mori nDNA sequences cantain the Bmnumt sequences,

including coding genes and control region (non-coding) sequences, and the same mtDNA sequence can be repeatedly inserted into different nDNA sequences. After mtDNA sequence was inserted into the nDNA sequence, point mutations could occur as well as insertion and deletion mutations, and finally the formation of different Bmnumt copies.

Lopez et al. (1994) reported that the 7.946 kb numt mitochondrial genome to a specific nuclear chromosomal position in the domestic cat was due to the transfer of a complete large fragment of the mtDNA from the control region (D-loop) to the CO II gene, so that the transfer of mtDNA may be a large fragment. The mtDNA gene structure and features at both ends of numt that were homologous with B. mori mtDNA sequences led us to try to understand whether or not there had been transfer of large fragments of mtDNA in B. mori genome, a sequence analysis of B. mori genome was done. The results show that the transfer of large fragments of mtDNA did not exist in B. mori genome, and the longest fragment was Bmnumt564, and most Bmnumt fragments in nDNA were relatively short. We have used mtDNA sequences of different species for blast analysis that was carried out with the Bmnumt sequence. However, we have reason to believe that there are numt sequences in B. mori genome far more than shown in our analysis of these sequences, that originated in different periods of evolution but numt was not found that formed from the transfer of mtDNA fragments late in evolution. From features of the end of the sequence of these Bmnumt sequences, was also difficult to speculate whether the Bmnumt sequences are processed pseudogenes or a non-processed pseudogene that direct formed by transfer of mtDNA fragments (Huang and Xue, 2006). As the homologous fragments of the control region also appear in the nDNA, and thus presumably at least Bmnumt formed directly from transfer of mtDNA to nDNA. There appears to be several types of conserved sequence repeats after carefully comparing these to the Bmnumt sequences. In view of the existence of different types of transposons in B. mori genome (Ichimura et al., 1997; Robertson and Walden, 2003; Kawanishi et al., 2008), we can guess that if these Bmnumt sequences were processed pseudogenes, they may be dependent on different transposase enzymes for transposon. Because some transposon target sequences were too short, such as the mariner transposon into the target genome that caused the target sequence TA repeat, in addition, these Bmnumt earlier origins, as well as the conservation of Bmnumt end sequences was not high without being collected and analyzed (the analysis of Bmnumt sequences at both ends was not necessarily true), thus also difficult to find the characteristics and rules of the end of the sequence.

In the multi-cellular animals, numt lost the function of mtDNA after being transferred to the nucleus (Gellissen and Michaelis, 1987), therefore, the way of Bmnumt

Table 9. Homologous region of mtDNA and Bmnumt-O.

Bmnumt Accession No.	mtDNA (Dazao) Accession No	region	Xiafang AY048187	Aojuku AB083339	C-108 AB070264	Backokjam AF149768	Ankang AY301620	Tsukuba AB070263
BAAB01212268		—	521–589	10 853–10 921	10 876–10 944	10 863–10 931	10 902–10 970	11 148–11 216
BABH01003279	AADK01034881	214–259	1 493–1 538	11 825–11 870	11 848–11 893	11 835–11 880	11 876–11 921	12 122–12 167
BABH01006274	BAAB01163697	842–899	5 662–5 719	359–416	361–418	361–418	364–421	361–418
BABH01017611	BABH01049001	574–766	6 583–6 775	1 253–1 445	1 279–1 471	1 259–1 451	1 290–1 482	1 284–1 476
BABH01019913	AADK01058254	800–749	8 606–8 657	3 275–3 326	3 299–3 350	3 282–3 333	3 310–3 361	3 304–3 355
BABH01012405	AADK01058254	337–251	9 069–9 155	3 738–3824	3 762–3 848	3 745–3 831	3 773–3 858	3 767–3 853
BAAB01023567	BABH01045778	584–654	9 976–10 046	4 645–4 715	4 669–4 739	4 652–4 722	4 683–4 753	4 674–4 744
BABH01017047	BABH01045778	680–731	10 072–10 123	4 741–4 792	4 765–4 816	4 748–4 799	4 779–4 832	4 770–4 823
AADK01028330	BABH01045778	1 498–1 579	10 893–10 974	5 562–5 643	5 587–5 668	5 571–5 652	5 609–5 690	5 600–5 681
BABH01033821	BABH01045778	1 559–1 594	10 954–10 989	5 623–5 658	5 648–5 683	5 632–5 667	5 670–5 705	5 661–5 696
BAAB01133008	AADK01040309	364–414	11 957–12 007	6 626–6 676	6 650–6 700	6 635–6685	6 675–6 725	6 666–6 716
AADK01000378		—	13 811–13 990	8 482–8 661	8 505–8 684	8 488–8 668	8 535–8 715	8 520–8 700
BABH01013212		—	13 988–14 027	8 659–8 698	8 682–8 721	8 665–8704	8 713–8 752	8 698–8 737

Table 10. The substitution of Bmnumt564 compair with mtDNA sequence [a].

	Bmnumt564	Dazhao	Qingzhou	Xiafang	Aojuku	C-108	Backokjam	Ankang	Tsukuba
Bmnumt564		0.1738	0.2358	0.1738	0.2340	0.3085	0.2642	0.1862	0.2535
Dazhao	0.1310		0.0000	0.0000	0.0000	0.0106	0.0000	0.0142	0.0000
Qingzhou	0.0890	1.0000		0.0000	0.0000	0.0000	0.0000	0.0319	0.0000
Xiafang	0.1160	1.0000	1.0000		0.0000	0.0106	0.0000	0.0142	0.0000
Aojuku	0.0870	1.0000	1.0000	1.0000		0.0106	0.0000	0.0124	0.0000
C-108	0.0570	0.1720	1.0000	0.1710	0.0640		0.0035	0.0904	0.0000
Backokjam	0.0710	1.0000	1.0000	1.0000	1.0000	0.2300		0.0355	0.0000
Ankang	0.1120	0.2720	0.1310	0.2740	0.2700	0.0520	0.1660		0.1223
Tsukuba	0.0770	1.0000	1.0000	1.0000	1.0000	1.0000	1.0000	0.0010	

a): Below diagonal: genetic distance; above diagonal: standard error of the genetic distance.

evolution was different from that of the functional mtDNA. In the absence of purifying selection, they rapidly accumulated frameshift mutations (Fukuda et al., 1985). The Bmnumt564 compared with homologous region of B. mandarina (Qingzhou) show that it contains 101 mutation sites which include 33 transitions and 68 transversions (conversion / transversion ratio: 0.4853). Mutations occurred mainly in the A ↔ T (56 times) followed by T ↔ C (25 times).

Subject to different selective pressures leading to different rates of evolution in each region in the mtDNA gene sequences, and the numt in the nuclear genome has been subject to selection pressure with different mtDNA, so the calculated evolutionary distance was only an approximate average with analysis of combined different structural gene sequences. In order to understand the evolutionary relationships of Bmnumt564 fragment, blast analysis of the genome database of different species showed that there are

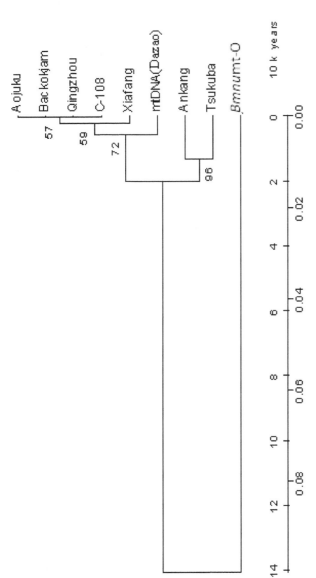

Figure 5. ME-TREE according to mtDNA and *Bmnumt*-O homologous sequence. The phylogenetic analysis was performed based on the concatenated nucleotide sequences of the *Bmnumt*-O (***Bmnumt*** sequence was low homologous with **o**ther insects mtDNA sequence) using the minimum evolution (ME) programs of the MEGA3 software. The divergence of the different geographic varieties of the *B. mandarina* has been inferred to have occurred 0.02 Mya (20 k years).

Table 11a. The substitution of *Bmnumt*-H compair with mtDNA sequence [a].

	Bmnumt-H	Dazhao	Qingzhou	Xiafang	Aojuku	C-108	Backokjam	Ankang	Tsukuba
Bmnumt-H		3.3710	0.0359	0.0000	0.0000	0.0000	0.0000	0.1736	0.0819
Dazhao	0.0000		3.9355	3.5174	3.5440	3.5166	3.5246	3.8356	3.6752
Qingzhou	0.2080	0.0000		0.0157	0.0074	0.0093	0.0098	0.0393	0.0017
Xiafang	1.0000	0.0000	0.0540		0.0000	0.0007	0.0000	0.0613	0.0000
Aojuku	1.0000	0.0000	0.1330	1.0000		0.0000	0.0000	0.0525	0.0000
C-108	1.0000	0.0000	0.1140	0.2350	1.0000		0.0000	0.0688	0.0072
Backokjam	1.0000	0.0000	0.1080	1.0000	1.0000	1.0000		0.0635	0.0014
Ankang	0.0310	0.0000	0.0600	0.0200	0.0310	0.0170	0.0270		0.0071
Tsukuba	0.0970	0.0000	0.3230	1.0000	1.0000	0.2620	0.3400	0.2050	

a): Below diagonal: genetic distance; above diagonal: standard error of the genetic distance.

Table 11b. The substitution of *Bmnumt*-L compair with mtDNA sequence [a].

	Bmnumt-L	Dazhao	Qingzhou	Xiafang	Aojuku	C-108	Backokjam	Ankang	Tsukuba
Bmnumt-L		54.8002	0.7669	0.8677	0.8581	0.8045	0.8325	0.5923	0.3555
Dazhao	0.0000		55.9024	57.3465	57.2468	55.5651	55.7706	57.8060	54.9479
Qingzhou	0.0070	0.0000		0.0000	0.0000	0.0000	0.0000	0.0610	0.0458
Xiafang	0.0030	0.0000	1.0000		0.0000	0.0029	0.0081	0.0234	0.0673
Aojuku	0.0000	0.0000	1.0000	1.0000		0.0031	0.0000	0.0560	0.0739
C-108	0.0020	0.0000	1.0000	0.2950	0.2280		0.0000	0.0634	0.0539
Backokjam	0.0030	0.0000	1.0000	0.0340	0.0000	1.0000		0.0470	0.0606
Ankang	0.0040	0.0000	0.0260	0.1650	0.0710	0.0310	0.0470		0.0817
Tsukuba	0.0360	0.0000	0.0820	0.0840	0.0600	0.0860	0.0750	0.0080	

a): Below diagonal: genetic distance; above diagonal: standard error of the genetic distance.

Table 11c. The substitution of *Bmnumt*-O compair with mtDNA sequence [a].

	Bmnumt-O	Dazhao	Qingzhou	Xiafang	Aojuku	C-108	Backokjam	Ankang	Tsukuba
Bmnumt-O		1.1977	0.5655	0.4701	0.4856	0.4856	0.4608	0.5707	0.5871
Dazhao	0.0010		1.2273	1.1683	1.1779	1.1779	1.1477	1.0702	1.1573
Qingzhou	0.0190	0.0000		0.0005	0.0005	0.0005	0.0015	0.0000	0.0000
Xiafang	0.0350	0.0000	0.2880		0.0000	0.0000	0.0000	0.0000	0.0000
Aojuku	0.0210	1.0000	0.4770	1.0000		0.0000	0.0000	0.0000	0.0000
C-108	0.0270	1.0000	0.4790	1.0000	1.0000		0.0000	0.0000	0.0000
Backokjam	0.0330	1.0000	0.2300	1.0000	1.0000	1.0000		0.0000	0.0000
Ankang	0.0250	1.0000	1.0000	1.0000	1.0000	1.0000	1.0000		0.0044
Tsukuba	0.0290	1.0000	1.0000	1.0000	1.0000	1.0000	1.0000	0.2630	

a): Below diagonal: genetic distance; above diagonal: standard error of the genetic distance.

homologous sequences of *Bmnumt*564 fragment in nDNA, and there are multi-copy sequences in some species, such as *Culex quinquefasciatus*, where there are two homologous sequences of *Bmnumt*564 in one sequence (GenBank accession number: AAWU01031902), and four homologous sequences of *Bmnumt*564 in one genome sequence of *Drosophila virilis* (GenBank accession number: AANI01013925), and 11 homologous sequences of *Bmnumt*564 in one genome sequence of *Monodelphis domestica* (GenBank accession number: AAFR03065773), and a number of *M. domestica* genome sequences with multiple copies of the *Bmnumt*564 homologous sequences. Analysis of these nDNA sequences of different species show that the sequences are highly homologous to its corresponding mtDNA sequence of the species, presumably these species suggest the presence of high-frequency transfer of mtDNA to nDNA. Because these sequences did not have the feature of a "molecular fossil" of the mtDNA, a phylogenetic analysis cannot be done with the *Bmnumt*564 sequence, and therefore it is difficult to determine the relative differentiation time of the *Bmnumt*564 sequence in evolution.

The phylogenetic trees that were identical or very similar in topological structure, were obtained through different *Bmnumt* sequence comparisons, but were slightly different in different *B. mori* strains that clustered into a group. It did not reflect the geographical origin of *B. mori* whether consistent with the "multi centers" or "mono center". But we can speculate that *B. mori* was originally

derived from a region ("mono center"), afterwards, because different regions of human production and living requirements, for example, the thickness of silk, pupa be used food, different voltine, and as well as other breeding characteristics, *B. mori* and the local *B. mandarina* were backcross breeding separately ("multi centers"). The feature of *B. mori* and *B. mandarina* hybrid sterility can support this hypothesis, and this was similar to conclusions drawn by Lu et al., (2002) obtained by a RAPD study, that *B. mori* may include a variety of eco-types of mixed domestication events from *B. mandarina*.

The *numt* sequences have a very good value in phylogenetic studies. Using mtDNA and *numt* two kinds of sequences were used to construct phylogenetic trees, and to compare the phylogenetic results of the study with these two sequences, more objectively reflecting the evolutionary relationships of species, and also checking the traditional method with mtDNA phylogenetic analysis. There are relatively short *Bmnumt* fragments in *B. mori* genome, furthermore, evolutionary analysis shows that the *Bmnumt* fragments derived from silkworm mtDNA in *B. mori* genome could not be found after *B. mori* was evolutionarily split from *B. mandarina*, so a phylogenetic tree based on the *numt* sequences could not be constructed, and it is impossible to verify the phylogenetic trees which were constructed by using traditional methods based on mtDNA.

Conclusion

By the *numt* analysis of *B. mori* genome sequence database, the following conclusions can be inferred:

(1) *B. mori* nDNA sequences have *numt* (*Bmnumt*), that include coding genes and control region (non-coding genes) sequences. There was no EST evidence to support that *Bmnumt* had the genetic characteristics of pseudogenes.
(2) *Bmnumt* terminal sequence may have the same characteristics of consensus sequences.
(3) The same mtDNA sequence can be repeatedly inserted into different nDNA sequences and form repeated sequences.
(4) The point mutations of *Bmnumt* may be random. After mtDNA sequence sequence is inserted into the nDNA, further insertion and deletion mutation may occur in addition to point mutations.
(5) *B. mori* genome mtDNA is not transfered in large fragments, most *Bmnumt* of nDNA were relatively short.
(6) The *Bmnumt* that transfer mtDNA fragments may

occur during different periods of evolution, but we did not find *Bmnumt* that formed during the transfer of mtDNA to the nDNA that occurred after *B. mori* evolution. For example, the analysis of the origin of *Bmnumt* fragment showed that *Bmnumt564* may be transfered after formation of the Lepidoptera, and may occur before the families of Lepidoptera evolved.
(7) *Bmnumt* from foreign groups suggest that *B. mori* may have originated about 7,000 years ago, indicates the origin of *B. mori* was from the Chinese wild silkworm, *B. mandarina*.

ACKNOWLEDGEMENTS

Authors gratefully acknowledge the financial support of the National Natural Science Foundation of China (30671590), the Science and Technology Support Program (Agriculture) of Jiangsu Province (BE2010426), the "Talents in Six Fields" Project of Jiangsu Province (2009-D-Agr18), and the Key Fostering Project for Application Research of Soochow University (Q3134991).

REFERENCES

Altschul S, Gish W, Miller W, Myers E, Lipman D (1990). Basic local alignment search tool. J. Mol. Biol., 215(3): 403-410.
Avise JC, Arnold J, Ball RM, Bermingham E, Lamb T, Neigel JE, Reeb CA, Saunders NC (1987). Intraspecific phylogeography: the mitochondrial DNA bridge between population genetics and systematics. Annu. Rev. Ecol. Syst., 18(1): 489-522.
Bensasson D, Petrov DA, Zhang DX, Hartl DL, Hewitt GM (2001a). Genomic gigantism: DNA loss is slow in mountain grasshoppers. Mol. Biol. Evol., 18(2): 246-253.
Bensasson D, Zhang DX, Hartl DL, Hewitt GM (2001b). Mitochondrial pseudogenes: evolution's misplaced witnesses. Trends. Ecol. Evol., 16(6): 314-321.
Blanchard JL, Schmidt GW (1996). Mitochondrial DNA migration events in yeast and humans: integration by a common end-joining mechanism and alternative perspectives on nucleotide substitution pattern. Mol. Biol. Evol., 13(6): 537-548.
Brown WM, George MJr, Wilson AC (1979). Rapid evolution of animal mitochondrial DNA. Proc. Natl. Acad. Sci. USA., 76(4): 1967-1971.
Chen L, Zhao Q, Shen X, Zhang Z, Tang S, Xu A, Zhang G, Guo X (2007). Nucleotide sequences in the A+T-rich regions of mitochondrial DNA from local races of *Bombyx mori* and their molecular evolution. Acta Sericologica Sinica 33(1): 5-13.
Fu YX, Li WH (1997). Estimating the age of the common ancestor of a sample of DNA sequences. Mol. Biol. Evol., 14: 195-199.
Fukuda M, Wakasugi S, Tsuzuki T, Nomiyama H, Shimada K, Miyata T (1985). Mitochondrial DNA-like sequences in the human nuclear genome. Characterization and implications in the evolution of mitochondrial DNA. J. Mo1. Biol., I86(2): 257-266.
Gellissen G, Michaelis G (1987). Gene transfer: mitochondria to nucleus. Ann. N.Y. Acad. Sci., 503: 391-401.
Goldsmith MR, Shimada T, Abe H (2005). The genetics and genomics of the silkworm, *Bombyx mori*. Annu. Rev. Entomol., 50: 71-100.
Goldsmith MR (1995). Genetics of the silkworm: revisiting an ancient model system. In: Goldsmith MR, Wilkins AS, editors. *Molecular model systems in the Lepidoptera*, Cambridge University Press, pp. 21–76.
Haag-Liautard C, Coffey N, Houle D, Lynch M, Charlesworth B, Keightley PD (2008). Direct estimation of the mitochondrial DNA mutation rate in *Drosophila melanogaster*. PLoS Biol., 6(8): e204.
Hebert PDN, Cywinska A, Ball SL, de Waard JR (2003). Biological identifications through DNA barcodes. PLoS Biol., 270(1512): 313-321.

Hemudu Relics Archaeological Team (1980). Main discoveries of the second excavation of Hemudu sites in Zhejiang. Culture Relics, 5: 1-15.

Hlaing T, Tun-Lin W, Somboon P, Socheat D, Setha T, Min S, Chang MS, Walton C (2009). Mitochondrial pseudogenes in the nuclear genome of Aedes aegypti mosquitoes: implications for past and future population genetic studies. BMC Genet., 10: 11.

Hu X, Cao G, Xue R, Zheng X, Zhang X, Duan H, Gong C (2009). The complete mitogenome and phylogenetic analysis of Bombyx mandarina strain Qingzhou. Mol. Biol. Rep., 37(6): 2599-2608.

Huang Z, Xue Q (2006). Composition and distribution of pseudogenes and their molecular evolution. Chin. Bull. Bot., 7(4): 402-408.

Ichimura S, Mita K, Sugaya K (1997). A major non-LTR retrotransposon of Bombyx mori, L1Bm. J. Mol. Evol., 45(3): 253-264.

Kawanishi Y, Takaishi R, Morimoto M, Banno Y, Nho SK, Maekawa H, Nakajima Y (2008). A novel maT-type transposable element, BmamaT1, in Bombyx mandarina, homologous to the B. mori mariner-like element Bmmar6. J. Insect Biotechnol. Sericol., 77(1): 45-52.

Kim J-H, Antunes A, Luo S-J, Menninger J, Nash WG, O'Brien SJ, Johnson WE (2006). Evolutionary analysis of a large mtDNA translocation (numt) into the nuclear genome of the Panthera genus species. Gene., 366(2): 292-302.

Kumar S, Tamura K, Nei M (2004). MEGA3, integrated software for molecular evolutionary genetics analysis and sequence alignment. Brief. Bioinform., 2: 150-163.

Li WH, Gojobori T, Nei M (1981). Pseudogenes as a paradigm of neutral evolution. Nature, 292(5820): 237-239.

Lopez JV, Yuhki N, Masuda R, Modi W, O'Brien SJ (1994). Numt, a recent transfer and tandem amplification of mitochondrial DNA to the nuclear genome of the domestic cat. J. Mol. Evol., 39: 174-190.

Lu C, Yu H, Xiang Z (2002). Molecular Systematic Studies on Chinese mandarina silkworm (Bombyx mandarina M.) and domestic silkworm (L.). Scientia Agricultura Sinica, 35(1): 94-101.

Mita K, Kasahara M, Sasaki S, Nagayasu Y, Yamada T, Kanamori H, Namiki N, Kitagawa M, Yamashita H, Yasukochi Y (2004). The Genome Sequence of Silkworm, Bombyx mori. DNA Res., 11: 27-35.

Nugent JM, Palmer JD (1991). RNA-mediated transfer of the gene coxII from the mitochondrion to the nucleus during flowering plant evolution. Cell, 66(3): 473-48l.

Pamilo P, Viljakainen L, Vihavainen A (2007). Exceptionally high density of Numts in the honeybee genome. Mol. Biol. Evol., 24(6): 1340-1346.

Pan M, Yu Q, Xia Y, Dai F, Liu Y, Lu C, Zhang Z, Xiang Z (2008). Characterization of mitochondrial genome of Chinese wild mulberry silkworm, Bomyx mandarina (Lepidoptera: Bombycidae). Sci. China C. Life Sci., 51(8): 693-701.

Perna NT, Kocher TD (1996). Mitochondrial DNA: molecular fossils in the nucleus. Curr. Biol., 6(2): 128-129.

Purugganan MD (1998). The molecular evolution of development. Bioessays, 20(9):700-7l1.

Ricchetti M, Fairhead C, Dujon B (1999). Mitochondrial DNA repairs double-strand breaks in yeast chromosomes. Nature, 402: 96-100.

Richly E, Leister D (2004). Numts in sequenced eukaryotic genomes. Mol. Biol. Evol., 21: 1081-1084.

Robertson HM, Walden KK (2003). Bmmar6, a second mori subfamily mariner transposon from the silkworm moth Bombyx mori. Insect Mol. Biol., 12(2): 167-71.

Sambrook J, Russell DW (2001). Molecular cloning: a laboratory manual. 3rd edition. New York, Cold Spring Harbor Laboratory Press.

Song H, Buhay JE, Whiting MF, Crandall KA (2008). Many species in one: DNA barcoding overestimates the number of species when nuclear mitochondrial pseudogenes are coamplified. Proc. Natl. Acad. Sci. USA., 105(36): 13486–13491.

Sorenson MD, Quinn TW (1998). Numt: A challenge for avian systematics and population biology. The Auk., 115(1): 214-221.

Thompson JD, Gibson TJ, Plewniak F, Jeanmougin F, Higgins DG (1997). The CLUSTAL_X windows interface: flexible strategies for multiple sequence alignment aided by quality analysis tools. Nucleic Acids Res., 25: 4876-4882.

Woischnik M, Moraes CT (2002). Pattern of organization of human mitochondrial pseudogenes in the nuclear genome. Genome Res., 12(6):885-893.

Xia Q, Zhou Z, Lu C, Cheng D, Dai F, Li B, Zhao P, Zha X, Cheng T, Chai C (2004). A draft sequence for the genome of the domesticated silkworm (Bombyx mori). Sciences, 306: 1937-1940.

Zakharov EV, Caterino MS, Sperling FA (2004). Molecular phylogeny, historical biogeography, and divergence time estimates for swallowtail butterflies of the genus Papilio (Lepidoptera: Papilionidae). Syst. Biol., 53: 193-215.

Zhang DX, Hewitt GM (1996). Nuclear integrations: challenges for mitochondrial DNA markers. Trends Ecol. Evol., 11(6): 247-251.

Zhang Z, Lü H (2005). The evidence of molecular biology to support the "multi-center" hypotheses of origin of silkworm, Bombyx mori. China Sericulture, 26(4): 11-12.

Zischler H (2000). Nuclear integrations of mitochondrial DNA in primates: inference of associated mutational events. Electrophoresis, 21(3): 531-536.

6

Distribution of insertion sequences in Tn*1546* element in vancomycin-resistant *Staphylococcus aureus* in Sulaimani, Kurdistan of Iraq

Dlnya A. Mohammed and Dana Sabir Khder*

College of Science, University of Sulaimani, Sulaimani 964, Iraq.

In 2008, nine clinical isolates of vancomycin-resistant *Staphylococcus aureus* containing Tn*1546* were recovered in Sulaimani, Iraq. The genetic diversity in Tn*1546*-like elements has been documented previously. The differences described thus far have included the integration of insertion sequence (IS) elements IS*1216V* and IS*1251*. With polymerase chain reaction (PCR) and deoxyribonucleic acid (DNA) sequence analysis of Tn*1546*, the distribution of ISs among 9 *vanA*-containing *S. aureus* isolates were investigated. Only one VRSA element was identical to the prototype Tn*1546* element. Structural analyses of the *van* gene detected IS*1216* and IS*1251* in the genomes of 8 isolates. In addition, IS*19* was detected in the *vanS-vanH* region of one of the 8 isolates. Two of the 8 vancomycin-resistant *Staphylococcus aureus* (VRSA) elements showed a deletion, which eliminated the *orf1* region, and IS*1216* inserted in place of it and also another copy of IS*1216* inserted into the *vanSH* region. The distribution of ISs associated with Tn*1546*-like elements among the Sulaimani isolates was found to be different from that of American vancomycin-resistant Staphylococci population. From this study, it was concluded that identification and analysis of the IS within the *vanA* gene could be a useful tool in epidemiological investigations.

Key words: Vancomycin-resistant *Staphylococcus aureus* (VRSA), insertion sequence (IS), Tn*1546*, Sulaimani, Kurdistan.

INTRODUCTION

Vancomycin-resistant enterococci (VRE) containing the *vanA* gene have been isolated from humans and animals worldwide (Woodford, 1998). Epidemiologic studies of VRE indicate that there are geographic differences (Dahl et al., 1999). *Staphylococcus aureus* is a major cause of potentially life-threatening infections acquired in health care settings and in the community worldwide. Only four vancomycin-resistant *S. aureus* (VRSA) isolates have been reported so far from the USA (Arthur et al., 1993; Brown et al., 2001; Dahl et al., 1999; Darini et al., 1999; Donabedian et al., 2000).

There has been no report of the *van* gene-mediated VRSA (Vancomycin-resistant *Staphylococcus aureus*), from Asia, except for vancomycin-intermediate *S. aureus*

(ISA) in Japan (Dutka-Malen and Courvalin, 1995), Korea (Handwerger and Scoble, 1995), India (Hashimoto et al., 2000), Southern Asia (Jensen et al., 1998). Vancomycin, a glycopeptide antibiotic, acts against Gram-positive bacteria only by inhibiting the incorporation of N-acetyl-muramic acid- N-acetyl-glucose amine polypeptide into the growing peptidoglycan (PG) chain. This is achieved by interacting with D-Alanine-D-Alanine which subsequently blocks the release of terminal D- alanine and intra-chain bond formation. Vancomycin-resistant *Enterococcus faecium* harbours the *vanA* operon, which contain five genes, including vanS, -R, -H, -A and -X, respectively (Perichon et al., 2000).

It had been known that the *vanA* gene cluster is carried as a part of Tn*1546*-like elements and this indicate that the horizontal transfer of Tn*1546*-like elements play an important role in the dissemination of *vanA*-type VRE. Therefore, investigation of the genetic variations within

---

*Corresponding author. E-mail: dlnyaasan@gmail.com

Tn1546-like elements would be essential to have an understanding of the mechanism of evolution of the VRSA, particularly in cases that involve horizontal gene transfer.

The majority of the variations comprises of integration of insertion sequences (ISs) with or without a deletion at the insertion site, point mutations, and deletions (Brown et al., 2001). Epidemiological studies of vanA gene indicate that there are geographic differences associated with this genetic element (Stobberingh et al., 1999). Thus, it is important to understand the underlying molecular mechanisms for the dissemination of VRSA in order to have an effective mechanism for controlling the threat associated with this potentially hazardous microbe in Iraq and elsewhere.

Generally, the primary mechanism for dissemination of the van gene in Staphyllococci could be the clonal dissemination of VRSA where horizontal transfer of resistance gene cluster also plays a prominent role. Pulsed-field gel electrophoresis (PFGE) has been widely carried out to have an understanding of this clonal dissemination of VRE and structural analyses of the van gene have already been introduced to establish an understanding of the horizontal transfer of the resistance gene cluster. In the present study, a set of nine isolates of vancomycin-resistant Staphylococcus aureus (VRSA) containing Tn1546, recovered from Iraq were analyzed to understand the distribution pattern of insertion sequences in Tn1546.

MATERIALS AND METHODS

Bacterial strains

During the period from 2008 to 2009, 10 clinical isolates of vanA-containing S. aureus isolates were collected from patients at the Sulaimani emergency hospital, Iraq. Organisms were identified by conventional biochemical reactions using the API 20 Strep system (BioMérieux).

DNA extraction and PCR

Extraction of bacterial DNA was performed with a Qiagen DNeasy kit (Qiagen, Germany) according to the instructions of the manufacturer. The vancomycin resistance genotypes were determined by PCR with oligo-nucleotide primers specific for the van gene sequences as described previously (Dahl et al., 1999; Dutka-Malen and Courvalin, 1995). For structural analysis of Tn1546-like elements, PCR amplification of internal regions of Tn1546 was performed. The primer sequences for specific Tn1546 regions were listed in Table 1. Primers ISV650F and ISV132R were designed based on the published sequence of IS1216V using the OLIGO program (version 6.0; National Biosciences Inc., Plymouth, Minn.). The melting temperatures of the individual primers were computed by using the same software (Table 1).

Sequence analysis

PCR amplicons of vanA gene cluster were purified using Gene

clean kit (Qiagen, Germany). The purified PCR products were directly sequenced by using an ABI 377 genetic analyzer. DNA fragments amplified with a combination of a Tn1546 and IS1216V-specific primer pairs were also purified and subsequently sequenced to determine the exact integration site and orientation of the S1216V insertion. The DNASIS program for Windows (version 2.6; Hitachi Software Engineering, South San Francisco, Calif.) was used for bioinformatic analysis of nucleotide sequences.

RESULTS AND DISCUSSION

The horizontal transfer of the resistance gene cluster has been regarded as the main mechanism in the dissemination of van gene (Lee et al., 2001; Shin et al., 2003). VanB VRE was predominantly isolated in Korean hospitals in the initial years, whereas isolates recovered between years 1998 and 2000 were predominant VanA type (Lee et al., 2001; Shin et al., 2003). Hence, structural analysis of the vanA gene cluster is critical to investigation of the epidemiology of vanA-containing Staphylococci in this research program. The vanA gene cluster is carried as a part of Tn1546-like elements. The heterogeneity of Tn1546 has previously been reported and comprises of point mutations, deletions, and integration of the IS elements. Among these variations, the presence of IS elements accounts for a major part of the heterogeneity.

Till date, IS1216V, IS1542, IS1251, and IS1476 have been reported in VanA VRE. IS1216V is known to be ubiquitous in vanA elements (Jensen et al., 1998; Willems et al., 1999) whereas the other three IS elements appear to be geographically restricted. For example, IS1542 is frequently found in clinical as well poultry-originating VRE isolates from the United Kingdom and Ireland (Schouten et al., 2001; Woodford et al., 1998). IS1251 and IS1476 have been reported in the vanA elements of enterococci from the United States (Donabedian et al., 2000; Handwerger and Scoble, 1995) and Canada (Mackinnon et al., 1997), respectively.

The present study involved characterization of the structures of Tn1546-like elements among S. aureus isolates from burnt patients admitted to emergency hospital from different parts of Sulaimani governorate using PCR and nucleotide sequencing analysis. Three main types of vanA gene clusters were identified according to the distributions of ISs that is, IS1216V, IS1251 and IS19 in the Tn1546-like elements. In contrast IS1476 and IS1542 were not detected in the Sulaimani isolates. IS1216V and IS1251 were identified in the genomes of all isolates from Sulaimani emergency hospital. Isolate no. 2 was characterized by a Tn1546 sequence identical to the prototype Tn1546 element (GenBank accession no. M97297).

The DNA sequences of the other 7 isolates were not identical to those of the prototype Tn1546 element and divided into two groups, one contained IS1216 and IS1251, the other contained IS19, IS1216 and IS1251. Sequence analysis of isolate no.3, was characterized by

Table 1. Nucleotide sequences of PCR (primers).

Primer	Sequences (5' →3')
Tn1546-specific primers	
42F	ATT TTC CTG ACG AAT CCC TCG
349R	TCG GAA AAC AAG GTG AGC TTA GA
164F	AAC CTA AGG GCG ACA TAT GGT G
921R	AAA AGG AGC CAC AT CTA CCG
170F	AGG GCG ACA TAT GGT GTA ACA
1913R	CGT CCT GCC GAC TAT GAT TAT TT
949F	GCA TGT AGT GAT GAA ACA CCT AGC TGC
2976R	TGA AGA TGA ATG GAT ACT GGG GAC C
1871F	ACC GTT TTT GCA GTA AGT CTA AAT
3726R	AGC CCT AGA TAC ATT AGT AAT T
3514F	ACT GTA ATG GCT GGT GTT AAC
3978R	CAT AGT TAT CAC CCC TTT CAC TAT
3907F	ATG CTT ATA AAT TCG GCC C
4794R	ATC CAA TCC CCA AGT TTC CC
3992F	TTA TTG TGG ATG ATG AAC ATG
4511R	TCG GAG CTA ACC ACA TTC
4676F	AAC GAC TAT TCC AAA CTA GAA C
5769R	GCT GGA AGC TCT ACC CTA AA
5235F	ATA TCA CGT TGG ACA AAG C
7035R	TTA CGT CAT GCT CCT CTG AG
8082F	ACT TGG GAT AAT TTC ACC GG
8505R	TGC GAT TTT GCG CTT CAT TG
8448F	GAT GAA CGC TCT CAT CAT GC
9138R	TTC CTG AGA AAA CAG TGC TTC A
8544F	GCA TAT AGC CTC GAA TGG
9580R	TCG TCA AGC TTG ATC CTA C
10446F	AAT ACT GTT GGA GGC TTT CTT GG
10577R	GGT ACG GTA AAC GAG CAA TAA TAC G
IS1216V-specific primers	
650F	ACC TTC ACG ATA GCT AAG GTT
132R	AGG ATT ATA TAA GAA AAC CCG

a 1,499-bp sequence designated "IS1251-like" in the orf2-vanR intergenic region.

This element was inserted downstream from position 5820 in the opposite orientation relative to the transposon but was in the same position and orientation as an insertion described by Donabedian et al. (2000) in a Tn1546-like element from an *E. faecium* isolate, and an 810 bp IS1216V insertion in the vanX-vanY intergenic region. Isolate no. 3 and 4 was characterized by two copies of IS1216V at the left ends of Tn1251-like elements, the first copy revealing truncation of the 5′ region of the Tn1546-like element resulting in the loss of nucleotides 1 to 3100, which eliminated the orf1 region. Upstream from the truncated Tn1546 element was a 419-bp sequence with homology to bases 58293 to 58711 of *E. faecalis* V583 pTEF1 (GenBank accession no. AE016833).

This sequence, represented by the dotted line in Figure 1, was followed by an 810-bp sequence designated an "IS1216V-like" element that is in the same 5′→ 3′ orientation as the transposon, and a second copy of IS1216 in the vanX-vanY intergenic region as well as IS1251 in the orf2-vanR intergenic region. Isolate no. 5, 6, 7, and 8 was characterized by two copies of IS1216V at the left ends of Tn1546-like elements and in the vanX-vanY intergenic region as well as IS1251 in the orf2-vanR intergenic region. Isolate no 9, was characterized by the presence of IS19 in the vanS-vanH intergenic region, in addition to IS1251 in the orf2-vanR intergenic region and IS1216V in the vanX-vanY intergenic region. IS1216V was present in the vanX-vanY intergenic regions of the genomes of 8 isolates, but at various points of

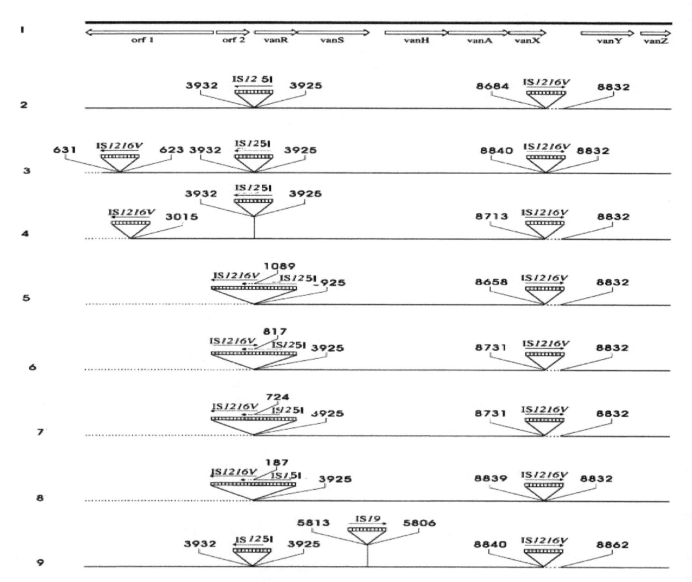

Figure 1. Genetic maps of Tn*1546* types of *S. aureus* isolates from Sulaimani emergency hospital. The positions of genes and open reading frames (orf1 and orf2) and the direction of transcription are marked by open arrows at the top. Boxes with vertical lines represent IS elements

integration. Among these 8 isolates, the insertions in 4 isolates were accompanied by small deletions adjacent to the insertion site. Also, IS*1216V* was present at the left ends of Tn*1546*-like elements of 6 isolates, with or without large deletions encompassing the *orf1* and/or *orf2* region. IS*1251* was detected in the *orf2-vanR* intergenic regions of all 8 isolates (Figure 1)

IS*1216V* was inserted at the left ends of the *vanA* elements, with a deletion that included the *orf1* and/or *orf2* regions. IS*1216* was found in the Tn*1546*-like element at right ends of Van A gene exactly at intragenic of *Van* XY at the same position in all the isolates as describe previously (Darini et al., 1999; Schouten et al., 2001; Woodford, 1998). Interestingly, the 3′ end of IS*1251* belonging to isolates no. 6, 7, and 8 was deleted

at various points by the IS*1216V* insertion. This finding suggests that IS*1216V* at the left end of Tn*1546* was acquired later than IS*1251*. Moreover, importantly, to our knowledge, our study is the first to demonstrate the presence of IS*19* in the *vanS-vanH* intergenic region of the *vanA* gene cluster. Perichon et al. (2000) reported that IS*19* was inserted in the d-Ala-d-Ala ligase gene of VanD strain *E. faecium* BM*4416*, resulting in inactivation of the *ddl* ligase. However, IS*19* has never been documented in Tn*1546*-like elements. The movement of ISs frequently causes structural alterations in Tn*1546*-like elements. Furthermore, several investigators have documented the functional changes associated with IS integration with or without the adjacent deletion, as in the loss of VanY activity by an IS*1476* insertion (Mackinnon et al., 1997) and inactivation of the *ddl* ligase by IS*19* (Perichon et al., 2000).

In our study, it was unlikely that the integration of an IS would affect the function of the *vanA* gene cluster. The genetic differences among Tn*1546*-like elements have been investigated in several studies (Brown et al., 2001; Hashimoto et al., 2000; Jensen et al., 1998; Simonsen et al., 2000; Stobberingh et al., 1999; Willems et al., 1999; Woodford et al., 1998). However, the Tn*1546* subtypes of the enterococci investigated were not comparable, since various molecular techniques were used. Finally the identification of ISs within the *vanA* gene cluster to analyze and compare the structures of Tn*1546*-like elements could be a useful tool in epidemiological studies.

REFERENCES

Arthur M, Molinas C, Depardieu F, Courvalin P (1993). Characterization of Tn*1546*, a Tn*3*-related transposon conferring glycopeptide resistance by synthesis of depsipeptide peptidoglycan precursors in *Enterococcus faecium* BM4147. J. Bacteriol., 175: 117-127.

Brown AR, Townsley AC, Amyes SGB (2001). Diversity of Tn*1546* elements in clinical isolates of glycopeptide-resistant enterococci from Scottish hospitals. Antimicrob. Agents Chemother., 45: 1309-1311.

Dahl KE, Simonsen GS, Olsvik Ø, Sundsfjord A (1999). Heterogeneity in the *vanB* gene cluster of genomically diverse clinical strains of vancomycin-resistant enterococci. Antimicrob. Agents Chemother., 43: 1105-1110.

Darini ALC, Palepou MI, Woodford N (1999). Nucleotide sequence of IS1542, an insertion sequence identified within VanA glycopeptide resistance elements of enterococci. FEMS Microbiol. Lett., 173: 341-346.

Donabedian S, Hershberger E, Thal LA, Chow JW, Clewell DB, Robinson-Dunn B, Zervos MJ (2000). PCR fragment length polymorphism analysis of vancomycin-resistant *Enterococcus faecium*. J. Clin. Microbiol., 38: 2885-2888.

Dutka-Malen S, Evers S, Courvalin P (1995). Detection of glycopeptide resistance genotypes and identification to the species level of clinically relevant enterococci by PCR. J. Clin. Microbiol., 33: 24-27.

Handwerger S, Scoble J (1995). Identification of chromosomal mobile element conferring high-level vancomycin resistance in *Enterococcus faecium*. Antimicrob. Agents Chemother., 39: 2446-2453.

Hashimoto Y, Tanimoto K, Ozawa Y, Murata T, Ike Y (2000). Amino acid substitutions in the VanS sensor of the VanA-type vancomycin-resistant *Enterococcus* strains result in high-level vancomycin resistance and low-level teicoplanin resistance. FEMS Microbiol. Lett., 185: 247-254.

Jensen LB, Ahrens P, Dons L, Jones RN, Hammerum AM, Aarestrup FM (1998). Molecular analysis of Tn*1546* in *Enterococcus faecium* isolated from animals and humans. J. Clin. Microbiol., 36: 437-442.

Lee WG, Jernigan JA, Rasheed JK, Anderson GJ, Tenover FC (2001). Possible horizontal transfer of the *vanB2* gene among genetically diverse strains of vancomycin-resistant *Enterococcus faecium* in a Korean hospital. J. Clin. Microbiol., 39: 1165-1168.

Mackinnon MG, Drebot MA, Tyrrell GJ (1997). Identification and characterization of IS*1476*, an insertion sequence-like element that disrupts VanY function in a vancomycin-resistant *Enterococcus faecium* strain. Antimicrob. Agents Chemother., 41: 1805-1807.

Perichon B, Casadewall B, Reynolds P, Courvalin P (2000). Glycopeptide-resistant *Enterococcus faecium* BM4416 is a VanD-type strain with an impaired d-alanine:d-alanine ligase. Antimicrob. Agents Chemother., 44: 1346-1348.

Schouten MA, Willems RJL, Kraak WAG, Top J, Hoogkamp-Korstanje JAA, Voss A (2001). Molecular analysis of Tn*1546*-like elements in vancomycin-resistant enterococci isolated from patients in Europe shows geographic transposon type clustering. Antimicrob. Agents Chemother., 45: 986-989.

Shin JW, Yong D, Kim MS, Chang KH, Lee K, Kim JM, Chong Y (2003). Sudden increase of vancomycin-resistant enterococcal infections in a Korean tertiary care hospital: possible consequences of increased use of oral vancomycin. J. Infect. Chemother., 9: 62-67.

Simonsen GS, Myhre MRM, Dahl KH, Olsvik Ø, Sundsfjord A (2000). Typeability of Tn*1546*-like elements in vancomycin-resistant enterococci using long-range PCRs and specific analysis of polymorphic regions. Microb. Drug Resist., 6: 49-57.

Stobberingh E, van den Bogaard A, London N, Driessen C, Top J, Willems R (1999). Enterococci with glycopeptide resistance in turkeys, turkey farmers, turkey slaughterers, and (sub)urban residents in the south of The Netherlands: evidence for transmission of vancomycin resistance from animals to humans? Antimicrob. Agents Chemother. 43: 2215-2221.

Willems RJL, Top J, van den Braak N, van Belkum A, Mevius DJ, Hendriks G, van Santen-Verheuvel M, van Embden JDA (1999). Molecular diversity and evolutionary relationships of Tn*1546*-like elements in enterococci from humans and animals. Antimicrob. Agents Chemother., 43:483-491.

Woodford N (1998). Glycopeptide-resistant enterococci: a decade of experience. J. Med. Microbiol., 47: 849-862.

Woodford N, Adebiyi AMA, Palepou MI, Cookson BD (1998). Diversity of VanA glycopeptide resistance elements in enterococci from human and nonhuman sources. Antimicrob. Agents Chemother., 42: 502-508.

7

An intelligent system with the model-view-controller pattern querying visual objects: Application in the malaria control domain

Guillaume Koum[1]*, Augustin Yekel[1], Bernabé Batchakui[1] and Josiane Etang[2]

[1]Laboratoire D'Informatique, de Mathématiques et de Simulation des Systèmes- ENSP. B. P. 8390, Yaoundé, Cameroun.
[2]Organisation de Coordination pour la lutte contre les Endémies en Afrique Centrale B. P. 288, Yaoundé, Cameroun.

Malaria affects hundreds of millions of people in the world, particularly in the tropics. This results in particularly high death rates among children and pregnant women, especially the poor living in squalid conditions. This situation is not only due to the increasing drug resistance of malaria and the resistance of the main vector to pesticide control, but also the lack of awareness on the part of communities to fight the disease. In this view, vector control is a cornerstone of the strategy that needs to be implemented and monitored. In this regard, the problem of estimating malarial transmission rate is still very important. It is the aim of this paper.

Key words: Model-view-controller (MVC) pattern, visual object, web programming, malaria transmission, malaria vector.

INTRODUCTION

Many studies have been performed to estimate malaria transmission rates in some villages in Africa. A comparison of three sampling methods has been presented (Le Goff et al., 1997). To get a good view of the vector-borne disease transmission, the entomologist must select a catching method that meets a main requirement: Get the best evaluation of host/infective vectors relationship in a given situation. In Antonio-Nkondjo et al. (2006), the contribution of the so-called secondary malaria vectors to the overall parasite transmission intensity is highlighted. High malaria transmission intensity is studied in Antonio-Nkondjo et al. (2002) and in Cohuet et al. (2004). In the current paper, a system is described that significantly results in increasing malaria transmission rate understanding. The measure of malaria transmission depends on qualitative statistics.

The final result is not to quantify the rate of malaria transmission but to qualify it into four levels: Weak, average, fairly strong and strong.

Model-view-controller (MVC) is a classic design pattern often used by applications that need the ability to maintain multiple views of the same data (Crane et al., 2006). The MVC pattern hinges on a clean separation of objects into one of three categories: Models for maintaining data, views for displaying all or a portion of the data, and controllers for handling events that affect the model or view(s). A developer needs to take care in linking between all views and appropriate controllers. Because of this separation, multiple views and controllers can interface with the same model. Even new types of views and controllers that never existed before can interface with a model without forcing a change in the model design.

On another plan, one of the most fundamental approaches in software engineering is the layered architecture. It implies dividing a system into several interacting layers with certain limitations imposed on how layers may interact

*Corresponding author. E-mail: g_koum@yahoo.fr.

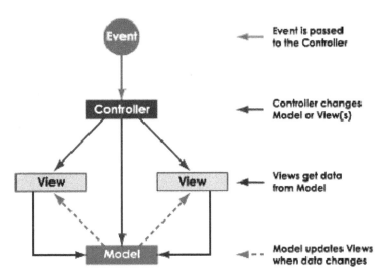

Figure 1. MVC pattern.

Layered architecture finds its application in various systems for example: Internet protocols (TCP/IP layers), operating systems (three layers: Core, drivers, applications), information systems (database management systems, geographic information systems, etc) and others.

A particular case of layered architecture is the 3-tier architecture with its variation (Cloux et al., 2002): Model-view-controller. All this can be implemented in a heterogeneous environment containing a geographic information system (GIS), a database management system (DBMS) and an expert system (ES). Views are performed to present visual objects. Visual objects may be textual, graphical, and geographic. Derived data are expressed through particular graphical objects that are points. Usually, graphical objects are points, lines, ellipses, rectangles and other polygons.

An intelligent system is implemented generally when an expert system is involved. In GIS-based surveillance applications, successful expert systems have a well defined focus and are confined to a specific domain like malaria transmission.

An application of MVC pattern in the field of malaria transmission dynamics is the base of this prototype; four levels of malaria transmission rate are defined as: Weak, average, fairly strong, and strong.

MATERIALS AND METHODS

In model-view-controller (MVC) based applications, maintaining an application logic layer may require considerable efforts and may not be easy to implement. When this problem is taking place in a heterogeneous environment comprising a variety of systems, every view and controller may be attached to a particular system so that a better understanding of the whole system can be obtained. This simplifies and speeds up the development of such applications. This paper aims at implementing a model-view-controller pattern in

an intelligent system constituted of a geographic information system (GIS), a database management system (DBMS), and an expert system (ES). This is applied in malaria control to measure the rate of malaria transmission. A qualitative approach is used, estimating the levels of disease transmission in localities of Cameroon. Views display objects which can be textual, geographic or derived and are called visual objects.

MVC patterns

According to MVC objects, the presentation layer consists of view objects and application logic consists of controller objects. For each view object, a corresponding controller exists and vice versa. Views process presentation needs and controllers handle application logic. The MVC pattern has two major characteristics:
1. MVC controllers receive and process user input.
2. MVC controllers affect their views by changing the intermediate presentation model, which the views are subscribed to (by observer patterns). This makes views pure observations without any direct access to the controllers.

The MVC abstraction can be graphically represented as shown in Figure 1.

Events typically cause a controller to change a model, or view, or both. Whenever a controller changes a model's data or properties, all dependent views are automatically updated. Similarly, whenever a controller changes a view, for example, by revealing areas that were previously hidden, the view gets data from the underlying model to refresh itself. There can be as many controllers and views. An event is directly related to a particular controller. For this purpose, we consider the task concept. A task unites several views with their controllers in fulfilling a particular job.

In this case, a querying task on malaria control may consist of three views: One to return a point in a map situating a locality, another one to return basic information belonging to a geographic information system (GIS) and/or a database management system (DBMS), and the last to return deduced information stemming from an expert system (ES). All these data are called visual objects. All controllers within a task are given a link to the task object. Generally a task can be expressed as a workflow or a state machine.

Application developers do not have to care about associating each view with its controller. Views and controllers get connected

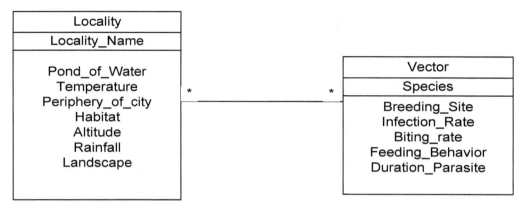

Figure 2. Class diagram.

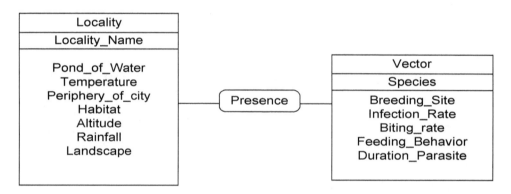

Figure 3. Entity relationship diagram.

automatically. This is the case of MVC# framework which automatically establishes links between views and corresponding controllers.

Since there are multiple controllers, the MVC pattern allows any number of controllers to modify the same model. The GIS, the DBMS and the ES are considered as the whole model. The dictionaries of the GIS, the DBMS and the ES are merged to create a single dictionary.

Interfacing GIS, DBMS and expert system

Interfacing a GIS, DBMS, and ES is a known exercise. In this prototype, the concern is to navigate through views generated from the interfacing of the GIS, DBMS and the ES. Generally speaking, operations that represent different working situations to the user should be kept in different parts of the user interface. The user interface is designed with usability and ergonomy in mind.

Basic data

The basic data are constituted of data belonging to the GIS and the DBMS (Contensin, 2004). The UML (Unified Modeling Language) class diagram of this association is as shown in Figure 2 (Fannader and Leroux, 1999).

Locality is a GIS class while vector is a DBMS class. A locality can comprise breeding sites of a variety of mosquito types such as ponds, marshlands and streams. A mosquito type can be found in many localities as well as a locality can contain a variety of mosquito types. When translating this class diagram in an entity/relationship model the following schema is obtained (Figure 3).

Using the normalization theory, the relational schema shown in Figure 4 through the transformation of the many-to-many association is realized.

The relation presence can contain a specific attribute called abundance. This attribute is deduced from the ES. The attribute period indicating the season must be defined in this relation, because the abundance of vectors usually depends on the season.

Deduced data

Deduced data are produced by the ES and indicate the level of malaria transmission through many factors. This choice provides measured feedback to appreciate the rate of malaria transmission. The malaria vector situation in a locality is given in Table 1. The locality name and the species name constitute a composite key of the table. The ES works very close with the table to deduce knowledge. This knowledge is expressed as points in the deduced view, showing the rate of malaria transmission.

Some of the rules used in the ES to predict the rates are:

1. If a locality has no ponds and if its temperature is higher than 40 °C, then the malaria transmission rate is weak.
2. If a locality has ponds, with a forest landscape, then the malaria transmission rate is strong.

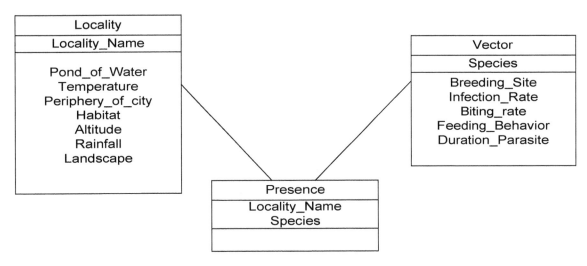

Figure 4. Relational diagram.

Table 1. Outputs explained.

Malaria transmission rate	Number of point
Weak	1
Average	2
Fairly strong	3
Strong	4

3. If a locality has an altitude more than 1000 m with an average rainfall, then the malaria transmission rate is average.
4. If the season is such that vector abundance is at its peak and the locality is urban, then the malaria transmission is fairly strong.
5. If the season is such that vector abundance is at its peak and the locality is rural, then the malaria transmission is strong.

Many other rules which belong to one of the categories aforementioned can be inserted in the ES. These rules are not visible to a user. The system administrator is the one in charge of handling them as he does for the DBMS and the GIS. The system administrator has as tasks to introduce rules and data in the system. The system is perceived as a mono-user system in its functioning but it is distributed.

In practice, problems can be found on environmental data concerning vegetation, land use, rainfall, temperature, and include:

1. The spatial scale of data may not be appropriate for many types of analyses (land cover may be appropriate for district-wide analysis but not for local/village analysis since small features such as ponds and localized wetlands may not be shown).
2. Weather data (rainfall and temperature) is not usually available at the scale needed for analysis, there are usually only one or two weather stations in a district and some parameters relevant to malaria transmission may not be measured at all, such as wind speed and direction which affects the vector-people interaction.

Solution

Generating the domain classes

Generating Java code: As in eclipse modeling framework (EMF)

(Crane et al., 2006), two models, the ".ecore" and the ".genmodel" model can be created. Based on these two models, Java code is generated. So, the two domain classes, GIS class (Locality) and DBMS class (Vector) are generated in Java code. This creates the Java implementation of the EMF model in this application.

Review the generated code: The generated code consists out of the following:

1. Model: Interfaces and the factory to create the Java classe.
2. Model.impl: Concrete implementation of the interfaces defined in model.
3. Model util: The adapter factory.

The central factory has methods for creating all defined objects via createObjectName() methods.

Rule-based systems

Among the most popular rule engines, JESS (Java Expert System Shell) is probably of the most interest to Java developers. It is the reference implementation of JSR 094 Java Rule Engine API and it has plug-ins to support development of rule systems in Eclipse. It is helpful to introduce JESS and take a glimpse of its programming syntax. JESS is software that interprets rules and facts expressed in its programming language. Just as Java is a language for expressing objects and Java compiler is software that interprets Java code, JESS has a language for expressing rules and facts and a compiler to interpret the code. JESS is developed in Java by Ernest Friedman-Hill at Sandia National Laboratories. Here is what

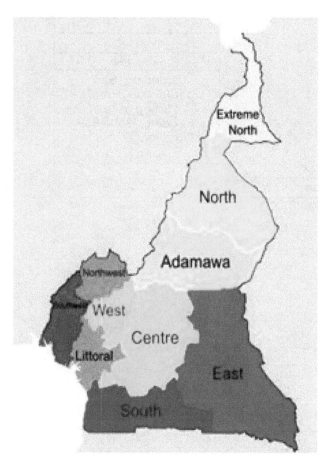

Figure 5. Map of Cameroon.

the rules and facts in our weather example look like in JESS code.

```
(defrule rule-1 (rainy-season) = > (advise-people malaria))
(defrule rule-2 (ponds-many) => (advise-people hygiene))
(defrule rule-3 (rainy-season) => (assert ponds-many))
(ponds-many)
(rainy-season)
```

The last two lines in the list are the two facts. The first three lines are the three rules. Rules in JESS take this form: defrule rule-name conditions => actions. Rules are defined using the defrule construct. Rule-1, rule-2, and rule-3 are the names of the rules respectively. Rule-1 has a condition: rainy-season. In this case, rainy-season is also called a pattern. It is so called because the rule engine treats it as a pattern for matching facts. The pattern (rainy-season) in rule-1 will match only one fact: The (rainy-season) fact in the last line of the code list. When it is matched, the action (advise-people malaria) of rule-1 will be executed.

RESULTS

The model in the MVC comprising a DBMS, a GIS and an ES contains factual, geographic and graphic data. The application allows a user to query the system and displays all those internal objects which become visual. The intelligence of the system is due to the fact that

derived data converted to points are obtained with JESS Rule Engine, and returned through maps. The number of points indicates the rate of malaria transmission in a given locality. For prototyping, trial data stemming from studies in Cameroon are injected into the system to give the results. The trial data is not exhaustive as it is limited only to the test localities.

Global results

The application displays a map of Cameroon through its ten regions according to the SVG format. While clicking on a region, the application may:

1. Perform a zoom. This operation is applied to the GIS. It represents one view of the MVC pattern. We call it geographic view.
2. Permit a user to enter the locality name as a parameter.
3. Display information on the locality and the vectors concerned.

Geographic view- geographic controller

The map of Cameroon according to the SVG format is divided in ten SVG files, each file corresponding to a region as follows: Adamawa.svg, Centre.svg, East.svg, Extreme-North.svg, Littoral.svg, North.svg, North-West.svg, West.svg, South.svg and South-West.svg (Figure 5). For each region, an SVG code is written that delivers a zoom on the region.

Deduced view- deduced controller

The malaria transmission rate is the relationship between the vector density contained in the Table 1 and some specific factors of the locality. JESS is used in this view as a rule engine for the Java platform; it is a superset of CLIPS programming language.

Rather than a procedural paradigm, where a single program has a loop that is activated only one time, the declarative paradigm used by JESS continuously applies a collection of rules to a collection of facts by a process called *pattern matching*. Rules can modify the collection of facts, or they can execute any Java code. The JESS rules engine uses the Rete algorithm.

The malaria transmission rate is then determined. We adopt its graphical representation through a number of points as followings.

Basic view - basic controller

The PHP code infosRegionVectors sends the request to the DBMS. The result is analyzed and then is displayed

Figure 6. Mosquito picture.

The vector section receives this information. Mosquito data are factual and the application may be extended to store image data in this regard. Figure 6 is general and is not particular to a type of vector.

Detailed results

Here, we present different functionalities of the application. The prototype is web-oriented. So, it runs with the perspective to be under the n-tier architecture.

The essential basic functionalities of the application are the following:

1. Create a new locality (or region) in the table locality of the GIS
2. Modify a locality (to modify its features).
3. Create a vector in the table vector of the DBMS.
4. Delete a vector from the DBMS.
5. Add a vector in a locality.
6. Delete a vector from a locality.

The main interface of the application is as shown in Figures 7a and b.

In Figures 7, the application shows a map of Cameroon in the section called map of Cameroon and the map of a region in the section map of region. When a locality is selected, features are displayed in the locality information zone. When a user clicks on a region on the general map of Cameroon, the specific map of that region is displayed. The user is asked to select a locality. For this example, the locality selected is Ntui, the divisional headquarters of Mbam-and-Kim Division in the Centre region of Cameroon. This region appears zoomed on, in the section map of region. The distribution of the different vectors of this locality also is displayed as well as features of this locality in the locality information zone. The user can also visualize the list of vectors present in this locality with their properties in vector zone.

In this example, the Ntui town presents average malaria transmission rate. This is the reason why two

points are displayed at the left of the vertical arrow. On the right of the arrow corresponding to the East of Ntui, there are two localities with one point each displayed; the malaria transmission rate deduced by the system in these localities is weak. *A. gambiae* is the only vector species studied here.

Comparison

Here, we compare the results of a longitudinal entomological follow-up on malaria transmission dynamics conducted in the town of Mbalmayo, in the centre region of Cameroon (Antonio-Nkondjo et al., 2005). Sampling was also conducted in the village of Olama, not far from Mbalmayo in a rural environment. This study assesses the impact of urbanization and deforestation on local malaria vector populations and their effects on malaria transmission dynamics.

Mbalmayo is an urban area situated along the river Nyong, 50 km south of Yaounde, the capital of Cameroon. The village of Olama is situated 15 km south of Mbalmayo, downstream on the River Nyong. The climate is a typical equatorial, characterized by two rainy seasons extending from March to June and from September to November. Average annual rainfall during the study period was 1600 mm. The average minimum and maximum monthly temperature recorded by the national meteorological services ranged from 18 to 25 °C in July to 20 to 29 °C in March.

In Mbalmayo, *Anopheles gambiae* was the most anopheline species caught throughout the survey period (Figure 8). The HBR (human biting rate) was 11.3 bites/person/night for *A. gambiae* varied with the season. The maximum HBR was 27.8 bites/person/night.

As Ntui town in our study, Mbalmayo is an urban area within the equatorial forest zone. The average HBR is respectively 7 and 11.3. This is quite normal. The climate is sensitively the same, as the annual rainfall. Some differences depending on the season are observed at the temperatures side. Mainly in our work, we deduce the

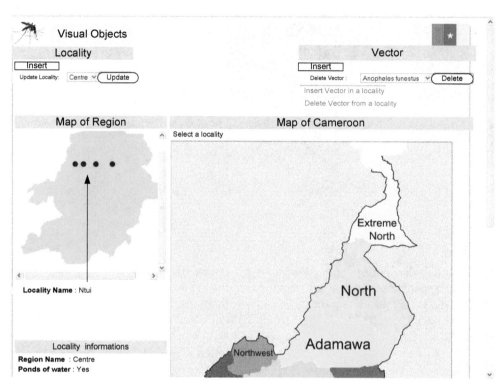

Figure 7a. Only localities information.

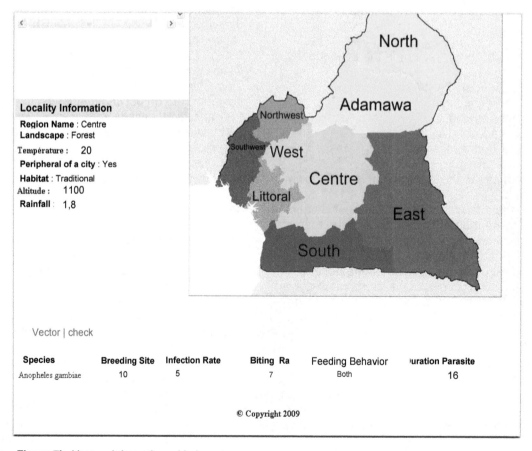

Figure 7b. Vectors information added

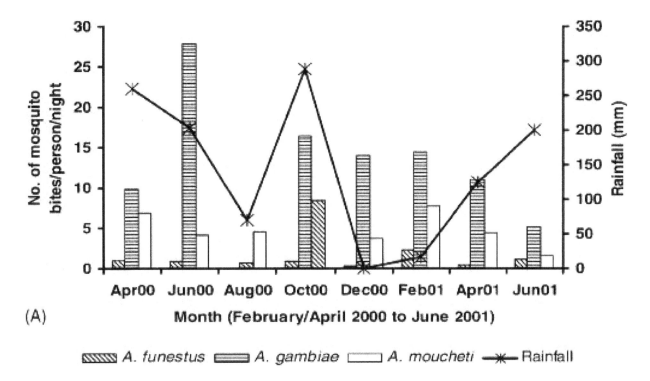

Figure 8. Rainfall and human biting rate for malaria vectors.

malaria transmission rate.

The results of the test for CSP (circumsporozoite protein) are shown in Table 2. They are infective rates *Plasmodium falciparum.* For *A. gambiae* in Ntui, the infective rate obtained by our system is 5%, whereas in Mbalmayo, the survey carried out in the current section gives 4.5%. In the nearby village of Olama, for *A. gambiae,* the CSP rate is equal to 10.8%. In our system the CSP rates in the localities at the east of Ntui were not calculated.

DISCUSSION

Maps generated by this application give indications on malaria transmission rate. The system analyzes parameters that determine malaria transmission. The peak season for the species is a period during which malaria transmission can be high. But in general, malaria transmission in Africa is a dynamic and complex system. Through this study, four levels of malaria transmission rate are established. It is an interesting factor in the fight against the disease. The risk of malaria transmission can be assessed in this consideration. This prototype can be completed with much more exhaustive data for the different stakeholders in the fight against malaria to use.

Conclusion

The lack of awareness on the part of communities to fight

the malaria disease is one the most important issue in public health policies. Decision support systems or medical expert systems are created as an aid in decision making in health care.

The goals of such systems are to provide a methodological and accurate system that can mimic or model some aspect of health care knowledge. The system built in this paper gives an opportunity for decision makers to control the situation of malaria pandemic in the field in order to efficiently curb it. The system is intended to give visual information for a better understanding of the phenomena. The system is technically founded and obeys MVC patterns framework associating JESS environment. It displays graphically the malaria transmission rate in a qualitative approach expressed as points. The system may be extended by some functions like vectors spatial distribution, species identification, infected zones. Including a more exhaustive data set, developing the other functionalities previously listed will transform this prototype to a reliable application for malaria control.

ACKNOWLEDGEMENTS

The authors thank members of OCEAC particularly F. Simard and C. Antonio-Nkondjo for helpful discussions. Many thanks are also to J. Noutchegueme and J.M. Moto for their contribution to this paper through their masters' dissertation.

Table 2. CSP rates.

Location	Species	No. tested	Positive	CSP rate (95% CI)
Mbalmayo	A. moucheti	299	4	1.3% (0.02-2.6)
	A. gambiae	714	32	4.5% (3-6)
	A. funestus	44	2	4.5% (0.56-15.5)
Olama	A. moucheti	4084	85[a]	2.1%(1.6-2.6)
	A. gambiae	37	4	10.8% (1-2.6)
	A. marshallii	8	1	12.5%(0.3-52.7)

[a]Two were plasmodium malariae, all the rest were *P. falciparum*.

REFERENCES

Antonio-Nkondjo C, Awono-Ambene P, Toto JC, Meunier JY, Zebaze-Kemleu S, Nyambam R, Wondji C, Tchuinkam T and Fontenille D (2002). High malaria transmission intensity in a sub urban area of Yaounde, the capital city of Cameroon. J. Med. Entomol., 39: 350-355.

Antonio-Nkondjo C, Simard F, Awono-Ambene P, Ngassam P, Toto JC, Tchuinkam T, Fontenille D (2005). Malaria vectors and urbanization in the equatorial forest region of south Cameroon. Trans. Roy. Soc. Trop. Med. Hyg. Elsevier, 97: 347-354.

Antonio-Nkondjo C, Hinzoumbe Kerah C, Simard F, Awono-Ambene P, Mohamadou Chouaibou, Tchuinkam T, Fontenille D (2006). Complexity of the Malaria Vectorial System in Cameroon: Contribution of Secondary Vectors to Malaria Transmission. J. Med. Entomol., 43(6): 1215-1221.

Cloux PY, Doussot D, Geron A (2002). Technologies et architectures internet: corba, com, xml, j2ee, .net, web services. Dunod.

Cohuet A, Simard F, Wondji C, Antonio-Nkondjo C, Awono-Ambene P, Fontenille D (2004). High malaria transmission intensity due to Anopheles funestus (Diptera: Culicidae) in a village of savannah-forest transition area in Cameroon. J. Med. Entomol., 41: 901-905.

Contensin M (2004). Databases and internet with PHP and MYSQL. Dunod.

Crane D, Pascarello E, Darren J (2006). Ajax in practice. Campus Press Ref. Pearson edu.

Fannader R and Leroux H (1999). UML. Modeling principles. Dunod.

Le Goff G, Carnevale P, Fondjo E, Robert V (1997). Comparison of three sampling methods of man-biting anophelines in order to estimate the malaria transmission in a village of South Cameroon. J. Parasite, 4: 75-80.

8

An insight into blood clotting disorders in humans

Parul Johri[1]*, Sagar Nagare[1], Kakumani Venkateswara Swamy[2] and Chitta Suresh Kumar[2]

[1]Department of Biotechnology and Bioinformatics, Dr. D. Y. Patil University, Navi Mumbai, India.
[2]Bioinformatics Facility, Department Biochemistry, Sri Krishnadevaraya University, Anantapur, Andhra Pradesh, India.

The structure of thrombin protein *Oncorhynchus mykiss* had not yet been resolved by NMR or X-ray diffraction method. In the present work, we have modeled the structure of protein using Modeller 9v1, taking human thrombin protein as the template. Furthermore, the antithrombin protein was docked with the best model generated by R-dock and Z-dock module of INSIGHT II and the nine potential amino acids involved in anchoring of antithrombin with thrombin were identified as: Leu3, Trp27, Asn120, Glu123, Pro133, Ile148, Ser152, Gly204 and Phe215, respectively. The study also showed surface complimentarily between *O. mykiss* thrombin and antithrombin which can be helpful for designing new antithrombin molecules for the treatment of blood clotting disorders in humans.

Key words: Antithrombin protein, homology modeling, r-dock, thrombin, z-dock.

INTRODUCTION

The mechanism of coagulation needs to be clearly understood for determining the preoperative bleeding risk to patients undergoing surgery and managing haemostatic therapy preoperatively. The coagulation cascade of hemostasis has two pathways, the contact activation pathway (formerly known as the intrinsic pathway), and the tissue factor pathway (formerly known as the extrinsic pathway), which lead to fibrin formation. It was previously thought that the coagulation cascade consisted of two pathways of equal importance joined to a common pathway. It is now known that the primary pathway for the initiation of blood coagulation is the tissue factor pathway (Tanaka et al., 2009). The pathways are a series of reactions, in which a zymogen (inactive enzyme precursor) of a serine protease and its glycoprotein co-factor are activated to become active components that then catalyze the next reaction in the cascade, ultimately resulting in cross-linked fibrin. Coagulation factors are generally indicated by roman numerals, with a lowercase 'a' appended to indicate an active form. The coagulation factors are generally serine proteases (enzymes). The main role of the tissue factor

pathway is to generate a "thrombin burst," a process by which thrombin, the most important constituent of the coagulation cascade in terms of its feedback activation roles, is released instantaneously. Anti-coagulation factor VIIa (FVIIa) circulates in a higher amount than any other activated coagulation factor.

The contact activation pathway begins with formation of the primary complex on collagen by high-molecular-weight kininogen (HMWK), prekallikrein, and factor XII (FXII) (Hageman factor). Prekallikrein is converted to kallikrein and FXII becomes activated factor XII (FXIIa). FXIIa converts factor XI (FXI) into activated factor XI (FXIa). Activated factor XI (XIa) activates factor IX (FIX), which with its co-factor activated factor FVIII (FVIIIa) form the tenase complex, which activates factor X (FX) to activated factor X (Fxa). Thrombin has a large array of functions. Its primary role is the conversion of fibrinogen to fibrin, the building block of a hemostatic plug. In addition, it activates Factors VIII and V and their inhibitor protein C (in the presence of thrombomodulin), and it activates Factor XIII, which forms covalent bonds that crosslink the fibrin polymers that form from activated monomers (Vine 2009).

The serine protease thrombin plays pivotal roles in activation of additional serine protease zymogens (inactive enzymatic precursors), co-factors, and cell-

*Corresponding author. E-mail: pjohri_14@yahoo.co.in.

```
thrombin    ------------------------------------------------------------Q   1
1JWT|A      TFGSGEADCGLRPLFEKKSLEDKTERELLESYIDGRIVEGSDAEIGMSPWQVMLFRKSPQ  60
                                                                       *


thrombin    ELLCGASLISDEWILTAAHCILYPPWNKNFTINDILVRLGKHNRAKFEKGTEKIVAIDEI  61
1JWT|A      ELLCGASLISDRWVLTAAHCLLYPPWDKNFTENDLLVRIGKHSRTRYERNIEKISMLEKI 120
            **********.*:******:*****:**** **:***:***.*:::*:. ***  :::*


thrombin    IVHPKYNWKENLNRDIALLHMRRPITFTDEIHPVCLPTKQVAKTLMFAGYKGRVTGWGNL 121
1JWT|A      YIHPRYNWRENLDRDIALMKLKKPVAFSDYIHPVCLPDRETAASLLQAGYKGRVTGWGNL 180
            :**:***:***.****:::::*::*:* ******* ::..* :*: *************


thrombin    YETWSSSP-KSLPTVLQQIHLPIVEQDICRDSTSIRITDNMFCAGFKPEEQKTGDACEGD 180
1JWT|A      KETWTANVGKGQPSVLQVVNLPIVERPVCKDSTRIRITDNMFCAGYKPDEGKRGDACEGD 240
            ***::.  *. *:*** ::*****: :*:*** *********:**:* * ******


thrombin    SGGPFVMKSPDDNRWYQIGIVSWGEGCDRDGKYGFYTHLFRMRRWMKKVIDKTGGDDDD- 239
1JWT|A      SGGPFVMKSPFNNRWYQMGIVSWGEGCDRDGKYGFYTHVFRLKKWIQKVIDQFGEDFEEI 300
            **********  :****:*******************:**:::*::****: * *  ::


thrombin    -----
1JWT|A      PEEYL 305
```

Figure 1. Alignment of the amino acid sequences of *O. mykiss* thrombin *Homo sapience* thrombin PDB: 1JWT. * strong similarity, : Weak similarity, – gap between alignment of both the sequences.

surface receptors. The thrombin generation is closely regulated to achieve locally rapid haemostatic effect subsequent to injury without causing uncontrolled systemic thrombosis (Samama, 2008). The prothrombin complex concentrates are haemostatic blood products containing four vitamin K-dependant clotting factors (II, VII, IX and X). They are useful, reliable and fast alternative to fresh frozen plasma for the reversal of the effects of oral anticoagulant treatments (vitamin K antagonists). These are sometimes used for factor II or factor X replacement in patients with congenital or acquired deficiencies (Gumulec et al., 2009; Mackman et al., 2007). Thrombin receptor activation mechanisms are: Direct activation and transactivation. In direct activation, soluble thrombin directly cleaves the extracellular domain of the receptor to unmask receptor activation. In transactivation, soluble thrombin, in low concentrations, interacts with the first receptor and the thrombin-receptor complex itself serves as an enzyme to cleave the second receptor (Esmon, 1989, 2008).

Till date, the structure of the thrombin protein had not yet been resolved by any of the structure prediction method like NMR or X ray diffraction. Without the structural details of the protein, it is very difficult to understand antithrombin interactions. In the present work, we have modeled the *Oncorhynchus mykiss* thrombin protein, which is structurally very similar to human thrombin protein, and analyzed antithrombin interactions using *In-silico* molecular modeling techniques. Thrombin is an endolytic serine protease that selectively cleaves the Arg - Gly bond of fibrinogen to form fibrin and release fibrinopeptides A and B. To understand the blood clotting

in lower animals, we have selected the animal model of *O. mykiss* for studying its thrombin and antithrombin interactions. However, due to unavailability of thrombin structure for the organism in the Protein Data Bank, we have followed a *in silico* approach to model this protein using homology modeling technique and investigated the binding mode of antithrombin protein.

MATERIALS AND METHODS

Homology modeling for *O. mykiss* thrombin protein (GI: 213487) was done using MODELLER 9v1 (Windows Platform) (Altschul et al., 1990; Lévesque et al., 2001; Thompson et al., 1994; Fiser and Sali, 2003). Nine models were generated, using *Homo sapiens* thrombin (1JWT) as template. (Figure 1 in supplementary material). All the generated models were validated using PROCHECK (Laskowski et al., 1993). After validation, model 09 was found to be the best model, and was further used for active site analysis. The RMSD of the structure was calculated using SPDBV 4.01 that came out to be 3.7 Å (Guex and Peitsch, 1997).

The active site on the modeled protein was identified with the amalgamation of two approaches namely, superimposing the modeled structure of *O. mykiss* on the *H. sapiens* thrombin protein using INSIGHT II (Unix Platform), and also by the active site finder module of INSIGHT II, which provides the number of hollow cavities that can be the potential active site.

Finally, the binding mode of thrombin of *O. mykiss* was studied by docking strategies. Antithrombin protein of human (2AX2) was used as a ligand (Lange et al., 2006). The energy of both the proteins was minimized with CHARMM force field (Brooks et al., 1983). Furthermore, the channel surface mapping was done using multi channel surfaces (MCS) module in INSIGHT II with a 1.4 Å probe radius. The docking of antithrombin protein with modeled thrombin was achieved using traction beam docking (TBD) and protein - protein docking technique with z-dock module with the

Table 1. Geometric parameters of the nine thrombin models developed by MODELLER9v1 and statistics of PROCHECK.

Model no.	Core region (%)	Allowed regions (%)	Generously allowed region (%)	Disallowed region (%)	Bad contacts	G factor	M/c bond lengths	M/c bond angles (%)	Planar groups (%)
1	80	17	2	1	1	-0.15	90	73	100
2	82	14	3	1	2	-0.17	81	70	95
3	80	16	2	2	1	-0.14	85	75	94
4	80	18	1	1	2	-0.16	84	80	90
5	81	16	2	1	3	-0.14	82	72	85
6	81	10	4	5	2	-0.13	83	78	72
7	79	14	3	4	1	-0.12	81	71	70
8	78	15	4	3	2	-0.15	82	75	75
9	82.5	16	1	0.5	0	-0.16	89	86	100

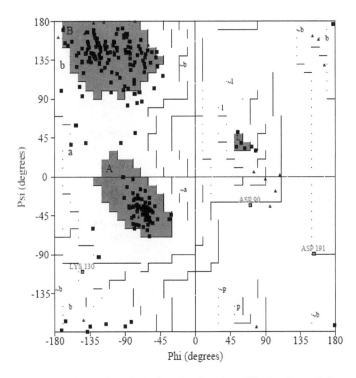

Figure 1. Ramachandran plot showing the phi/psi values of the modeled thrombin protein. Red color- most favorable regions, yellow color region- allowed region, pale yellow- generously allowed region and white color- disallowed regions.

default parameters (Chen et al., 2003). The models were further refined using r-dock. The model with best score was finally selected (Li et al., 2003).

RESULTS

Nine protein models were generated using Modeller 9v1 considering loops and site specific residues. All nine models were subjected to energy minimization with

CHARMM force field of DISCOVER module. Refined model was validated with PROCHECK and the values are depicted in Table 1.

Amongst the nine models generated, model 09 was found to give better results as compared to the other eight models. Ramachandran plot for the model 09 shows residues falling in: Core regions, favorable allowed regions, generously allowed regions and disallowed regions as 82.5, 16, 1.0 and 0.5%, respectively (Figure 1). Overall plot gave 99.5% of residues within favorable

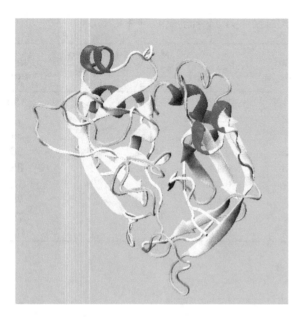

Figure 2. Homology model 9 of the thrombin protein. Yellow color with β sheets, pink color with helices and blue color with 3^{10} helices cyan color turns, white color denotes loops.

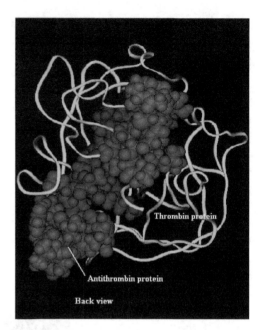

Figure 4. Antithrombin of *H. sapience* (red balls) and modeled thrombin structure in tubes in binding mode (back view).

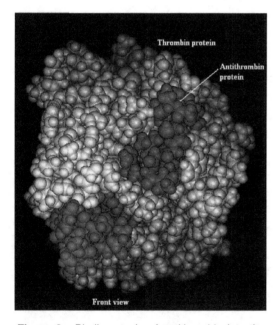

Figure 3. Binding mode of antithrombin into the thrombin protein of *O. mykiss* (yellow balls) and antithrombin (red balls) (front view).

modeled *O. mykiss* protein and 1JWJ, and found to be 3.7 was 0.56Å. The best structure modeled was then energy minimized using CHARMM force field by the Builder module of molecular simulation option of INSIGHT II. The protocol for energy minimization was as follows: Steepest descents (1000 cycles), conjugate gradient methods (1000 cycles) and Newton's methods (1000 cycles). The final model had -240.6 kcal energy.

After energy minimization, the protein-protein docking of modeled thrombin structure with 2AX2 was performed using the z-dock module of INSIGHT II. The z-dock scoring function was obtained as pairwise shape complementarily (PSC) while the r-dock score on the CHARMM force field. The binding modes were based on electrostatic interaction and desolvation energy of z-dock results. Z-dock pro filters all the hits obtained from z-dock conformations with the cutoff of 0.4Å. R-dock module was applied for optimizing a selected range of poses from filtered z-dock output file by running a CHARMM optimization. The 71 pose (Table 1 supplementary information) was found to be the best one with the following residues involved in protein-protein interaction: Leu3, Trp27, Asn120, Glu123, Pro133, Ile148, Ser152, Gly204 and Phe215. Figure 3 shows the front and Figure 4 shows the back view of the complex along with protein-protein interaction.

DISCUSSION

Comparative protein modeling is increasingly gaining interest since it is of great assistance during the rational design of mutagenesis experiments. The availability of

regions and only two residues, Ala10 and Arg13 out of the 305 (0.05%) were found in disallowed regions of Ramachandran plot. This showed that model No. 9 can be taken for further study (Figure 2).

We used SPDBV 3.7 for calculating the root mean square deviation between the backbone Cα atoms of the

Table 1. Comparisons of energy partitioning of the thrombin and antithrombin models.

Index	First: ELEC	First: VDW	First: ACE	Second: ELEC	Second: VDW	Second: ACE	Second: ELEC+First:ACE
1	1.01928	-83.855	6.77	28.9216	-87.241	6.18	35.6916
2	7.13E-02	-78.217	21.42	-5.4253	-80.721	21.54	15.9947
3	0.760335	-103.78	11.28	-5.6824	-103.93	11.5	5.59763
4	0.711845	-98.415	9.38	-6.3226	-99.984	10.12	3.05737
5	0.368667	-79.923	19.26	7.66821	-88.306	19.06	26.9282
6	-6.02233	-90.621	12.01	-15.777	-88.112	12.41	-3.767
7	-4.371	-77.751	8.46	-15.526	-85.583	7.96	-7.0663
8	0.891797	-87.119	19.41	14.5822	-88.346	19.03	33.9922
9	-1.19519	-74.081	18.24	6.78098	-90.955	17.95	25.021
10	-1.52123	-78.518	8.18	26.2327	-83.878	7.67	34.4127
11	-0.326596	-82.709	21.59	-11.043	-83.32	21.45	10.547
12	6.70E-02	-96.738	19.79	11.5243	-95.748	19.14	31.3143
13	-3.6275	-86.396	8.02	13.2991	-89.408	7.77	21.3191
14	-2.38796	-91.277	18.68	7.97121	-88.019	18.83	26.6512
15	-0.779055	-29.356	8.21	-2.4955	-85.281	9.15	5.71446
16	0.142032	-76.608	22.36	-2.9611	-80.282	22.28	19.399
17	-0.152473	-97.516	24.67	-7.1571	-94.146	24.07	17.513
18	-3.82267	-79.825	16.7	1.28911	-82.398	16.77	17.9891
19	-2.97702	-41.149	9.9	14.3042	-65.896	9.67	24.2042
20	-4.30691	-73.812	9.14	-12.297	-79.978	9.45	-3.157
21	1.17375	-65.171	9.7	-16.609	-65.789	9.6	-6.9092
22	-2.64026	-104.94	10.18	-3.1532	-100.16	10.94	7.02683
23	-0.435228	-92.408	19.6	11.3764	-90.086	18.95	30.9764
24	-2.71088	-79.854	9.94	-15.026	-86.629	9.59	-5.0864
25	-5.19762	-80.177	10.92	-11.969	-82.496	11.1	-1.0489
26	-1.76E-02	-85.764	8.78	-4.5681	-89.549	8.97	4.21186
27	-1.75131	-83.473	17.33	13.7749	-90.337	16.93	31.1049
28	-1.11241	-88.057	22.08	-12.139	-84.985	22.2	9.9407
29	2.05465	-60.924	-4.17	11.2079	-67.18	-4.5	7.0379
30	0.111097	-76.123	14.51	9.74233	-78.733	14.65	24.2523
31	0.532499	-96.633	18.2	7.84957	-94.796	18.3	26.0496
32	2.48308	-59.403	-3.46	13.1424	-67.472	-4.39	9.6824
33	-3.02588	-70.949	8.87	14.8738	-79.361	8.13	23.7438
34	-1.46E+00	-37.003	6.79	-17.56	-69.242	7.45	-10.77
35	2.24883	-78.046	24.59	-7.6378	-87.664	24.21	16.9522
36	-0.706516	-83.253	15.15	12.138	-83.996	15.04	27.288
37	0.254395	-72.491	20.85	15.764	-93.206	20.51	36.614
38	-2.70567	-71.963	19.97	16.9473	-82.336	19.45	36.9173
39	-2.70567	-71.963	19.97	0.0012	-80.42	12.29	19.97
40	-3.20533	-76.521	15.57	-5.7807	-79.605	15.16	9.78931
41	1.25129	-101.97	10.91	-6.0359	-103.43	10.76	4.87411
42	0.264408	-87.092	10.43	-6.77	-98.019	10.61	3.66002
43	3.22347	-91.395	2.8659	-68.447	-4.24	12.4095	-75.301
44	1.21148	1047	-3.4583	-65.133	14.82	-13.286	-73.661
45	-0.422204	-948	2.27314	-75.598	10.16	-9.4149	-76.978
46	2.8659	-68.447	-449	-0.3839	-71.57	7.77	-0.368
47	-3.45832	-65.133	14.825	0.26685	-86.857	19.59	5.371
48	2.27314	-75.598	10.1651	0.34029	-90.426	-6.3681	-92.44
49	-0.383874	-7152	4.35569	-64.718	-5.49	10.0478	-66.593
50	0.266847	2.42759	-89.651	24.71	-520233	-88.257	24.51

Table 1. Contd.

51	0.34029	-54	-1.3977	-86.579	18.04	6.81777	-85.805
52	4.35569	-64.55	-4.2363	-80.943	11.82	3.09053	-84.9
53	2.42759	-89.651	-0.4267	-89.779	8.38	-7.4247	-98.54
54	-1.39771	-86.579	18.0466	0.77679	-61.799	8.65	-15.455
55	-4.23625	-80.943	11.8258	-3.0586	-72.007	8.96	19.1394
56	-0.426688	-89.779	-0.4611	74.8113	5.98	-24.46	-71.181
57	0.776786	1.69415	-85.108	-2.1879	-87.352	10.91	8.74208
58	-3.05859	-72.007	8.96	19.1395	-0.4267	-89.779	8.59
59	-0.461046	-74.812	5.98	-24.46	-71.181	5.57	0.77678
60	1.69415	-85.108	1.69415	-85.108	-0.461	-759	-24.46
61	-0.461046	-759	-24.921	-95.641	-71.186	1.69415	-85.6
62	1.69415	-2.1879	-89.538	-87.352	1.58871	-73.299	15.51
63	8.89848	-85.6	1.69415	-2.1879	-89.538	-87.352	1.58871
64	-73.2991	15.51	8.89848	-77.989	14.53	24.4085	20.3442
65	-74.5256	22.19	-7.4298	-78.556	22.48	14.7602	3.4406
66	-1.20488	-59.431	30.07	-5.5472	-76.877	29.69	24.5228
67	1.65E-02	-82.554	26.47	-6.1258	-91.37	26.02	20.3442
68	1.58871	-73.299	15.51	8.89848	-77.989	14.53	24.4085
69	-4.4345	-75.388	20.47	-8.8429	-80.794	20.51	11.6271
70	0.403804	-65.043	-4.27	1.60433	-72.642	-3.62	-2.6657
71	3.23762	-74.42	20.43	18.9617	-79.101	19.52	39.3917
72	-0.585221	-95.629	10.18	3.23002	-97.297	10.2	13.41
73	-0.852606	-94.584	7.6	-18.035	-93.54	8.01	-10.435
74	3.23762	-74.42	20.43	15.4758	-93.903	19.97	35.9058
75	-0.585221	-95.629	10.18	3.23002	-97.297	10.2	13.41
76	3.23762	-74.42	20.43	15.4758	-93.903	19.97	22.342
77	-0.86017	-45.174	8.34	-18.03	-62.188	9.25	-9.6896
78	-0.625388	-83.255	7.55	-9.2091	-89.557	7.95	-1.6591
79	0.920641	-65.959	26.59	-1.3051	-89.292	26.39	25.285
80	0.567431	70.0444	4.87	-12.88	-80.112	5.3	-8.0095
81	5.79E-02	-71.082	11.71	82	-1.2504	-74.526	22.19
82	-1.25044	-74.526	22.19	-7.4298	-78.556	22.48	14.7602
83	-2.0713	-65.005	12.93	21.8927	-76.487	12.95	34.8227
84	-2.18725	-97.96	7.38	16.2724	-92.197	6.61	23.6524
85	1.20686	-80.569	19.7	10.4356	-83.813	19.14	30.1356
86	0.699904	-59.622	16.58	-13.139	-62.21	17.07	3.4406
87	0.281504	83.8491-	19.14	13.3934	-82.763	18.97	32.5334
88	1.20686	-80.569	19.7	10.4356	-83.813	19.14	30.1356
89	0.699904	-59.622	16.58	-13.139	-62.21	17.07	3.4406
90	0.281504	-83.849	19.14	13.3934	-82.763	18.97	32.5334
91	-0.222227	-91.475	21.91	4.41301	-64.883	21.55	26.323
92	1.68769	-77.213	15.88	11.8388	-86.166	15.54	27.7188
93	-1.41945	-89.75	5.89	-3.3334	-81.209	4.62	2.55658
94	-0.222227	-91.475	21.91	3.48324	-83.618	21.86	25.3932
95	1.44938	-61.912	9.64	-3.0252	-72.889	8.84	6.61476
96	-3.38229	-74.599	22.38	-7.6016	-75.513	22.9	14.7784
97	-2.20916	-78.62	19.03	9.88363	-79.87	18.47	28.9136
98	1.21651	-52.286	7.62	15.7976	-92.389	7.41	23.4176
99	-3.14873	-79.036	21.54	-6.0083	-79.167	21.35	15.5317
100	-3.23081	-73.298	13.97	20.3782	-77.479	13.53	34.3482

First ELEC: First electrostatic potential; First VDW: First Vander Wal potentials. First ACE: Desolvation energy.

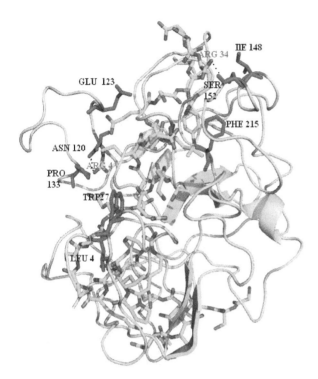

Figure 5. *O. mykiss* protein binding pocket of ILE 4, TRP 27, ASN 120, GLU 123, PRO 133, ILE 148, SER 152, PHE 215 in magenta color and antithrombin in stick model. Antithrombin of ARG 34 and ARG 4 are showing polar hydrogen bonding with SER 152 and ASN 120, respectively.

this method, and the resulting models, has however been restricted by the availability of expensive computer hardware and software. To overcome these limitations, programs like Modeller had been developed, which can generate protein models based on homology. Furthermore, two protein docking algorithms, designed to operate in succession: A rigid-body docking program, z-dock, and a refinement program, r-dock are used for docking studies.

Bleeding is one of the most feared complications of anticoagulant therapy, and is a risk of all anticoagulants. Whereas, unfractionated heparin and warfarin, the oldest and most widely used anticoagulants have specific antidotes for their anticoagulant effect, many of the newer agents (direct and indirect inhibitors of coagulation factors Xa and/or IIa) do not have specific antidotes to reverse their actions. The use of novel anticoagulants is further complicated by a lack of easily available laboratory tests to measure their levels and thereby optimize their benefit and safety in clinical practice. Our *In silico* modeling studies provides a comprehensive picture of the 3-D structure of *O. mykiss* protein. The docking studies and the active site analysis proposed the specific contacts with: Leu3, Trp27, Asn120, Glu123, Pro133, Ile148, Ser152, Gly204 and Phe215 residues (Figure 5). This provides a different perspective for

designing new antithrombin molecule to arrest the bleeding in patients suffering from clotting disorders, as the template protein was a human thrombin.

REFERENCES

Altschul SF, Gish W, Miller W, Myers EW, Lipman DJ (1990). Basic local alignment search tool. J. Mol. Biol., 215: 403-410

Brooks BR, Bruccolerr RE, Olafson BD, States DJ, Swaminathan S, Karplus M (1983). CHARMm: A program for macromolecular energy minimization and dynamics calculations. J. Comp. Chem., 4: 187-217.

Chen R, Li L, Weng (2003). ZDOCK: An initial stage protein docking algorithm. Proteins, 52: 80-87.

Esmon CT (1989). The roles of protein C and thrombomodulin in the regulation of blood coagulation. J. Biol. Chem., 264: 4743-4746.

Esmon CT (2008). Crosstalk between inflammation and thrombosis. Maturitas, 61: 122-131.

Fiser A, Sali A (2003). Modeller: generation and refinement of homology-based protein structure models. Methods in Enzymology, 374: 461-491.

Guex N, Peitsch MC (1997). SWISS-MODEL and the Swiss-PdbViewer: An environment for comparative protein modeling. Electrophoresis, 18: 2714-2723.

Gumulec J, Kessler P, Procházka V, Brejcha M, Penka M, Zänger M, Machytka E, Klement P (2009). Bleeding complications of anticoagulant therapy. Vnitr. Lek., 55: 277-289.

Lange UE, Baucke D, Hornberger W, Mack H, Seitz W, Höffken HW (2006). Orally active thrombin inhibitors. Part 2: optimization of the P2-moiety. Bioorg. Med. Chem. Lett., 15: 2648-2653.

Laskowski RA, MacArthur MW, Moss DS, Thornton JM (1993). PROCHECK: a program to check the stereo chemical quality of protein structures. J. Appl. Cryst., 26: 283-291.

Lévesque S, St-Denis Y, Bachand B, Préville P, Leblond L, Winocour PD Edmunds JJ, Rubin JR, Siddiqui MA (2001). Novel bicyclic lactam inhibitors of thrombin: Potency and selectivity optimization through P1 residues. Bioorg. Med. Chem. Lett., 11: 3161-3164.

Li L, Chen R, Weng Z (2003). RDOCK: refinement of rigid-body protein docking predictions. Proteins, 53: 693-707.

Mackman N, Tilley RE, Key NS (2007). Role of the extrinsic pathway of blood coagulation in hemostasis and thrombosis. Arterioscler. Thromb. Vasc. Biol., 27: 1687-1693.

Samama CM (2008). Prothrombin complex concentrates: a brief review. Eur. J. Anaesthesiol., 25: 784-789.

Tanaka KA, Key NS, Levy JH (2009). Blood coagulation: hemostasis and thrombin regulation. Anesth. Anal., 108: 1433-1446.

Thompson JD, Higgins DG, Gibson TJ (1994). CLUSTAL W: improving the sensitivity of progressive multiple sequence alignment through sequence weighting, position-specific gap penalties and weight matrix choice. Nucleic Acids Res., 22: 4673 -4680.

Vine AK (2009). Recent advances in haemostasis and thrombosis. Retina, 29: 1-7.

9

In silico structure assessment analysis of core domain of six protein data bank entries of HIV-1 Integrase

Salam Pradeep Singh* and B. K. Konwar

Bioinformatics Infrastructure Facility, Department of Molecular Biology and Biotechnology, School of Science and Technology Tezpur University, Tezpur 784028, Assam, India.

HIV integrase is a 32 kDa protein produced from the C-terminal portion of the Pol gene product, and is an attractive target for new anti-HIV drugs. Its main function is to insert the viral DNA into the host chromosomal DNA, a step that is essential for its replication. However there are six different Protein Data Bank (PDB) entries of the same protein with the same amino acids with PDB IDs 1BIS, 1BIU, 1BIZ, 1HYV, 1HYZ and 1QS4. The present work focuses on the structure analysis of chain A of the different PDB entries of the same protein using *in silico* approaches via the Swiss Model structure assessment server, ANOLEA Assessment server and Ramachandran plot analysis. The structure assessment analysis reveals that there is a major difference among these PDB entries based on the energy assessment and structural analysis. The PDB ID 1BIU chain A is found to be the most stable and reliable structure for assisting computer aided drug designing.

Key words: *In silico* structure, core domain, protein data bank, HIV integrase.

INTRODUCTION

The integration of viral DNA into the host chromosome is a necessary process in the HIV replication cycle (Brown, 2000). The key steps of DNA integration are carried out by the viral integrase protein, which is one of three enzymes encoded by HIV. Combination antiviral therapy with protease and reverse transcriptase inhibitors has demonstrated the potential therapeutic efficacy of antiviral therapy for the treatment of AIDS (Vandamme et al., 1998). Integrase is an attractive target for antivirals because it is essential for HIV replication and unlike protease and reverse transcriptase, there are no known counterparts in the host cell. Furthermore, integrase uses a single active site to accommodate two different configurations of DNA substrates, which may constrain the ability of HIV to develop drug resistance to integrase inhibitors. Unlike protease and reverse transcriptase, for which several classes of inhibitors have been developed and co crystal structures have been determined, progress with the development of integrase inhibitors has been

slow. A major obstacle has been the absence of good lead compounds that can serve as the starting point for the structure based inhibitor development. Although numerous compounds have been reported to inhibit integrase activity *in vitro*, most of these compounds exhibit little specificity for integrase and are not useful as lead compounds (Pommier et al., 1997). HIV-1 integrase is a 32-kDa enzyme that carries out DNA integration in a two-step reaction (Brown, 2000). Integrase is comprised of three structurally and functionally distinct domains and all three domains are required for each step of the integration reaction (Engelman et al., 1993). The isolated domains form homodimers in solution and the three-dimensional structure(s) of all three separate dimers have been determined (Dyda et al., 1994; Goldgur et al., 1998; Maignan et al., 1998; Lodi et al., 1995; Eijkelenboom et al., 1995; Cai et al., 1997). Although little is known concerning the organization of these domains in the active complex with DNA substrates, integrase is likely to function as at least a tetramer (Dyda et al., 1994). Extensive mutagenesis studies mapped the catalytic site to the core domain (residues 50–212), which contains the catalytic residues Asp-64, Asp-116, and Glu-152 (Engelman et al., 1992; Kulkosky et al., 1992). The

*Corresponding author. E-mail: salam10@tezu.ernet.in.

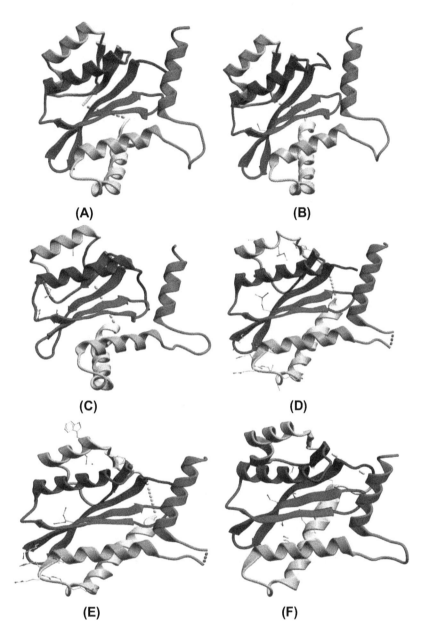

Figure 1. Secondary structure of Chain A's of (A) 1BIS Chain A; (B) 1BIU Chain A; **(C)** 1BIZ Chain A; (D) 1HYV Chain A; (E) 1HYZ Chain A; (F) 1 QS4 Chain A.

structure of this domain of HIV-1 integrase has been determined previously in several crystal forms (Dyda et al., 1994; Goldgur et al., 1998; Maignan et al., 1998) describes structures with bound magnesium and predicts that these structures would provide a more suitable platform for inhibitor binding than the earlier structure of the apoenzyme.

The present study aims at the *in silico* structure assessment analysis of six different PDB entries of integrase protein of HIV in finding the best stable structure from these six different PDB entries for assisting computer aided drug designing. This *in silico* analysis will add up for designing a more reliable and accurate class of HIV inhibitors.

MATERIALS AND METHODS

The PDB ID of 1BIS, 1BIU, 1BIZ, 1HYV, 1HYZ and 1QS4 (Goldgur et al., 1998; Molteni et al., 2001; Goldgur et al., 1999) were retrieved from the Protein Data Bank (http://www.pdb.org/). Their three-dimensional structures are shown in Figure 1. The three-dimensional structures of chain A's of 1BIS, 1BIU, 1BIZ, 1HYV, 1HYZ and 1QS4 were analysed for structure assessment.

Initially the 3D structures of these proteins were assessed with Atomic Non- Local Environment Assessment (ANOLEA) a server that performs energy calculations on a protein chain, evaluating the "Non- Local Environment" (NLE) of each heavy atom in the molecule in which the energy of each pair wise interaction in the non-local environment is taken from a distance-dependent knowledge-based mean force potential that has been derived from a database of 147 non-redundant protein chains with a sequence

Table 1. ANOLEA energy assessment showing high energy amino acids and the total non-local energy of chain A's of 1BIS, 1BIU, 1BIZ, 1HYV, 1HYZ and 1QS4.

S/n	PDB ID and Chain	Total amino acids	high energy (percentage)	Total non-local energy (E/kT units)	Non-local normalized energy Z-score
1	1BIS-A	146	15 (10.27)	-1014	-0.69
2	1BIU-A	147	13(8.84)	-1043	-0.75
3	1BIZ-A	147	18(12.2)	-889	-0.23
4	1HYV-A	142	16(11.27)	-929	-0.75
5	1HYZ-A	142	16(11.27)	-922	-0.73
6	1QS4-A	150	16 (10.67)	-955	-0.32

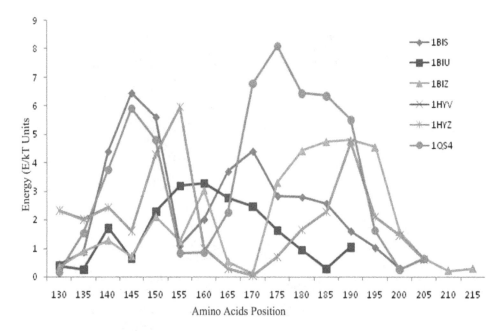

Figure 2. High energy amino acid residue plot of chain A's of 1BIS, 1BIU, 1BIZ, 1HYV, 1HYV and 1QS4. 1BIU chain A (Red) has an overall lower energy as compared to the other five chains.

identity below 25% and solved by X-Ray crystallography with a resolution lower than 3 Å (Melo and Feytmans, 1998).

Further the chain A's of the six three dimensional structures were accessed with PROCHECK (Laskowski et al., 1993) via the Swiss Model - Protein Structure and Model Assessment Tools (http://swissmodel.expasy.org/) for analyzing the Ramachandran plot (Ramachandran et al., 1963) and for visualizing the dihedral angles ψ against φ of the amino acid residues.

RESULTS AND DISCUSSION

Table 1 with ANOLEA energy assessment of chain A's of 1BIS, 1BIU, 1BIZ, 1HYV, 1HYZ, 1QS4 shows the total number of high energy amino acids of 1BIU with 13 high energy amino acids out of 147 amino acids and a total non-local energy of −1043 E/kt units. The table also shows 1BIZ with 18 high energy amino acids out of 147 amino acid residues with a total non-local energy of -889 E/kT units as the highest energy. This assessment shows that chain A of 1BIU is more stable in terms of low

number of high energy amino acids (13/147 [8.84 %]), lowest total non-local energy (-1043 E/kT units) and lowest non-local normalized energy Z-score with -0.23 as compared to the chain A's of 1BIS, 1BIZ, 1HYV, 1HYZ and 1QS4.

The ANOLEA energy assessment analysis of high energy amino acid residues of chain A of 1BIS, 1BIU, 1BIZ, 1HYV, 1HYV and 1QS4 is shown in Table 2. In most of the cases the high energy amino acid was located between the CYS130 to ALA196. Chain A of 1BIU accounts an overall of 20.91 E/kT units of high energy amino acids as compared to 40.1 E/kT units of 1BIS chain A , 34.95 kT units of 1BIZ chain A, 33.64 E/kT units of both 1HYV and 1HYZ chain A and E/kT 55.88 units of 1QS4. The energy analysis of each high energy amino acid also revealed that each of the high energy residues of 1BIU chain A has a lower energy as compared to the other five chains which is shown in Figure 2. The superimposition of the six chain A's of the

Table 2. ANOLEA energy assessment showing the energy values of the high energy amino acids of the chains A's of 1BIU, 1BIU, 1BIZ, 1HYV, 1HYV and 1QS4. 1 BIU chain A accounts with a minimum energu of 20.91 E/kT units.

1BIS Chain A		1BIU Chain A		1BIZ Chain A		1HYV Chain A		1HYZ Chain A		1QS4 Chain A	
Amino acid position	Energy (E/kT units)	Amino acid position	Energy (E/kT units)	Amino acid position	Energy (E/kT units)	Amino acid position	Energy (E/kT units)	Amino acid position	Energy (E/kT units)	Amino acid position	Energy (E/kT units)
CYS130	0.42	CYS 130	0.39	SER56	0.35	ALA129	2.33	ALA129	2.33	CYS130	0.16
TRP132	0.86	GLU 131	0.26	GLY 118	0.89	TRP131	2.03	TRP131	2.0	TRP132	1.54
ILE141	4.40	TRP 132	1.71	CYS130	1.28	TRP132	2.44	TRP132	2.44	PRO145	3.76
PRO142	6.45	LYS 188	0.65	TRP131	0.72	PHE139	1.61	PHE139	1.61	GLN 146	5.92
ILE151	5.60	GLY 189	2.29	TRP132	2.11	GLY140	4.30	GLY140	4.30	SER147	4.80
ARG187	1.09	GLY 190	3.19	PHE139	1.24	GLN148	5.96	GLN148	5.96	GLN148	0.83
LYS188	2.01	ILE 191	3.27	GLY140	3.03	GLY149	1.00	GLY149	1.00	ARG187	0.85
GLY189	3.69	GLY 192	2.77	GLY149	0.54	ALA169	0.29	ALA169	0.29	LYS188	2.25
GLY190	4.40	GLY 193	2.46	ALA169	0.12	ARG187	0.05	ARG187	0.05	GLY189	6.78
ILE191	2.83	TYR 194	1.64	GLY189	3.30	LYS188	0.70	LYS188	0.70	GLY190	8.10
GLY192	2.79	SER 195	0.95	GLY 190	4.43	GLY189	1.66	GLY189	1.66	ILE191	6.44
GLY193	2.57	ALA 196	0.28	ILE191	4.75	GLY193	2.29	GLY193	2.29	GLY192	6.35
TYR 194	1.60	ASP 207	1.05	GLY192	4.80	TYR194	4.73	TYR194	4.73	GLY193	5.51
SER195	1.02			GLY193	4.56	SER195	2.11	SER195	2.11	TYR194	1.62
ALA196	0.28			TYR194	1.59	ALA 196	1.46	ALA196	1.46	SER195	0.26
				SER195	0.65	ILE208	0.62	ILE208	0.62	ASP207	0.64
				ALA196	0.22						
				GLY197	0.29						
Sum = 40.1		Sum = 20.91		Sum = 34.95		Sum= 33.64		Sum = 33.64		Sum = 55.88	

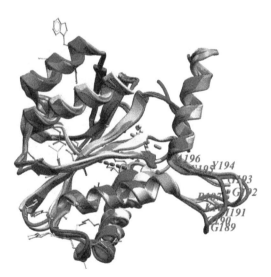

Figure 3. Superimposition of the Chain A's of 1BIS (Green), 1BIU (Blue), 1BIZ (Pink), 1HYV (Yellow), 1HYZ (Violet), 1QS4 (Purple) showing the deviation in the residues form GLY189 to ALA196.

PDB ID 1BIS, 1BIU, 1BIZ, 1HYV, 1HYZ, 1QS4 is shown in Figure 3 and it shows the region of the high energy amino acid region ranging from GLY189 to ALA196.

Further Ramachandran plot analysis reveals that 96.0% amino acid residues of chain A of 1BIS, 93.6% of Chain A 1BIU, 96.1% of Chain A of 1BIZ, 95.8% of

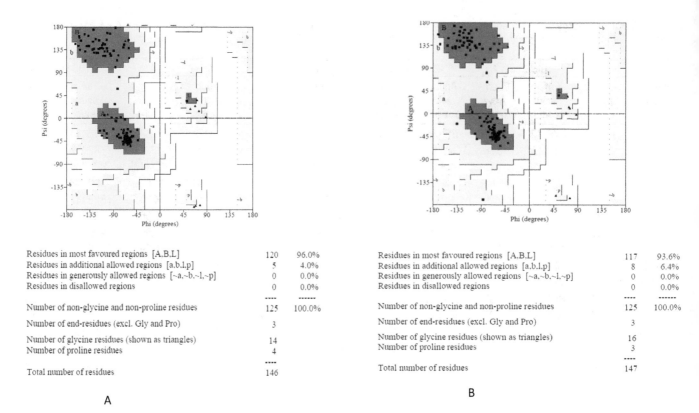

Residues in most favoured regions [A.B.L]	120	96.0%
Residues in additional allowed regions [a.b.l.p]	5	4.0%
Residues in generously allowed regions [~a,~b,~l,~p]	0	0.0%
Residues in disallowed regions	0	0.0%
	----	------
Number of non-glycine and non-proline residues	125	100.0%
Number of end-residues (excl. Gly and Pro)	3	
Number of glycine residues (shown as triangles)	14	
Number of proline residues	4	

Total number of residues	146	

A

Residues in most favoured regions [A.B.L]	117	93.6%
Residues in additional allowed regions [a.b.l.p]	8	6.4%
Residues in generously allowed regions [~a,~b,~l,~p]	0	0.0%
Residues in disallowed regions	0	0.0%
	----	------
Number of non-glycine and non-proline residues	125	100.0%
Number of end-residues (excl. Gly and Pro)	3	
Number of glycine residues (shown as triangles)	16	
Number of proline residues	3	

Total number of residues	147	

B

Figure 4A. Ramachandran plot showing chain A's of (A): 1BIS; (B): 1BIU.

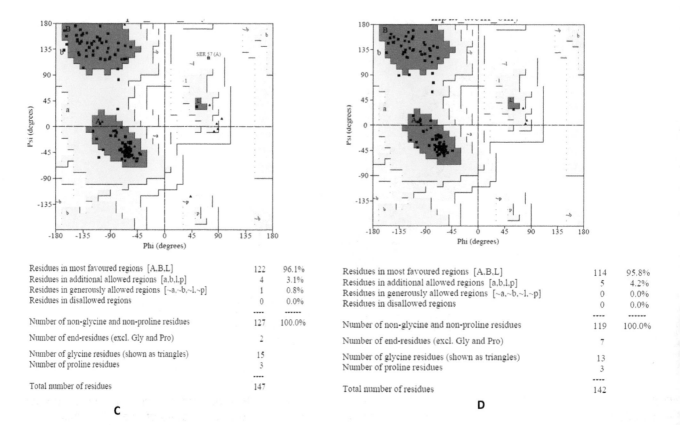

Residues in most favoured regions [A.B.L]	122	96.1%
Residues in additional allowed regions [a.b.l.p]	4	3.1%
Residues in generously allowed regions [~a,~b,~l,~p]	1	0.8%
Residues in disallowed regions	0	0.0%
	----	------
Number of non-glycine and non-proline residues	127	100.0%
Number of end-residues (excl. Gly and Pro)	2	
Number of glycine residues (shown as triangles)	15	
Number of proline residues	3	

Total number of residues	147	

C

Residues in most favoured regions [A.B.L]	114	95.8%
Residues in additional allowed regions [a.b.l.p]	5	4.2%
Residues in generously allowed regions [~a,~b,~l,~p]	0	0.0%
Residues in disallowed regions	0	0.0%
	----	------
Number of non-glycine and non-proline residues	119	100.0%
Number of end-residues (excl. Gly and Pro)	7	
Number of glycine residues (shown as triangles)	13	
Number of proline residues	3	

Total number of residues	142	

D

Figure 4B. Ramachandran plot showing chain A's of (C): 1BIZ; (D) 1HYV.

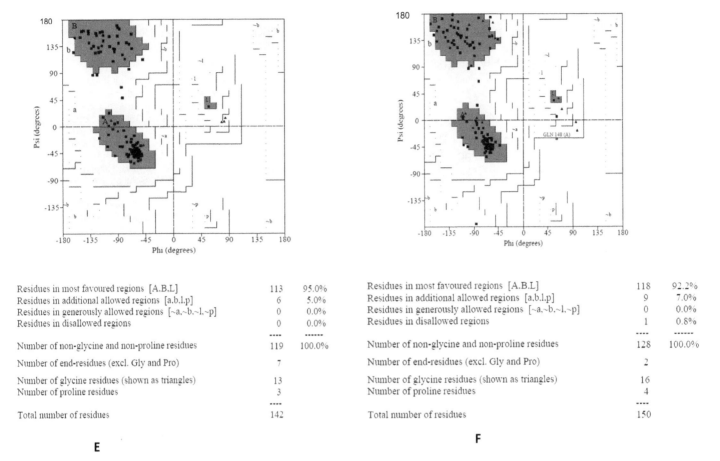

Residues in most favoured regions [A.B.L]	113	95.0%
Residues in additional allowed regions [a.b.l.p]	6	5.0%
Residues in generously allowed regions [~a.~b.~l.~p]	0	0.0%
Residues in disallowed regions	0	0.0%
Number of non-glycine and non-proline residues	119	100.0%
Number of end-residues (excl. Gly and Pro)	7	
Number of glycine residues (shown as triangles)	13	
Number of proline residues	3	
Total number of residues	142	

E

Residues in most favoured regions [A.B.L]	118	92.2%
Residues in additional allowed regions [a.b.l.p]	9	7.0%
Residues in generously allowed regions [~a.~b.~l.~p]	0	0.0%
Residues in disallowed regions	1	0.8%
Number of non-glycine and non-proline residues	128	100.0%
Number of end-residues (excl. Gly and Pro)	2	
Number of glycine residues (shown as triangles)	16	
Number of proline residues	4	
Total number of residues	150	

F

Figure 4C. Ramachandran plot showing chain A's of (E): 1HYV; (F): 1QS4.

Table 3. Ramachandran plot result showing chains A's of 1BIS, 1BIU, 1BIZ,1HYV, 1HYV and 1QS4 in favoured region, additional allowed regions, generously allowed region and disallowed region.

PDB ID	Residues in most favoured regions [A,B,L] (%)	Residues in additional allowed regions [a,b,l,p] (%)	Residues in generously allowed regions [~a,~b,~l,~p] (%)	Residues in disallowed regions (%)
1BIS Chain A	120 (96.0)	5 (4)	0 (0.0)	0 (0.0)
1BIU Chain A	117 (93.6)	8 (6.4)	0 (0.0)	0 (0.0)
1BIZ Chain A	122 (96.1)	4 (3.1)	1 (0.8)	0 (0.0)
1HYV Chain A	114 (95.8)	5 (4.2)	0 (0.0)	0 (0.0)
1HYZ Chain A	113 (95.0)	6 (5.0)	0 (0.0)	0 (0.0)
1QS4 Chain A	118 (92.2)	9 (7.0)	0 (0.0)	1 (0.8)

Chain A of 1HYV, 95.0% of Chain A of 1HYZ and 92.2% of Chain A of 1QS4 are in the most favoured region of Ramachandran plot. While 4% amino acid residues of Chain A of 1BIS, 6.4% of Chain A 1BIU, 3.1% Chain A of 1BIZ, 4.2% Chain A of 1HYV, 5.0% Chain A of 1HYZ and 7.0%of Chain A of 1QS4 are in the additional allowed regions. The plot also reveals that only one residue of Chain A of 1BIZ is in generously allowed regions and only one residue of Chain A of 1QS4 is in the disallowed region. Ramachandran plot and its details are shown in

Figures 4A to 4C and Table 3.

Conclusion

The chain A's of 1BIS, 1BIU, 1BIZ, 1HYV, 1HYZ and 1QS4 has been assessed for stability, energy analysis and geometrical errors using various assessment servers and programmes and found that the Chain A of 1BIU is more reliable and accurate as compared to chain A's of

1BIS, 1BIZ, 1HYV, 1HYZ and 1QS4. Chain A of 1BIU would be a promising structure for assisting computer aided drug designing in targeting HIV Integrase inhibitors.

ACKNOWLEDGEMENT

The authors thank Department of Biotechnology, Government of India for providing Bioinformatics Infrastructure Facility to carry out this research.

REFERENCES

Brown PO (2000). Retroviruses Integration. In: Coffin JM, Hughes SH, Varmus HE. (Eds), Cold Spring Harbor Lab. Press, Plainview, New York; p.161–203.

Cai ML, Zheng R, Caffrey M, Craigie R, Clore GM, Gronenborn AM (1997). Solution structure of the N-terminal zinc binding domain of HIV-1 Integrase. Nat. Struct. Biol., 4:839–840.

Dyda F, Hickman AB, Jenkins TM, Engelman A, Craigie R, Davies DR (1994). Crystal structure of the catalytic domain of HIV-1 integrase: similarity to other polynucleotidyl transferases. Sci., 266:1981–1986.

Eijkelenboom AP, Lutzke RA, Boelens R, Plasterk RH, Kaptein R, Hard K (1995). The DNA-binding domain of HIV-1 integrase has an SH3-like fold. Nat. Struct. Biol., 2:807–810.

Engelman A, Bushman FD, Craigie R (1993). Identification of discrete functional domains of HIV-1 integrase and their organization within an active multimeric complex. EMBO J., 12:3269–3275.

Engelman A, Craigie R (1992). Identification of conserved amino acid residues critical for human immunodeficiency virus type 1 integrase unction in vitro. J. Virol., 66:6361–6369.

Goldgur Y, Craigie R, Cohen GH, Fujiwara T, Yoshinaga T, Fujishita T, Sugimoto H, Endo T, Murai H, Davies DR (1999). Structure of the HIV-1 integrase catalytic domain complexed with an inhibitor: a platform for antiviral drug design. Proc. Natl. Acad. Sci. USA., 96:13040-13043

Goldgur Y, Dyda F, Hickman AB, Jenkins TM, Craigie R, Davies DR (1998). Three new structures of the core domain of HIV-1 integrase: an active site that binds magnesium. Proc. Natl. Acad. Sci. USA., 95:9150–9154.

Kulkosky J, Jones KS, Katz RA, Mack JP, Skalka AM (1992). Residues critical for retroviral integrative recombination in a region that is highly conserved among retroviral/retrotransposon integrases and bacterial insertion sequence transposases. Mol. Cell Biol., 12:2331–2338.

Laskowski RA, MacArthur MW, Moss D, Thornton JM (1993). PROCHECK: a program to check the stereochemical quality of protein structures. J. Appl. Cryst., 26:283-291.

Lodi PJ, Ernst JA, Kuszewski J, Hickman AB, Engelman A, Craigie R, Clore GM, Gronenborn AM (1995). Solution structure of the DNA binding domain of HIV-1 integrase. Biochem., 34:9826–9833.

Maignan S, Guilloteau JP, Zhou-Liu Q, Clement-Mella C, Mikol V (1998) Crystal structures of the catalytic domain of HIV-1 integrase free and complexed with its metal cofactor: high level of similarity of the active site with other viral integrases. J. Mol. Biol., 282:359–368.

Meloc F, Feytmans E (1998). Assessing protein structures with a non-local atomic interaction energy. J. Mol. Biol., 277(5):1141-1152.

Molteni V, Greenwald J, Rhodes D, Hwang Y, Kwiatkowski W, Bushman FD, Siegel JS, Choe S (2001). Identification of a small-molecule binding site at the dimer interface of the HIV integrase catalytic domain. Acta Crystallogr. Sect. D., 57:536-544

Pommier Y, Pilon AA, Bajaj K, Mazumder A, Neamati N (1997). HIV-1 integrase as a target for antiviral drugs. Antiviral Chem. Chemother. 8:463–485.

Protein Data Bank <http://www.pdb.org/pdb/home/home.do>.

Ramachandran GN, Ramakrishnan C, Sasisekharan V (1963). Stereochemistry of polypeptide chain configurations. J. Mol. Biol., 7:95–9

Swiss Model Protein Structure and Model Assessment Tools <http://swissmodel.expasy.org/>.

Vandamme AM, Van Vaerenbergh K, De Clercq E (1998). Anti-human immunodeficiency virus drug combination strategies. Antiviral Chem. Chemother., 9:187–203.

10

Pattern clustering of forest fires based on meteorological variables and its classification using hybrid data mining methods

Yong Poh Yu[1], Rosli Omar[1], Rhett D. Harrison[2], Mohan Kumar Sammathuria[3] and Abdul Rahim Nik[4]

[1]Department of Electrical Engineering, University of Malaya, 50603 Lembah Pantai, Kuala Lumpur, Malaysia.
[2]Xishuangbanna Tropical Botanical Garden, Menglun, Mengla, 666303, Yunnan, China.
[3]Malaysia Meteorological Department, Jalan Sultan, 46667 Petaling Jaya, Malaysia.
[4]Forest Research Institute, 52110 Kepong, Selangor, Malaysia.

This paper outlines two hybrid approaches to investigate the nonlinear relationship between size of a forest fire and meteorological variables (temperature, relative humidity, wind speed and rainfall). Self organizing map was used to cluster the historical meteorological variables. The clustered data were then used as inputs for two different approaches, the back-propagation neural network and the rule generation approaches. A back-propagation neural network was trained based on these inputs to classify the output (burnt area) in categorical form, namely; small, medium, large and extremely large. Several sets of rules were also generated from the data clustered by the self organizing map. Experimental results showed that both approaches gave considerable accuracy. Back-propagation neural network achieved a higher rate of accuracy than rule generation approach because the rule generation approach could not predict any criterion that goes beyond the set of rules.

Key words: Forest fire, self organizing map, back-propagation neural network, rule-based system.

INTRODUCTION

Forest fire is one type of significant disturbance to the forest ecosystem. There is increasing evidence to show that the global climate change may cause a significant effect on the forest fire (Torn and Fried, 1992; Williams et al., 2001). New evidence shows that the more forests burn the more susceptible to future burning they become (Rowell and Moore, 2000). Forest fire eventually causes destruction to the community. For example, greater than 2.7 million hectares of forest area were burnt in Portugal, from 1980 to 2005. Some fire seasons caused human deaths and losses of large territory (Cortez and Morais, 2007).

Earlier studies have shown that there is a relationship between meteorological conditions and forest fire occurrence. It is believed that fire is largely a function of meteorological variables, that is temperature, relative humidity, wind speed and precipitation (Cortez and Morais, 2007; Amiro et al., 2004). Some numerical indices incorporate these meteorological variables into their calculations. An example is the Canadian forest fire weather index (FWI). This index was adopted and used by several countries including those from developing countries (de Groot et al., 2005).

Investigation on forest fire modeling and its nonlinear relationship with meteorological conditions keep increasing. Data mining technique is one of the common approaches to determine the relationship. In the study done by Stojanova et al. (2006), they built different models based on different data mining techniques to predict the forest fire in different regions. They concluded that bagging of decision trees gave best results

*Corresponding author. E-mail: ypyu@siswa.um.edu.my

compared to logistic regression, random forest, and decision tree. However, a study from Cortez and Morais (2007) showed that support vector machine (SVM) was the technique that gave the best performance. Thus, there is still lack of comprehensive studies on the performance and effectiveness of data mining techniques in predicting and clustering the forest fires.

In this research, two different hybrid approaches are presented. Basically, a self organizing map (SOM) was applied in the first stage to cluster the characteristics of the meteorological conditions. The clustered patterns were then used in subsequent approaches to classify the forest fire. Two approaches, namely back-propagation neural network and rule-based system, were developed.

Self organizing map was selected as the clustering method so that the system could be trained without any supervision. Self organizing map is able to cluster those samples with similar characters (inputs) into a same category (neuron) by itself, where no target or output is needed in first stage. The dimensionally reduced map was then projected to the back-propagation neural network for a supervised training. As the data were clustered at first stage, it would not be too time consuming at second stage.

A rule-based system was selected as part of the hybrid system too. The generated sets of rules can be integrated and incorporated with other models (such as blackboard system) as well. Thus, the results from rule-based system can be used as the pre-condition and post-condition criteria in other model (McManus, 1992). For instance, in a biodiversity change blackboard model, this rule-based system can be used to predict the forest fires and subsequently, the respective biodiversity change.

DATA MINING TECHNIQUES

Self organizing map

The self organizing map (SOM) is an unsupervised learning algorithm proposed by (Kohonen, 1982). It is quite often used as a tool for clustering, classification, and data mining (Vesanto, 2000). Typically, it provides a way to reduce the topology information from high dimension to lower dimension, which is normally represented by one or two dimensional layer of neurons. Number output or target is given to the SOM for the training as it is capable of self-learning.

According to Kalteh et al. (2008), there are 3 types of procedures required to apply a SOM, namely data gathering and normalization, training and information extraction. In the data gathering and normalization step, the input variables are normalized so that all variables have equal importance in the SOM. The SOM trains itself by finding a best match unit (BMU) or winning neuron in its output map. The common criterion used to find a best match unit is Euclidean distance. Let input vector $X_i = \{x_{i1},$

$x_{i2}, x_{i3}... x_{in}\}$ and SOM neuron $X_j = \{x_{j1}, x_{j2}, x_{j3}... x_{jn}\}$, then the Euclidean distance between X_i and X_j, denoted by d_{ij}, is defined as

$$d_{ij} = \sqrt{\sum_{k=1}^{n} (x_{ik} - x_{jk})^2} \tag{1}$$

The weights of BMU and its topological neighbouring neurons are updated in such a way as to reproduce the input pattern (Kalteh et al., 2008). The process is continued by other input vectors until convergence, this is known as incremental training algorithm. There is another type of training known as batch training algorithm. Batch training algorithm determines the BMU for each input vector. Then every BMU (and its topological neighbouring neurons) is updated based on the average of all of input vectors that fire that particular BMU. Batch training algorithm was implemented in this research.

Back-propagation neural network

Back-propagation neural network system is also a common approach in data mining (Sunar and Ozkan, 2001; Antonie et al., 2001). Back-propagation algorithm is often used to train a feed-forward multilayer perception (MLP) network. A MLP network contains two or more layers. A typical 3 layer MLP network consists of an input layer, a hidden layer and an output layer. Number of input neurons in an input layer is equal to the number of elements existing in an input vector. Hidden layer is the internal layer where the number of neurons can be chosen in trial and error manner. Output layer has the output neurons where the number of neurons is same as the number of desired output variables.

In back-propagation neural network, MLP network is trained iteratively until the difference of values (or error) between output neurons and output targets has converged. MLP forwards the input vectors or training samples from the input layer, to the hidden layer and lastly to the output layer. During the feed-forward propagation, the weight of each MLP neuron is updated based on an activation function. A common activation function is the sigmoid activation function (Gardner and Dorling, 1998).

There are many types of training algorithms that can be used to train the back-propagation neural network (Cha et al., 2008). A common training algorithm is Levernberg Marquardt algorithm (Mas et al., 2004; Atluri et al., 1999) Levernberg-Marquardt algorithm for neural network training was developed by (Hagan and Menhaj, 1994) They concluded that Levernberg-Marquardt algorithm was much more efficient than other techniques such as conjugate gradient algorithm and variable learning rate algorithm. They found that Levernberg-Marquardt algorithm was efficient for network that contained no more than a few hundred neurons. Thus, this algorithm is widely used now. In this research, the network that is used is also within this size.

DATA COLLECTION AND METHODOLOGY

Forest fire data

Forest fire data have been collected from the study of Cortez and Morais (2007) which are available in the UCI machine learning repository. The dataset contains forest fire occurrence, forest fire weather index (FWI) components in Montesinho Natural Park, a northeast region of Portugal. Weather observations were collected by Braganca Polytechnic Institute and integrated to the forest fire dataset. The park was divided into 81 distinct locations by placing a 9×9 grid onto the map of the park. The dataset has a total of 517 samples, from 2000 until 2007.

In our research, four meteorological variables, yield temperature, relative humidity, wind speed and rainfall, had been used to classify the size of forest fire. The data were categorized into two different sets, randomly, which were used as training dataset, and testing dataset. The training dataset contained 80% or 414 samples out of the total samples, including both of non-fire occurrence and fire occurrence samples. The remaining 103 samples were used as testing data, which were not projected to self organizing map and back-propagation neural network. Every sample was defined as a 5×1 vector, where first four elements were the meteorological variables and the last element was the burnt area of that particular sample. Thus, a 5×414 matrix was formed to represent the training samples.

Self organizing map (SOM)

Prior to the self organizing map system training, all the training data samples were normalized so that the mean of each variable was 0 and the standard deviation (SD) of each variable was 1. The training data samples were then projected to the SOM training phase using MATLAB version R2009b. Batch unsupervised weight algorithm was implemented using MATLAB. There were only four meteorological variables included in the SOM training. The burnt area variable was not used for the SOM training. As the outputs (burnt area) of testing samples may be unknown or unidentified, burnt area was excluded as part of the training inputs. Thus, every training and testing sample was defined as 4×1 vector and a 4×414 matrix was formed to be trained. Another 4×103 matrix was formed to be tested.

After the SOM was trained, training samples with similar characteristics (in terms of the meteorological variables) would be mapped to the same neurons (clusters) in the output map (Kalteh et al., 2008). In this research, each of the training samples was mapped to the neuron that had the shortest Euclidean distance with that particular sample.

Figure 1 shows the distribution of training data samples in the output map. From the figure, some neurons (clusters) had more samples, such as neuron at (2, 1) position had 45 training samples. All these 45 samples were said to have similar characteristics.

The testing data samples were then classified into the map. Euclidean distance between every SOM output neuron and the testing data sample was calculated. Similarly, each testing data sample was mapped into the neuron that had the shortest Euclidean distance.

Back-propagation neural network

The samples were classified into 16 different clusters. Every cluster was then projected to its own back-propagation neural network. Four meteorological variables of training samples in each cluster were the inputs of the neural network. The 5th element, namely burnt area, was the output of the training set in the neural network. The output (burnt area) was used in this stage for training purpose. Then, the results of testing samples (extracted from SOM map) will be projected to respective back-propagation neural network that was trained earlier.

Back-propagation neural network does not necessarily need to have testing samples with known outputs (burnt area). It is good to be used to make classification on those testing samples with unknown outputs. It is also suitable to train (and test) the SOM neurons that have no outputs, which was proposed in this research. Levenberg-Marquardt training algorithm was used for the neural network training.

The testing samples in each cluster were projected to the trained neural network to classify the burnt area of forest fire. Both of the experimental and original values of burnt area were in continuous form. In order to have better representation, the burnt area was transformed from continuous value to categorical form, namely small, medium, large, and extremely large. Empirical rule was adopted and implemented into the transformation. Empirical rule states that for a normal distribution, about 68% of the data will fall within 1 standard deviation of the mean, about 95% of the data will fall within 2 standard deviation of the mean, and about 99.7% of the data will fall within 3 standard deviation of the mean. With zero mean and unity standard deviation, the transformation was based on the following rules:

If $\left|normalized\ burnt\ area\right| < 1$, then it is small;

If $1 \leq \left|normalized\ burnt\ area\right| < 2$, then it is medium;

If $2 \leq \left|normalized\ burnt\ area\right| < 3$, then it is large;

If $\left|normalized\ burnt\ area\right| \geq 3$, then it is extremely large.

Rule-based system

Apart from the back-propagation neural network, a rule-based system was also generated from each cluster for the classification. Meteorological variables and burnt area of every training sample in each cluster were analyzed. Rule-based system was then developed based on the range of input (meteorological) variables and output variable (burnt area). IF... THEN... type of rules was implemented.

To prevent bias on the results, variables of testing samples were not used for the rule generation. The testing samples were only used to validate the effectiveness of the proposed system.

Table 1 shows some examples of the rules that were generated from SOM. Rule 1 in Table 1 can be interpreted as, "if a testing sample in SOM cluster has the normalized temperature between 0.7299 and 2.3845, normalized relative humidity between -1.3499 and -0.1316, normalized wind speed between -1.585 and -0.0406, normalized rainfall of -0.0818, then the burnt area of that particular testing sample is classified as small".

RESULTS AND DISCUSSION

Self organizing map outputs

Table 2 summarizes the distribution of the training

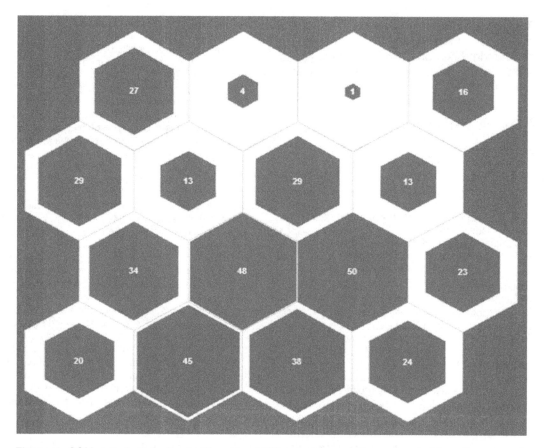

Figure 1. SOM output map after training. The SOM output neuron is represented by a hexagon. A number is shown in each SOM neuron to indicate the number of training samples that is mapped into that SOM neuron. The more number of training samples in the neuron, the more area is shaded.

samples and testing samples in the output map. The ratio of number of testing samples over number of training samples for each cluster was between 0 to 47%.

Comparison between outputs of back-propagation neural network and rule-based system approaches

Table 3 summarizes the accuracy of the burnt area classification for the testing samples, based on back-propagation neural network and rule-based system approaches. Overall, it provides agreement to the hypothesis that SOM is a good clustering method where the samples with similar characteristics are mapped into the same cluster. For this research, a single SOM could not predict the burnt area since the burnt area was not projected into the SOM training.

Thus, a subsequent approach is needed to predict the burnt area, yields the back-propagation neural network or rule-based system.

One of the back-propagation neural network issues is the non-representativeness of training samples (Chang et al., 1993). If the training samples are not representative

of the testing samples, the network may not be classified very well due to the limitation of the training samples (the training samples are too few). For instance, a testing sample with the normalized burnt area of 12.1952 (extremely large burnt area) was classified as a small burnt area by the neural network system.

The result extracted from back-propagation is slightly better than the result extracted from rule-based system. The proposed rule-based system has a weakness where if a testing sample has a criterion that goes beyond the set of rules, then the system cannot recognize and classify it accurately. As a back-propagation neural network can be trained and used to classify all kinds of patterns, it has a better position to achieve higher accuracy. Future studies may include the SOM training with 5 variables (4 meteorological variables and burnt area) and its hybrid approaches of back-propagation neural network or rule-based system.

Comparison with existing methods

The datasets were used by other researchers using

Table 1. Examples on rule generation (from SOM cluster 2).

Rules	1	2
Normalized Temperature TP	0.7299 ≤ TP ≤ 2.3845	0.9587 ≤ TP ≤ 1.5748
Normalized Relative Humidity RH	-1.3499 ≤ RH ≤ -0.1316	-1.0528 ≤ RH ≤ -0.5001
Normalized Wind Speed WS	-1.585 ≤ WS ≤ -0.0406	-0.5532 ≤ WS ≤ -0.5532
Normalized Rainfall RF	-0.0818 ≤ RF ≤ -0.0818	-0.0818 ≤ RF ≤ -0.0818
Burnt area BA	SMALL	MEDIUM

Table 2. Distribution of dataset in SOM output map.

Position of SOM output neuron	Number of training samples	Number of testing samples	Number of testing samples/number of training samples (%)
1	20	6	30
2	45	12	27
3	38	11	29
4	24	9	38
5	34	16	47
6	48	10	21
7	50	7	14
8	23	8	35
9	29	2	7
10	13	2	15
11	29	6	21
12	13	2	15
13	27	5	19
14	4	0	0
15	1	0	0
16	16	7	44
Total	414	103	20

different approaches, such as the work done (Cortez and Moraisv 2007; Ku Ruhana and Khor, 2009). Cortez and Moraisv (2007) concluded that support vector machine (SVM) was the best among the approaches they used. They found that it was better to use weather conditions (meteorological variables) rather than FWI variables. Also, the spatial and temporal variables (irrelevant variables) will not improve the performances of SVM. Reason was not stated to support or discuss the results. Ku Ruhana and Khor (2009) used sliding window technique to extract the patterns. The inputs were also based on meteorological variables. The rules were then generated from the patterns extracted from the sliding window technique. They concluded that the proposed method is able to produce a high-accuracy result. Irrelevancy issue was not discussed in the paper.

Issues on irrelevant variables may occur in the data mining model. If irrelevant variables are chosen, accuracy and performance may be greatly influenced. In this paper, SOM approach is suggested to be one of the alternatives to reduce the impact. As SOM algorithm is able to reduce the data dimensions, irrelevancy issue can be reduced to minimum. Thus, future studies may include some other conditions that potentially contribute to the forest fires, such as topology factors, types of forest and location, etc.

Conclusion

The nonlinear relationship between size of forest fire and meteorological variables (temperature, relative humidity, wind speed and rainfall) was investigated using self organizing map together with its hybrid approaches, namely back-propagation neural network or rule-based system. The rules or outputs generated from these approaches can be used to classify the size of forest fire. This study was wholly based on the qualitative analysis on the 4 meteorological variables to predict the size of forest fire. It can be much more challenging in a real time forest fire management and analysis. More data mining techniques are needed to analyze the relationships. As

Table 3. Accuracy of burnt area prediction.

Position of SOM output neuron	Number of testing samples	Number of successful prediction	
		Back-propagation network	Rule-based system
1	6	5	4
2	12	9	10
3	11	10	8
4	9	9	7
5	16	15	14
6	10	9	9
7	7	5	6
8	8	8	6
9	2	2	2
10	2	2	1
11	6	5	4
12	2	2	2
13	5	5	4
14	0	0	0
15	0	0	0
16	7	7	7
Total	103	93	84

SOM is able to reduce the data dimension, irrelevancy issue can be reduced. Future studies may include some other conditions that potentially contribute to the forest fires, such as topology factors, types of forest and location, etc.

REFERENCES

Amiro BD, Logan KA, Wotton BM, Flannigan MD, Todd JB, Stocks BJ, Mattell DL (2004). Fire weather index system components of large fires in the Canadian boreal forest. Int. J. Wildland Fire, 13: 391–400.

Antonie M, Zaiane OR, Coman A (2001). Application of Data Mining Techniques for Medical Image Classification. In: Second International Workshop on Multimedia Data Mining (MDM/KDD), pp. 94-101.

Atluri V, Hung CC, Coleman TL (1999). An artificial neural network for classifying and predicting soil moisture and temperature using Levenberg-Marquardt algorithm. In: Proceedings IEEE Southeastcon '9, pp.10-13.

Chai SS, Veenendaal B, West G, Walker JP (2008). Back propagation Neural Network for Soil Moisture Retrieval Using NAFE'05 Data: A Comparison of Training Algorithms. In: Proceedings of the International Society for Photogrammetry and Remote Sensing (ISPRS) XXIth Congress, pp. 1345-1350.

Chang W, Bosworth B, Carter GC (1993). Empirical results of using back-propagation neural networks to separate single echoes from multiple echoes. Neural Networks, IEEE Trans., 4(6): 993-995.

Cortez P, Morais A (2007). A data mining approach to predict forest fires using meteorological data. In: Proceedings of the 13th Portugese Conference on Artificial Intelligence, pp. 512-523.

de Groot WJ, Field RD, Brady MA, Roswintiarti O, Mohamad M (2005). Development of the Indonesian and Malaysian fire danger rating systems. Mitigation Adaptation Strat. Global Change, 12(1): 165-180.

Gardner MW, Dorling SR (1998) .Artificial neural networks (the multi-layer perceptron) – a review of applications in the atmospheric sciences. Atmos. Environ., 32: 2627–2636.

Hagan MT, Menhaj MB (1994). Training feedforward networks with the Marquardt algorithm. Neural Networks, IEEE Trans., 5(6): 989-993.

Kalteh AM, Hjorth P, Berndtsson R (2008). Review of the self-organizing map (SOM) approach in water resources: Analysis modelling and application. Environ. Model. Softwar, 23(7): 835-845

Kohonen T (1982). Self-organized formation of topologically correct feature maps. Biological Cybernetics, 43: 59–69

Ku Ruhana KM, Khor JY (2009). Pattern Extraction and Rule Generation of Forest Fire Using Window Sliding Technique. Comput Inf. Sci., 2(3): 113-121

Mas JF, Puig H, Palacio JL, Sosa-Lopez A (2004). Modelling deforestation using GIS and artificial neural networks. Environ Model. Software, 19(5): 461-471.

McManus JW (1992). Design and Analysis Techniques for Concurrent Blackboard Systems. PhD Thesis. The College of William and Mary in Virginia. pp. 35-41

Rowell A, Moore DPF (2000). Global review of forest fires. International Union for Conservation of Nature and Natural Resources. p. 3

Stojanova D, Panov P, Kobler A, Dzeroski S, Taskova K (2006). Learning to Predict Forest Fires with Different Data Mining Techniques. In: Conference on Data Mining and Data Warehouses pp. 255-258.

Sunar F, Ozkan C (2001). Forest fire analysis with remote sensing data Int. J. Remote Sens., 22: 2265-2277.

Torn MS, Fried JS (1992). Predicting the impact of global warming on wildfire. Clim. Change, 21: 257-274.

Vesanto J (2000). Using SOM in data-mining. Dissertation, Helsink University of Technology. pp. 26-38

Williams AAJ, Karoly DJ, Tapper N (2001). The Sensitivity of Australian Fire Danger to Climate Change. Clim. Change, 49: 171-191.

11

SNP model to address cytosine trios

Sriram Kannan

Graduate Studies, Molecular Mechanism of Disease, NCMLS, Radboud University, K603, Erasmuslaan17, 6525GE, Nijmegen, Netherlands. E-mail: sriram.kannan@student.ru.nl.

DNA methylation maintains allele specific gene expression (Chan et al., 2003) in which miRNA influences allele-specific protein expression and SNPs, found inside miRNA, in turn influences tumor susceptibility (Nicoloso et al., 2010). Further, methylated CpGs have been correlated to *APC* gene in colorectal cancer (Zhang et al., 2007) and retrotranspositions have also been correlated to *APC* gene (Miki et al., 1992). Another aspect unrelated to it is *Tet1* gene, which has been associated with the conversion of methylcytosine to hydroxymethyl cytosine (Tahiliani et al., 2009). DNA methylation might also have a role in the prevention of normal differentiation in pediatric cancers (Diede et al., 2009). As the difference between a nucleobase and its methylated form is its structure and its molecular weight, this research article is focussed on using the molar mass of nucleobases to find out if there is any uniqueness as for the position of occurrence of a nucleotide in a given model. SNPs occurrence position was used as a model in this research for addressing the cytosine trios (cytosine, 5methyl cytosine, hydroxy methyl cytosine) based on molar mass of the nucleobase. As the conditions for occurrence of SNP, at a given position in a sequence, were found to uniformly conform with all 140,000 SNPs analysed, including all clinically associated SNPs from NCBI SNP database, it intrigued conformity to be cross checked with SNPs near experimentally proven methylation sites.

Key words: SNP, molar mass, *Tet1,* colorectal cancer, methylation.

INTRODUCTION

SNPs could influence miRNA as seen with rs334348 associated with germline allele specific expression of *TGFBR1* correlated to colorectal cancer (Nicoloso et al., 2010). Methylated cytosines have been experimentally proven in CpG islands of *APC* gene promoter region (Genbank accession: U02509, CpG Position 687) (Zhang et al., 2007) and rs35417795, which is another SNP, occurs at close proximity in this island. Further, the tumor suppressor gene, *Tet1*, is known for its conversion of methylated cytosine to hydroxymethylcytosine.

Hence, the intriguing question was to find out if there are SNP occurrence positions that might be influenced by methylation positions. The first step was to find out if there are any global SNP occurrence positions, while the second step was to find out if this could be changed by substituting methylated cytosine molar mass instead of cytosine and subsequently, with hydroxy methyl cytosine as *Tet1* does.

After analyzing, all the validated biallelic SNPs of chromosome 21, X, Y, mitochondrial and all the clinically associated SNPs of the other chromosomes by the novel, excel the based algorithm as described in the methods

that conform globally to the occurrence position of SNPs (Table 2). This pattern was used to find out if any deviation occurs, when the experimentally proven methylated cytosine was substituted in flanking regions of SNP occurrence and then replaced by hydroxymethylcytosine.

MATERIALS AND METHODS

Global SNP occurrence pattern

The algorithm takes an input of a DNA sequence as:

"............N_a N_b N_c N_d N_e N_f N_g N_h N_i N_j N_k N_l N N_m N_n N_o N_p N_q N_r N_s N_t N_u N_v N_w ...."

where N is the position of interrogation of being x or y nucleotide representing a single nucleotide change and {a, b, c, d, e, f, g, h, I, j, k, X/Y, m, n, o, p, q, r, s, t, u, v and w) are the positions of nucleobases in an ascending order. It then substitutes the nucleobases nucleobase occurrence position with a numerical constant value "NC" for each base as shown in Table 1 substitution values. After the substitution with any one type of NC, there are four ratio values that are calculated (R1, R2, R3 and R4) as shown in Table 2. The ratio value is calculated with this formula:

Table 1. Molar mass based on substitution values.

	A	G	C	T	Methyl cytosine	Hydroxy methyl cytosine
Type one substitution	24	40	1	15	13	30
Logic used	Difference in molar mass from cytosine with decimals rounded off with an addition of one so as not to assign cytosine a zero value					
Name assigned	Nucleobase value (NBV)					
Type two substitution	23.03	39.03	1	13.94	13.19	30.03
Logic used	Absolute difference in molar mass from cytosine					
Name assigned	Absolute NBV					
Type three substitution	135.13	151.03	111.1	126.04	125.29	141.13
Logic used	Absolute molar mass value (1)					
Name assigned	Absolute value					

Table 2. Global SNP occurrence positions with type 1 substitutions.

Set	R1(NC1.5)/(NC1.5)	R2(NC1.5)/(NC1.5)	R3(NC1.5)/(NC1.5)	R4(NC1.5)/(NC1.5)
Set 1	a,b,c,d,e / g,h,i,j,k	b,c,d,e,f / h,i,j,k,x	a,b,c,d,e / g,h,i,j,k	b,c,d,e,f / h,i,j,k,y
Set 2	b,c,d,e,f / h,i,j,k,x	c,d,e,f,g / i,j,k,x,m	b,c,d,e,f / h,i,j,k,y	c,d,e,f,g / i,j,k,y,m
Set 3	c,d,e,f,g / i,j,k,x,m	d,e,f,g,h / j,k,x,m,n	c,d,e,f,g / i,j,k,y,m	d,e,f,g,h / j,k,y,m,n
Set 4	d,e,f,g,h / j,k,x,m,n	e,f,g,h,i / k,x,m,n,o	d,e,f,g,h / j,k,y,m,n	e,f,g,h,i / k,y,m,n,o
Set 5	e,f,g,h,i / k,x,m,n,o	f,g,h,i,j/ x,m,n,o,p	e,f,g,h,i / k,y,m,n,o	f,g,h,i,j/ y,m,n,o,p
Set 6	f,g,h,i,j/ x,m,n,o,p	g,h,i,j,k/ m,n,o,p,q	f,g,h,i,j/ y,m,n,o,p	g,h,i,j,k/ m,n,o,p,q
Set 7	g,h,i,j,k/ m,n,o,p,q	h,i,j,k,x / n,o,p,q,r	g,h,i,j,k/ m,n,o,p,q	h,i,j,k,y / n,o,p,q,r
Set 8	h,i,j,k,x / n,o,p,q,r	i,j,k,x,m/ o,p,q,r,s	h,i,j,k,y / n,o,p,q,r	i,j,k,y,m/ o,p,q,r,s
Set 9	i,j,k,x,m/ o,p,q,r,s	j,k,x,m,n / p,q,r,s,t	i,j,k,y,m/ o,p,q,r,s	j,k,y,m,n / p,q,r,s,t
Set 10	j,k,x,m,n / p,q,r,s,t	k,x,m,n,o /q,r,s,t,u	j,k,y,m,n / p,q,r,s,t	k,y,m,n,o /q,r,s,t,u
Set 11	k,x,m,n,o /q,r,s,t,u	x,m,n,o,p /r,s,t,u,v	k,y,m,n,o /q,r,s,t,u	y,m,n,o,p /r,s,t,u,v
Set 12	x,m,n,o,p /r,s,t,u,v	m,n,o,p,q /s,t,u,v,w	y,m,n,o,p /r,s,t,u,v	m,n,o,p,q /s,t,u,v,w

Set	Condition (Any one of these)	SNP	Conditions
1,6,7,12	R1 = R2 = R3; R1 = R3 = R4; R2 = R3 = R4; R2 = R4 = R1	+	1
2,3,4,5,8,9,10,11	R1 = R2 and R3 = R4; R1 = R2 and R3≠R4; R3 = R4 and R1≠R2	+	2
1,6,7,12	R1 = R2 and R3 = R4; R1 = R2 and R3 ≠ R4; R3 = R4 and R1 ≠ R2	-	3
2,3,4,5,8,9,10,11	R1 = R2 = R3; R1 = R3 = R4; R2 = R3 = R4; R2 = R4 = R1	-	4
All sets	R1 = R2 = R3 = R4	-	5
All sets	All four Rs are not equal	+	6

$R = \sum (NC1.5) / \sum (NC1.5),$

Where NC1.5 depicts: (NC1 + NC2 + NC3 + NC4 + NC5) as for positions mentioned in Table 2.

The positions are dynamic as the algorithm calculates "NC" along the sequence for positions in the sequence {a, b, c, d, e, f, g, h, I, j, k, X/Y, m, n, o, p, q, r, s, t, u, v and w) including only five positions for one set as in Table 1, whereas there are twelve sets calculated for each R value altogether. Based on the four R values for the twelve sets, six different conditions were concluded as for the occurrence positions of SNPs that are summarised in Table 2. R1 and R2 calculates for positions with "x" as nucleobase at position "N", while R3 and R4 calculates for positions with "y" as nucleobase at position "N". The DNA substitutions were simulated with the following values as in Table 1. Table 2 values are based on type one substitutions.

RESULTS AND DISCUSSION

The global SNP occurrence position as in Table 2 was found to conform with 140,000 SNPs analysed, but not with rs35417795 of *APC* gene promoter region lying close to the methylated CpG island if anlaysed with molar mass of methylated cytosine instead of cytosine.

This could mean that protein encoded genes like *tet1* could probably use this strategy of hydroxymethyl cytosine conversion from methylated cytosine to prevent the occurrence of a random nucleotide change in a nearby flanking region which could be pathogenic sometimes. This model could serve as a tool for cancer researchers to validate this experimentally.

Key points

(1) SNP occurrence positions are correlated with methyl cytosine and a tumor suppressor gene function.
(2) In special attention to colorectal cancer related attributes.

REFERENCES

Chan HW, Kurago ZB, Stewart CA, Wilson MJ, Martin MP, Mace BE, Carrington M, Trowsdale J, Lutz CT (2003). DNA methylation maintains allele-specific KIR gene expression in human natural killer cells. J. Exp. Med., Jan 20; 197(2):245-55.

Miki Y, Nishisho I, Horii A, Miyoshi Y, Utsunomiya J, Kinzler KW, Vogelstein B, Nakamura Y (1992). Disruption of the APC gene by a retrotransposal insertion of L1 sequence in a colon cancer. Cancer Res., Feb 1; 52(3):643-5.

Nicoloso MS, Sun H, Spizzo R, Kim H, Wickramasinghe P, Shimizu M, Wojcik SE,Ferdin J, Kunej T, Xiao L, Manoukian S, Secreto G, Ravagnani F, Wang X, Radice P,Croce CM, Davuluri RV, Calin GA (2010). Single-nucleotide polymorphisms inside microRNA target sites influence tumor susceptibility. Cancer Res., Apr 1; 70(7):2789-98.

Tahiliani M, Koh KP, Shen Y, Pastor WA, Bandukwala H, Brudno Y, Agarwal S,Iyer LM, Liu DR, Aravind L, Rao A (2009). Conversion of 5-methylcytosine to 5-hydroxymethylcytosine in mammalian DNA by MLL partner TET1. Science, May 15; 324(5929):930-5.

Zhang LX, Pan SY, Chen D, Xie EF, Gao L, Shu YQ, Lu ZH, Cheng L,Yang D,Zhang JN (2007). Effect of adenomatous polyposis coli (APC) promoter methylation on gene transcription in lung cancer cell lines. China J.Cancer, 26(6):576-80.

12

Querying formal concepts containing transcription factors: A case study using multiple databases

Mathilde Pellerin[1,2], and Olivier Gandrillon[1]*

[1]Université de Lyon, Université Lyon 1, Centre de Génétique et de Physiologie Moléculaire et Cellulaire (CGPHIMC), CNRS UMR5534, F-69622 Lyon, France.
[2]Statlife, Espace Maurice Tubiana, 39 rue Camille Desmoulins, 94805 VILLEJUIF, France.

In order to reduce the amount of information when querying from large databases, one has to develop new approaches. We present here a new way to query our SQUAT database. SQUAT contains formal concepts representing an association between a number of genes that are simultaneously overexpressed and the biological situations in which those genes are overexpressed. We explored the relevance of querying "self-explaining" formal concepts obeying a double constraint: (1) The concept should contain, within the genes of the concepts, at least one transcription factor (TF), and (2) At least one gene in the concept, should contain in its promoter a transcription factor binding site (TFBS) for the identified TF. The present work demonstrated that: (1) there are such "self-explaining" formal concepts in SQUAT. (2) Mining only those "self-explaining" formal concepts severely reduces the number of concepts that have to be analyzed. (3) Two such "self-explaining" concepts have been further analyzed, and their biological relevance has been demonstrated.

Key words: Data mining, gene expression, large database, formal concepts.

INTRODUCTION

The generation of very large gene expression databases by high-throughput technologies like microarray (Gershon, 2002), SAGE (Velculescu et al., 1995) or RNA-seq (Hanriot et al., 2008) calls for similarly high-throughput exploration tools of the possible functional links between gene expression levels and biological situations. Various techniques have been used for exploring such relationships, including global techniques like hierarchical clustering (Ng, 2001) or local techniques like local pattern extraction (Prelic et al., 2006). For the biologist, a local pattern is an association between a number of genes displaying specific expression pro-perties and the situations in which those genes display such properties. A recent review highlights the relevance of mining local patterns with respect to clustering analyses (Madeira and Oliveira, 2004).

We have been developing local pattern extraction such as association rule discovery (Becquet et al., 2002; Creighton and Hanash, 2003; Georgii et al., 2005; Li et at., 2003) or formal concepts (Rioult et al., 2003; Blachon et al., 2007) to capture groups of genes displaying a simultaneous behavior in a number of biological situations. We have been focusing on the gene overexpression property (for a discussion about overexpression, see Becquet et al., 2002 and Pensa et al., 2004). A formal concept is a special case of a local pattern that harbors an association between genes that are simultaneously overexpressed and the biological situations in which those genes are overexpressed. We have recently described a web-available database called SQUAT containing different types of data, including raw SAGE expression values and local patterns in the form of formal concepts (Leyritz et al., 2008) allowing the biologist to query the resulting information.

One of the main drawbacks of every local pattern approach is the huge number of extracted patterns. This is especially true in noisy data, such as transcriptomic data. As an example, the human part of SQUAT database contains 532,073 formal concepts, and the murine part contains 1,141,895 formal concepts. We have therefore developed over the years a number of techniques to reduce the amount of information to be displayed to the final end-user, that is, the biologist.

This includes:

(1) a simple color-coding approach by function

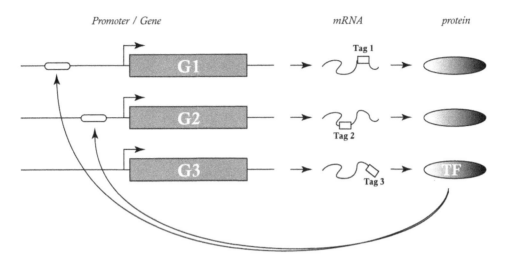

Figure 1. Schematic description of the "self-explaining" concept. SQUAT was used to establish a "tag-to-TFBS" relationship. This allowed to query for concepts containing autoregulated genes (genes harboring in their promoter at least one TFBS for the TF that is present within the concept). The percentage of autoregulated genes is then calculated (in the example it is 66.6%).

(Becquet et al., 2002).

(2) a regrouping of formal concepts using clustering techniques (Blachon et al., 2007) implemented in SQUAT (Leyritz et al., 2008).

(3) the simultaneous use of various sources of information, including text mining approaches (Klema et al., 2008).

In the present work, we decided to focus on "self-explaining" formal concepts. For this the basic idea was to find concepts responding to the following query: "find all concepts, containing within the genes of the concepts, at least one transcription factor (TF), and in which at least one gene in the concept contains in its promoter a transcription factor binding site (TFBS) for the identified TF."

Our hope was that this TF/TFBS relationship should be able to explain at least part of the molecular link explaining why some of those genes were found in the same concept, which is why those genes are simultaneously overexpressed.

METHODS

The SQUAT database was used for performing the tag-to-transcript relationship (Keime et al., 2004), followed by the tag-to-transcript-to-TSS relationship (Leyritz et al., 2008). Starting from TSS positions, promoter sequences were defined as ranging from 5 kbp in 5' of the TSS to 1 kbp in 3' of the TSS. All promoters corresponding to a 1 tag – 1 transcript – 1 TSS were kept, as well as promoters corresponding to a 1 tag – 1 transcript – n TSS, if all TSS were contained within a 2 kpb distance. In the first case, the most 3' TSS was used for further studies. This left us with a total of 12,951 human promoters.

The MATCH program (Kel et al., 2003, 2008 version 4) was run using the resources of the commercial version of TRANSFAC® for finding all TFBS on these promoter sequences. In order to reduce

the number of false positives, the profile contained in the "vertebrate_non_redundant_minFP.prf" file was used.

In the end, we obtain a tag-to-TFBS relationship (Figure 1) that is the basis for future queries. The query is a two step process. All concepts containing at least one TF were isolated from SQUAT. The percentage of autoregulated genes was then calculated for each of the concepts.

The L2L-based queries were performed using the stand alone version of L2L (http://depts.washington.edu/l2l/; Newman and Weiner, 2005). This tool, given a gene list, provides categories that are statistically overrepresented as compared to a gene random sampling. We therefore took as an entry a list of genes, belonging to one concept, a well as lists belonging to the following categories:

1. The Gene Ontology organizing principle: biological process,
2. The Gene Ontology organizing principle: molecular function.
3. The L2L specific category: microarray data. For this L2L compare the list of genes contained within a concept to lists of genes that have been experimentally determined as being over expressed in response to a particular stimulus - in other words, published lists of microarray results.

The program first calculates the number of expected matches for that list, then the relative enrichment of actual matches, and finally a binomial probability for the relative enrichment. The results are logged, and written to a raw output file. The best p-values were retrieved and one therefore obtains, for each formal concept, three values: the best p value obtained when trying to find an enrichment regarding a biological process, a molecular function or a microarray experiment.

STRING was queried using the default parameters values.

RESULTS

The first purpose of this work was to find "self explaining concepts" obeying a double constraint regarding the presence of a TF in the concept and of potential target genes among the other genes of the concept (Figure 1). The second purpose was to see if that would lead to a

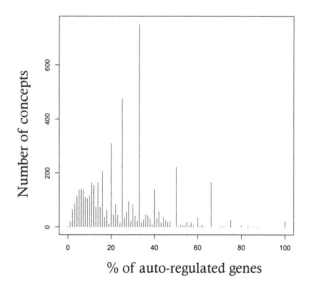

Figure 2. The number of concepts as a function of the autoregulated genes it harbors. 5013 concepts containing at least one autoregulated gene (mean size = 14.74 genes, as compared with the mean size of 5.43 for all SQUAT concepts) were obtained. 561 concepts harbored at least 50 % of autoregulated gene (mean size = 6,65 genes) and 20 concepts harbored 100 % of autoregulated gene (mean size = 3,15 genes).

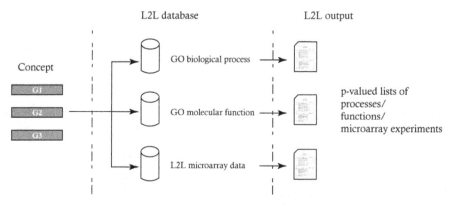

Figure 3. Schematic description of the use of L2L. Each individual concept can be seen as a list of genes. Each list was then compared to three types of lists of genes present within L2L. This results in the calculation of the p-value estimating the statistical significance of the redundancy between the two lists.

reduction in the number of formal concepts that have to be studied, and the third was to investigate their biological relevance.

We first checked for the presence of concepts that would fit such a double constraint. The results of the corresponding queries are displayed in Figure 2. Three things are readily apparent from Figure 2:

1. There indeed are concepts obeying the double constraint.
2. The percentage of auto-regulated gene can vary over the full range of 1 to 100% of the genes

3. Although the number of concepts is severely reduced from more than 500,000 to a few hundreds, it nevertheless still represents an unmanageable amount of information

We therefore decided to explore the possible biological relevance of the queried concepts, using L2L. For each identified concept, three files, representing three types of categories were retrieved from L2L (Figure 3):

1. Biological process,
2. Molecular function

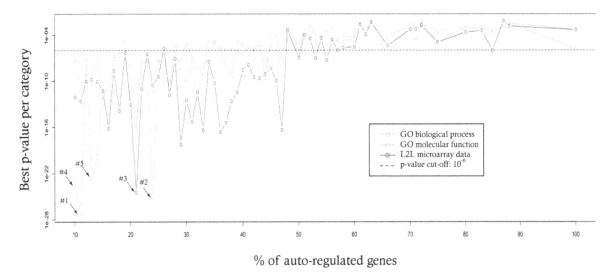

% of auto-regulated genes

Figure 4. Most significant concepts for varying values of the percentage of auto-regulated genes.
Shown is the best p-value among all of the possible p-values for all of the gene belonging to all of the concept that were extracted at a certain value of x, the percentage of auto-regulated genes. The best p-value was selected each for of the three L2L categories examined. The five concepts displaying the lowest p-values are indicated and labeled 1 to 5.

Table 1. The four CRX concepts.

Rank	List Name	Binomial p-value	Number of libraries	Number of tags	% of CRX-regulated genes
1	visual perception	4.94 10 -28	2	168	11,00
2	visual perception	5.46 10-26	2	150	11,00
4	visual perception	1.73 10-24	3	84	10,00
5	visual perception	2.34 10-23	2	139	13,00

Column 1: The rank of the concept among the 5 best p-values (Figure 4); Column 2: L2L list name providing the best p-value; Column 3: the actual p-value; Columns 4 and 5: the number of libraries (i.e. biological situations) and tags (i.e. genes) in each concept; Columns 6: the percentage of auto-regulated genes (via CRX binding sites) in each concept.

3. Microarray data.

All concepts for values of x (the percentage of auto-regulated gene) ranging from 1 to 100% were extracted. Then for one value of x, one obtains a large amount of concepts. All of the genes belonging to those concepts were processed through L2L, and the best p-value obtained for a given value of x, for the three categories chosen, for any concept, was selected. The best p-value, for the three categories chosen, is displayed in Figure 4.

Although this might be counterintuitive, it is nevertheless clear that there are much more biologically significant concepts arising for the lower values of x. For concepts where more than half of the genes are auto-regulated, there is almost no concept displaying a significant p-value using L2L.

The five most significant extracted concepts were then examined. Among those, 4 harbored the same transcription factor, named CRX (Table 1). It is immediately apparent that the best p-values were all obtained for the "Visual perception" category of the GO biological

processes.

We then interrogated SQUAT in order to estimate the global number of concepts which contained CRX. We found a total of 7 concepts, 4 of them containing more than one gene. It therefore appears that among the 5 best p-values we obtained all four CRX concepts among the 532073 concepts contained within our SQUA database. This demonstrates the power of the approach to extract a very small number of closely related concepts.

We then investigated the nature of the three libraries found within the concepts. It turned out that all three libraries were made from normal retina. At that stage we investigated the nature of CRX. Using the hyperlink from SQUAT to Entrez Gene, we could find the following description of the function of CRX: "The protein encoded by this gene is a photoreceptor-specific transcription factor which plays a role in the differentiation of photoreceptor cells. This homeodomain protein is necessary for the maintenance of normal cone and rod function". It was therefore clear that we had extracted information regarding the overexpression for a

A

Gene product	TFBS	Description
RAX2	1	Homo sapiens retina and anterior neural fold homeobox 2
RDH8	1	Homo sapiens retinol dehydrogenase 8 (all-trans)
GUCA1A	1	Homo sapiens guanylate cyclase activator 1A (retina)
RLBP1	1	Homo sapiens retinaldehyde binding protein 1
PDE6G	2	Homo sapiens phosphodiesterase 6G, cGMP-specific, rod, gamma
RCVRN	1	Homo sapiens recoverin
PPEF2	1	Homo sapiens protein phosphatase, EF-hand calcium binding domain 2

B

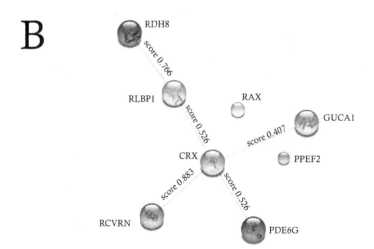

Figure 5. Analysis of the biological meaning of the CRX concepts. **A:** Shown are all the genes that 1. were common to all four concepts and 2. harbored at least one TFBS for CRX in their promoter. For each gene is shown its HUGO name, the number of CRX-binding sites in its promoter, and its full name. **B.** STRING output showing the known relationship between the 8 genes, indicated by a yellow line representing text-mining-based evidence. The combined score are computed as the joint probability of the probabilities from the different evidence channels, correcting for the probability of randomly observing an interaction (see the STRING website for more information).

photoreceptor-specific transcription factor in retinal cells Finally, we identified all genes that (1) were common to all four concepts and (2) harbored at least one TFBS for CRX in their promoter. This resulted in a list of 7 genes (Figure 5A). Those were still linked to "visual perception" with a very highly significant score (p= 2.48 10-12), which is due to the fact that all individual gene products could be shown to be related to eye development and vision (not shown).

In order to explore possible known relationship between CRX and any of those gens, we turned to the STRING database (http://string-db.org/; Figure 5B). Among the 7 genes, 2 (RAX and PPEF2) had no known relationship with CRX,1 (RDH8) had an indirect relationship, and the 4 left displayed weak text-mining-based relationship. When explored in details, the most

relevant relationship was between Recovering and CRX whereas only anecdotal co-occurrence-based linked CRX to RLBP-1, GUCA1 andPDE6G.

We therefore have isolated 7 new putative direct CRX target genes involved in the visual ability of retinal cells previously uncharacterized as CRX target genes. As a next step in the analysis, we decided to relax the stringency of the p-value constraint. For this, we analyzed the concepts harboring the 54 best p-values. Among those it was immediately apparent that the TEAD2 (TEA domain family member 2) transcription factor was the most prominent one, since it appeared in 40% of the concepts. One should note that 466 concepts containing TEAD2 and with more than one gene and more than one situation appear in SQUAT. So this is different from the previous situation: here we selected a subpart of all of the

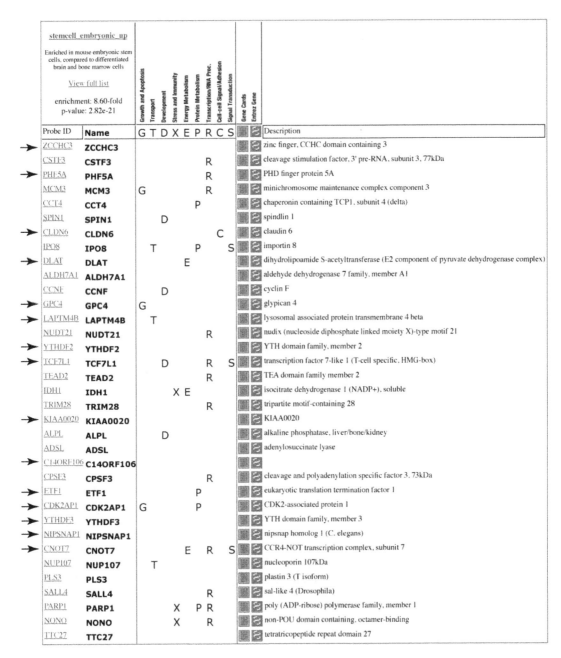

Figure 6A. Analysis of the biological meaning of the TEAD2 concepts.L2L output of the 35 genes that match between our TEAD2 targets and the L2L microarray list "stemcell_embryonic_up". The first column displays the name of the genes, the second, the GO functional category to which they are related, and the third indicates their complete name. Arrows points toward those genes harboring at least one TEAD2-binding site in their promoter.

TEAD2-containing concepts.

Among the 21 concepts containing TEAD2 and appearing among the 54 best p-values, 15 were harboring homogeneous situations consisting of Embryonic Stem Cells. Pubmed was then searched using as an entry "TEAD2 embryonic stem cells". Such a query returned 4 papers, mostly non relevant for establishing a link between TEAD2 and ES cells.

We then analyzed the function of the genes contained

in the concepts, by making a complete list of all the genes appearing in the 15 concepts. This left us with a list of 116 genes that we submitted to L2L. We obtained a very significant match (p= 2.82 10-21) with a microarray-based list called "stemcell_embryonic_up (Enriched in mouse embryonic stem cells, compared to differentiated brain and bone marrow cells)". The 35 genes that match between our TEAD2 targets and the L2L microarray list are displayed in the Figure 6A. We also performed a

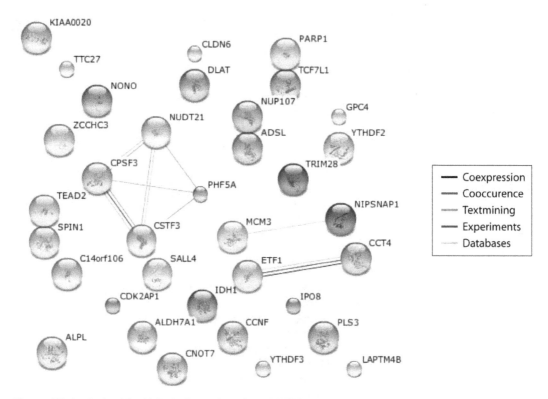

Figure 6B. Analysis of the biological meaning of the TEAD2 concepts.
STRING output showing the known relationship, indicated by a line, between the 35 genes. The color code of the lines is shown in the box on the right (see the STRING website for more information).

STRING analysis, that revealed that none of those genes are known to be connected to TEAD2, and are mostly non connected with each other (Figure 6B).

Altogether our analysis suggest a role for TEAD2 in embryonic stem cells which has until now not been described, together with a list of TEAD2-target genes that might be relevant for its function in human ES cells, half of them being putative direct TEAD2 targets.

DISCUSSION

We have developed a querying process of our SQUAT database, which allows querying simultaneously various sources of information. This allowed us to search for "self-explaining" concept containing a TF together with putative target genes of that TF. We further refined our search by relying on an automatic L2L-based indexing. We finally analyzed two groups of concepts. Both of those were found to be biologically significant with a mixture of both known and new information that indicates a successful data mining quest.

In this work various databases have been used in a sequential fashion, to progressively reduce the amount of extracted information. One possible future direction would consist in mining simultaneously different sources of information. Such a process could be viewed as computing all maximal homogeneous clique sets from

different subgraphs. Preliminary evidence that this could be feasible has been obtained recently (Mougel et al., 2010).

Furthermore, it would be of interest to automate the search for interesting concepts. This would require the combination in a single solver of various information sources, an effort that is presently the subject of intense research (Medina et al., 2010; Cao et al., 2011 and references therein).

ACKNOWLEDGEMENTS

This work has been funded by the ANR (French Research National Agency) project BINGO2 (https://bingo2.greyc.fr/) ANR-07-MDCO-014 which is a follow-up of the first BINGO project (2004-2007). We thank all members of the BINGO2 project for stimulating discussion.

REFERENCES

Becquet C, Blachon S, Jeudy B, Boulicaut JF, Gandrillon O (2002). Strong-association-rule mining for large-scale gene-expression data analysis: a case study on human SAGE data. Genome Biol., 3, RESEARCH0067.

Blachon S, Pensa RG, Besson J, Robardet C, Boulicaut J-F, Gandrillon O (2007). Clustering formal concepts to discover biologically relevant knowledge from gene expression data. In Silico Biol., 7: 0033.

Cao L, Zhang H, Zhao Y, Luo D, Zhang C (2011). Combined mining: discovering informative knowledge in complex data. IEEE Trans Syst Man Cybern B Cybern, 41: 699-712.

Creighton C, Hanash S (2003). Mining gene expression databases for association rules. Bioinformatics, 19: 79-86.

Georgii E, Richter L, Ruckert U, Kramer S (2005). Analyzing microarray data using quantitative association rules. Bioinformatics, 21 Suppl 2, ii123-ii129.

Gershon D (2002). Microarray technology: an array of opportunities. Nature, 416: 885-891.

Hanriot L, Keime C, Gay N, Faure C, Dossat C, Wincker P, Scote-Blachon C, Peyron C, Gandrillon O (2008). A combination of LongSAGE with Solexa sequencing is well suited to explore the depth and the complexity of transcriptome. BMC Genomics, 9: 418.

Keime C, Damiola F, Mouchiroud D, Duret L, Gandrillon O (2004). Identitag, a relational database for SAGE tag identification and interspecies comparison of SAGE libraries. BMC Bioinform., 5: 143.

Kel AE, Gößling E, Reuter I, Cheremushkin E, Kel-Margoulis OV, Wingender E (2003). MATCHTM : A tool for searching transcription factor binding sites in DNA sequences. Nucleic Acids Res., 31: 3576-3579.

Klema J, Blachon S, Soulet A, Crémilleux B, Gandrillon O (2008). Constraint-Based Knowledge Discovery from SAGE Data. ISB, 8: 0014.

Leyritz L, Schicklin S, Blachon S, Keime C, Robardet C, Boulicaut J-F, Besson J, Pensa RG, Gandrillon O (2008). SQUAT: a web tool to mine human, murine and avian SAGE data. BMC Bioinform., 9: 378.

Li J, Liu H, Downing JR, Yeoh AE, Wong L (2003). Simple rules underlying gene expression profiles of more than six subtypes of acute lymphoblastic leukemia (ALL) patients. Bioinformatics, 19: 71-78.

Madeira SC, Oliveira AL (2004). Biclustering algorithms for biological data analysis: a survey. IEEE/ACM Transactions on Computational Biol. Bioinform., 1: 24-45.

Medina I, Carbonell J, Pulido L, Madeira SC, Goetz S, Conesa A, Tarraga J, Pascual-Montano A, Nogales-Cadenas R, Santoyo J (2010). Babelomics: an integrative platform for the analysis of transcriptomics, proteomics and genomic data with advanced functional profiling. Nucleic Acids Res., 38, W210-213.

Mougel PN, Plantevit M, Rigotti C, Gandrillon O, Boulicaut JF (2010). Constraint-based Mining of Sets of Cliques Sharing Vertex Properties. In Proc Workshop on the Analysis of Complex Networks ACNE 2010 co-located with ECML PKDD 2010 (Barcelona, M. Berlingerio, B. Bringmann, A. Nürnberger), pp. 48-62.

Newman JC, M Weiner AM (2005). L2L: a simple tool for discovering the hidden significance in microarray expression data. Genome Biol., 2005, 6:R81.

Ng TR, Sander J, Sleumer M (2001). Hierarchical Cluster Analysis of SAGE Data for Cancer Profiling. workshop on Data Mining in BioInformatics with SIGKDD '01.

Pensa R, Leschi C, Besson J, Boulicaut JF (2004). Assessment of discretization techniques for relevant pattern discovery from gene expression data. Paper presented at: 4th ACM SIGKDD Workshop on Data Mining in Bioinformatics BIOKDD'04 co-located with ACM SIGKDD'04 (Seattle, USA).

Prelic A, Bleuler S, Zimmermann P, Wille A, Buhlmann P, Gruissem W, Hennig L, Thiele L, Zitzler E (2006). A systematic comparison and evaluation of biclustering methods for gene expression data. Bioinform., 22: 1122-1129.

Rioult F, Robardet C, Blachon S, Crémilleux B, Gandrillon O, Boulicaut JF (2003). Mining concepts from large SAGE gene expression matrices. Paper presented at: 2nd Int Workshop Knowledge Discovery in Inductive Databases KDID'03 co-located with ECML-PKDD 2003 (Cavtat-Dubrovnik (Croatia)) STRING. http://string.embl.de/.

Velculescu VE, Zhang L, Vogelstein B, Kinzler KW (1995). Serial analysis of gene expression. Sciences, 270:484-487.

13

A new biophysical metric for interrogating the information content in human genome sequence variation: Proof of concept

James Lindesay[1], Tshela E. Mason[2], Luisel Ricks-Santi[3], William Hercules[1], Philip Kurian[1] and Georgia M Dunston[2,4]*

[1]Computational Physics Laboratory, Howard University, Washington, DC, 20060, U.S.
[2]National Human Genome Center, Howard University, Washington, DC, 20060, U.S.
[3]Cancer Center, Howard University, Washington, DC, 20060, U.S.
[4]Department of Microbiology, Howard University, Washington, DC, 20060, U.S.

The 21st century emergence of genomic medicine is shifting the paradigm in biomedical science from the population phenotype to the individual genotype. In characterizing the biology of disease and health disparities in population genetics, human populations are often defined by the most common alleles in the group. This definition poses difficulties when categorizing individuals in the population who do not have the most common allele(s). Various epidemiological studies have shown an association between common genomic variation, such as single nucleotide polymorphisms (SNPs), and common diseases. We hypothesize that information encoded in the structure of SNP haploblock variation in the human leukocyte antigen-disease related (HLA-DR) region of the genome illumines molecular pathways and cellular mechanisms involved in the regulation of host adaptation to the environment. In this paper we describe the development and application of the normalized information content (NIC) as a novel metric based on SNP haploblock variation. The NIC facilitates translation of biochemical DNA sequence variation into a biophysical quantity derived from Boltzmann's canonical ensemble in statistical physics and used widely in information theory. Our normalization of this information metric allows for comparisons of unlike, or even unrelated, regions of the genome. We report here NIC values calculated for HLA-DR SNP haploblocks constructed by Haploview, a product of the International Haplotype Map Project. These haploblocks were scanned for potential regulatory elements using ConSite and miRBase, publicly available bioinformatics tools. We found that all of the haploblocks with statistically low NIC values contained putative transcription factor binding sites and microRNA motifs, suggesting correlation with genomic regulation. Thus, we were able to relate a mathematical measure of information content in HLA-DR SNP haploblocks to biologically relevant functional knowledge embedded in the structure of DNA sequence variation. We submit that NIC may be useful in analyzing the regulation of molecular pathways involved in host adaptation to environmental pathogens and in decoding the functional significance of common variation in the human genome.

Key words: Information theory, entropy, genomic variation, biological information.

INTRODUCTION

The human genome is arguably the most sophisticated knowledge system ever discovered, as evidenced by the exquisite information it encodes and communicates via the structure of its DNA sequence. Such information underpins the structure, function, and regulation of complex molecular pathways and network systems transmitted from cell to cell, individual to individual, and

---

*Corresponding author. E-mail: gdunston@howard.edu.

generation to generation via the genome. New knowledge derived from sequencing the human genome (International Human Genome Sequencing Consortium, 2001) and researching genome variation (International Human Genome Sequencing Consortium, 2003) challenges traditional views of biological identity and how biology works at the molecular level. The integration of this new knowledge into theoretical models of living systems demands a more complete and comprehensive understanding of the life sciences in general and the science of the human genome in particular. In many respects, the human genome displays features of communication systems based in information theory, such as pattern recognition, data compression, signal processing, and regulation that are also seen from a biophysical perspective of life and living systems.

The concept of information as a basic conserved property of the universe has been successfully demonstrated in the physical sciences from cosmology (Susskind and Lindesay, 2005) to telecommunications (Shannon, 1948). In both classical and quantum physics there is a sense that information is conserved. The information content (IC) of an isolated system can be quantified using the fundamental thermodynamic concept of entropy (Susskind and Lindesay, 2005). Complex biophysical systems, like the human genome, are not isolated but rather evolve within external environments which can be assumed to have quasi-static properties. This environmental contact leads to fluctuations of the entropy associated with the system. IC is measured as a difference between the maximum possible entropy and the entropy of a coherently maintained population distribution. In the biological realm, a coherent system maintains its characteristics over generations until perturbed or modified by external forces from the environment.

When applied to whole genome sequence-based biology, we hypothesize that genomic IC can be measured by identifying the "dynamic sites" of the genome and examining variation within and among populations. We identify dynamic sites as single nucleotide polymorphisms (SNPs) for statistical analysis of the genome (Mason et al., 2009). Almost all common SNPs have only two alleles and are therefore bi-allelic. SNP haplotype blocks (haploblocks) can be identified, within which the variability of nucleotides can be interrogated and the occurrence of particular combinations can be determined. Analysis of the frequencies of these SNP combinations leads to a statistical distribution of haplotypes within the population. Since the sizes of SNP haploblocks within the genome are of variable lengths, it is nontrivial to directly compare the IC associated with different haploblocks in a meaningful manner. In order to compare the IC among different haploblocks across the genome, as well as among different human populations, a normalized IC (NIC) was developed. The concept for NIC we developed from statistical physics was discovered to be similar to Shannon's concept of *redundancy* (Shannon,

1948). Because our focus is the genome, NIC values here apply to the transmission of information in this biological system. If the NIC value of a SNP haploblock for a population is high compared to 50%, we can deduce that there are likely environmental factors skewing the distribution of haplotype frequencies in the population. Similarly, a low NIC value implies high variability and substantially fewer external factors biasing the haplotype frequency distribution in the population. In particular, a SNP haploblock that is completely homogeneous for a population has identical nucleotides at all dynamic sites for all members, thereby exhibiting no variability in the alleles encoded in that haploblock. Such a *monomorphic* haploblock has a NIC value of unity. Likewise, a population with maximum variation in the alleles will have a NIC value of zero. We assert that populations maintain themselves by establishing coherent SNP haplotype frequencies.

In this paper, we seek to explore the biophysical underpinnings of common variation in the genome. This perspective makes the physics of DNA sequence variation in the human genome relevant in new ways to concepts in biology and biomedical science. In so doing, the intent is to connect the genomic frontiers of biology and the health sciences with the biophysical frontiers of information theory and quantum physics.

MATERIALS AND METHODS

Derivation of the normalized information content equation

The degree of variability within a SNP haploblock population can provide a measure of the maintained order associated with that haploblock. SNP haplotype diversity will vary across different SNP haploblocks. Each population group is defined by the maintained order of its SNP haplotype diversity within the SNP haploblock structure; however the latter might be defined. Thus, haplotype diversity is herein reflected in the frequencies with which the SNP haplotypes occur within a given haploblock structure.

In order to provide a meaningful comparison of the information content among different regions of the genome as well as amongst different populations, the normalized information content (NIC) parameter was developed. NIC measures the difference between the entropy and the maximum possible entropy of a SNP haploblock within a given population. Since we expect that the external environment will significantly influence the state of the genome, we choose a form for the entropy measure as illustrated in equation 1.

$$S_{A,coherent} = -k \sum_{j}^{N_A} P^A_{\ j} \log_2 P^A_{\ j} \ . \tag{1}$$

where $P^A_{\ j}$ represents the probability or frequency with which a particular SNP haplotype j occurs within the particular haploblock A, and $N_A = 2^{N^A_{SNPs}}$ represents the number of mathematically possible SNP combinations for N^A_{SNPs} active biallelic SNP sites. For our purposes, $S_{coherent}$ has the potential of being an additive genostatic parameter that can be used to quantify the information in a system. Since all probabilities are non-negative, the minimum value this entropy can take occurs when one of the probabilities itself is unity. This defines a *homogeneous* population yielding $S_{A,min}=0$. The maximum value this entropy can take occurs when all the probabilities are equal, $P^A{}_j = \dfrac{1}{N_A}$, defining an informationally *gray population*. In this case, one obtains the result for the entropy as $S_{A,max} = k \log_2 N_A = k N^A_{SNPs}$. This represents the mathematical maximum of entropy for the SNP haploblock A across all human populations, giving a universal upper bound for this value. A given population will generally not have all possible SNP combinations expressed as viable SNP haplotypes, so that a population made up of equal frequencies for just the expressed haplotypes would not represent a universal maximum across populations. However, some of the SNP combinations that are not expressed in the populations *do* contribute to the informa-tion content of the haploblock. For these reasons, the chosen form for the maximum entropy is both universal and complete. Since the maximum entropy represents the upper limit that any entropy can attain, genomic information can be expected to relate to the difference between the maximum entropy of a gray population and the coherent frequency distribution maintained by a given popula-tion. However, the number of SNPs haplotypes that completely describe all populations varies for different regions of the genome. The information measure is most useful when it represents a dimensionless parameter that can be used to compare the informa-tion content of different SNP haploblocks as well as the same block amongst different populations. We have therefore chosen to normalize our measure of information content in a manner that gives zero for a gray population with no information content and unity for a homogeneous population that has a single maintained SNP haplotype. This can be mathematically expressed for haploblock A as follows:

$$NIC_A = \frac{S_{A,max} - S_{A,coherent}}{S_{A,max}} = \frac{N^A_{SNPs} + \sum_{j=1}^{2^{N^A_{SNPs}}} P^A{}_j \log_2 P^A{}_j}{N^A_{SNPs}}$$

(2)

This information measure is bounded by $0 \leq NIC \leq 1$, allowing for an informational comparison of apples to oranges. Normalization of the information metric therefore provides a means to interrogate genomic information from different regions of the genome. Besides limiting the range of the *NIC*, the maximum entropy state of specified block A is common to all populations; only the frequency distribution varies amongst the populations. This dimensionless form allows one to gain considerable insights into genomic informa-tion without a need for detailed information about the dynamics and history of the genome or knowledge of the form of all genomic parameters. The NIC is similar to an independently derived from (Nothnagel et al., 2004) where an entropic measure was used to construct haploblocks rather than interrogate the information content of SNP haploblock variation.

Analysis of NIC for the human leukocyte antigen-disease related (HLA-DR) region of the major histocompatibility complex (MHC)

The human MHC encoding the HLA system is the most highly expressed polymorphic system in the genome, and it plays an essential role in regulation of the immune response in host adaptation to environmental stimuli. It is a strong genomic marker of historical changes in environmental conditions. The NIC values were calculated for the HLA-DR region located on chromosome 6 between positions 415,611 and 3,908,995 (HLA-DRA1, HLA-DRB1, HLA-DRB5) and between positions 32,515,990 and 32,663,637 (HLA-DRB2, HLA-DRB3, HLA-DRB4). SNP haploblocks were constructed using the confidence interval algorithm (Gabriel et al., 2002) in Haploview v 4.2 from HapMap phase III data on the African American population from the southwest United States (N=98). Haploview uses a two marker expectation-maximization algorithm with a partition-ligation approach which creates highly accurate population frequency estimates of the phased haplotypes based on the maximum-likelihood as determined from the unphased input (Barrett et al., 2005; Haploview, 2003). The confidence interval algorithm defines the haploblock as a region over which a very small proportion (<5%) of comparisons among "informative SNP pairs" shows strong evidence of historical recombination and within which independent measures of pairwise linkage disequilibrium (LD) did not decline substantially with distance. Informative SNP pairs were in "strong LD" if the one-sided upper 95% confidence bound on the pairwise correlation factor D' was > 0.98 and the lower bound above 0.7. Conversely, "strong evidence of historical recombination" was defined by an upper confidence bound on D' less than 0.9 (Gabriel et al., 2002). The NIC values for the various blocks were collectively plotted in order to assess the statistical features of the distribution. We defined outliers on the distribution by identifying those values proximal to or beyond two root mean squared (RMS) deviations (2σ) of the mean, 0.61 (RMS (σ) =0.13; standard error=0.01). Root mean squared deviation is defined by $\sigma = \sqrt{<(p-<p>)^2>}$, where <p> represents the mean of the distribution with discrete elements p_j. Lastly, all of these regions were scanned for potential regulatory elements using the publicly available bioinformatics tools ConSite and miRBase.

RESULTS

Haploview generated 189 haploblocks for the HLA-DR region for the ASW population. As illustrated in Figure 1, the NIC values were distributed between zero and one. There were ten blocks with values proximal to the lower bound (between 0.28 and 0.39), and those blocks were comprised of twenty-three SNPs. All twenty-three SNPs proximal to the lower bound were located in intergenic regions (Table 1). Conversely, there were no blocks with NIC values beyond the upper bound (0.86). The sequences of the ten blocks located proximal to the lower bound were scanned for potential regulatory elements, such as transcription factor binding sites (TFBS) and micro RNA (miRNA) motifs. Putative TFBS were identified for the ten blocks proximal to the lower bound which are listed in Table 2. Of the TFBS found, FOXI1, SOX5, and SOX17 sites were present in all ten blocks. Also, there were five SNPs that had TFBS changes when their minor alleles were present (Table 3). Lastly, we found that all ten blocks had miRNA motifs (Table 4).

DISCUSSION

The advent of geographically-defined, population-based genome-wide variation resources such as the haplotype

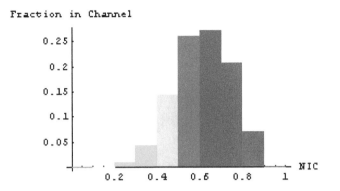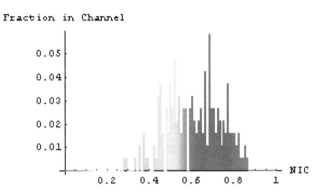

Figure 1. NIC Values for HLA-DR in an African American Population from the Southwest, US. The height of each bar is the fraction of all NIC values that fall within the channel given by the width of each bar.

Table 1. Location of SNPs proximal to the Lower Bound. In order to determine the location of each SNP in the region proximal to the lower bound, each reference sequence (rs) number was searched through the SNP database (dbSNP) maintained by the National Center for Biotechnology Information (NCBI).

Block ID	NIC Value	SNPs	SNP Location
DRB234-174	0.28	rs9378385	Intergenic Region
		rs9503746	Intergenic Region
DRB234-63	0.29	rs1028380	Intergenic Region
		rs7774941	Intergenic Region
DRB234-17	0.33	rs1890366	Intergenic Region
		rs2788212	Intergenic Region
DRB234-182	0.35	rs9405676	Intergenic Region
		rs9378389	Intergenic Region
DRB234-23	0.35	rs7751939	Intergenic Region
		rs6597267	Intergenic Region
		rs2317217	Intergenic Region
DRB234-38	0.37	rs11970370	Intergenic Region
		rs845896	Intergenic Region
DRB234-132	0.37	rs6924630	Intergenic Region
		rs9378763	Intergenic Region
		rs6596945	Intergenic Region
DBR234-22	0.37	rs9392155	Intergenic Region
		rs9505192	Intergenic Region
		rs9505153	Intergenic Region
DRB234-108	0.38	rs2449447	Intergenic Region
		rs1773015	Intergenic Region
DRB234-40	0.39	rs1764136	Intergenic Region
		rs845883	Intergenic Region

Table 2. Putative TFBS for the Haploblocks proximal to the Lower Bound. The sequence for the ten haploblocks located proximal to the lower bound region were scanned for putative TFBS using ConSite, which is a web-based tool that finds cis-regulatory elements in genomic sequences via high quality transcription factor models and cross species filters.

Block ID	ARNT	cFOS	COUP-TF	COUP-TF2	E4BP4	EVI-1	FOXD1	FOXD2	FOXD3	FOXI1	FOXQ1	HNF-1	MEF2	MYC-MAX	MYF	nMYC	NF-κB	NRF-2	PPARB	PPARG6	PPARG5	RORA1	RORA2	RREB-1	RXR-VDR	SOX5	SOX17	SP1	STAF	TEF-1	USF
DRB234-174	X	X	X	X	X	X	X	X	X	X				X		X		X				X	X	X			X	X			X
DRB234-63	X	X	X	X	X	X	X	X	X	X	X		X	X		X		X				X	X	X			X	X			X
DRB234-17	X	X	X	X	X	X	X	X	X	X	X		X	X		X		X	X		X	X	X	X			X	X	X	X	X
DRB234-182	X	X	X	X	X	X	X	X	X	X			X	X		X		X	X	X		X	X	X			X	X			X
DRB234-23	X	X		X	X	X	X	X	X	X		X	X	X	X	X		X				X	X	X			X	X			X
DRB234-38	X	X			X	X	X	X	X	X				X		X	X	X				X	X	X			X	X			X
DRB234-132	X	X	X	X	X	X	X	X	X	X		X	X	X		X	X	X	X			X	X	X			X	X	X	X	X
DRB234-22				X	X	X	X	X				X									X						X	X			
DRB234-108	X	X	X	X	X	X	X	X	X	X	X	X	X	X	X	X		X				X	X	X			X	X		X	X
DRB234-40	X	X	X	X	X	X	X	X	X	X	X	X	X	X	X	X	X	X	X			X	X	X	X		X	X	X	X	X

Table 3. SNPs proximal to the Lower Bound with TFBS changes when their minor allele is present. Of the twenty three SNPs interrogated for putative TFBS, these five SNPs were found to have a gain or loss of a TFBS when scanned using ConSite.

SNPs	Alleles	TFBS Change
rs9378763	A>C	Gain of FOXI1 site
rs17464136	C>G	Gain of SOX-17 site
rs11970370	A>C	Loss of SOX-5 site
rs6924630	A>T	Loss of TEF-1 site
rs7751939	C>A	Loss of IRF-1 and gain of FOXA2, FOXD3 & FOXI1 sites

map (i.e. HapMap) has opened a new era in human population genetics. Single nucleotide polymorphisms (SNPs), the most common type of natural variation in the human genome, offer an unprecedented opportunity to investigate evolutionary forces that have shaped human genome variation in natural populations. Information content (IC), as a new metric grounded in biophysical matrix of DNA-sequence based biology, has been used to explore the biomedical significance of natural variation in the human genome. As the most polymorphically expressed biological system, the HLA region was examined for proof of concept that natural variation encodes fundamental information about the biology of host adaptive mechanisms in response to environmental pathogens. The data on the normalized information content (NIC) of SNP haploblocks in the HLA-DR region relate natural variation to pathways of innate immunity. The molecules and cells of the innate immune system are the first

Table 4. Characterized miRNAs located proximal to the lower bound. The sequence for the ten blocks proximal to the lower bound was scanned for miRNA motifs via the web-based tool miRBase.

Block ID	miRNA
DRB234-23	let-7e
DRB234-17	miR-16
	miR-93
	miR-222
DRB234-63	miR-29
DRB234-132	miR-142-p
	miR-548
DRB234-38	miR-21

responders to environmental disturbances of homeostasis. This system can initiate the inflammatory response by activating the cellular release of cytokines, chemokines, reactive oxygen (ROS), and reactive nitrogen (RNS) species. However, when the inflammatory response is sustained at a chronic level, these molecules can inflict a variety of damaging effects.

In our analysis, the transcription factor binding sites (TFBS) present in all ten of the blocks proximal to the lower bound have been reported to be regulated by the p38 mitogen activated protein kinase (MAPK) and Wnt (wingless) pathways (Gazel et al., 2008; Perreault et al., 2001; Zorn et al., 1999). These two pathways are activated in response to oxidative stress and inflammation (Maiese et al., 2008; Nagata et al., 1998). p38 is a kinase that is localized to the cytoplasm until activated, when it translocates to the nucleus. Its activity is critical for normal immune and inflammatory responses. p38 is activated by macrophages, neutrophils, and T cells in response to cytokines, chemokines, and bacterial lipopolysaccharide (LPS) (Roux and Blenis, 2004). It is known to phosphorylate its cellular targets such as the following transcription factors: ATF-1 and -2, MEF2A, Sap-1, Elk-1, NF-κB, Ets-1, and p53 (Roux and Blenis, 2004). An interesting feature of the p38 pathway is that it can regulate the Wnt pathway when activated by ROS and other stressors. Wnt signaling controls a variety of signal transduction pathways that involve protein kinases, caspases, NF-κB, GSK-3β, iNOS and FOXes (Maiese et al., 2008; Du et al., 2006; Savage et al., 2010).

Thus, it is possible that cross-talk between the p38 and Wnt pathways represents a network that has formed in response to oxidative stress. This proposed network would be advantageous to a population under constant challenge in a tropical environment with a plethora of pathogenic agents, such as *Schistosoma mansoni* (*S. mansoni*). In innate immunity, dendritic cells (DCs)

exposed to helminth products (such as Lacto-N-Fucopentaose III (LNFPIII), a milk sugar containing the Lewis[x] trisaccharide found in the schistosome egg antigen (SEA)), have been reported to activate NF-□B by stimulating its nuclear translocation (Carvalho et al., 2008). It is worth noting that Lewis structures can occur on both N-glycan and mucin-type O-glycan cores, and these fucosylated glycans have been involved in many functions, like selecting recognition (Haltiwanger, 2009). Selectins are known for mediating extravasation of leukocytes and lymphocytes, pathogen adhesion, and modulation of signal transduction pathways (Becker and Lowe, 2003). The hallmark of *S. mansoni* infection is the switching of the host immune response from Th1 to Th2, resulting in the persistent survival of the parasite. One of the key components involved in modulating the host immune response from Th1 to Th2 is NF-□B. Studies conducted by Goodridge et al. (2007) and Thomas et al. (2005), found that neither SEA nor LNFPIII-dextran pulsed NF-κB [-/-] DCs were able to induce a Th2 response. Interestingly, increased levels of IL-4, a Th2 cytokine, have been demonstrated in murine schistosomiasis to control the generation of reactive oxygen and nitrogen intermediates in the liver (LaFlamme et al., 2001).

Additionally, our analysis showed that all the blocks proximal to the lower bound contained putative miRNA structures. This is consistent with findings of miRNAs in intronic and intergenic regions (Bartel, 2004). There were four blocks that contained well characterized miRNAs (Table 4). These miRNAs have been identified as tumor suppressors in a multitude of cancers (Calin and Croce, 2006; Esquela-Kerscher and Slack, 2006). Furthermore, miRNA expression has been shown to regulate the inflammatory response. For example, O'Connell et al. (2010) reported that an increase in miR-155 and a decrease in let-7e levels enhanced the response of Akt[-/-] macrophages to LPS.

Particularly noteworthy was the SNP variation proximal to the lower bound, which reflected that five SNPs had TFBS changes when their minor alleles were present (Table 3). rs9378763 and rs1764136 had a gain of FOXI1 and SOX-17 sites, respectively. rs11970970 and rs6924630 had a loss of SOX-5 and TEF-1 sites, respectively. rs7751939 was the only SNP whose minor allele resulted in loss of an IRF-1 site and gain of FOXA2, FOXD3 and FOXI1 sites. These FOX transcription factors have been shown to activate and be activated by the Wnt pathway (Pohl and Knochel, 2001; Zorn et al., 1999). In the study by Zhang et al. (2008), SOX-17 was shown to negatively regulate the Wnt pathway via suppression of β-catenin/T-cell factor-regulated transcription. IRF-1 is constitutively expressed in various cell types and induces the expression of pro-inflammatory cytokines in response to the activation of pathogen recognition receptors, such as the Toll-like receptor and nucleotide-binding oligomerization domain (NOD)-like receptor families (Tamura et al., 2008). Also, IRF1 transcriptionally targets a number of genes, and is required for Th1 differentiation of interferon (IFN)-stimulated macrophages. When IRF-1 is absent, the induction of Th2-type immune responses occurs (Taki et al., 1997). In addition, when p38 is activated by IFN, it contributes to the phosphorylation of NF-☐B, AP-1, IRF-1, IRF-4, IRF-8, and PU.1 (van Boxel-Dezaire et al., 2006). It has been reported that transcription enhancer factor 1 (TEF-1) directly binds to poly (ADP-ribose) polymerase 1(PARP-1) which is known to participate in DNA repair processes (Ha et al., 2002). Under conditions of oxidative stress, the activation of PARP1 results in greater expression of AP-1 and NF-☐B-dependent genes (Virag and Szabo, 2002). Also, in a study conducted by Braam et al. (2005) using endothelial cells, SOX-5 had more pronounced representation in genes regulated by nitrous oxide (NO) than the other transcription factors studied. Interestingly, in *falciparum* malaria NO inhibits the adhesion of parasitized red cells to vascular endothelium (Clark et al., 2004). Hence, it is possible that not only has schistosomiasis acted as an environmental stressor in shaping the allelic variation in the proposed p38-Wnt compensatory network, but so has malaria. It is intriguing that independent of the potential gains and losses of transcription factor binding sites, there is continued regulation of the oxidative stress process irrespective of specific allele selection.

We also assessed the performance of the measure by comparing blocks with NIC values most proximal to the upper bound with those most proximal to the lower bound. It is noteworthy that more than 96% of SNPs in the blocks proximal to the upper bound were located in genic regions, in contrast to the SNPs in the blocks proximal to the lower bound, *none* of which were found in genic regions. The identification of genic haploblocks with high information content and a more in-depth assessment of the biological significance of the entire NIC distribution are being investigated.

This paper has introduced a biophysical metric for analyzing the information content of SNP haploblock variation. NIC values in the HLA-DR region highlighted common variants involved in regulation of host immunity to environmental stressors. This supports our hypothesis that information encoded in the structure of SNP haploblock variation can elucidate molecular pathways and cellular mechanisms involved in the regulation of host adaptation to the environment. Using our analysis, p38 and Wnt, are proposed as a communication network connected by transcription factors and miRNAs in population adaptation to pathogens. Since the genetic variation highlighted by NIC values is in a representative sample of the population, its relevance in disease association studies remains to be determined. Because our motivation has been to use common variation in a reference population to interrogate the biology of health, the further understanding of disease using this approach would be a by-product. Finally, NIC values derived from common variation in the HLA-DR region suggest its involvement with regulation of innate immune mechanisms.

ACKNOWLEDGMENTS

The research is supported in part by NIH Grants NCRR 2 G12 RR003048 from the RCMI Program, Division of Research Infrastructure; NIGMS S06 GM08016, and NCI 5U54 CA091431.

Abbreviations: IC, Information content; **SNPs,** single nucleotide polymorphisms; **Haploblocks,** SNP haplotype blocks; **NIC,** normalized information content; **HLA-DR,** human leukocyte antigen-disease related; **MHC,** major histocompatibility complex; **TFBS,** transcription factor binding sites; **miRNA,** MicroRNA; **ARNT,** aryl hydrocarbon receptor nuclear translocator; **c-FOS,** proto-oncogene c-FOS; **CHOP,** DNA damage-inducible transcript 3 protein; **COUP-TF,** COUP transcription factor; **CREB1,** Cyclic AMP responsive element binding protein 1; **c-REL,** proto-oncogene c-REL; **E2F,** transcription factor E2F; **E4BP4,** nuclear factor interleukin 3 related protein; **FOXA2,** Hepatocyte nuclear factor 3-beta; **FOXD1,** forkhead box protein D1; **FOXD3,** forkhead box protein D3; **FOXF2,** Forkhead box protein F2; **FOXI1,** Forkhead box protein I1; **FOXQ1,** Forkhead box protein Q1; **EVI-1,** MDS1 and EV-1 complex locus protein EV1; **HEN1,** helix-loop-helix protein 1; **HLF,** endothelial PAS domain containing protein 1; **IRF-1,** interferon regulatory factor 1; **MAX,** protein Max; **MEF2,** myocyte-specific enhancer factor 2A; **MYC-MAX,** MYC proto-oncogene protein-protein MAX; **MYF,** myogenic factor; **n-MYC,** N-myc proto-oncogene protein; **NF-☐☐,** NF-kappa beta; **NRF2,** Nuclear factor erythroid 2-related factor 2; **PAX6,** paired box protein PAX6; **PBX,** Pre-B cell leukemia transcription factor; **p65,** Transcription factor p65; **ROR-α1,** Nuclear receptor ROR- α1; **ROR- α2,** nuclear receptor ROR-α2; **RUNX1,** runt related transcription factor 1; **RXR-VDR,** retinoic acid receptor RXR-vitamin D receptor complex; **SAP1,** Receptor type tyrosine protein phosphatase H; **SOX5,** transcription factor SOX5; **SOX17,** transcription factor SOX17; **SPZ1,** Spermatogenic leucine zipper protein 1; **STAF,** zinc finger protein 143; **TEF1,** transcriptional enhancer factor TEF-1; **USF,** upstream stimulatory factor; **HapMap,** haplotype map project; **ROS,** reactive oxygen species; **MAPK,** mitogen activated protein kinase; **Wnt,** Wingless; **LPS,** lipopolysaccharide; **ATF1,** cyclic AMP dependent transcription factor ATF-1; **ATF2,** cyclic AMP dependent transcription factor ATF-2; **Elk1,** ETS domain containing protein Elk1; **Ets1,** protein C-ets-1; **p53,** cellular tumor antigen p53; **GSK-3β,** glycogen synthase kinase 3 beta; **iNOS,** inducible nitric oxide synthase; ***S. mansoni,*** *Schistosoma mansoni;* **LNFPIII,** lacto-N-Fucopentaose III; **SEA,** schistosome egg antigen; **Th1,** T-helper 1 cells;

Th2, T-helper 2 cells; DCs, dendritic cells; IL-4, interleukin 4; NOD, nucleotide binding oligomerization domain; IFN, interferon; AP1, transcription factor AP1; PARP1, poly(ADP-ribose) polymerase 1.

REFERENCES

Barrett JC, Fry B, Maller J, Daly MJ (2005). Haploview: analysis and visualization of LD and haplotype maps. Bioinformation, 21: 263-265.

Bartel D (2004). MicroRNAs: genomics, biogenesis, mechanism and function. Cell, 116: 281-297.

Becker D, Lowe J (2003). Fucose: biosynthesis and biological function in mammals. Glycobiology, 13: 41R-53R.

Braam B, de Roos R, Bluyssen H, Kemmeren P, Holstege F, Joles JA, Koomans H (2005). Nitric oxide-dependent and nitric oxide-independent transcriptional responses to high shear stress in endothelial cells. Hypertension, 45: 1-9.

Calin G, Croce C (2006). MircoRNA signatures in human cancers. Nat. Rev. Cancer, 6: 857-866.

Carvalho L, Sun J, Kane C, Marshall F, Krawczyk C, Pearce EJ (2008). Review series on helminths, immune modulation and the hygiene hypothesis: Mechanisms underlying helminth modulation of dendritic cell function. Immunol., 126: 28-34.

Clark I, Alleva L, Mills AC, Cowden W (2004). Pathogenesis of malaria and clinically similar conditions. Clin. Microbiol. Rev., 17: 509-539.

Du Q, Park KS, Guo Z, He P, Nagashima M, Shao L, Sahai R, Geller DA, Perwez Hussain S (2006). Regulation of human nitric oxide synthase 2 expression by Wnt □-catenin signalling. Cancer Res., 66:7024-7031.

Esquela-Kerscher A, Slack F (2006). Oncomirs-microRNAs with a role in cancer. Nat. Rev. Cancer 6: 259-269.

Gabriel SB, Schaffner SF, Nguyen H, Moore JM, Roy J, Blumenstiel B, Higgins J, DeFelice M, Lochner A, Faggart I, Liu-Cordero SN, Rotimi C, Adeyemo A, Cooper R, Ward R, Lander ES, Daly MJ., Altshuler D (2002). The Structure Blocks in the Human Genome. Sciences, 296: 2225-2229.

Gazel A, Nijhawan RI, Walsh R, Blumenberg M (2008). Transcriptional profiling defines the roles of ERK and p38 kinases in epidermal keratinocytes. J. Cell. Physiol., 215: 292-308.

Goodridge H, McGuiness S, Houston KM, Egan CA, Al-Riyami L, Alcocer MJC, Harnett MM, Harnett W (2007). Phosphorylcholine mimics the effects of ES-62 on macrophages and dendrictic cells. Parasite Immunol., 29: 127-137.

Ha H, Hester L, Snyder S (2002). Poly (ADP ribose) polymerase-1 dependence of stress-induced transcription factors and associated gene expression in glia. PNAS, 99: 3270-3275.

Haltiwanger R (2009). Fucose is on the TRAIL of colon cancer. Gastroenterol., 137: 36-39.

Haploview (2003). http://www.broadinstitute.org/scientificcommunity/science/programs/medical-and population-genetics/Haploview/Haploview

International Human Genome Sequencing Consortium (2003). The International HapMap project. Nat., 426: 789-794.

International Human Genome Sequencing Consortium (2001). Initial sequencing and analysis of the human genome. Nat., 409: 860-921.

LaFlamme AC, Patton EA, Bauman B, Pearce EJ (2001). IL-4 plays a crucial role in regulating oxidative damage in the liver during schistosomiasis. J. Immunol., 166: 1903-1911.

Maiese Y, Li F, Chong ZZ, Shang YC (2008). The Wnt signalling pathway: Aging gracefully as a protectionist. Pharmacol. Ther., 118: 58-81.

Mason TE, Ricks-Santi L, Lindesay J, Kurian P, Hercules W, Dunston GM (2009). Mining the Information Content of Natural Variation in Health Disparity Research. The American Society of Human Genetics, 59th Annual Meeting, Honolulu, Hawaii, US, October 2009; 1942/T/Poster Board #491.

Nagata Y, Takahashi N, Davis RJ, Todokoro K (1998). Activation of p38 MAP kinase and JNK but not ERK is required for erythropoietin-induced erythroid differentiation. Blood, 92: 1859-1869.

Nothnagel M, Furst R, Rohde K (2004). Entropy as a measure for linkage disequilibrium over multilocus haplotype blocks. Hum. Hered., 54: 186-198.

O'Connell R, Rao D, Chaudhuri A, Baltimore D (2010). Physiological and pathological roles for MircoRNAs I the immune system. Nat. Rev. Immunol., 10: 111-122.

Perreault N, Katz JP, Sackett SD, Kaestner KH (2001). FOXI1 controls the Wnt/β-catenin pathway by modulating the expression of proteoglycans in the gut. J. Biol. Chem., 276: 43328-43333.

Pohl B, Knochel W (2001). Overexpression of the transcriptional repressor FOXD3 prevents neural crest formation in Xenopus embryos. Mech. Dev., 103: 93-106.

Roux P, Blenis J (2004). ERK and p38 MAPK-activated protein kinases: a family of protein kinases with diverse biological functions. Microbiol. Mol. Biol. Rev., 68: 320-344.

Savage J, Voronova A, Mehta V, Sendi-Mukasa F, Skerjanc IS (2010). Canonical Wnt signalling regulated FOXC1/2 expression in P19 cells. Differentiation, 79: 31-40.

Shannon C (1948). A mathematical theory of communication. Bell Syst. Tech. J., 27: 379-423.

Susskind L, Lindesay J (2005). An Introduction to Black Holes, Information and the String Theory Revolution. World Scientific Publishing Company, New Jersey, US.

Taki S, Sato T, Ogasawara K, Fukuda T, Sato M, Hida S, Mitsuyama M, Shin EH, Kojima S, Taniguchi T, Asano Y (1997). Multistage regulation of Th1 type immune responses by the transcription factor IRF1. Immunity, 6: 673-679.

Tamura T, Yanai H, Savitsky D, Taniguchi T (2008). The IRF family transcription factors in immunity and oncogenesis. Annu. Rev. Immunol., 26: 535-584.

Thomas PG, Carter MR, Da'dara AA, DeSimone TM, Harn DA (2005). A helminth glycan induces APC maturation via alternative NF-kappa B activation independent of I kappa B alpha degradation. J. Immunol., 175: 2082-2090.

van Boxel-Dezaire A, Rani M, Stark G (2006). Complex modulation of cell type-specific signalling in response to Type 1 interferons. Immunity, 25: 361-372.

Virag L, Szabo C (2002). The therapeutic potential of Poly (ADP-ribose) polymerase inhibitors. Pharmacol. Rev., 54: 375-429.

Zhang W, Glockner S, Guo M, Machida EO, Wang DH, Easwaran H, Van Neste L, Herman JG, Schuebel KE, Watkins DN, Ahuja N, Baylin SB (2008). Epigenetic inactivation of the canonical Wnt antagonist SRY-Box containing gene 17 in colorectal cancer. Cancer Res., 68: 2764-2772.

Zorn AM, Barish GD, Williams BO, Lavender P, Klymkowsky MW, Varmus HE (1999). Regulation of Wnt signalling by SOX proteins: XSoxa/b and XSox3 physically interact with β-catenin. Mol. Cell., 4: 487-498.

URLs:

dbSNP (http://www.ncbi.nlm.nih.gov/projects/SNP/)
HapMap (http://hapmap.ncbi.nlm.nih.gov/)
ConSite (http://asp.ii.uib.no:8090/cgi-bin/CONSITE/consite)
miRBase (http://www.mirbase.org/search.shtml)

14

In silico study of the binding parameters of various antioxidants with human Paraoxonase 1

K. Shyamala*, Suhasini Cherine A., Nandha Devi E. and Deepa Gaauthem

Department of Bioinformatics, Stella Maris College, 17, Cathedral Road, Chennai – 600 086, India.

Paraoxonases are a group of enzymes involved in the hydrolysis of organophosphates. Human Paraoxonase 1 is synthesized in liver and secreted into blood, where it is associated exclusively with High Density Lipoproteins and may protect against the development of atherosclerosis. Paraoxonase was identified as a genetic risk factor for cardiovascular disease. An enhancement of Paraoxonase 1 activity by well-known anti oxidant flavonols like Quercetin and its derivatives are therefore of interest. The aim of this study is to investigate the binding parameters of Quercetin and its derivatives such as Quercetin dihydrate, Quercetin pentaacetate and Quercetin -3-methylether with Paraoxonase. Human Paraoxonase 1 was modeled using Modeller and binding parameters were studied using Arguslab software. The interactions show the differences in their binding and will throw light on new ways of effecting High Density Lipoprotein content and action. The docking studies helped in understanding the binding parameters thereby giving a direction for future anti-atherosclerotic treatment options.

Key words: Paraoxonases, quercetin, anti-oxidant, high density lipoproteins (HDL), atherosclerosis.

INTRODUCTION

Paraoxonase

In serum, Paraoxonase (PON) is a high-density lipoprotein associated esterase that hydrolyses lipoperoxides and inhibits Low Density Lipoprotein oxidation. Paraoxonase 1 serves as a protective factor against oxidative modification of LDL, suggesting that it may play an important role in the prevention of atherosclerotic process. Paraoxonase, a member of the A-oxonzse family, breaks down acetylcholinesterase inhibitors before they bind to the cholinestarases, thus protecting from harm by low dose organophosphate pesticide exposure. Paraoxonase-1 possesses both arylesterase and organophosphatase activities.

The Paraoxonase gene family includes 3 genes, PON1, PON2, and PON3 aligned next to each other on chromosome 7. The human paraoxonase-1 (PON-1) is a serum high-density lipoprotein-associated phosphotriesterase secreted mainly by the liver. The enzyme encoded by this gene is an arylesterase that mainly hydrolyzes paroxon to produce p-nitrophenol Paroxon is an organophosphorus anticholinesterase compound that is produced in vivo by oxidation of the insecticide parathion. Polymorphisms in this gene are a risk factor in coronary artery disease. Next to the PON1 gene is a gene that codes for 1 of the pyruvate dehydrogenase kinases and may explain the linkage of Paraoxonase (PON) genotypes with diabetic glycemic control in some studies.

The product of PON2 has not yet been identified in biological tissue, but the PON3 gene product has recently been identified as a lactonase located on rabbit high

*Corresponding author. E-mail: shyamala@stellamariscollege.edu.in or shyamala.katragadda@gmail.com.

Abbreviations: PON, Paraoxonase; **OP,** organophosphates; **CHD,** coronary heart disease; **NCBI,** national center for biotechnology information; **BLAST,** basic local alignment search tool; **PDB,** protein data bank; **PFam,** protein family database; **SAVS,** structural analysis and validation server.

density lipoprotein.

In addition to its detoxification function, paraoxonase-1 is involved in the metabolism of endogenous substrates (Aviram et al., 1998). This enzyme metabolizes oxidized phospholipids in high- and low density lipoproteins, homocysteine thiolactoneactivating factor. It was shown that PON-1–deficient mice are more susceptible to atherosclerosis than wild-type littermates, and several clinical studies report that paraoxonase-1 plays a role in the physiological prevention of cardiovascular disease (Mackness et al., 2001).

Quercetin and its derivatives

Quercetin is a phytochemical found in the skins of apples and red onions. Quercetin - a powerful antioxidant is also natural anti-histamine (Boesch-saadatmandi et al., 2010). Research shows that Quercetin may help to prevent cancer, especially prostate cancer. Quercetin has demonstrated significant anti-inflammatory activity by inhibiting both manufacture and release of histamine and other allergic/inflammatory mediators. In addition, it exerts potent antioxidant activity and vitamin C-sparing action. Cultured skin and prostate cancer cells showed significant mortality when treated with a combination of Quercetin and ultrasound. Ultrasound also promotes topical absorption up to 1,000 times more, making the use of topical Quercetin and ultrasound an interesting proposition.

Quercetin is a member of a group the flavonoids, which have a common flavone nucleus composed of two benzene rings linked through a heterocyclicpyrone ring. Epidemiological data suggest an inverse relation between flavonoid intake and the risk for cardiovascular disease [Aviram and Fuhrman 2001]. Although there is some evidence from cell culture studies that the dietary flavonoid Quercetin may induce the expression of PON1, systematic studies investigating the influence of a Quercetin supplementation on PON2 gene expression are missing.

The therapeutic effects of plasmid DNA containing the human PON1 gene (pcDNA/PON1) in hyperlipidemic model rats suggest the potential therapeutic effect of pcDNA/PON1 on hyperlipidemia (Fu and Shao, 2010). The role of PON1 in development of cardio-vascular disease has drawn considerable attention in recent years. Studies have shown decreased levels of High Density Lipoprotein and PON1 activity in CRF patients on hemodialysis and reported this to be a risk factor in the development of CVD. Prakash et al. (2010) enhancement or maintenance of the PON1 activity may prevent development of CVDs and its consequences in patients on hemodialysis.

PON1 and PON2 were associated with increased systemic oxidative stress and increased risk for CVD (Shih and Lusis, 2009) and atherogenesis (Thomas van

Himbergen, 2006). They are basically Lactonases (Gupta et al., 2009). PON1 expression protected against *Pseudomonas aeruginosa* lethality in Drosophila, suggesting that PON1 can interfere with quorum sensing *in vivo*. PON2 attenuated macrophage triglyceride accumulation via inhibition of diacylglycerol acyltransferase 1. Over expression of PON2 protected against endoplasmic reticulum stress-induced apoptosis when the stress was induced by interference with protein modification but not when endoplasmic reticulum stress was induced by Ca^{2+} deregulation. Elucidation of the physiologic substrates of the PON proteins is of particular importance.

MATERIALS AND METHODS

The target protein was zeroed in as Paraoxonase 1 after screening the proteins involved in hyperlipidemia and atherosclerosis. The sequence was retrieved from the NCBI database whose SWISSPROT id is P27169. The protein sequences which have a similarity above 40% have been identified using the BLASTP tool. The protein 1V04 was chosen as the template as the similarity was 83%. The Template sequence and structure was retrieved from PDB database. Homology modeling was done using Modeller 9v5 and the 3-D structure of the target protein (Paraoxonase 1) was generated with the template structure (1V04) (Figure 1). Validation was done using the SAVS-PROCHECK. Q-site finder was used to identify the active site of the target protein (Paraoxonase 1) and the template protein.

Docking Studies: The 3-D structure of the ligands – Quercetin and its derivatives were downloaded from PUBCHEM. The Docking Analysis was done with the help of ArgusLab. The binding parameters of Paroxanase 1 with Quercetin and its derivatives are shown in Figures 4 to 7.

RESULTS

Blast results

The structure similarity for the sequence was carried out with the help of basic local alignment search tool. The similar structure for PON1_Human sequence was search against the PDB database.

The result indicates the degree of similarity between target and query sequences. Paraoxonase 1 from Homo sapiens had 83% similarity with 1V04 (Figure 2). Identities 83% indicate same amino acid, positives 91% indicates same group of amino acid and gaps 0%. As the criteria of the template selection is satisfied, 1V04 is used for homology modeling to model Paraoxonase1 (target).

Domain selection using PFAM

The domain region for Paraoxonase 1 was from 168 – 253. This family consists of arylesterases EC: 3.1.1.2. These enzymes hydrolyse organophosphorus esters such as paraoxon and are found in the liver and blood.

Selection of the protein (NCBI)

⬇

Retrieval of the sequence (NCBI)

⬇

Check the 3D structure is solved or not using similarity search (BLAST)

⬇

Generating 3D structure (MODELLER)

⬇

Model Validation (SAVS-PROCHECK)

⬇

Active site prediction (Q-Site Finder)

⬇

Effector Selection (PUBCHEM)

⬇

Docking Analysis (Argus Lab)

Figure 1. Methodology .

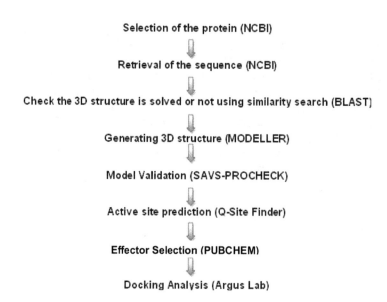

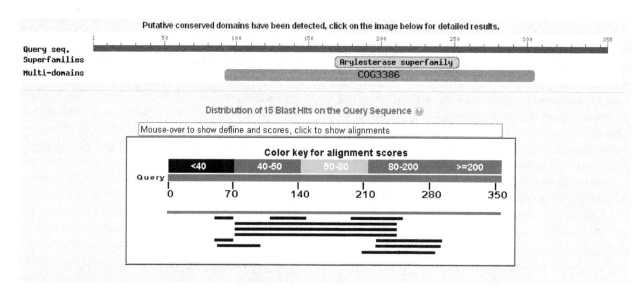

Figure 2. Graphical representation of sequence alignment from BLAST.

They confer resistance to organophosphate toxicity. Human arylesterase (PON1) is associated with HDL and may protect against LDL oxidation.

The structure model obtained was evaluated further using SAVS server. The RMSD value of 0.23Å revealed deviation between target and template structure.

SAVS server result

SAVS server analyzed the target (PON1) protein structure and showed the validity. PON1 had 88.3% residues in core region, 10.4% residues in allowed region, 1.3% residues in generously allowed region and 0.0% in disallowed region (Figure 3).

Protein ligand binding and the orientation within the targeted binding site by a suitable ligand is chosen and docked with the help of ArgusLab.

The docking result of Paraoxonase 1 with Quercetin is as follows

Best Ligand Pose: energy = -8.34 kcal/mol

ArgusLab predicted 117 poses with minimum energies. It had 69 final unique configurations. The pose 1 has the least energy of -8.34 kcal/mol. The best pose is selected

PROCHECK

Ramachandran Plot
target.B99990003

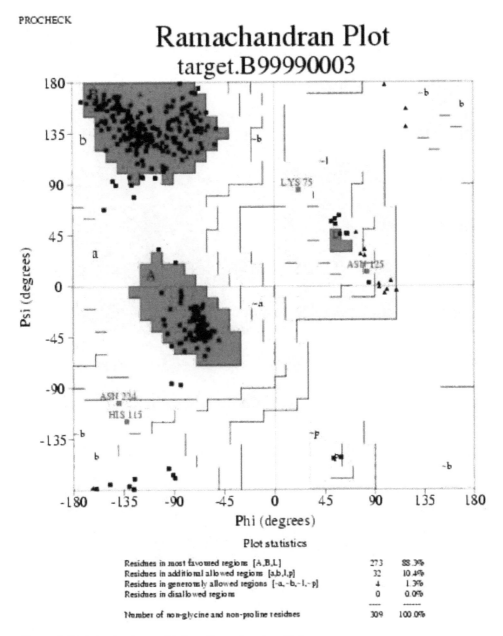

Phi (degrees)

Plot statistics

Residues in most favoured regions [A,B,L]	273	88.3%
Residues in additional allowed regions [a,b,l,p]	32	10.4%
Residues in generously allowed regions [-a,-b,-l,-p]	4	1.3%
Residues in disallowed regions	0	0.0%
	---	---
Number of non-glycine and non-proline residues	309	100.0%

Figure 3. Protein structure validation: Ramachandran Plot.

for viewing the hydrogen bond interactions. The docking result shows six hydrogen bond interactions with the Paraoxonase 1 protein (Figure 4).

Hydrogen bond information dialog box shows the hydrogen bond interaction with the distance in angstrom.

The docking result of Paraoxonase 1 with Quercetin dihydrate is as follows:

Best Ligand Pose: energy = -8.55557 kcal/mol

ArgusLab predicted 120 poses with minimum energies. It had 69 final unique configurations. The first pose has the least energy of -8.555 kcal/mol. The best pose is selected for viewing the hydrogen bond interactions. The docking result shows seven hydrogen bond interactions with the Paraoxonase 1 protein (Figure 5).

The docking result of Paraoxonase 1 with Quercetin pentaacetate is as follows:

Best Ligand Pose: energy = -7.90468 kcal/mol

Paraoxonase 1 with Quercetin pentaacetate – 8 hydrogen bonds. ArgusLab predicted 115 poses with minimum energies. It had 72 final unique configurations.

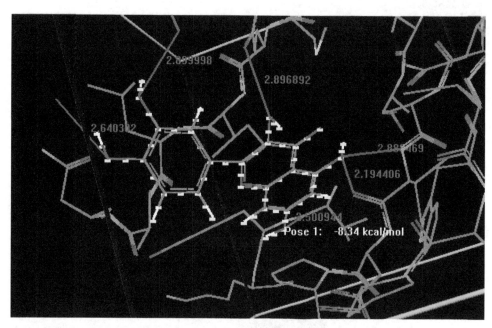

Figure 4. Docking result of Paraoxonase 1 with Quercetin.
Pose 115 fitness=-1.90066; pose 116 fitness=0.926483; pose 117 fitness=26.4906.
Refining candidate poses
Clustering the final poses:69 final unique configurations; number of local searches that succeeded in locating new minima=3; re-clustering the final poses: 69final unique configurations.
Best Ligand Pose: energy=-8.33652 kcal/mol.

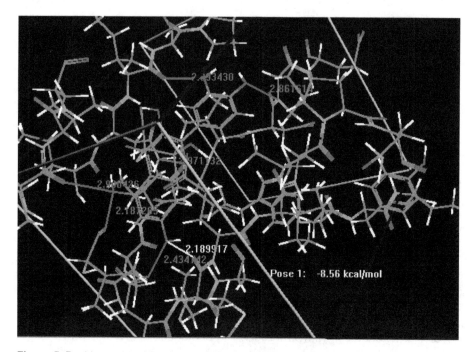

Figure 5. Docking result of Paraoxonase 1 with Quercetin dehydrates.

The first pose has the least energy of -7.90468 kcal/mol. The best pose is selected for viewing the hydrogen bond interactions. The docking result shows eight hydrogen bond interactions with the Paraoxonase 1 protein (Figure

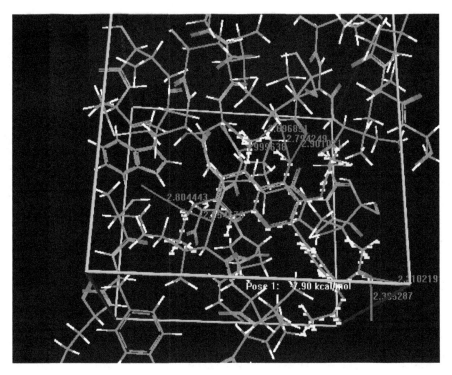

Figure 6. Docking result of Paraoxonase 1 with Quercetin pentaacetate. Best Ligand pose: energy = -7.90468 kcal/mol

6).

The docking result of Paraoxonase 1 with Quercetin -3-methylether is as follows:

Best Ligand Pose: energy = -7.5832 kcal/mol

Paraoxonase 1 with Quercetin -3- methylether – 5 hydrogen bonds. ArgusLab predicted 109 poses with minimum energies. It had 72 final unique configurations. The first pose has the least energy of -7.5832 kcal/mol. The best pose is selected for viewing the hydrogen bond interactions. The docking result shows five hydrogen bond interactions with the Paraoxonase 1 protein (Figure 7).

DISCUSSION

Of the 69 unique configurations with Quercetin the one with the least energy of -8.34 kcal/mol was selected for viewing the hydrogen bond interactions. The six hydrogen bonds had lengths ranging from 2.1 to 2.89 Angstrom, the lesser the distance, the stronger the interaction. In this context the aliphatic and hydrophobic amino acid Valine (VAL273) of Paraoxonase 1 has a length of 2.1944 Angstrom thus showing the strongest interaction with the Quercetin.

The docking result of Paraoxonase 1 with Quercetin dihydrate showed seven hydrogen bond interactions with distances ranging from 2.1 to 2.97 Angstrom. It is interesting to note that Methionine (MET55) and Isoleucine (ILE117) had lesser distances of 2.189 and 2.187 Angstrom. Therefore Paraoxonase 1 with Quercetin derivative has two strong interactions. That could be involved in binding. The residues of the predicted active site are different in the modified ligand, which can be taken up for further study.

Quercetin pentaacetate shows eight hydrogen bond interactions with distance ranging from 2.2 to 2.99 Angstrom. The distance of Threonine (THR121) with Quercetin pentaacetate was found to be 2.21 Angstrom. The active site also has Threonine which mimics hydrophobicity. Of the various amino acids that have hydrogen bonding Threonine is common in the base Quercetin and the pentaacetate derivative. It should be noted that the pentaacetate and the dihydrate derivatives have Asparagine in the active site and its mode of action could be similar

The methyl ether of Quercetin showed five hydrogen bond interactions with distance ranging from 2.2 to 2.69 Angstrom with Isoleucine (ILE117) having a distance of 2.245 Angstrom suggesting stronger interaction. Only one residue Isoleucine has a strong hydrogen bonding capacity in this derivative.

The present study infers that Paraoxonase 1 with Quercetin derivatives like Quercetin dihydrate, Quercetin pentaacetate has more number of stronger interactions when compared to Quercetin itself and the methyl ether

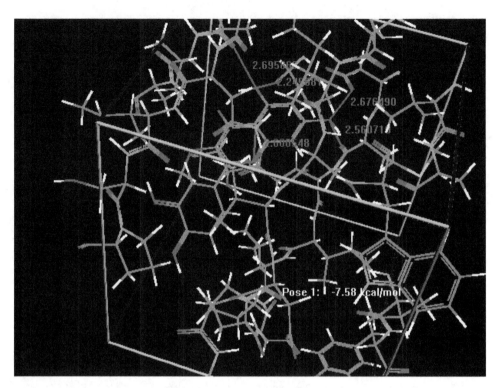

Figure 7. Docking result of Paraoxonase 1 with Quercetin -3-methylether. Clustering the final poses: 72final unique configurations.Number of local searches that succeeded in locating new minima = 2.
Re-clustering the final poses: 72 final unique configurations. Best Ligand Pose: energy = -7.5832 kcal/mol.

derivative has less binding. These results can be used to further research on the effect of various functional groups on the Quercetin molecule to increase the impact on Paroxonase, thereby leading to effective treatment of Hyperlipidemia especially to increase the high density lipoprotein which is the need of the hour.

Conclusion

The presence of Paraoxonase 1 in High Density Lipoprotein may thus be a major contributor to the anti-atherogenicity of this lipoprotein. In the presence of Quercetin HDL, up-regulation is increased thereby giving indications of alternative therapy modules. The various derivatives such as Quercetin dihydrate, Quercetin pentaacetate showed more number of stronger interactions when compared to Quercetin itself, but the methyl ether derivative has less binding. These results can be used for further research to identify derivatives for maximum impact on Paroxonase. The study demonstrates that a Quercetin supplementation may up-regulate Paraoxonase 1 activity giving us a valuable tool to treat or manage Hyperlipidemia.

REFERENCES

Fu Ai Ling, Shao Ping Wu (2010). Single intravenous injection of plasmid DNA encoding human paraoxonase-1 inhibits hyperlipidemia in rats. Biochem. Biophys. Res. Commun., 397(2):257-62.

Aviram M, Fuhrman B (2001). Flavonoids protect LDL from oxidation and attenuate atherosclerosis. Curr Opin Lipidol., 12(1):41-8, PMID:11176202

Aviram M, Rosenblat M, Bisgaier CL, Newton RS, Primo-Parmo SL, La Du BN (1998). Paraoxonase inhibits high-density lipoprotein oxidation and preserves its functions. A possible peroxidative role for paraoxonase. J. Clin. Invest., 101(8): 1581–1590, PMC508738.

Boesch-saadatmandi C, Egert S, Schrader C, Coumoul X, Barouki R, Muller MJ, Wolffram S, Rimbach G (2010). Effect Of Quercetin On Paraoxonase 1 Activity – Studies In Cultured Cells, Mice And Humans. J. Physiol. Pharmacol., 61(1):99-105, PMID: 20228421

Mackness B, Davies GK, Turkie W, Lee E, Roberts DH, Hill E, Roberts C, Durrington PN, Mackness MI (2001). Paraoxonase status in coronary heart disease: are activity and concentration more important than genotype?. Arterioscler Thromb Vasc Biol., 21(9):1451-7.

Gupta N, Kirandip G, Surjit S (2009). Paraoxonases: Structure, gene polymorphism & role in coronary artery disease. Indian J. Med. Res., 130, 361-368

Prakash M, Phani NM, Kavya R, Supriya M (2010). Paraoxonase: Its antiatherogenic role in chronic renal failure. Indian. J. Nephrol. 20(1):9-14, PMID: 20535264

Shih DM, Lusis AJ (2009). The roles of PON1 and PON2 in cardiovascular disease and innate immunity. Curr Opin Lipidol. 20(4):288-92, PMID: 19474728

Thomas van H (2006). Paraoxonase in cardiovascular disease: actions and interactions. The Netherlands J. Med., 64(2).

15

Potential of mangrove derived compounds against dihydrofolate reductase: An *in-silico* docking study

Senthilraja P.[1]*, Sunil Kumar Sahu[2] and Kathiresan K.[2]

[1]Department of Zoology, Annamalai University, Annamalai Nagar, Chidambaram-608002, TN, India.
[2]CAS in Marine Biology, Faculty of Marine Sciences, Annamalai University, Parangipettai-608502, TN, India.

Approximately 3 billion people, one half of the world's population, live in at-risk regions for malaria infection leading to about 250 million malaria cases every year and nearly one million deaths. Once the malarial parasite *Plasmodium vivax* and *Plasmodium falciparum* enters the red blood cells its growth is inhibited by Proguanil, a prophylactic antimalarial drug which inhibits the enzyme, dihydrofolate reductase leading to the inhibition of the growth of malarial parasites. Considering the side effects of the antimalarial drugs, the present study was undertaken to substantiate the inhibition potential of mangrove-derived compounds against the receptor protein dihydrofolate reductase. Docking studies by using Argus lab software revealed that among nine mangrove-derived compounds five compounds namely stigmasterol, triterpenoid, tretinoin, pyrethrin and rubrolide-N showed good docking energy score of -14.2239, 12.4725, -11.689, -11.1828 and -10.884 Kcal/mol, respectively against dihydrofolate reductase.

Key words: Malaria, dihydrofolate reductase, mangrove-derived compounds, Pdb, Argus lab.

INTRODUCTION

Malaria continues to be a major public health threat, with over two billion people at risk of contracting this deadly disease. It continues to represent a major threat to world health infecting between 300 and 500 million people annually and causing 1.5 to 2.7 million deaths-equal to 150 to 300 deaths each hour (Snow et al., 2005; WHO, 2008; Breman, 2009). The disease results from infection by parasites belonging to the Plasmodium species and is transmitted by the female mosquitoes of the Anopheles genus. Of the four species of parasite (*Plasmodium falciparum*, *Plasmodium vivax*, *Plasmodium malariae*, and *Plasmodium ovale*) that infect humans, P. *falciparum* is responsible for the majority (95%) of fatalities (Murray and Perkins, 1996). In areas where malaria is prevalent, one of the most crucial obstacles for eradicating malaria is a widespread resistance of malarial parasite to almost all classical antimalarial agents such as chloroquine,

mefloquine, and antifolates (Hyde, 2007) has prompted researchers worldwide to consider and to search for other antimalarial drugs of ideally different molecular mechanism(s) of action from those against which malaria parasites have developed resistance (Borstnik et al., 2002a). Therefore, it is very necessary to seek for new drugs that are effective against drug resistant strains in order to combat and relieve this tremendous prevalence.

Dihydrofolate reductase plays an essential role in the building of DNA and other processes. It manages the state of folate, a snaky organic molecule that shuttles carbon atoms to enzymes that need them in their reactions of particular importance, the enzyme thymidylate synthase use these carbon atoms to build thymine bases, an essential component of DNA. After folate has released its carbon atoms, it has to be recycled. Proguanil is a prophylactic antimalarial drug, a biguanide derivative which stops the reproduction of the malaria parasite, P. *falciparum* and P. *vivax*, once it is entered in the red blood cells by inhibiting the enzyme, dihydrofolate reductase, which is involved in the reproduction of the parasite that is, it blocks the

*Corresponding author. E-mail: lionbioinfo@gmail.com.

Table 1. Dihydrofolate reductase binding site.

S/N	Amino acids in the binding pocket	Binding site of amino acids in the structural unit
1	ALA9,ARG137,ASN185	Beta strand
2	ALA86, ASP29	Coil
3	ALA96, ARG36, ASP94	Alpha helix

biosynthesis of purines and pyrimidines, which are essential for DNA synthesis and cell multiplication. This leads to failure of nuclear division at the time of schizont formation in erythrocytes and liver. Common side effects include stomach ache, sore throat, loss of hair, abnormal bruising or bleeding, fever and pale yellow urine. Sometimes, overdose of Proguanil also creates problems. Dihydrofolate reductase has been a primary target for the Proguanil drug (http://www.emedicinehealth.com/drug-atovaquone_ and_proguanil/article_em.htm). Molecular docking is an application, wherein molecular modeling techniques are used to predict how a protein (enzyme) interacts with small molecules (ligands). The ability of a protein (enzyme) to interact with small molecules plays a major role in the dynamics of the protein which may enhance/inhibit its biological function. The necessity of new improved drugs is being felt due to the side effects of antimalarial drugs. Hence, in the present *in silico* study we try to find the suitable analogues with high binding affinity, which could be a possible lead molecule. Moreover, the obtained docking results will enhance an understanding of drug–receptor interactions, which enables a modification of the drug's structure to achieve suitable interactions. Hence, this can bring about a development of new and more effective drugs.

MATERIALS AND METHODS

Protein structure

The targeted protein dihydrofolate reductase (ID: 1MVT), having the resolution of 1.80 A° was retrieved from the protein data bank (PDB) (www.rcsb.org/pdb). Structural and active site studies of the protein were done by using CASTP (Computed Atlas of Surface Topography of Proteins) and pymol molecular visualization software.

Chemicals screened

Nine chemicals namely triterpenoid, stigmasterol, tretinoin, rubrolide-N, pyrethrin, tricin, Heritonin, Haloprogin and N-methylflindersine identified from the coastal mangrove ecosystems (Kathiresan and Qasim, 2005) were screened against the dihydrofolate reductase.

Amino acid binding site

The phytochemical molecules were retrieved the pubchem

database. The selected chemical structures were generated from SMILES notation (Simplified Molecular Input Line Entry Specification) by using the Chemsketch Software (www.acdlabs.com). The predicted binding sites, based on the binding energy, and amino acids make up the binding cavity. The predicted ligand binding site residues are listed in Table 1.

Docking methods

Argus Lab 4.01 was used for docking analysis, which is widely distributed public domain molecular docking software. The inhibitor and target protein were geometrically optimized and docked using docking engine Argus dock.

RESULTS

Nine chemicals derived from mangrove ecosystem were docked with dihydrofolate reductase. The docked ligand molecules were selected based on docking energy and good interaction with the active site residues and the results are shown in Table 2. Of the nine ligand molecules, 5 showed the activation energy of greater than -10 Kcal/mol and the remaining four compounds exhibited the values <10 kcal/mol. The highest activation energy (-14.2239 Kcal/mol) was found in stigmasterol (Figures 1a and 1b) followed by triterpenoid, tretinoin, pyrethrin and rubrolide-N (12.4725, -11.689, -11.1828 and -10.884 Kcal/mol respectively). While, the lowest activation energy of -6.74187 Kcal/mol was found in tricin. Thus, the *in silico* docking results, revealed that mangrove derived compounds have the great potential against inhibition of dihydrofolate reductase.

DISCUSSION

Anti-malarial drugs such as proguanil inhibit the dihydrofolate reductase of plasmodia thereby blocking the biosynthesis of purines and pyrimidines, which are essential for DNA synthesis and cell multiplication. This leads to failure of nuclear division at the time of schizont formation in erythrocytes and liver. But, there are several side-effects of Proguanil too. Hence, realizing the necessity of new potential dihydrofolate reductase inhibitory drug, in this present study we screened nine mangrove derived compounds against dihydrofolate reductase protein Molecular docking is a key tool in structural molecular biology and computer-assisted drug

Table 2. Docking results of mangrove derived compounds against dihydrofolate reductase.

Compound name	Pubchem ID	Compound structure	Molecular weight (g/mol)	Hydrogen donor/acceptor	Docking energy level (Kcal/mol)
Stigmasterol	CID: 5280794		269.082	(1,1)	-14.2239
Triterpenoid	CID: 9804218		458.6041	(2,3)	-12.4725
Tretinoin	CID:444795		300.43512	(1,2)	-11.689
Pyrethrin	CID:6433155		372.454	(0,5)	-11.1828
Rubrolide-N	CID: 5472704		472.51196	(2,4)	-10.884
Heritonin	CID:130118		258.31232	0,3	-9.89708
Haloprogin	CID:3561		361.39093	0,1	-9.82504

Table 2. Cont'd.

| N-Methylflindersine | CID: 72819 | 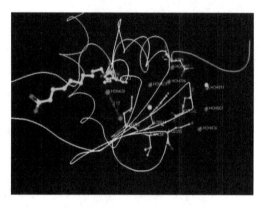 | 241.2851 | (0,2) | -8.09744 |
| Tricin | CID: 5281702 | | 330.288 | (3,7) | -6.74187 |

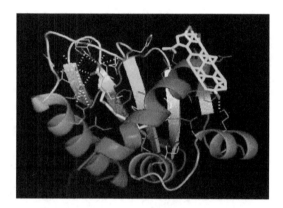

(A) Stigmasterol   (b) Hydrogen bond, Neighbor residues

Figure 1. Molecular visualization of stigmasterol (a) and its hydrogen bond and neighbor residues (b) by using Pymol software.

design. Our previous docking studies have already proved the efficacy of mangrove derived compounds against oncoprotein of cervical cancer, sterol containing protein (AeSCP-2) and breast cancer protein BRCA1 (Senthilraja et al., 2011; Senthilraja and Kathiresean, 2011ab; Senthilraja et al., 2011). Our docking results showed the highest activation energy (-14.2239 Kcal/mol) in stigmasterol which is much better than the activation energy of the antimalarial drug proguanil (-6.59 Kcal/mol) (Prakash et al., 2010).

Thus, the present *in-silico* docking study also proved that mangrove-derived compounds are capable of blocking dihydrofolate reductase, ultimately which could lead to inhibition of the growth of malaria parasite.

Conclusion

Mangroves are rich source of ecofriendly, safer and cheaper compounds (phenolic) which possess great medicinal value. In this study we have docked the receptor dihydrofolate reductase with the nine different mangrove derived compounds and from the results it can be concluded that these compounds derived from mangrove ecosystem (stigmasterol, triterpenoid, tretinoin, pyrethrin and rubrolide-N) could be a novel inhibitor for dihydrofolate reductase. All the compounds passed the Lipinski rule of five (Lipinski et al., 2001), hence further studies such as ADME/T (Absorption, Distribution, Metabolism, Excretion/Toxicity) properties of the compound could be tested further.

ACKNOWLEDGEMENTS

Authors are thankful to the authorities of Annamalai University for providing necessary facilities to carry out this work, and one of the authors (Sunil Kumar Sahu to Department of Science and Technology, Government of India, New Delhi for financial support.

REFERENCES

Borstnik K, Paik IH, Posner GH (2002a). Malaria: new chemotherapeutic peroxide drugs. Mini-Rev. Med. Chem., 2:573–583.

Lipinski CA, Lombardo F, Dominy BW, Feeney PJ (2001). Experimental and computational approaches to estimate solubility and permeability in drug discovery and development settings. Adv. Drug Del. Rev., 46: 3–26.

Hyde JE (2007). Drug-resistant malaria-an insight. FEBS J., 274:4688-4698.

Kathiresan K, Qasim SZ (2005). Biodiversity of mangrove ecosystems. Hindustan Publishing Corporation Limited, New Delhi 251 pp.

Murray MC, Perkins ME (1996). Chemotherapy of Malaria. Ann. Rep. Med. Chem., 31:141-150.

Prakash N, Patel S, Faldu NJ, Ranjan R, Sudheer DVN (2010). Molecular Docking Studies of Antimalarial Drugs for Malaria. J. Comput. Sci. Syst. Biol., 3:070-073.

Senthilraja P, Kathiresan K, Sunil KS (2011). *Insilico* docking analysis of mangrove-derived compounds against breast cancer protein (BRCA1). IRMJ-Health Sci., 1(1): 09-12.

Senthilraja P, Kathiresan K (2011a). Computational selection of mangrove-derived compounds as mosquito larvicide's by blocking the sterol carrying protein, AeSCP-2. Res Bioscientia., 2(1):1-6.

Senthiraja P, Kathiresan K (2011b). Computational selection of compounds derived from mangrove ecosystem for anti-cervical cancer activity. J. Recent Sci. Res., 2(4):93-98.

Snow RW, Guerra CA, Noor AM, Myint HY, Hay HI (2005). The global distribution of clinical episodes of. *Plasmodium falciparum* malaria. Nature, 434:214-217.

World Health Organisation (2008). WHO- World Malaria Report. Geneva Switzerland.

16

Chloride anation reaction of aqua (diethylenetriamine) platinum (II): Density functional studies "Dedicated to Prof. H. B. Gray"

Partha Sarathi Sengupta[1*], Snehasis Banerjee[2] and Ashish Kumar Ghosh[3]

[1]Chemistry department, Vivekananda Mahavidyalaya, Burdwan, India, 713103.
[2]Darjeeling Government College India, Darjeeling, 734101, India.
[3]Central Institute of Mining and Fuel Research Institute, Dhanbad, India 828108.

The nucleophilic and solvolytic path for the chloride anation reaction of aqua(diethylenetriamine)platinum (II) is computationally investigated at the Hartee-Fock (HF) and Density functional theory (B3LYP and mPW1PW91) of levels of calculation in gas phase and on the self- consistent reaction field (SCRF) model. All the stationary points are fully optimized and characterized. The kinetic and thermodynamic properties of all the species involved are investigated and compared with the available experimental data. The transition state is described by local reactivity descriptors. A point of inflection of Fukui function and local softness of the incoming nucleophile for both the solvolytic and nucleophilic path at the transition state (Saddle point), corresponds to both bond breaking and bond making processes. The existence of the solvolytic path (k_1) along with nucleophilic path (k_2) has been supported by DFT studies. From the enthalpy of activation ($\Delta H^{\ast}$), entropy of activation ($\Delta S^{\ast}$) and the structures of the transition states, an inter change associative mechanism (I_a) is established for both nucleophilic and solvolytic path for the chloride anation reaction

Key words: Anation reactions, aqua (diethylenetriamine) platinum (II), DFT, self consistent reaction field, Fukui function.

INTRODUCTION

Theoretical and computational studies of transition metal complexes in solution are of great importance due to their applications in drug design, organometallic energetics, kinetics and in industrial processes (Carloni et al., 2000; Wong et al., 1999; Zeigler, 1995; Michelle et al., 2000). The kinetics of ligand substitution reaction of platinum (II) has shown to follow a two term rate law.

$PtX_3L + Y \longrightarrow PtYX_3 + X$
$Rate = (k_1 + k_2 [Y]) [PtX_3L]$

The k_2 term relates the associative bimolecular attack of the nucleophile Y on the substrate, the first order rate constant is known to involve the associative solvolysis, followed by rapid anation. Grey et al. (1962) have shown that for the complex [Pt (dien) Cl]$^+$ in aqueous solution proceed through the solvolytic path and [Pt (dien) (H$_2$O)]$^+$

is the active intermediate of the reaction. The kinetics of the same reaction was revisited by Kotowski et al. (1980)and they demonstrate that $k_{2(obs)}$ is adequately represented by $k_2[Y]$ and appearance of k_1 is within the experimental error limit.

In the present work, the author attempts to analyze the chloride anation reaction via nucleophilic path (1) along with the solvolytic path (2), by *ab-initio* and Density Functional theory

$$[Pt(dien)(H_2O)]^{2+} + Cl^- \xrightarrow{k_2} [Pt(dien)(Cl)]^+ + H_2O \qquad (1)$$

$$[Pt(dien)(H_2O)]^{2+} + H_2O \xrightarrow{k_1} [Pt(dien)(H_2O)]^{2+} + H_2O \qquad (2)$$

The structures, thermodynamic properties and rate constants were calculated as a function of different leve of theory and compared with the experimental data. The solvent effect on thermodynamic and kinetic parameters for this reaction was analyzed in Onsager SCRF model Finally, the nature of the transition state was described by local reactivity descriptor.

METHODOLOGY

Full unconstrained geometry optimization and frequency calculation for all the distinct species involve in the chloride anation reaction of aqua(diethylenetriamine)platinum(II) have been carried out at the Hartee-Fock (HF) and two Density Functional methods. These are three parameter fit non-local correlation provided by LYP expression and VWN functional III for local correction and exchange functional suggested by Becke (1988,1993,1996), Perdew et al. (1992, 1994), Vosko et al. (1980)] [B3LYP] b) modified Perdew-Wang exchange and Perdew-Wang 91 correlation (MPW1PW91) Adamo et al. (1998). The standard split valence basis set 6-31G (d) (Dtchfield et al., 1971; Hehre et al., 1972) was applied for O and H, N, C and Cl atoms. The relativistic effective core potential (ECP) and associated valence double ξ basis set of Hay and Wadt (Hay et al., 1985), Wadt et al. (1985) (LANL2DZ) was employed for Pt. This includes electrons in the 6s, 6p, and 5d orbitals. All stationary points located on the potential energy surface were characterized as minima (no imaginary frequencies) or first order transition state (characterized by having one imaginary frequency) through harmonic frequency calculations. To gain deeper insight into the reaction pathway, the intrinsic reaction coordinate (IRC) was calculated using Gonzalez–Schlegel second order path following algorithm (Gonzalez et al., 1989, 1990) starting from the optimized transition state structure with a step size 0.100 (a. m. u.)$^{1/2}$ bohr. The minimum energy path used in IRC is defined as the path that would be taken by a classical particle sliding downhill with infinitesimal velocity from the transition state to each minima. Thermal contributions to the energetic properties were also calculated at 298.15 K and 1 atm.

To incorporate the solvent effects in this reaction, self-consistent reaction field model of Onsager (1936), Wong et al. (1991, 1992) has been utilized. In Onsager reaction field model, the solvent is considered as a continuous unstructured dielectric with a given dielectric constant surrounding a solute embedded in a spherical cavity. The rate constant (k) have been evaluated according to Eyring's transition state theory,

$$k(T) = (k_B \, T)/h \, \exp(-\Delta G^{\ddagger}/ RT)$$

where k_B is the Boltzmann constant, T the absolute temperature and h the Planck constant. $\Delta G^{\ddagger}$ is the free energy of activation for each step.

The density–functional theory (Parr et al., 1989; Lewars, 2003) is highly pertinent for chemical concepts. The electronic chemical potential was defined as $\mu = (\partial E / \partial N)_V$, where E and V are the energy of the system and external potential due to the nuclei respectively with N number of electrons. The negative of the electronic chemical potential, μ, that is $-\mu$ is the electronegativity of the species. The hardness of the system has been defined as $2\eta = (\partial \mu / \partial N)_V$. These are the global properties. In order to understand the reaction mechanism, local parameters are very important which varies from point to point and be a measure of reactivity of the different sites in a supermolecule. Parr and Yang (1989) introduced frontier electron density, $\rho(r)$ of the frontier orbital concept of Fukui into the DFT theory (Parr et al., 1989). They defined Fukui function, the space dependent local function, as $f(r) = [\partial \rho(r) / \partial N]_V = [\delta \mu / \delta v(r)]_N$. This measures the sensitivity of the system's chemical potential to an external perturbation at a particular point in a molecular species, with the change of number of electrons.

In chemical reaction, change of electron density changes from one species to another occurs at the transition state. The addition or removal of electron to LUMO or HOMO of the species respec-

tively, the Fukui Function is therefore related to the properties of Frontier orbital (HOMO and LUMO).

The approximate definition of chemical potential μ and chemical hardness η of the system can be obtained by the method of finite difference. These are- $\mu = \chi = (I\,E. + E\,A.)/2$. $\eta = (I.\,E. - E\,A)/2$, where χ, I. E. and E. A. are the electronegativity, vertical ionization potential and electron affinity of the system.

Within the validity of Koopman's theorem (Szabo et al., 1996) for closed shell electronic systems, the frontier orbital energies is expressed as

$$-\varepsilon_{HOMO} = I.\,E. \quad \text{and} \quad -\varepsilon_{LUMO} = E.\,A.$$

Due to the discontinuity of electron density $\rho(r)$ with respect to the number of electrons, N, the finite difference method leads three different type of Fukui Function for a system, these are;

$f^{-}(r) = \rho_N(r) - \rho_{N-1}(r)$ for electrophilic attack, $f^{+} = \rho_{N+1}(r) - \rho_N(r)$ for nucleophilic attack and $f^{0} = \frac{1}{2}[\rho_{N+1}(r) - \rho(r)]$ for radical attack. In practice, the condensed Fukui function (Geerlings et al., 2003; Chattaraj et al., 2005) for an atom k in the molecule was determined. The Fukui Function has therefore used to predict and rationalize the variation of reactivates in different sites of the molecule concerned. The condensed Fukui Function measures the sensitivity of small changes in the number of electrons at atom k in HOMO and LUMO.

They are expressed as $f_k^{+} = [q_k(N+1) - q_k(n)]$, $f_k^{-} = [q_k(N) - q_k(N-1)]$ and
$f_k^{0} = 1/2[q_k(N+1)q_k - (N-1)]$

The Fukui function and local softness are related as $s(r) = f(r).S$

where S is the global softness and is the inverse of global hardness, $S = 1/2\eta = 1/2(\partial N / \partial \mu)_V$.

The philicity parameter is also another local parameter and has been defined as

$\omega = W. \, f(r)$ where W is the global philicity.

To determine the Fukui function and local softness, separate calculations were done for N, (N+1) and (N-1) electron system with the same geometry along the IRC path. The Mulliken population analysis scheme was used for the necessary charges. The B3LYP protocol and 6-31(G) basis set have been used for these calculations. All the quantum mechanical calculations have been carried out with the GAUSSIAN 03(RevisionC.02), program (Frisch et al., 2004, GAUSSIAN 03)

RESULTS AND DISSCUSSION

Structural analysis

Figure 1 shows all optimized structures found on the potential energy surface for the species involved in the chloride anation reaction of aqua(diethylenetriamine)platinum(II). To save the space, only the B3LYP structures are shown. A systematic search for the intermediate structures was done and five stationary points along the reaction pathway were found as can be seen in Figure 1. The reactant molecule shows quasi square planar geometry around the central Pt atom. The three Pt -N bond lengths are 2.031, 2.098 and 2.099 Å and Pt -O bond

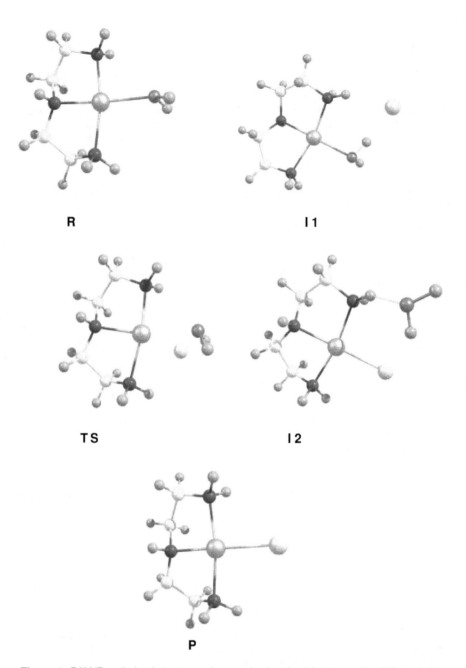

Figure 1. B3LYP optimized structures for species involved in the nucleophilic path for the chloride anation reaction of [Pt(dien)(H₂O)]²⁺

length is 2.14 Å. O-H bond lengths are 0.976 and 0.977 Å at B3LYP level of theory. The bond angles $\angle$N(T)- Pt – N₂, $\angle$N(T)- Pt –N₃ and $\angle$N₂- Pt –N₃, are 83.21°, 84.26° and 165.68° respectively. The $\angle$O-Pt-N₂ and $\angle$O-Pt-N₃ bond angles are 101.01° and 91.5° respectively. Both the five member rings of diethylenetriamine (dien) bound with platinum are out of plane with N-C-C-N dihedral angles 39.15° and 51.05° degrees respectively. The structural parameter of the aqua ion [Pt(dien)(H₂O)]²⁺ are unique (Briton et al., 1982) (Table 1) as X ray crystallographic data of this ion was unavailable due to the synthetic pro-

blem.

In the intermediate **I1**, [Pt(dien)(H₂O)]²⁺...Cl, the incoming chloride ion is weakly hydrogen bonded with the hydrogen of the aqua ligands at a intermolecular distance of 1.907 Å . The O-H bond distance changes from 0.975 to 1.038 Å. The angle $\angle$O-H-Cl is 171.2° degrees. The existence of hydrogen bond was supported by the depression of stretching frequencies by 510 cm⁻¹ (Cotton et al., 1999).

In this substitution reaction, a five-coordinated trigonal-bi-pyramid like transition state with a small angle ($\angle$ leav-

Table 1. Structural data for optimized aqua ion, $[Pt(dien)(H_2O)]^{2+}$ in different protocol in gas phase. In parentheses are the respective values in Onsager reaction field model.

Bond lengths (Å)	HF	B3LYP	mPW1PW91
Pt-N(T)[a]	2.031(2.032)	2.029(2.031)	2.012(2.009)
Pt-N$_2$	2.101(2.094)	2.105(2.098)	2.075(2.0746)
Pt-N$_3$	2.098 (2.108)	2.098(2.099)	2.075(2.0753)
Pt-O	2.148 (2.143)	2.148(2.141)	2.123(2.119)
N(T)-C$_3$	1.524 (1.505)	1.512(1.511)	1.522(1.5107)
C$_3$-C$_4$	1.531 (1.529)	1.53(1.531)	1.522(1.523)
N(T)-C$_5$	1.512(1.493)	1.512(1.511)	1.519(1.511)
N(T)-H	1.020(1.018)	1.025(1.025)	1.024(1.0235)
C$_5$-C$_6$	1.529(1.526)	1.530(1.531)	1.522(1.5229)
N-H	1.021(1.009)	1.024(1.025)	1.021(1.022)
O-H	0.975(0.956)	0.975(0.975)	0.972(0.9723)
C-H	1.095(1.094)	1.092(1.092)	1.092(1.092)
Bond angles(in degrees)			
N(T)-Pt-N$_2$	83.09 (83.21)	83.09(83.21)	83.32(83.36)
N$_2$-Pt-N$_3$	84.25(83.66)	84.24(84.26)	84.46(84.48)
N$_2$-Pt-O	91.54(91.01)	91.54(91.57)	91.50(91.46)
N$_3$-Pt-N$_2$	165.6 (164.89)	165.60(165.68)	165.99(166.06)
N(T)-Pt-O	179.8(179.9)	179.9(179.93)	179.97(180.01)
Dihedral angle			
N(T)-C$_3$-C$_4$-N$_2$	39.28 (39.68)	39.28(39.15)	39.82(39.66)
N(T)-C$_5$-C$_6$-N$_3$	51.22(51.52)	51.22(51.05)	51.53(51.44)

a N(T) is the trans nitrogen with respect to the H_2O.

ing H_2O- Pt - entering Cl that is, 70.14° was found. The TS structure has an imaginary frequency of -129.1 cm^{-1} computed at B3LYP level of theory (Foresman et al., 1996) in which Pt - O (2.341 Å) bond is breaking and Pt - Cl (2.728 Å) bond is forming, the Pt - N(T) bond length in the equatorial plane has larger value than the two axial Pt - N bond length (Figure 2(a) of supporting information). The imaginary frequency at mPW1PW91 level is -130.8 cm^{-1}.

In the intermediate structure I2, the leaving aqua ligand, H_2O is hydrogen bonded with intermolecular distance of 1.759 Å, the O atom of H_2O and one of the amine hydrogen of dien are involved in hydrogen bonding. The leaving H_2O is above the quasi-square plane of the complex with N-H...O bond angle 157.6° and the two five membered (Pt-N-C-C-N) ring of the diethylenetriamine ligand are on the opposite side of the leaving H_2O.

This anation reaction was characterized by replacement of H_2O by chloride ion (Cl$^-$) and proceed via a collision between the reactant $[Pt(dien)(H_2O)]^{2+}$ with the nucleophilc species Cl$^-$. In such substitution process, a five coordinated distorted trigonal bi-pyramid like transition structure, with entering ligand, leaving ligand and the metal complex being weakly bound was found. This was found to be true from the structural analysis (Table 1). The small angle between entering H_2O and leaving Cl$^-$ minimizes the repulsion between the d orbital

electrons of Pt and the electron pairs of entering and leaving group.

From structural analysis for the transition state (Table 1 of supporting information), it was concluded that the main geometric change took place in the equatorial plane of the transition structure (in both gas and SCRF model). In the d^8 trigonal-bi-pyramid transition state, there occurs greater interaction among the filled dπ orbital electrons with the equatorial ligands compared to the axial ligand. Henceforth dπ -pπ^* back bonding and dπ -pπ nonbonding repulsion affect the trigonal plane mainly (Atwood, (1997).

In the product $[Pt(dien)Cl]^{+1}$, Pt atom is tetra-coordinated, the angles around the central Pt atom are deviated from their optimal values. The optimized parameters for the product are compared with X-ray crystallographic data (Briton et al., 1982) (Table 2).

The geometries I and II [Figure 3(a), curve E) in intrinsic reaction coordinate were fully optimized at B3LYP level of theory and were found to be the correct intermediate structures (I 1 and I 2).

Population analysis of the transition state from the optimized structure in B3LYP levels of theory reveals that main contribution of HOMO and LUMO comes from d atomic orbital of Pt atom (Figure 2a). It was also observed that through out the reaction path, the energy of HOMO remain constant but the energy of LUMO increases

Table 2. Structural data for optimized [Pt(dien)(Cl)]⁺ in different protocol (Onsager reaction field model). The data are compared with the experimental X-ray crystallographic data.

Bond lengths (Å)	HF	B3LYP	mPW1PW91	Experimental data[b]
Pt-N(T)[a]	2.068	2.076	2.054	2.002(8)
Pt-N_2	2.087	2.078	2.054	2.063(10)
Pt-N_3	2.097	2.088	2.064	2.063(9)
Pt-Cl	2.375	2.330	2.332	2.312(3)
N(T)-C_3	1.498	1.491	1.502	1.48(1)
C_3-C_4	1.530	1.539	1.528	1.53
N(T)-C_5	1.487	1.510	1.491	1.46(2)
N_2-C_3	1.490	1.508	1.4952	1.50(1)
C_5-C_6	1.528	1.536	1.525	1.53
N_3-C_5	1.496	1.508	1.500	1.49(2)
Bond angles(degrees)				
N(T)-Pt-N_2	83.09	84.132	83.89	83.5(4)
N_2-Pt-N_3	83.70	84.78	84.68	84.5(4)
N_2-Pt-Cl	96.79	95.48	95.77	95.6(3)
N_3-Pt-N_2	164.27	165.97	165.90	165.7(4)
N(T)-Pt-Cl	177.90	177.30	177.85	175.6(3)
Dihedral angle(degrees)				
N(T)-C_3-C_4-N_2	40.76	39.96	40.68	-54 ±1
N(T)-C_5-C_6-N_3	51.94	52.20	52.32	-53 ±1

a N(T) is the trans nitrogen with respect to the leaving chloride (Cl⁻) ion
b From reference Briton (1992) (for single [Pt(dien)(Cl)]Cl crystal

HOMO   LUMO

Figure 2a. Isodensity surface of HOMO and LUMO for the TS calculated at the B3LYP level for the nucleophilic path, (Two different views).

HOMO   LUMO

Figure 2b. Isodensity surface of HOMO and LUMO for the TS calculated at the B3LYP level for the solvolytic path.

steadily leading to a decrease in gap between HOMO and LUMO.

Solvolytic path

The Figure 3 shows the existence of all optimized struc-

tures of the transition state along with the corresponding reaction intermediate and product intermediate on the potential energy surface for the species involved in the for the solvolytic path. This solvolysis reaction was characterized by replacement of H_2O by H_2O and proceed via a collision between the reactan $[Pt(dien)(H_2O)]^{2+}$ with the solvent H_2O in Onsager self consistent reaction field model. The TS structure has a imaginary frequency of -160.3 cm⁻¹, computed at B3LYF level of theory. The Pt - O (2.536 Å) bond is breaking and Pt - O (2.499 Å) bond is forming In such substitution pro cess, a five coordinated distorted trigonal bi-pyramid like transition structure, with entering ligand (H_2O), leaving ligand (H_2O) and the metal complex being weakly bound

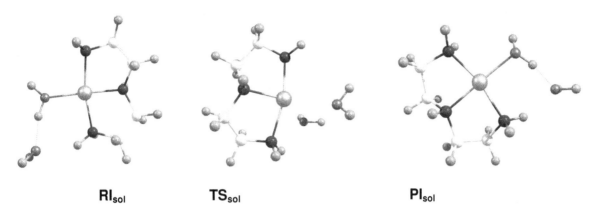

Figure 3. B3LYP optimized structures for species involved in the solvolytic path for the chloride anation reaction of $[Pt(dien)(H_2O)]^{2+}$.

was found. This was found to be true from the structural analysis (Table 2 of supporting information). The small angle between entering H_2O and leaving Cl^- minimizes the repulsion between the d orbital electrons of Pt and the electron pairs of entering and leaving group.

Solvent effect on the structural properties

This section compares the structural data in Onsager self-consistent reaction field model that is, solution phase with the gas phase data for the transition state. All the bond lengths (including Pt...Cl and Pt...OH_2 partial bonds) increase in Onsager model except the equatorial Pt- N bond of the distorted trigonal bi-pyramid like transition state (Table 1). The changes in bond angles are less significant except the equatorial angles. The angle between the entering H_2O and leaving Cl changes significantly from 70.1 to 67.23 degrees. The other two equatorial angle changes their values in all the level of theory concerned. This also favors the conclusion that main geometric change took place in the equatorial plane during the anation process.

Properties of the transition state

Figure 4a and 4b depicts the Fukui functions (f^+), local softness(s) and the energy(E) of the incoming neucleophile (Cl^-) and leaving H_2O along the intrinsic reaction coordinates (IRC) connecting the reactant intermediates, the transition states (TS) and the product intermediates along the minimum energy path. Figure 4(b) depicts the Fukui functions (f^+), local softness(s) and the energy (E) of the solvolytic path (where both incoming and leaving groups are H_2O) along the intrinsic reaction coordinates (IRC) connecting the reactant intermediates, the transition states (TS) and the product intermediates along the minimum energy path. The optimized intermediates

were found by full optimization of I and II for both Figure 4a and 4b. The data are superimposed for clear clarification. The nucleophilicity gradually increases for Cl^- (Figure 4a) and H_2O (Figure 4b) and pass through the transition state with an inflection and reach the final level. This indicates that the reactivity depends on the nature and distances of other species present in the transition state (at zero IRC) and is not an absolute property. The reactivity of outgoing H_2O decreases with intrinsic reaction coordinate due to it's involvement in the bond breaking process for the nucleophilic path and ultimately attain a stable closed shell configuration. On the other hand, the reactivity of the chloride ion (Cl^-) increases, passes through the inflection point at IRC zero, due to the formation of Pt - Cl bond. In the transition state, the reactivates of Cl^- and H_2O are same; this implies that the system can proceed to either side on equal ease. The Fukui function of f_k^+ of H_2O and Cl^- coincides at the saddle point and this may be used to locate the transition state for a chemical reaction. This is also true for the solvolytic path.

Energy and activation parameters

The total energy (E) and Gibbs free energy (G) of the intermediate species and the transition state for both the neucleophilic and solvolytic paths are presented in Table 3 and 4. The enthalpy of activation ($\Delta H^{\neq}$) for the nucleophilic path and the entropy of activation ($\Delta S^{\neq}$) for the forward reaction on mPW1PW91 protocol with the general basis set are 54.27 kJ/mol and -37.6 J/K/mol. This is indicative of an associative interchange mechanism for the nucleophilic path (Basolo et al., 1967; Langford et al., 1966). The enthalpy of activation ($\Delta H^{\neq}$) for the nucleophilic path and the entropy of activation ($\Delta S^{\neq}$) for the forward reaction on mPW1PW91 protocol with the general basis set are 54.27 kJ/mol and -37.6 J/K/mol (Table 4 of supporting information). This is indicative of

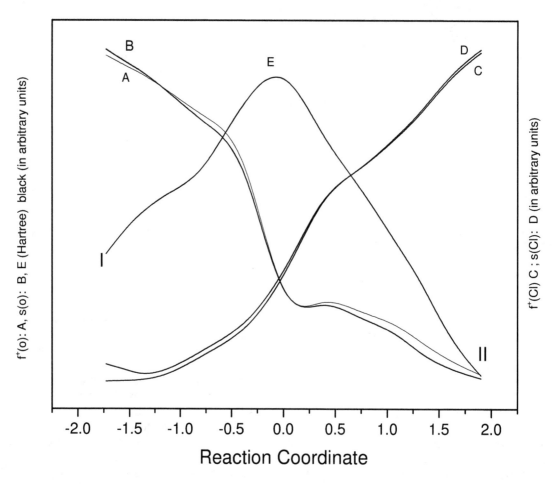

Figure 4a. Profiles of different local reactivity descriptor along the IRC in the nucleophilic path for the chloride anation reaction of $[Pt(dien)(H_2O)]^{2+}$

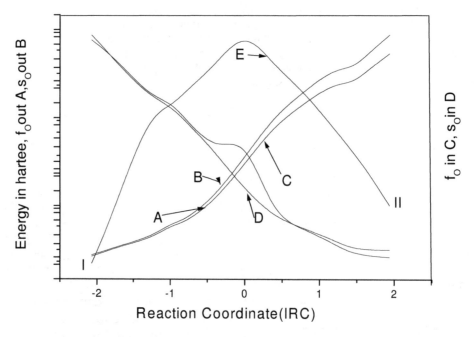

Figure 4b Profiles of different local reactivity descriptor along the IRC in the solvolytic path for the chloride anation reaction of $[Pt(dien)(H_2O)]^{2+}$

Table 3. Total energy (E) and Gibbs Free energy (G), in hartees for the reaction intermediates (**I1** and **I2**) and the transition state of the chloride anation reaction.

		HF	B3LYP	mPW1PW91
I1				
Gas	E	-976.003803	-980.135066	-980.075214
	G	-975.560991	-979.735922	-979.6707803
Onsager	E	-976.045542	-980.166970	-980.101179
	G	-975.605154	-979.764272	-979.696881
TS				
Gas	E	-975.996523	-980.122909	-980.063938
	G	-975.560592	-979.720418	-979.653715
Onsager	E	-976.010203	-980.134484	-980.080130
	G	-975.574876	-979.732079	-979.672822
I2				
Gas	E	-976.038423	-980.165328	-980.1066934
	G	-975.606128	-979.763986	979.700244
Onsager	E	-976.051024	-980.172893	-980.114938
	G	-975.617742	-979.771289	979.707968

Table 4. Total energy (E) and Gibbs free energy (G), in hartees for the reaction intermediates (**I1** and **I2**) and the transition state of the solvolytic reaction.

		HF	B3LYP	mPW1PW91
I1				
Onsager	E	-592.239186	-596.029187	-595.941891
	G	-591.755116	-595.575389	-595.482117
TS				
Onsager	E	-592.208894	-595.993239	-595.905521
	G	-591.726608	-595.543712	-595.449862
I2				
Onsager	E	-592.241316	-596.029098	-595.941859
	G	-591.752263	-595.575872	-595.486048

an associative interchange mechanism for the nucleophilic path.

For solvolytic path, the enthalpy of activation ($\Delta H^{\neq}$) and the entropy of activation ($\Delta S^{\neq}$) values are 82.08 kJ/mol and -8.73 J/K/mol respectively in mPW1PW91 protocol. In the B3LYP protocol, the values are 79.2685 kJ/mol and -12.82 J/K/mol respectively (Table 5 of supporting information). The small negative value for the solvolytic path is a characteristic of the self-exchange associative reaction where both the bond breaking and bond making at the transition state have been playing the important role (Wilkins, 1991).

The rate constants in gas phase for all the protocols are very high this is due to the electrostatic interaction of a bi-positive $[Pt(dien)(H_2O)_2]^{2+}$ ion with the uni-negative Cl^- ion in absence of any retarding force. All the bond lengths increase in Onsager model except the equatorial Pt–O bond of the distorted trigonal-bipyramid-like transition

state (**TS** in Figure 1). The changes in bond angle are less significant except the equatorial angle ($\angle$O-Pt-Cl 66.79° in mPW1PW91 protocol). The angle between the entering chloride ion (Cl^-) and the leaving H_2O is almost constant but the other two equatorial angles change their values in all the levels of theory concerned. This also favors the conclusion that main geometric change took place in the equatorial plane during the exchange process.

Conclusion

The extraordinary piece of experimental work of Grey et al. (1962) was experimentally solved after 27 years of the original work and in this paper; we revisited the same chloride anation reaction by *ab-initio* and two DFT methods. The existence of the associative solvolytic path

Table 5. Ratio of rate constants (k_2: k_1) for the nucleophilic path (k_2) and solvolytic path (k_1) are shown in different level of theory of protocol in SCRF (Onsager) model.

Forward reaction		HF	B3LYP	mPW1PW91	Calculated k_2/k_1	Expt k_2/k_1[*]
Onsager	k_2	7.33×10^{-2}	9.65×10^{-3}	20.69		$1:10^{-4} = 10000$
	k_1	18.24	4.47×10^{-2}	9.04×10^{-3}	1488.48 (mPW1PW91)	
					0.2158 (B3LYP)	
					0.004 (B3LYP)	
Reverse reaction						
Onsager	k_{-2}	1.18×10^{-7}	5.71×10^{-6}	3.92×10^{-4}		
	k_{-1}	10.35	1.009×10^{-2}	1.58×10^{-4}	2.48 (mPW1PW91)	
					5.7×10^{-4} (B3LYP)	
					1.1×10^{-8} (HF)	

a Reference Grey et al(1962)
Rate constants in sec^{-1}

and the ratio of nucleophilic and solvolytic rate constants (Table 5) are found to be comparable with the result of Marti et al. (1998).

ACKNOWLEDGMENTS

The author thanks the UGC, New Delhi for granting a minor Research Project No. F.PSW-108/06-07, (ERO Sl. No.82420). The author also thanks Dr. Parimal Kumar Das, Dr. T. Storr (Stanford) and Krisnendu Kundu (TIFR), for their cooperation. The author thanks CHEMCRAFT for their free internet version.

REFERENCES

Adamo C, Barone V (1998). Exchange Functionals with Improved Long-Range Behavior and Adiabatic Connection Methods without Adjustable Parameters: The mPW and mPW1PW Models, J. Chem. Phys., 108: 664–675.

Atwood JD (1997). Inorganic and organometallic Reaction mechanisms, 2nd edition, , p.49.

Basolo F, Pearson RG (1967). Mechanisms of inorganic reactions A Study of Metal Complexes in Solutions, John Wiely and Sons, Inc. 2nd edition, p.391.

Becke AD (1988). Density-Functional Exchange-Energy Approximation with Correct Asymptotic Behavior, Phys. Rev. A, 38: 3098–3100.

Becke AD (1993). Density-Functional Thermochemistry. III. The Role of Exact Exchange, J. Chem. Phys. 98: 5648–5652.

Becke AD A new dynamical correlation functional and implications for exact-exchange mixing, J. Chem. Phys. (1996) 104: 1040-1046.

Briton JF, Lock CJL, Pratt WMC (1982). The structures of chloro(diethylenetriamine)platinum(II) chloride and (diethylenetriamine)nitratoplatinum(II) nitrate and some comments on the existence of Pt^{II}-OH_2 and Pt^{II}-OH bonds in the solid state. Acta. Cryst 38: 2148-2155.

Carloni P, Sprik M, Andreoni W J (2000). Phys. Chem B. Structural and Energetic Study of cisplatin and derivatives: Comparison of the Performance of Density Functional Theory Implementations 104: 823-835.

Chattaraj PK Roy DR (2005). A Possible Union of Chemical Bonding, Reactivity, and Kinetics. J. Phys. Chem. A, 110 : 11401–11403.

Cotton FA, Wilkinson G, Murillo CA, Bochmann M (1999). Advanced Inorganic Chemistry Wiley, New York, p. 55

Ditchfield R, Hehre WJ (1971). Pople JA Self-Consistent Molecular-Orbital Methods. IX. An Extended Gaussian-Type Basis for Molecular-Orbital Studies of Organic Molecules, J. Chem. Phys. 54: 724-728

Foresman JB, Ortiz JV, Cui Q, Baboul AG, Clifford S (1996). Exploring chemistry with electronic structure methods, Gaussian, Inc. Pittsburgh, p. 70.

Frisch MJ, Trucks GW, Schlegel HB, Scuseria GE (2004). GAUSSIAN 03, Revision C.02, Gaussian, Inc., Wallingford CT,

Geerlings P, De Profit F (2003). Langenaeker W Computational Density Functional Theory Chem. Rev.103: 1793-1873

Gonzalez C, Schlegel HB (1989). An improved algorithm for reaction path following. J. Chem. Phys. 90: 2154-2161.

Gonzalez C, Schlegel HB (1990). Reaction path following in mass weighted internal coordinates. J. Phys. Chem., 94: 5523-5527

Gray HB, Olcott JR (1962). Kinetics of the reactions of diethylene tri-amineaquoplatinum(II). Inorg. Chem. 1: 481–485

Hay PJ, Wadt WR (1985). Ab-initio effective core potentials for molecular calculations. Potentials for K to Au including the outermost core orbitals. J. Chem. Phys. 82: 299-310.

Hehre WJ, Ditchfield R, Pople JA (1972). Self-Consistent Molecular-Orbital Methods. XII. Further Extensions of Gaussian-Type Basis Sets for Use in Molecular Orbital Studies of Organic Molecules, J Chem. Phys. 56: 2257-2261.

Langford C, Gray H (1966). Ligand Substition Processes, (Benjamin New Year,

Kotowski M, Palmer DA, Kelm H (1980). Kinetics of the anation of aquadiethylenetriamineplatinum(II) ions. Kotowski, M., Palmer, D.A., Inorg. Chim. Acta. pp. 113-114.

Lewars E (2003). Computational Chemistry, Kluwer Academic Publishers, p 431.

Marti M, Hoa GHB, KoZelka J (1998). Reversible hydrolysis of $[PtCl(dien)]^+$ and $[PtCl(NH_3)_3]^+$. Determination of the rate constants using UV spectrophotometry. Inorg. Chem. Communications. pp. 439-442

Michelle LS, Richard AJ, O'Hair W, McFadyen D, Lily TR, Holmes J, Robert WG (2000). Formation and gas phase fragmentation reactions of ligand substitution products of platinum (II) complexes via electrospray ionization tandem mass spectrometry. J. Chem. Soc. Dalton Trans pp. 93–99.

Onsager L (1936). Electric Moments of Molecules in Liquids J. Am. Chem. Soc. 58: 1486 -1493

Parr RG, Yang W (1989). Density functional Theory of atoms and molecules, Oxford University Press; pp 66- 96.

Perdew JP, Wang Y (1992). Accurate and Simple Analytic Representation of the Electron-Gas Correlation Energy, Phys. Rev B,). 45: 13244–13249

Perdew JP, Bruke K, Wang Y (1996). Generalized gradient approximation for the exchange-correlation hole of a many-electron system, Phys. Rev. B. 54: 16533 -16539.

Szabo A., Ostlund NS (1996). Modern Quantum Chemistry, 1st Edn, revised, McGraw-Hill
Publishing company, New York, p.127

Vosko SH, Wilk L, Nusair M (1980). Accurate Spin-Dependent Electron Liquid Correlation Energies for Local Spin Density Calculations: A Critical Analysis,Can. J. Phys. 58: 1200–1211.

Wadt WR, Hay PJ (1985). Ab-initio effective core potentials for molecular calculations. Potentials for main groups elements Na to Bi. J. Chem. Phys 82: 284 -298.

Wilkins RG (1991). Kinetics and Mechanism of Reactions of Transition Metal Complexes, VCH, Weinheim p.202

Wong MW, Wiberg KBM, Frisch J(1991). Solvent Effects. 1. The Mediation of Electrostatic Effects by Solvent. J. Am. Chem. Soc. 113: 4776-4782.

Wong MW, Wiberg KB (1992). Frisch M J Solvent Effects. 2. Medium Effect on the Structure, Energy, Charge Density, and Vibrational Frequencies of Sulfamic Acid. J. Am. Chem. Soc., 114: 523 - 529.

Wong MW, Wiberg KB (1991). Frisch MJ Hartree-Fock second derivatives and electric field properties in a solvent reaction field: Theory and application. J. Chem. Phys. 95: 8991-8998.

Wong MW, Wiberg KB, Frisch MJ (1992). Solvent Effects. 3. Tautomeric Equilibria of Formamide and 2-Pyridone in the Gas Phase and Solution. An ab Initio SCRF Study J. Am. Chem. Soc. 114: 1645 – 1652.

Wong E, Giandomenico CM (1999). Current status of platinum-based antitumor drugs. Chem Rev 99: 2451-2466.

Zeigler T (1995). The 1994 Alcan Award lecture Density Functional Theory as a practical tool in studies of organometallicenergatics and kinetics. Beating the the heavy metal blues with DFT. Can. J. Chem. 73: 743-760.

17

Analysis of structurally conserved atomic interactions in structural homologs of nicotinamide adenine dinucleotide binding dehydrogenases

P. S. Solanki[1], M. Krishna Mohan[1], P. Ghosh[1] and S. L. Kothari[2]

[1]Birla Institute of Scientific Research, Jaipur, India.
[2]Department of Botany, University of Rajasthan, Jaipur, India.

The stability of protein-ligand complex is decided by the strength of the forces and interaction that holds the overall structure. The binding of ligand to its receptor involves the participation of atomic interactions of key conserved amino acid residues which are essential for functional and structural integrity of protein molecule. Understanding the binding mechanism of ligand to its receptors is important in exploring the structure activity relationships of any protein. In the present study, a dataset of nicotinamide adenine dinucleotide (NAD) binding dehydrogenase was prepared by screening 19 structural homologues using the SCOP database to study the structurally conserved atomic interactions. An interaction profile of NAD against all structural homologues was determined using protein interaction analyzer and structure parser (PIASP) program and the structurally conserved atomic interactions were identified at 50% cut off level. We identified that out of 44 ligand atoms, only single interaction (ASP: O2B-OD1) was 100% conserved throughout the family members. Thus, it is clear from this study that ligand implements varying degree of orientation for binding with receptor molecule. However, there are certain critical amino acid residues that remain conserved throughout the family and participated in all orientations. However, the interaction of aspartate protease (ASP) residue is critical to the active site of selected protein family. This residue, which is common in active site of all the chosen structures, is found to be structurally conserved throughout the family.

Key words: Structurally conserved atomic interaction, conserved residues, protein interaction analyzer and structure parser (PIASP).

INTRODUCTION

Knowing the structures of biological macromolecules is always useful for predicting, interpreting, modifying, and designing their function. The aim of the structural genomics project is to deliver structural information about most proteins. It is not feasible to determine the structure of all proteins by experiment; useful models can be obtained by fold assignment and comparative modeling of those protein sequences that are related to at least one known protein structure. Since each enzyme is specific in their action, the active site of enzyme is structurally a very important part of the proteins, as it determines the binding proficiency of a protein. In all the members of a given protein family, the residues which forms the active site should remain conserved, however, not necessarily that all the residues should participate in binding. It was observed that few of them play a crucial role in binding with the ligand (Kasinos et al., 1992).

The Protein Data Bank (PDB) is the most important database with structural information of biological macromolecules, with over 77,000 protein structures. The majority of structures in PDB are resolved either through X-ray crystallography or NMR imaging techniques (Frances et al., 1977; Helen et al., 2000, 2004). X-ray crystallography enables details of covalent and non covalent interactions to be analyzed quantitatively in three dimensions, thus providing the basis for the understanding of binding of ligands to proteins (Palmer and Niwa, 2003). The PDB file of any biological complex contains diversified information in the form of record types exhibiting various attributes of protein structure such as atomic coordinates, protein sequence, secondary structural information, experimental remarks. Based upon the structural data, several tools have been developed to analyze protein-ligand interactions such as PLID (Reddy et al., 2008), LigBase (Stuart et al., 2002), 3DinSight (Jianghong et al., 1998), SitesBase (Nicola et al., 2006), ConSurf (Haim et al., 2010), PDB-Ligand (Jae-Min, 2005), ProLINT (Kitajima et al., 2002), LIGPLOT program (Wallace et al., 1995), and CKAAPs DB (Wilfred et al., 2002), but none them provides the information on structurally conserved atomic interactions at family level.

The formation of biological complex is fundamental to biological process and functionality of enzymes. The major manipulation may disrupt the functionality of molecules. But to understand the mechanism of molecular recognition between the receptors and ligand, manipulation of complexes is essential for studies on protein engineering and has many applications such as engineered enzymes, biosensors, genetic circuit, signal transduction pathways and chiral separations (Loren et al., 2003). The receptor-ligand interaction is very crucial in determining the functionality of given molecular complex, thus it has always attracted the attention of researchers. It is well known that the functional specificity of protein molecules is due to the structural conservation of three-dimensional structure and the amino acid residues present on surface which participates in catalytic activity. The conformational stability of receptor-ligand complex is governed by the strength of the forces and interactions that holds the overall structure. Among these interactions, H-bonding interaction acting upon the interacting atoms such as Donor-Donor and Donor-Receptor plays a key role in maintaining the structural integrity (Branden and Tooze, 1991).

Structure of NAD binding dehydrogenases

Dehydrogenase family is one of the most studied protein family, and has always been a good model system for carrying out research in structural bioinformatics. Primary sequence comparison has indicated that there is an evolutionary relation between many dehydrogenases. The first ever isolated alcohol dehydrogenase (ADH) was purified in 1937 from *Saccharomyces cerevisiae* (Negelein and Wulff, 1937). The dehydrogenases catalyze the oxidation of alcohol to the carbonyl compound or aldehydes. They utilize the coenzyme called nicotinamide adenine dinucleotide (NAD) for their action and this coenzyme participate in the dehydrogenation reaction (Zhi-Jie et al., 1997). The X-ray crystallographic

structure of dehydrogenases shown that it consist of two domains, namely the nucleotide-binding domain and the catalytic domain, the first domain play a role in binding the coenzyme, often NAD, and the second domain play a role in binding the substrate. Since the catalytic domain involves in catalysis it is variable in nature and depends upon the substrate specificity and contain amino acid involving in catalysis (Benyajati et al., 1981). Little sequence similarity has been found in the coenzyme-binding domain although there is a large degree of structural similarity, and it has therefore been suggested that structure of dehydrogenase has arisen through gene fusion of ancestral coenzyme nucleotide sequence with various substrate specific domain. The nucleotide-binding domain is formed from the similar overall folding of the polypeptide chain for all the dehydrogenases. The detailed geometry of this domain varies considerably from one enzyme to another. The nucleotide-binding domain composed of six strands of parallel beta sheet with parallel helix running anti-parallel to the sheet. The dehydrogenases family composed of different members based on their substrate specificity but all the members have similar nucleotide binding domain. For the present investigation only those proteins that possess NAD^+ binding specificity have been chosen.

Binding site analysis

Characterization of a protein function and understanding the specific nature of a proteins binding as a critical part of both protein engineering and structure based drug discovery. Binding site analysis combines several tools that enable you to identify and characterize a protein-binding site and then use those characteristics to the similar features in other proteins of known structures. Active sites are usually identified through homology with another protein or from biochemical data, but identification by this method is not always possible. Binding site analysis identifies functionally important residues by sequence variation across a family. This information can then help you modify or design drug that target such residues. The numerous successes of structural biology have shown that three-dimensional structure of the proteins adds vital information and insight into understanding a protein function are often found by mapping the result of protein sequence analysis onto a known protein structure with known function. The amino acids in the active site are near in space but not necessarily sequentially close to one another. The active site finding tools in binding site analysis allows us to search for crevices that are large enough to bind a ligand.

The importance of hydrogen bonding

The importance of H-bonding for the structure and function

Table 1. Represents dataset of dehydrogenase structural family (based upon SCOP database).

Enzyme name	No of structures	PDB-ID
Fatty oxidation complex alpha subunit	4	1WDK, 1WDL, 1WDM, 2D3T
GDP-mannose 6-dehydrogenase	2	1MUU, 1MV8
L-3-hydroxyacyl CoA dehydrogenase	8	1F0Y, 1TL0, 1LSJ, 1LSO, 1M75, 1M76, 3HAD, 3HDH
Mannitol 2-dehydrogenase	2	1LJ8, 1M2W
Prephenate dehydrogenase TyrA	2	2G5C, 2PV7
UDP glucose dehydrogenase	1	1DLI

of biomacromolecules has been demonstrated by extensive statistical, experimental and theoretical studies (Legon and Millen, 1992; Buckingham et al., 1988; Baker and Hubbard, 1984; Ippolito et al., 1990; McDonald and Thornton, 1994; Subbarao and Haneef, 1991). The detailed attribution of binding free energy has demonstrated the intrinsic importance of interaction; H-bonding to the detailed mechanisms of binding specificity, stabilization of antibody-antigen and protease-inhibitor complexes in solution (Fersht et al., 1985; Serrano et al., 1993). Although the resolution of the X-ray data is probably not sufficient to establish the complete interfacial H-bond system of protein complexes with absolute certainty (Morris et al., 1992), a significance number of interfacial hydrogen bonds with good distance and angular geometry for interaction, can reasonably be assumed to be formed in the crystal structures of the protease-inhibitor and antibody-antigen complexes within the PDB forming 8 to 13 and an average of ten hydrogen bonds between the docking surfaces. Moreover, only a few of the donor/acceptor atoms involved in these intermolecular interactions are capable of forming intramolecular hydrogen bonds suggesting their principal role is one of functional recognition. By comparison however, the subunit interfaces of oligomeric proteins form far fewer hydrogen bonds in proportion to the docking surface areas, some examples forming none. The majority of interfacial hydrogen bonds between oligomeric subunits involve charged donor or acceptor groups, which should make a significant contribution to the subunit interactions (Janin et al., 1988). The energy of Hydrogen bonding interaction depends critically on the donor-acceptor spatial separation and line of approach of the donor hydrogen to the acceptor lone pairs. Other factors such as specific environment of individual H-bonds and specific arrangement of an interfacial hydrogen bond system have also been demonstrated to be major determinants in the overall hydrogen bond stabilization of protein complexes (Smith-Gill et al., 1982; Fersht et al., 1985). On the basis of the physical nature of the H-bond, the interacting donor and acceptor sites of a protein complex intermolecular hydrogen bonding system are required to have a certain degree of spatial and directional complementarities. A graph theoretic method has been reported for the search of small ligand-protein hydrogen bonding sites based upon graph clique finding

(Subbarao and Haneef, 1991; Smellie et al., 1991). However, the computational time required for clique finding between two large proteins would be prohibitively long. A minimum of two potential intermolecular hydrogen bonds in the complex is required for the prediction of relative orientations of the components.

The present work focuses on analysis of binding sites of NAD in dehydrogenases for identifying the structurally conserved H-bonding interactions. This will help us to find out whether the active site is conserved or not, if conserved then what are the critical residues which are important in binding of NAD with protein. We can also find the superposability of the H-bond interaction in any given pair of binding sites in two different proteins. It will also help us to analyze whether the NAD binds in the same orientation in all the active sites or it binds differently in specific set of protein.

MATERIALS AND METHODS

There are large numbers of PDB structures available in the Brooke heavens protein data bank that utilizes NAD as a coenzyme. Since dehydrogenases binding to NAD are most commonly studied complexes, it will be interesting to analyze the active site of NAD binding regions for their structural conservation. NAD being the common ligand in these complexes and its H-bonding interactions can be calculated and analyze structurally conserved interactions.

Dataset preparation

In order to understand the behavior of interaction specificity in protein-ligand complexes of a family, NAD binding dehydrogenases family from SCOP database (Andreeva et al., 2004; Murzin et al., 1995) was selected. The family was 6-phosphogluconate dehydrogenase-like, N-terminal domain [51868]. The family attributes are: beta-sheet is extended to 8 strands, order 32145678, strands 7 and 8 are anti parallel to the rest. The six enzymes (Table 1) from the family carrying NAD as a cofactor were selected and all structural homologs were downloaded from Protein Data Bank. Finally, the dataset comprises 19 structural members of NAD binding dehydrogenases Figure 1.

Definition of hydrogen bond donors and acceptors

The following definition of H-bond donors and acceptors has been used for different atom types. The hydrogen bonding donor and acceptor groups at physiological pH are given in Table 2.

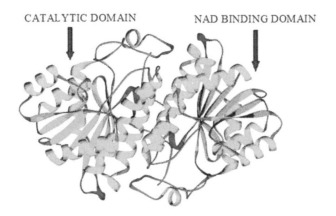

Figure 1. Structure representing catalytic and NAD binding domain of dehydrogenases family.

Table 2. Hydrogen bond donors and acceptors (Torshin et al., 2002; Subbarao and Haneef, 1991).

Donors
(1) N (main-chain N-H)
(2) Asn OD1, His NF2, His ND1, Lys NZ, Asn ND2, Gln NE2, Arg NH1, Arg NH2, Ser OG, Thr OG, Tyr OH, Trp NE1.
Acceptors
(1) O (main-chain C = O)
(2) Asp OD1, Asp OD2, Glu OE2, Glu OE1, His ND1, Asn OD1, Gln NE2, Asn ND2, Ser OG, Thr OG1, Tyr OH

Note: The names are corresponding to PDB id code.

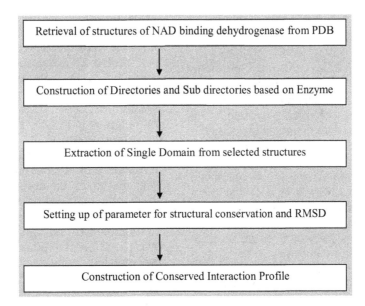

Figure 2. Flowchart of methodology of PIASP.

Analysis of interaction specificity

The analysis of protein-ligand complexes of NAD binding dehydrogenases was performed using in-house developed program, PIASP, stands for Protein Interaction Analyzer and Structure Parser. PIASP is a web based tool for mining protein-ligand interactions at atomic level. Flowchart of methodology implemented in PIASP is shown in Figure 2. It provides the complete interaction profile of all ligand atoms to its receptor and identifies interaction specificity in all structural homologs. It reports

Table 3. Structurally conserved atomic interactions. Cut-off for structural conservation is 50% and for atomic distance is 3.5 Angstrom. The row in red color indicates the 100% structural conserved of atomic interaction.

Number	Ligand atom	Residue name	Residue atom	Percentage (%)
1	O2A	GLY	CA	63.16
2	O4D	ASN	ND2	52.63
3	O3B	ASP	OD2	89.47
4	O2D	GLU	CD	63.16
5	O2D	GLU	OE2	63.16
6	O5B	GLY	CA	68.42
7	O3D	LYS	NZ	52.63
8	O2B	ASP	OD1	100.00
9	O2B	ASP	CG	57.89

the all conserved interactions essential for Receptor ligand interaction. In addition, PIASP has equipped with various utilities which are very useful for any researcher working on protein-ligand interactions. This tool enhances our understanding of protein ligand interaction at atomic interaction level and could be a great help when designing compounds for molecular docking like drugs. PIASP can be accessed from BISR website (http://bisr.res.in/cgi-bin/project/piasp/index.cgi).

All the selected structures were downloaded from PDB and categorized into name based classes for PIASP analysis. The single domain extracted using PIASP was further confirmed using Discovery Studio software from Accelrys Incorporation. The default parameters of structural conservation (that is, 70%) and RMSD (3.5 Angstrom) were chosen for analysis. Based upon the interaction profile of all NAD atoms, it constructs the result table for Structurally Conserved Atomic Interactions (Table 3).

RESULTS AND DISCUSSION

For decades, lot of research work has been done on catalytic mechanism of enzymes and on their binding strategies. The protein-ligand interaction is very crucial in determining the functionality of given protein. The interaction of ligand to its receptors molecule involves the participation of few atoms and the binding strategy is very important in understanding the mechanism of enzyme action. The present work focuses on nicotinamide adenine dinucleotide (NAD), which is one of the most commonly used organic cofactor in living cells, essential for many metabolic processes. Many NAD binding proteins which are responsible for variety of activities in cellular environment have been discovered. The binding of NAD to its receptor proteins is very specific and crucial for its activity. Thus, how NAD binds to various kinds of receptor protein is important to understanding the mechanism of enzyme action.

We investigated the interaction specificity of ligand, NAD, to the active site of its receptors (NAD binding dehydrogenases) using the in-house developed PIASP program. The structural homologues of NAD binding family of dehydrogenases were selected from SCOP database and all respective structure files were downloaded from the Protein Data Bank. The interaction profile of NAD against all the structural members was built at cutoff distance of 3.5Angstrom and structural Conservation of 50% (Table 3). The interaction profile at family level was generated successfully which represents the interaction of each of the ligand atom against atom of amino acid residues at the set parameter.

The interaction profile shows the strategy adopted by 44 atoms of NAD for interacting with the various atoms of receptor molecules. This profile shows the interaction of particular ligand atom with residual atom based upon the cutoff distance, so it becomes very clear how many atoms of ligands are participating in the binding. It was found that specific atom type of ligand behaves in different manner in different structures.

Based upon the interaction profile, a table of structurally conserved atomic interaction was generated in PIASP. We calculated structural conservation at 50% level (Table 3). It is obvious from the table that out of 44 atoms of NAD there were very few atoms found to participate in interaction with the atoms of amino acid residues of receptor molecule. It is clear from the table that interaction of O2B atom of NAD is 100% structurally conserved with OD1 (ASP) atom in all structural members of the family. Besides, there were few more interactions of NAD atoms (that is, O3B and O5B) which were found to be conserved at 50% level. From the structurally conserved table (Table 3), it may be inferred that the binding of NAD atoms was not exactly identical in all members of the family. NAD binds in different orientation in different structure. No two structures have shown the identical pattern of atomic interaction. Thus, this analysis shows that the binding of ligand to its receptor is very specific and depends upon the geometry of the active site pocket of receptor.

Conclusion

In the present research work, NAD binding protein families have been studied to understand the behavior of interaction specificity of NAD ligand against the structural homologs of dehydrogenases family. It is clear from the result obtained that different proteins have different binding specificity but there are few atoms of NAD, which participate in binding in all the structures. From interaction profile of NAD, it was clear that out of 44 atoms; only one atomic interaction was 100% structurally conserved throughout the family. The amino acid residue (ASP) is critical to the active site of selected protein family. This residue, which is common in active site of all the chosen structures, is found to be structurally conserved throughout the family. In active sites of all the family, it will present at specific position and also structurally conserved not only in the confined active sites but also in the entire molecular structure, when they are aligned pair wise.

Thus, it can be concluded that ligand implements varying degree of orientation for binding with receptor molecule. However, there were certain critical amino acid residues that remain conserved throughout the family and participated in all orientations.

ACKNOWLEDGEMENT

We are thankful to BTIS Centre funded by Department of Biotechnology, Government of India for providing infrastructure facilities at Birla Institute of Scientific Research, Jaipur.

REFERENCES

Andreeva A, Howorth D, Brenner SE, Hubbard TJP, Chothia C, Murzin AG (2004). SCOP database in 2004: refinements integrate structure and sequence family data, Nucleic Acids Research, 32:226-229.

Benyajati C, Place AR, Powers DA, Sofer W (1981). Alcohol dehydrogenase gene of Drosophila melanogaster: relationship of intervening sequences to functional domains in the protein. Proc. Natl. Acad. Sci. U.S.A., 78(5): 2717–2721.

Branden C, Tooze J (1991). Introduction to Protein Structure. Garland Publishing inc, New York and London.

Fersht AR, Shi JP, Knill-Jones J, Lowe DM, Wilkinson AJ, Blow DM, Brick P, Carter P, Waye MM, Winter G (1985). Hydrogen bonding and biological specificity analysed by protein engineering. Nature, 314(6008):235-8.

Haim A, Elana E, Eric M, Tal P, Nir B (2010). ConSurf 2010: calculating evolutionary conservation in sequence and structure of proteins and nucleic acids. Nucleic Acids Research, 38: W529–W533.

Ippolito JA, Alexander RS, Christianson DW (1990). Hydrogen bond stereochemistry in protein structure and function, J. Mol. Biol., 215(3):457-71.

Jae-Min S (2005). PDB-Ligand: a ligand database based on PDB for the automated and customized classification of ligand-binding structures. Nucleic Acids Research, 33:238-241.

Janin J, Miller S, Chothia C (1988). Surface, subunit interfaces and interior of oligomeric proteins. J. Mol. Biol., 204(1):155-64.

Jianghong A, Takao N, Yasushi K, Akinori S (1998). 3DinSight: an integrated relational database and search tool for the structure, function and properties of biomolecules, Bioinformatics, 14(2):188-195.

Kasinos N, Lilley GA, Subbarao N, Haneef I (1992). A robust and efficient automated docking algorithm for molecular recognition. Protein Eng., 5(1):69-75.

Kitajima K, Shandar A, Samuel S, Hideo K, Shinji S, Jianghong A, Akinori S (2002). Development of a Protein-Ligand Interaction Database, ProLINT and Its Application to QSAR Analysis. Genome Informatics, 13:498-499.

Loren LL, Dwyer MA, Smith JJ, Hellinga HW (2003).Computational design of receptor and sensor proteins with novel functions. Nature, 423:185-190.

McDonald IK, Thornton JM (1994), Satisfying Hydrogen Bonding Potential in Proteins, J. Mol. Biol., 238:777-793.

Morris AS, Thanki N, Goodfellow JM (1992). Hydration of amino acid side chains: dependence on secondary structure. Protein Eng., 5(8):717-28.

Murzin AG, Brenner SE, Hubbard T, Chothia C (1995). SCOP: a structural classification of proteins database for the investigation of sequences and structures. J. Mo.l Biol., 247(4):536-540.

Nicola DG, Richard MJ (2006). SitesBase: a database for structure-based protein–ligand binding site comparisons. Nucleic Acids Research, 34:231-234.

Reddy AS, Amarnath HS, Bapi RS, Sastry GM, Sastry GN (2008). Protein ligand interaction database (PLID). Comput. Biol. Chem., 32(5):387-90.

Serrano L, Day AG, Fersht AR (1993). Step-wise mutation of barnase to binase. A procedure for engineering increased stability of proteins and an experimental analysis of the evolution of protein stability. J. Mol. Biol., 233(2):305-12.

Smellie AS, Crippen GM, Richards WG (1991). Fast drug-receptor mapping by site-directed distances: a novel method of predicting new pharmacological leads. J. Chem. Inf. Comput. Sci., 31(3):386-92.

Smith-Gill SJ, Wilson AC, Potter M, Prager EM, Feldmann RJ, Mainhart CR (1982). Mapping the antigenic epitope for a monoclonal antibody against lysozyme. J. Immunol., 128(1):314-22.

Stuart AC, Ilyin VA, Sali A (2002). LigBase: a database of families of aligned ligand binding sites in known protein sequences and structures. Bioinformatics, 18(1):200-201.

Subbarao N, Haneef I (1991). Defining topological equivalences in macromolecules. Protein Eng., 4(8):877-84.

Wallace AC, Laskowski RA, Thornton JM (1995). LIGPLOT: a program to generate schematic diagrams of protein-ligand interactions. Protein Eng., 8(2): 127-134.

Wilfred WL, Boojala VBR, John GT, Ilya NS, Philip EB (2002). CKAAPsDB: a Conserved Key Amino Acid Positions DataBase. Nucleic Acids Res., 30(1):409-411.

Zhi-Jie L, Yuh-Ju S, John R, Yong-Je C, Chwan-Deng H, Wen-Rui C, Ingrid K, John P, Ronald L, John H, Bi-Cheng W (1997). The first structure of an aldehyde dehydrogenase reveals novel interactions between NAD and the Rossmann fold, Nat. Struct. Biol., 4:317-326.

18

Establishment of rice yield prediction model using canopy reflectance

K. W. Chang

Department of Leisure and Recreation Studies, Aletheia University, Tainan, 721, Taiwan, Republic of China.
E-mail: ckw550320@gmail.com.

The major objectives of this study were to identify spectral characteristics associated with rice yield and to establish their quantitative relationships. Field experiments were conducted at Shi-Ko experimental farm of TARI's Chiayi Station, during 2001 to 2005. Rice cultivar Tainung 67 (*Oryza sativa* L.), the major cultivar grown in Taiwan, was used in the study. Various levels of rice yield were obtained via nitrogen application treatments. Canopy reflectance spectra were measured during entire growth period and dynamic changes of characteristic spectrum were analyzed. Relationships among rice yields and characteristic spectrum were studied to establish yield estimation models suitable for remote sensing purposes. Spectrum analysis indicated that the changes of canopy reflectance spectrum were least during booting stages. Therefore, the canopy reflectance spectra during this period were selected for model development. Two multiple regression models, constituting of band ratios (NIR/RED and NIR/GRN) were then constructed to estimate rice yields for first and second crops separately. Results of the validation experiments indicated that the derived regression equations successfully predicted rice yield using canopy reflectance measured at booting stage unless other severe stresses occurred afterward.

Key words: Rice yield, canopy reflectance, prediction model.

INTRODUCTION

Yield maps are the basis of making precision management decisions. Through accumulated yield maps during past seasons, maps for field management can be produced. Regions always having higher or lower yields can be easily delineated, which can be very useful for diagnosing the causes responsible for low yield. Proper management strategies can then be applied. Where available, remotely sensed images showing spatial and spectral variations resulting from soil and crop characteristics are important source of data for making yield maps (NRC, 1997). A remote sensed yield map would not be affected by the inaccuracies (problems connected with grain flow dynamics and accurate logging of geographic position) associated with combine yield monitors, as suggested by Lark et al. (1997) and Arslan and Colvin (1999). However, difficulty results from a lack of valid regression models to convert imagery spectral information to a yield map.

Rice is one of the world's major staple foods, and paddy rice fields account for approximately 15% of the world's arable land (IRRI, 1993). Remote sensing data can acquire temporal, large spatial and vast spectrum data and also track the past data. Remote sensing, which quantitatively measures the light reflected from the surface of the earth, is a powerful tool for studying regional-scale ecosystem dynamics. So, remote sensing techniques have the potential to provide information on agricultural crops quantitatively, instantaneously and non-destructively over large areas. Ability to estimate rice yields within fields from remote sensing images is not only fundamental to applications of precision agriculture, but can also be very useful to governmental administrators for food provisions management. Though many researches have been devoted to rice planting acreage estimation (Leblon et al., 1991; Prince, 1991; Bouman, 1992; Wiegand et al., 1992; Field et al., 1995; Clevers and Leeuwen, 1996; Bach, 1998; Moulin et al., 1998; Reynolds et al., 2000; Serrano et al., 2000), few studies have been conducted attempting to relate canopy reflectance spectra measurements to grain yields. Basic

Table 1. Analysis of variance for rice yield at four nitrogen application rates (0, 45, 90, 180 kg N ha^{-1}) and five years (2001 to 2005).

Sources of variation	df	Mean squares	Pr
Year (Y)	4	4.19026276	<0.0001
Nitrogen rate (N)	3	7.00343400	<0.0001
Y × N	12	0.58496987	0.2310

studies regarding the timing of reflectance measurements and regression models for rice yield prediction/estimation are still very lacking. Our objectives were thus to collect the reflectance spectrum of rice canopies, to identify spectral characteristics associated with rice yield, and to establish their quantitative relationships.

MATERIALS AND METHODS

Study site and experimental treatments

The study was conducted at Shi-Ko experimental farm of TARI's Chiayi Station (23°35'4" N, 120°24' E) during 2001 to 2005 growing seasons. The soil at this site is a silt clay loam (mixed hyperthermic Haplaquepts). Rice cultivar Tainung 67 (*O. sativa* L.), the major cultivar grown in Taiwan, was used in the study. Different nitrogen levels, 0, 45, 90, 180 kg N ha^{-1}, were used in each year to affect rice yield. Field plots were shifted every year to other well-fertilized production fields to avoid any residue fertilizer effect from the previous year. The plots in each year were all arranged in randomized complete block design with three replications. Individual plot dimensions were at least 10 m × 10 m.

The rice was grown under conventional two-season cropping system. Three-leaf old rice seedlings were transplanted in early February for first season crop, and in early July for second season crop. Transplanting density was 0.15 m by 0.25 m with three plants per hill. Other than nitrogen, all plots were fertilized with 150 kg P$_2$O$_5$ ha^{-1} and 150 kg K$_2$O ha^{-1} at the time of transplanting as the basal dose. The nitrogen fertilizer, fractionated as three quotas, were applied as basal at transplanting, and top-dressed at active tillering and panicle initiation stages, respectively. In-season weed and pest controls were practiced according to regional recommendations.

Canopy reflectance measurement

Canopy reflectance spectra were measured during entire growth period of each cropping season using a portable spectroradiometer (LI-1800, LICOR) with remote cosine receptor (LI-1800-02, LICOR) attached to a 1.5 m extension arm. The arm was held 1 m above the canopy; at this height, a target area of 1 m-radius may have occupied 80% of the view. The man holding the extension arm always wore dark clothes and stands sideways to reduce measurement error. All the measurements were made near midday, within 2 h ± solar noon. Incident and reflected solar radiations were measured by facing the remote cosine receptor upward and downward, respectively. The measurements were taken over the wavelength range from 400 to 1100 nm at a scanning interval of 10 nm and executed consecutively three times per subplot to reduce the possible effect of changing sky conditions. The reflectance of canopies was then calculated from the mean of three repetitions.

Incremental values of spectral reflectance were averaged within 0.45 to 0.52 µm, 0.52 to 0.60 µm, 0.63 to 0.69 µm, and 0.76 to 0.90 µm to give, respectively, values of blue (BLU), green (GRN), red (RED), and near-infrared (NIR) bands of reflectance. Two normalized difference vegetation indices (NDVI and GNDVI) and two ratio vegetation indices (NIR/GRN and NIR/RED) were then calculated. The dynamic changes of these four vegetation indices during growing season were analyzed for each treatment at different year and crop season. The indices and timing best for yield prediction model development were then selected accordingly.

Grain yield estimation

At maturity, grain yield was estimated by hand harvesting three 1 m × 1 m area of each subplot. After threshing, fully filled grains sieved by wind selection were sun dried. After drying, grain yield per subplot was weighted and adjusted to a constant moisture basis of 13.5% water. Grain yield, vegetation index, year, and season were analyzed via ANOVA with a mixed model (Statistica Ver. 6, StatSoft, 2001).

Establishment and validation of rice yield prediction models

Rice yield prediction models were established by regression analysis of relationships between grain yields, spectral reflectance and vegetation indices using the General Linear Models procedure. Independent data of canopy reflectance at booting stage and grain yield from different nitrogen rate experiments conducted also at Shi-Ko experimental farm on the two crop growing seasons during 2002 to 2005. The experimental design of the nitrogen experiments, with levels of 0, 45, 90, 180 kg N ha^{-1}, was similar to those described earlier.

In this study, validation of rice yields prediction models was carried out using cross validation method. We judged the model fitting abilities with coefficients of determination (R^2) and root mean squared error of cross validation (RMSECV). Finally, we will conduct the model diagnostics with scatter plots and residual plots (Neter et al., 1999).

RESULTS AND DISCUSSION

The ground truth data of rice yield

The main effects of N rate and the interaction between N rate and year were statistically significant for yield (Table 1). Yields were also significantly different among the years and crop seasons. These results indicated that rice yield variability was not only affected by the amount of applied N fertilizers but also by the differences in climatic conditions between the years and crop seasons.

The features of rice canopy reflectance

Typical temporal changes of rice canopy reflectance spectra during first crop season were shown in Figure 1. Three weeks after transplanting, rice seedlings were just recovering from damages induced by transplanting. At this time, percent ground cover was less than 15%. Values of reflectance in the visible region were only slightly lower than those in the near-infrared region

Table 2. The results of RMSECV and R^2 for rice yield prediction models using different band of spectral reflectance.

First order linear models	RMSECV	R^2
BLUE	1.073	0.059
GRN	1.103	0.002
RED	1.023	0.130
NIR	0.886	0.336
BLUE GRN	1.077	0.062
BLUE RED	0.982	0.199
BLUE NIR	0.791	0.474
GRN RED	0.974	0.208
GRN NIR	0.684	0.605
RED NIR	0.742	0.535
BLUE GRN RED	0.945	0.261
BLUE GRN NIR	0.698	0.591
BLUE RED NIR	0.742	0.538
GRN RED NIR	0.695	0.592
BLUE GRN RED NIR	0.702	0.586

Table 3. The results of RMSECV and R^2 for rice yield prediction models by vegetation index.

First order linear models	RMSECV	R^2
NDVI	0.702	0.582
GNDVI	0.679	0.610
SR	0.710	0.573
NIR/GRN	0.705	0.580
NDVI GNDVI	0.688	0.601
NDVI SR	0.709	0.575
NDVI NIR/GRN	0.702	0.586
GNDVI SR	0.687	0.602
GNDVI NIR/GRN	0.718	0.570
SR NIR/GRN	0.712	0.573
NDVI GNDVI SR	0.703	0.585
NDVI GNDVI NIR/GRN	0.725	0.564
NDVI SR NIR/GRN	0.708	0.580
GNDVI SR NIR/GRN	0.727	0.562
NDVI GNDVI SR NIR/GRN	0.738	0.551

because underlying water and soil contributed most to the measured canopy reflectance spectrum. As rice plants grew, contribution from the plants gradually increased. At active tillering stage, six weeks and nine weeks after transplanting, tiller number and leaf area increased much more rapidly at rate about 1.3 tillers per day. Accordingly, reflectance in near-infrared region increased rapidly as a result of increased light scattering by leaves and stems. However, the reflectance in the visible region decreased due to absorption by pigments, chlorophyll in particular. About 12 weeks after transplanting, reflectance in the near-infrared region reached the highest value of the

season while reflectance in visible portion reached lowest value. At later stages, yellowing and wilting of rice plants gradually appeared. Therefore, reflectance in visible region increased as a result of decreasing chlorophyll concentration but reflectance in near infrared region decreased due to wilting, the exposing of soil background.

The rice yield prediction models

In this study, the rice yield prediction models were made using rice yields as dependent variable and different bands of spectral reflectance, band ratios and vegetation indexes as independent variables. After establishment of rice yield prediction models, we used RMSECV and R^2 values as criticism to judge the fitting abilities of models through cross validation.

Table 2 is the results of RMSECV and R^2 for rice yield prediction models using different band of spectral reflectance. From Table 2, we find that the simple regression models with BLUE, GRN, RED and NIR as independent variable have higher RMSECV values and lower R^2 values. So, the fitting abilities of these models are poor and not suitable for predicting rice yields. But the multiple regression models with GRN and NIR as independent variable have lower RMSECV values and higher R^2 values which fitting ability are well and suitable for predicting rice yields. Other multiple regression models with three or four independent variables have lower RMSECV values and higher R^2 values, their fitting abilities are most well and suitable for predicting rice yields.

Table 3 is the results of RMSECV and R^2 for rice yield prediction models by vegetation index (NDVI, GNDVI, SRVI and GRVI). From Table 3, we can clearly find that the simple regression models with vegetation indexes as independent variable have lower RMSECV and higher R^2 values than those of the simple regression models with different bands of spectral reflectance as independent variable. So, the fitting abilities of these models with vegetation indexes as independent variable are better and suitable for predicting rice yields than those models with different bands of spectral reflectance as independent variable. In all first order linear models, the model with GNDVI as independent variable has the lowest RMSECV and the highest R^2 values than others which is the best rice yield prediction model.

Diagnostics of rice yield prediction models

When a regression model is considered for an application, we can usually not be certain in advance that the model is appropriate for that application. Any one, or several, of the features of the model, such as linearity of the regression function or normality of the error terms, may not be appropriate for the particular data at hand. Hence, it is important to examine the aptness of the model for the data before inferences based on that model are

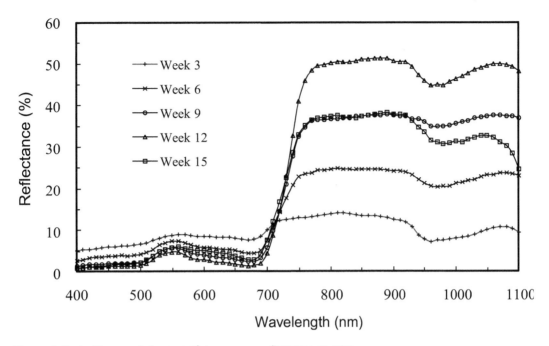

Figure 1. Typical temporal changes of rice canopy reflectance spectra.

undertaken.

Figure 2 is the plots of actual and predicted values of yield in first order linear models using BLUE, GRN, RED, and NIR as independent variable. From Figure 2, it is shown that the simple regression models with BLUE, GRN, and RED as independent variable appeared over or under estimation, but the model with NIR as independent variable has better performance. For multiple regression models, those performances are better than simple regression models. In general, multiple regression models with different bands of spectral reflectance as independent variables do not appear over or under estimation situation except those with BLUE and GRN, BLUE and RED, GRN and RED as independent variables.

Figure 3 is the plots of actual and predicted values of yield in linear models using vegetation indexes (NDVI, GNDVI, SRVI, GRVI, NDVI and GNDVI, NDVI and SRVI) as independent variables. From Figure 3, it is shown that the rice yield prediction models with vegetation indexes as independent variables do not appear serious over or under estimation situation.

Direct diagnostic plots for the response variable Y are ordinarily not too useful in regression analysis because the values of the observations on the response variable are a function of the level of the predictor variable. Instead, diagnostics for the response variable are usually carried out indirectly through an examination of the residuals. When a linear regression model is appropriate, the residuals fall within a horizontal band centered on 0, displaying no systematic tendencies to be positive and negative.

Figure 4 is the scatter plots of residual and actual value of yield in first order linear models using BLUE, GRN, RED, and NIR band values as independent variables. The simple regression models with BLUE, GRN, and RED as independent variable show declination situation of different levels between residual and actual value of yield from Figure 4, but the model with NIR as independent variable has better performance. For multiple regression models, those performances are better than simple regression models. In general, multiple regression models with three band values as independent variable do not show serious declination situations between residual and actual value of yield except that with BLUE, GRN and RED as independent variables.

Figure 5 is the scatter plots of residual and actual value of yield in linear models with vegetation indexes as independent variables. The simple regression models with NDVI, SRVI and NIR/GRN (GRVI) as independent variable showed declination situation of different levels between residual and actual value of yield from Figure 5, but the model with GNDVI as independent variable has better performance. The multiple regression models with two vegetation indexes as independent variables also showed declination situation of different levels between residual and actual value of yield, which means the fitting ability of these models are not so good. But the multiple regression models with three vegetation indexes as independent variables do not show serious declination situations between residual and actual value of yield; those models possess better fitting abilities.

Conclusion

Ability to estimate rice yields within fields   from   remote

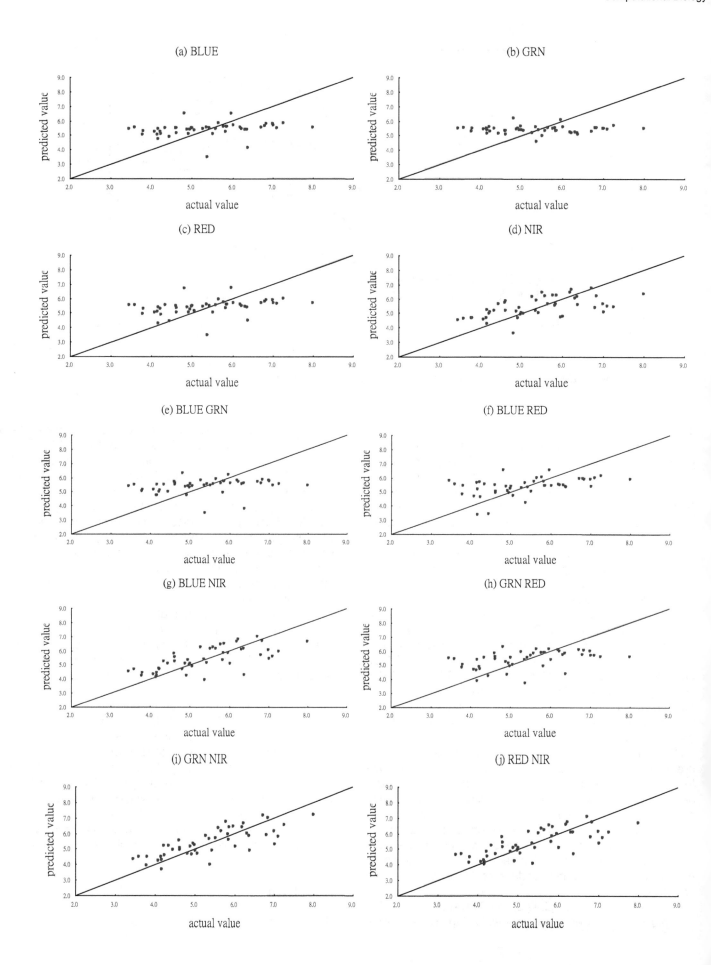

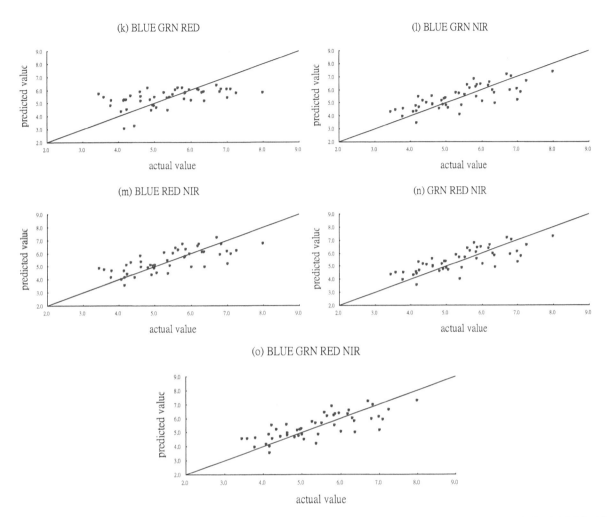

Figure 2. The plots of actual and predicted value of yield in first order linear models using (a) BLUE, (b) GRN, (c) RED, (d) NIR, (e) BLUE and GRN, (f) BLUE and RED, (g) BLUE and NIR, (h) GRM and RED, (i) GRN and NIR, (j) RED and NIR, (k) BLUE, GRN and RED, (l) BLUE, GRN and NIR, (m) BLUE, RED and NIR, (n) GRN, RED and NIR, (o) BLUE, GRN, RED and NIR.

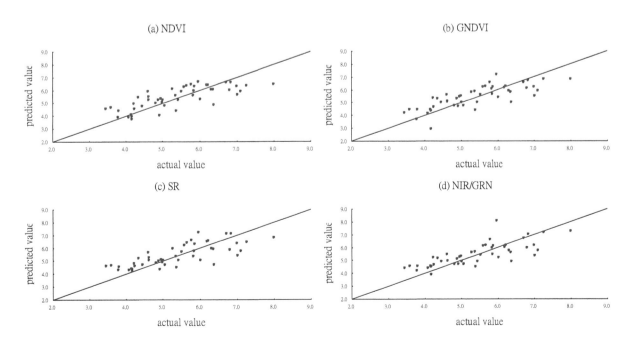

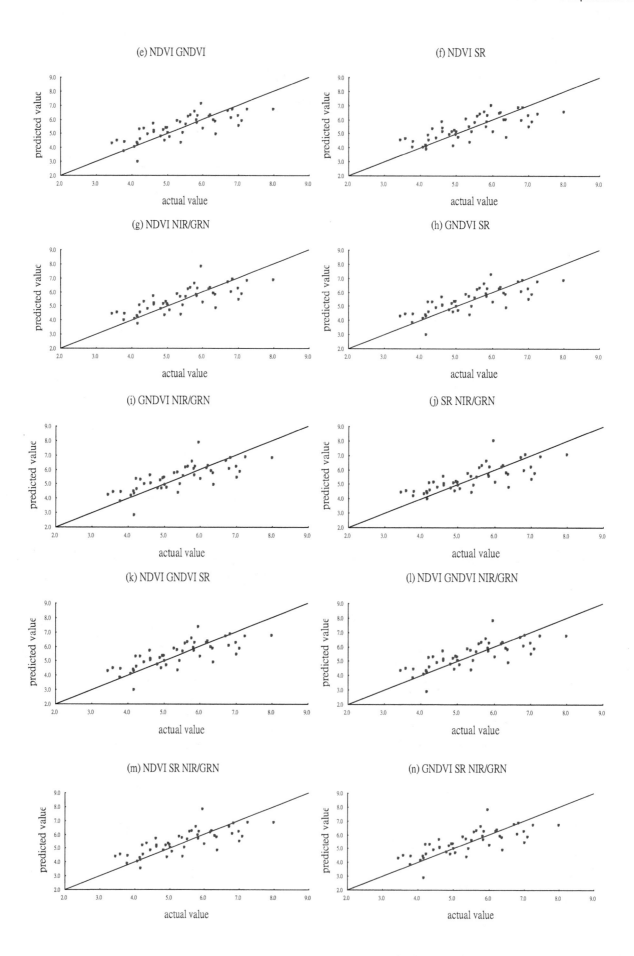

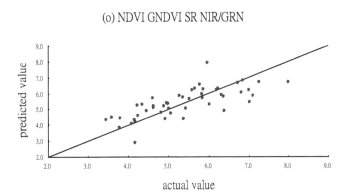

(o) NDVI GNDVI SR NIR/GRN

Figure 3. The plots of actual and predicted value of yield in linear models using (a) NDVI, (b) GNDVI, (c) SR, (d) NIR/GRN, (e) NDVI and GNDVI, (f) NDVI and SR, (g) NDVI and NIR/GRN, (d) GNDVI and SR, (i) GNDVI and NIR/GRN, (j) SR and NIR/GRN, (k) NDVI, GNDVI and SR, (l) NDVI, GNDVI and NIR/GRN, (m) NDVI, SR and NIR/GRN, (n) GNDVI, SR and NIR/GRN, and (o) NDVI, GNDVI, SR and NIR/GRN.

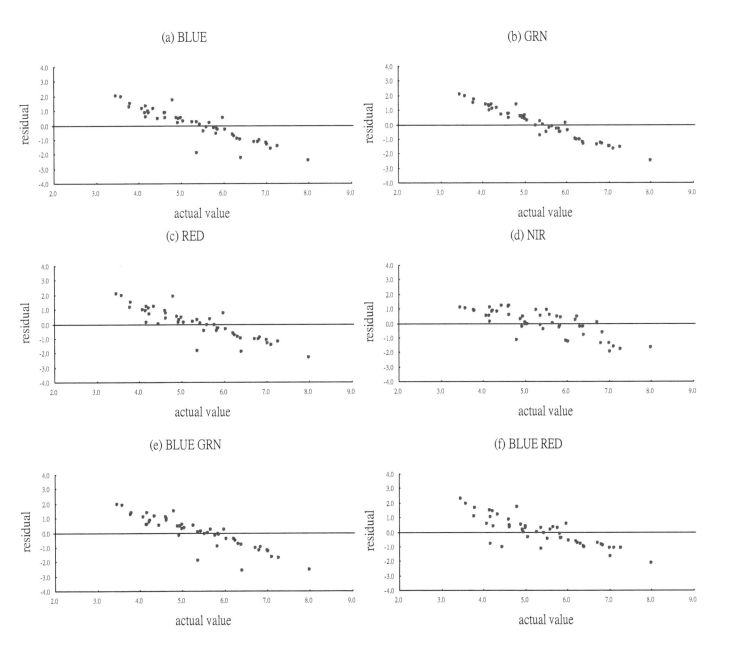

(a) BLUE

(b) GRN

(c) RED

(d) NIR

(e) BLUE GRN

(f) BLUE RED

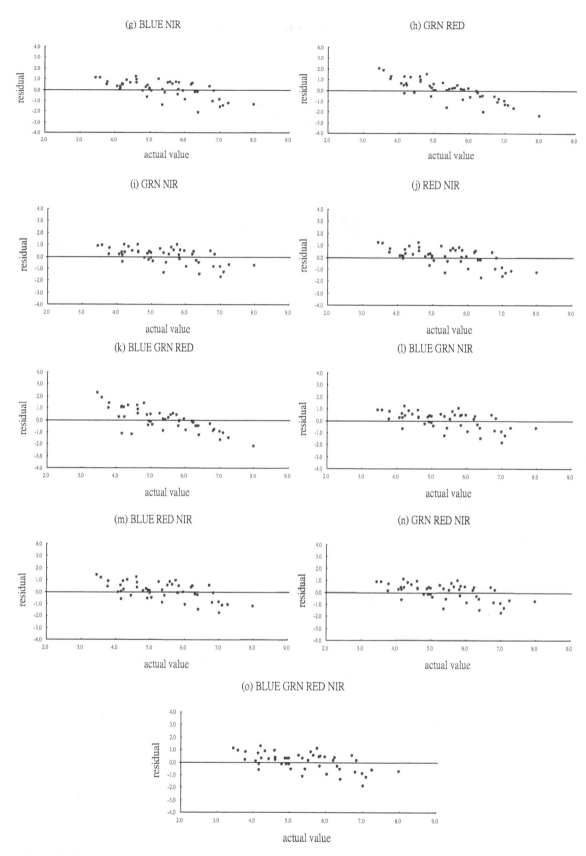

Figure 4. The scatter plots of residual and actual value of yield in first order linear models using (a) BLUE, (b) GRN, (c) RED, (d) NIR, (e) BLUE and GRN, (f) BLUE and RED, (g) BLUE and NIR, (h) GRM and RED, (i) GRN and NIR, (j) RED and NIR, (k) BLUE, GRN and RED, (l) BLUE, GRN and NIR, (m) BLUE, RED and NIR, (n) GRN, RED and NIR,(o) BLUE, GRN, RED and NIR.

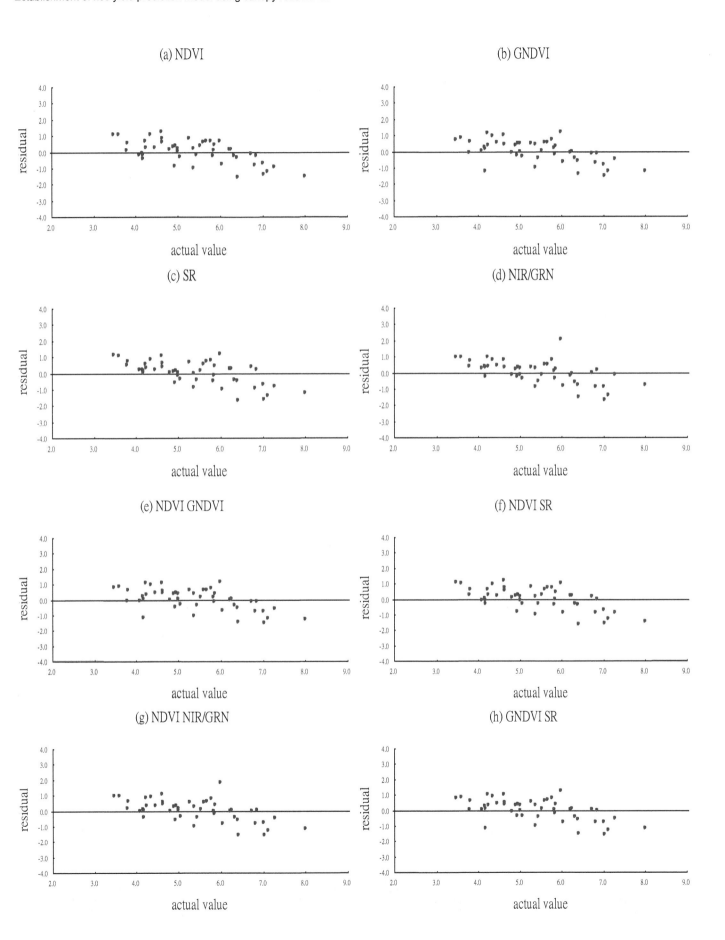

(a) NDVI

(b) GNDVI

(c) SR

(d) NIR/GRN

(e) NDVI GNDVI

(f) NDVI SR

(g) NDVI NIR/GRN

(h) GNDVI SR

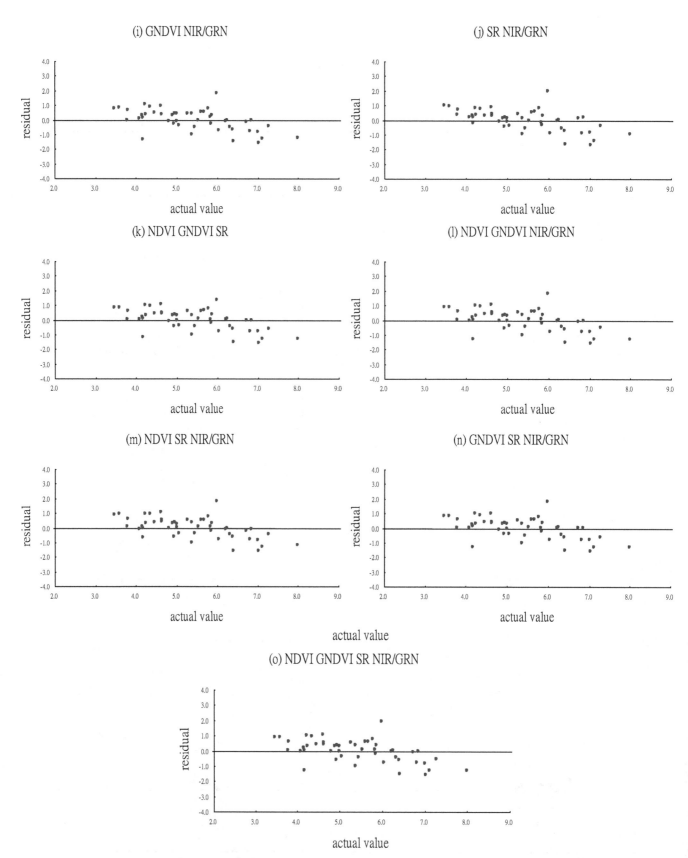

Figure 5. The scatter plots of residual and actual value of yield in linear models using (a) NDVI, (b) GNDVI, (c) SR, (d) NIR/GRN, (e) NDVI and GNDVI, (f) NDVI and SR, (g) NDVI and NIR/GRN, (h) GNDVI and SR, (i) GNDVI and NIR/GRN, (j) SR and NIR/GRN, (k) NDVI, GNDVI and SR, (l) NDVI, GNDVI and NIR/GRN, (m) NDVI, SR and NIR/GRN, (n) GNDVI, SR and NIR/GRN, (o) NDVI, GNDVI, SR and NIR/GRN.

sensing images is not only fundamental to applications of precision agriculture, but can also be very useful to food provisions management.

ACKNOWLEDGEMENT

Financial support for this research came from project (NSC 99-2632-H-156 -001 -MY3) of National Science Council, Taiwan, ROC.

REFERENCES

Arslan S, Colvin TS (1999). Laboratory performance of a yield monitor. Appl. Eng. Agric. 15:189-195.

Bach H (1998). Yield estimation of corn based on multitemporal Landsat-TM data as input for an agrometeorological model. Pure Appl. Optics 7:809-825.

Bouman BAM (1992). Linking physical remote sensing models with crop growth simulation models, applied for sugar beet. Int. J. Remote Sens. 13:2565-2581.

Clevers JGPW, van Leeuwen HJC (1996). Combined use of optical and microwave remote sensing data for crop growth monitoring. Remote Sens. Environ. 56:42-51.

Field CB, Randerson JT, Malmstrom CM (1995). Global net primary production: combining ecology and remote sensing. Remote Sens. Environ. 51:74-88.

Lark RM, Stafford JV, Bolam HC (1997). Limitations on the spatial resolution of yield mapping for combinable crops. J. Agric. Eng. Res. 66:183-193.

Leblon B, Guerif M, Baret F (1991). The use of remotely sensed data in estimation of PAR use efficiency and biomass production of flooded rice. Remote Sens. Environ. 38:147-158.

Moulin S, Bondeau A, Delecolle R (1998). Combining agricultural crop models and satellite observations: from field to regional scales. Int. J. Remote Sens. 19:1021-1036.

National Research council. [NRC] (1997). Precision agriculture in the 21st century: Geospatial and information technologies in crop management. Rep. 59-0700-4-139. NRC, Washington, DC.

Neter J, Kutner MH, Nachtsheim CJ, Wasserman W (1999). Applied linear statistical models. McGraw-Hill. pp. 54-56.

Prince SD (1991). A model of regional primary production for use with coarse-resolution satellite data. Int. J. Remote Sens. 12:1313-1330.

Reynolds CA, Yitayew M, Slack DC, Hutchinson CF, Huete A, Petersen MS (2000). Estimating crop yields and production by integrating the FAO crop specific water balance model with real-time satellite data and ground-based ancillary data. Int. J. Remote Sens. 21:3487-3508.

Serrano L, Fillela I, Penuelas J (2000). Remote sensing of biomass and yield of winter wheat under different nitrogen supplies. Crop Sci. 40:723-731.

Wiegand CL, Maas SJJ, Aase K, Hatfield JL, Pinter Jr PJ, Jackson RD, Kanemasu ET, Lapitan RL (1992). Multisite analyses of spectral-biophysical data for wheat. Remote Sens. Environ. 42:1-21.

19

Annotation of virulence factors in schistosomes for the development of a SchistoVir database

Adewale S. Adebayo[1] and Chiaka I. Anumudu[2]*

[1]Cell Biology and Genetics Unit, Department of Zoology, University of Ibadan, Oyo State, Nigeria
[2]Cellular Parasitology Programme, Department of Zoology, University of Ibadan, Oyo State, Nigeria.

Scientific efforts in the eradication of neglected tropical diseases, such as those caused by the parasitic helminthes, can be improved if a database of key virulence factors directly implicated in pathogenesis is available. As a first step towards creating SchistoVir, a database of virulence protein factors in schistosomes, in this study, we curated, annotated and aligned sequences of twenty virulence factors identified from the literature, using several bioinformatics tools including UniProtKB, SchistoDB, VirulentPred, InterProScan, ProtScale, MotifScan, TDRtarget, SignalP, MODBASE, PDB and MUSCLE. Among the protein entries, the most frequently occurring amino acid residues were lysine, serine, leucine, glutamine, glycine and cysteine in order of magnitude. Although sequence repeat regions (SRRs) of significant value were identified manually in fifty percent of the proteins (while dipeptide repeats (DiPs) and single amino acid repeats (SAARs) were not), nevertheless, seventy-two percent of the protein entries were classified as virulent by the prediction model, VirulentPred. Most of the entries (eighty percent) did not have target compounds based on the database of available chemical compounds at TDRtargets. Fourteen of the twenty entries (seventy percent) had more than 30 consecutively negative amino acid residues based on the ProtScale's Kyte and Doolittle hydrophobicity plot. Hence, they would be hydrophobic enough to be transmembrane in location or secretory in nature. Only 7 (tyrosinase, serine protease1, Tspan-1, VAL4, cathepsin b and L and calreticulin) had cleavage sites and signal peptides, while none had a significant signal anchor probability. The annotations and characterization provided by this work and the development of a SchistoVir database will aid in further research of schistosome pathogenesis and control.

Key words: Protein database, bioinformatics tools, virulence proteins/factors, annotation, schistosomes.

INTRODUCTION

Schistosomes are pathogenic helminthes, a group of parasites which constitute important sources of morbidity and mortality in several parts of the world, with 2 billion persons affected (Fumagalli, 2010). Of the several species of schistosomes known, *Schistosoma mansoni*, *Schistosoma haematobium* and *Schistosoma japonicum* are important in the spread of morbidity. Among the tropical diseases caused by parasites, schistosomiasis ranks second only to malaria as a cause of catastrophic worldwide morbidity and mortality. Besides, it is believed to infect 200 million persons (Dvorak et al., 2008; Chalmers et al., 2008). The control of schistosomiasis involves population-based chemotherapy with the use of praziquantel (PZQ) and metrifonate drugs. PZQ increa-ses antigen exposure, induces adenosine receptor bloc-kade and calcium influx, causes paralysis and distorts the parasite's morphology. Snail control (through habitat modification, environmental planning and molluscicides) and immu-nological control (vaccination) are also components of the disease control strategy. The identification and deve-lopment of vaccine candidates (usually protein antigens) will be useful in reducing morbidity drastically. Yet, a single actual potent vaccine is not within reach (WHO, 2010).

*Corresponding author. E-mail: chiaka.anumudu@mail.ui.edu.ng or walsaks002@yahoo.com.

Generally, parasites (including helminthes) use several mechanisms to attack hosts, while deriving nutrients and scheming for their own continued survival, and the success of parasites can be highly correlated with their ability to evolve a sophisticated immune evasion strategy (Matisz et al., 2011). Therefore, the key parasite proteins involved in these actions are critical to survival and they have been classified as virulence proteins (Fankhauser et al., 2007; Ramana and Gupta, 2009). These virulence proteins may be involved in attachment or adhesion to host membrane receptor cells, establishment and penetration within host cells, cleaving of host proteins and invasion (Ramana and Gupta, 2009). These proteins are strictly regulated and have also been identified as therapeutic agents; some of them are already at clinical trial stages (Gomez et al., 2010). A function-based classification of these virulence proteins was done by Ramana and Gupta (2009). The major classes identified were invasion, establishment, adhesion, proteases and others with unknown or putative function, although there is sometimes no sharp delineation amongst the different categories.

Schistosome virulence proteins have been evaluated for use as vaccine or drug targets. Chalmers et al. (2008), MacDonald et al. (2002) and Lopez-Quezada and McKerrow (2011) affirmed that SmVAL and serpins (serine protease inhibitors) are involved in immune system modulation. The SmVAL (S. mansoni venom allergen -like) have a conserved SCP/TAPS domain that possesses envenomation and larval penetration activity. The serpins are able to distort host proteases. Furthermore, proteomic studies have also shown that the Sm29, gluthatione-S-transferase, thioredoxin, tetraspanins, triose phosphate isomerase, Sm32 among others in schistosoma, are critical for host haemoglobin degradation, reduction of Th2 immune response and tissue invasion (Braschi et al., 2006; Hansell et al., 2008; Cardoso et al., 2008; Verjovski-Almeida and DeMarco, 2008; Sharma et al., 2009). There are also studies to indicate the importance of some of these proteins in treatment strategies. WHO /USAID partnership led to the establishment of the Schistosomiasis Vaccine Development Programme (SVDP) which identified epitopes of the triose phosphate isomerase (TPI), Sm14 and GST as virulence proteins with key vaccine candidates (WHO, 2010). Braschi et al. (2006), Reis et al. (2008) and Aslam et al. (2008) also highlighted the roles of tetraspanins, TPI and serpins in the preparation of efficacious vaccines.

In silico approaches have enhanced research in parasite pathogenesis and efforts in this direction continue till today (Devor, 2005; Hogeweg, 2011). This falls under the categorization of functional genomics (Garg and Gupta, 2008). Available databases of bacterial virulent proteins and toxins include VFDB (Virulence Factors Database), PRINTS (Protein Family fingerprints) and MVirDB (Microbial database of protein toxins and virulence factors) (Zhou et al., 2007; Tsai et al., 2009).

These are available at http://prediction centre. llnl. gov, provided by the Lawrence Livermore National Laboratory, US. ProtVirDB (http://bioinfo.icgeb.res.in/protvirdb) is a database for virulence factors in protozoans. The databases mentioned provide unified information portals for researchers interested in a panoramic or in-depth view of the virulent proteins in a parasite of interest or in comparison with other parasites.

In fact, many works available have indicated the roles of several virulence proteins in schistosomes pathogennesis, the full genome database of the *S. mansoni* (SchistoDB, www.schistodb.net/schistodb) has been made publicly available. Also, there are a number of public protein databases which offer information on the proteome of *S. mansoni, S. haematobium or S. japonicum,* for example, UniProt (http://uniprot.org). Nevertheless, there is no specialized and simplified public information portal for the virulence factors identified so far in the schistosomes, either in *S. mansoni, S. haematobium or S. japonicum.*

To the best of our knowledge, no database or classification to specifically annotate virulence proteins in parasitic worms exists, although substantial research has been done in characterizing proteins in different helminth species (Caprona et al., 2005; Braschi et al., 2006; Curwen et al., 2006; Cardoso et al., 2008; Aslam et al., 2008; Bos et al., 2009; Boumis et al., 2011). Such a database will give a simplified information portal for the researchers interested in a panoramic or in-depth view of the virulent proteins in a parasite or in comparison with other parasites. It will also facilitate sequence retrieval and analysis and will be a useful tool for the research community in the study of schistosome pathogenesis.

METHODOLOGY

In order to construct and develop a preliminary secondary database of schistosome virulence proteins (SchistoVir), annotation of selected proteins were done using some tools.

Catalogue of protein entries

Protein entries were curated from nucleotide sequences, genomic sequences and literature available in NCBI's RefSeq and PubMed (http://ncbi.nlm.nih)[1];GeneDB[2](http://genedb.org/genedb/smansoni); SchistoDB Release 2.0[3] ((http://schistodb.net) and UniProt KB[4] (http://www.uniprot.org/search). The criteria for choice of entry will be essentiality, decisiveness or crucial nature of the protein for survival in the host. The use of multiple databases is to ensure that all possible entries are obtained. The databases will provide literature sources, genomic sequences, contigs and protein sequences of schistosome entries.

---

1. National Centre for Biotechnology Information. It has a large depository of biomedical literature and genomic information. The RefSeq provides updated, universally confirmed genomic sequences and PubMed provides literature.
2. GeneDB provides genomic and proteomic data on species which have been completely sequenced
3. SchistoDB provides protein and genomic information on the Schistosoma mansoni genome
4. UniProtKnowledgebase is a mega database on proteomic data from hundreds of species

Coding and protein sequences, status and amino acid length were obtained from SchistoDB or UniProt queries with the use of keywords or gene names. Ontogenic expression which gives a measure of the protein's expression at different stages of the life cycle of schistosomes was obtained from SchistoDB using a number of ESTs (expressed sequence tags) in adults per total number of ESTs for all stages. The results were saved as complete html pages. Blastp searches were conducted using the UniProt Blast tool with default parameters.

Phylogenetic and secretory/transmembrane analysis

Homologous protein sequences to each of the virulence factors from selected species are obtained from NCBI and alignments were made using the MUSCLE multiple alignment tool (at http://ebi.ac.uk/tools/muscle) (Edgar, 2004) with default parameters and results are displayed in ClustalW format. Muscle is hosted by European Bioinformatics Institute-EMBL and provides for automated sequence analysis with multiple alignment.

Signal sequences in the proteins were recognized with SignalP 3.0 (http://www.cbs.dtu.dk/services/SignalP) hosted by the Technical University of Denmark, using both the neural network and Hidden Markov Model (HMM) methods (Nielsen et al., 1997; Bendtsen et al., 2004). In order to increase accuracy, presence or absence of signal peptides was defined by the default Neural Network D score thresholds. This is in accordance with the method of Bos et al. (2009). SignalP results present d, s and y scores. The D score is the average of the maximal Y-score (the most likely location of the cleavage site of the signal sequence) and the mean S-score, and is the best way to discriminate true signal sequences in proteins (Emanuelsson et al., 2007). In responding to query sequences, proteins with a D score greater than 55 and HMM greater than 90% were scored as having an N-terminal signal sequence (hence, transmembrane) and presented in our results. The default eukaryote setting of SignalP, with each sequence truncated after 70 residues, was used to avoid false positive detection of signal sequence outside the N-terminus. SignalP results were read off the query results directly from both the HMM and neural networks.

Domain, model and transmembrane predictions

Model search or prediction was done using protein data bank (PDB or MODBASE; http://rscb.pdb.org and http://salilab.org/modbase respectively), with the protein sequence as a query with default settings. The model predictions are presented as 3D structures obtained from MODBASE[1] query searches. Helices, beta sheets, turns or coils and loops are easily visible this way. PDB (protein data bank) 3D structures are displayed when available.

ProtScale[2] from ExPasy[3] (http://web.expasy.org/cgi-bin/protscale) was used to generate a hydropathy plot based on the calculated hydrophobicity of constituent amino acids. Interpretation is based on the fact that twenty consecutive hydrophobic amino acids are needed for a peptide/protein to be transmembrane. The Kyte-Doolittle hydrophobicity plot method was adopted while using ProtScale. ProtScale results from query sequence were generated in a numerical verbose format so as to be able to obtain numbers of consecutive hydrophobic residues. Prediction of motifs and domains was done using Motif Scan (http://myhits.isb-sib.ch/cgi-

bin/motif_scan) (Sigrist et al., 2010) of the Swiss Institute of Bioinformatics which makes use of the PROSITE database. Also, the InterPro Scan version 33.0 (Mulder et al., 2007) (http://www.ebi.ac.uk/Tools/services/web_iprscan) from European Bioinformatics Institute, an arm of European Molecular Biology Laboratory (EMBL) was used to discover conserved protein signatures and domains of individual entries.

Query sequences in plain format used in MotifScan and InterProScan returned results in html and SVG formats. Signatures, profiles and domains recognized are derived from these results and summarized. The relative hydrophobicity of a protein and the absence or presence of signal peptides with cleavage sites are important in determining if it is transmembrane or not.

Other tools in the annotation and characterization of entries

Protein entries were also characterized using the following tools:

1. VirulentPred (http:bioinfo.icgeb.res.in/virpred): a bacterial virulence factor prediction server, which relies upon amino acid composition, dipeptide composition, similarity search of known virulence factors in bacteria, and cascade support vector machine algorithms to predict likelihood of virulence.
2. TDRtargets version 4.0 (Crowther et al., 2010): Using homology to druggable proteins with specified modifiable criteria, the server generates possible drug targets. In the results, associated drugs or compounds represent the results of searches conducted on the TDR targets database for each entry. The GO terms display generally accepted terms of the function of a protein, the cellular component of which the protein is part and the interaction of the protein with other substances which is its molecular function.

RESULTS AND DISCUSSION

An initial twenty proteins derived from the literature were annotated in a simplified format using bioinformatics tools. Due to the large nature of the results or documentation generated, a summary of protein documentation and analysis are presented in Tables 1 and 2, respectively. The proposed schema is shown in Figure 1. Simply put, a database schema is a graphical depiction of the structure of the database and a similar pattern has been adopted by Ramana and Gupta (2009). A sample of the annotation pages for one of the protein entries is shown in Figure 2. The proteins included are discussed under the following headings.

Protein entries

Inclusion of the protein entries, data generated for the amino acid sequence, molecular weight, domains and signatures for the entries agree with the works of Chacon et al. (2003), Herve et al. (2003) for 28GST, Ramos et al. (2003, 2009) and Rabia et al. (2010) for Sm14, Fitzpatrick et al. (2007) for tyrosinase, Chalmers et al. (2008) for venom allergen like VAL, Kane et al. (2004) for major egg antigen p40, Berriman et al. (2009), Boumis et al. (2011) for thioredoxin, Lopez-Quezada and McKerrow (2011) for serpin and Wu et al. (2011).

Proteases, proteinase inhibitors and binding proteins

1. MODBASE predicts a protein's 3D structure, when it is not available in its data bank (Pieper et al., 2011). It is a tool for comparative protein structure modeling.
2. ProtScale analyses the profile of a query sequence using amino acid residues present
3. Protein analysis software from Swiss Bioinformatics

Table 1. The database proteins with their basic features and classification.

Systematic name	Name	Feature	Functional classification
Smp_155560	Serpin	50% (germball), 33% (cercariae), 43.62 kD, 4 paralogs Smp_062080,062120,155530,155550)	Establishment (Protease inhibitor)
Smp_000022	Tyrosinase	Female adults only, 56.3kD	Invasion (egg migration/formation
Smp_075800.1	Sm32	2 paralogs (Smp_075790,179170)	Protease
Smp_054470	Thioredoxin	85.7% adult, 7.1% schistosomula,1 paralog (Smp_008070),11.2kD	Establishment (redox homeostasis)
Smp_155310	Tetraspanin/Tspan-1	Adults only, 24.05kD, 8 paralogs	Establishment (Protective)
Smp_157090	Cathepsin L	2.8% (adult) 1.9% (schistosomula), 168.16kD, 3 paralogs (Smp_034410.1-3)	Protease
Smp_158420	Cathesspin B	36.6kD, 4 paralogs (Smp_067060, 103610,141610,179980)	Protease
Smp_072190	Sm29	58% (adult), 21.2kD, no paralogs	Establishment
Smp_095360	Fatty acid binding protein or Sm14 (fabp)	85% (adult), 9.8% (schistosomula), 14.9kD, 3 paralogs (Smp_174440.4,095360.1-2)	Establishment (Uptake of host fatty acid)
Smp_030350	Serine Protease 1 (Sp1)	54.28kD, no paralogs	Protease
Smp_003990	Triose phosphate isomerase	81.8% adult,12.7% expression (cercariae), 28.09kD	Establishment
Smp_054160	28GST	85% (adult), 23.82kD, no paralogs	Invasion
Smp_030370	Calreticulin	50.3% (adult), 45.4kD,no paralogs	Establishment (protein folding)
Smp_183000	Major egg antigen p40	21.07kD, 17 paralogs	Establishment (immune evasion)
Smp_018890	Phosphoglycerate kinase (Pgk)	75% (adult),18.47kD,1 paralog (Smp_187370)	Establishment
Smp_042160.2	Fructose 1,6 biphosphate aldolase	80.8% adult, 39.7kD,1 paralog (Smp_042160.1)	Establishment
Smp_002070	Venom allergen like (VAL)	28 paralogs, confirmed only as transcripts	Establishment

*All systematic names are derived from the SchistoDB (Berriman et al., 2009); *Paralogs are homologous or similar sequences found in same species; *All percentages are calculated from number of EST per total EST.

Table 2. Classification of database proteins based on different bioinformatics tools.

Parameter	Number of entries	Entry protein
Virulence using bacterial parameters and score (ViruPred)	13	Tyrosinase (0.6586); fabp1-97aa (0.6656); Sm14 (0.7938); Sp1 (0.6586); thioredoxin 2 (0.6586); Tspan-1 (1.2771); egg antigen p40 (1.1121); serpin (1.0287); cathepsin B(0.2498); cathepsin L(1.3629); calreticulin (0.2028); Sm29 (0.9471); Sm32
Non virulence according to Virupred	5	Triose p.isom (-1.742); thioredoxin!; Pgk (-0.816); 28GST (-0.572); fructose bp aldolase (-1.367)
Having known targets / compounds	4	Tyrosinase, t.p.isomearse, fabp3, 28GST
No known target compounds [Human ortholog target available*]	16	Fabp1, SP1*, calreticulin, thioredoxin1 and 2*, Tspan-1, p40, cathepsin b*, cathepsin L*, serpin* PGK*, Sm29, Sm23, fructose biphosphate aldolase*, Sm32*
MODBASE/PDB data available [both available*, MODBASE only^]	13	Fabp3*, 28GST*, Sm14*, aldolase^, Sm29^, pgk^, thioredoxin1&2^, sp1, cathepsin L and b^, tpi^, p40^

include Sm32, serine protease and cathepsins. 58 kD serine protease has been documented to be capable of mitigating the effects of IgE immune response through cleavage (Aslam et al., 2008). Involvement of protease inhibitors or proteinase inhibitors such as serpin 1 in direct virulence or pathogenesis has also been recognised by Dalton et al.

Table 2. Contd.

No PDB data/chain No MODBASE prediction model	3	Tspan-1, Sm23, Sm32
Hydrophobicity: Entries with highest number of consecutive negative residues		Calreticulin (130), cathepsin L (79), VAL 4 (65), cathepsin B (49), p40 (42), Sm32(40)
Largest number of Epitopes		Cathepsin L (55), Sm32 (40), Sm23 (35), 28GST (30), aldolase (26), SP1(20), Sm32 (20), serpin1 (17), Pgk 23

!: Predicted virulent based on dipeptide composition but non virulent based on other parameters, ^ no PDB structural data available.

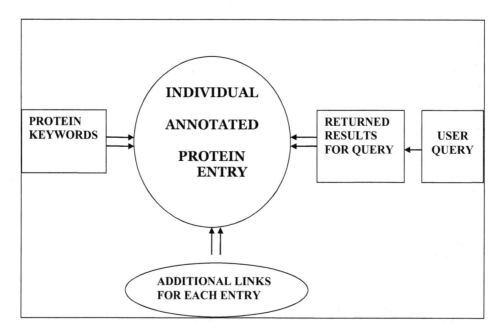

Figure 1. Schema (graphical structure) for the database.

al. (1997), Lin and He (2006) and Lopez-Quezada and McKerrow (2011).

Triose phosphate isomerase, aldolase, calreticulin and glutathione s-transferase (GST) are entries which have been identified as excretory-secretory (ES) products in *Schistosoma* by previous studies and these ES proteins have been implicated in invasion of host tissues by sporocysts, haemocyte encapsulation and eventual immunosuppression and immune evasion (Guillou et al., 2007; Reis et al., 2008).

None of the entries had a confirmed myristoylation site, an amino acid side chain to which a lipid group, myristic acid (14C saturated fatty acid) can be added to aid the localization of a cytosolic protein to a membrane. Although one entry, the major egg antigen p40 had probable sites. Nevertheless, this did not connote the absence of transmembrane proteins among the entries.

It is also noteworthy that some of the entries: Sm14, Sm23, 28GST, triose phosphate isomerase and Sm32 have already been identified as vaccine candidates (Cardoso et al., 2008; WHO, 2010). This is due to their high level of expression and antigenicity. Also, each protein entry had at least two GO ID and term/names to represent the function term (F) and the process terms (P). The GO terms aptly describe entries based on their status as a cellular component; in biological process and molecular function.

Amino acid sequence

The amino acid length of the protein entries and coding sequence varied from 97 to 1471 aa and 231 to 4413 bp. Protein length is apparently diverse although long-chained proteins are not in abundance among the entries. The more frequently occurring residues among the protein sequences were lysine, serine, leucine, glycine, cysteine, glutamine and aspartic acid. The first 5 residues have also been found to occur frequently among eukaryotic virulence proteins as reported by Garg and Gupta (2008). Quezada et al. (2009) also showed that conserved cysteine residues and leucine rich domains are key to virulence protein function.

SAMPLE ANNOTATION PAGE

Sm 14 Fatty acid binding protein (FaBP)
Status: putative, conserved in few eukaryotes
Protein/ coding sequence
MSSFLGKWKLSESHNFDAVMSKLGVSWATRQIGNTVTPTVTFTMDG DKMTMLTESTFKNLSCTFKFGEEFDEKTSDGRNVKSVVEKNSESKLT QTQVDPKNTTVIVREVDGDTMKTTVTVGDVTAIRNYKRLS 133aa
Coding sequence
ATGTCTAGTTTCTTGGGAAAGTGGAAACTTAGCGAGTCACACAAC TTCGATGCTGTCATGTCAAAGCTAGGTGTCTCATGGGCAACTCGAC AGATTGGGAACACAGTGACCCCAACTGTAACCTTCACAATGGATG GGGATAAAATGACTATGTTAACAGAGTCAACTTTCAAAAATCTTTC TTGTACGTTCAAGTTCGGCGAGGAATTCGATGAAAAAACAAGTGA CGGCAGAAATGTCAAGTCAGTTGTTGAAAAAAATTCCGAGTCGAA GTTAACGCAAACTCAAGTAGATCCCAAAAACACAACTGTAATCGT TCGTGAAGTGGATGGTGATACTATGAAAACGACTGTGACTGTTGG TGACGTTACTGCCATTCGCAATTATAAACGACTATCCTAA 402bp
Suggested Virulence category: Establishment
Associated compound (TDR): none human ortholog cmpd: 3-carbazol-9-ylpropanoic acid, 2 hexyldecanoic acid
Ontogenic/stage specific exp.(schistodb)
(no of EST/total ESTs)   Adult (139/163), schistosomula (16/163)

Model Prediction (A:MODBASE;B: PDB structure bound to oleic acid)
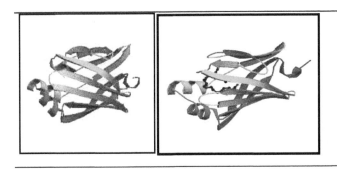

Homology	**3 paralogs**
Best blastp hits (% identity): *Homo sapiens* fabp, brain (48%); *Bos taurus* heart fabp(44%); *Mus musculus* adipocyte binding protein (43%)	

Figure 2. Sample annotation page for one of the protein entries.

None of the entries appeared to have single amino acid repeats (SAARS) or Di-peptide repeats (DiPs). On the other hand, sequence repeat regions (SRRs) of two amino acids in length were found in triose phosphate isomerase, tyrosinase, egg antigen p40, sp1, tspan-1, serpin, cathepsin L, calreticulin, 28GST and Sm14. These 2aa repeats were both heteropeptide and homopeptide repeats. The numbers of repeats found in the rest of the entries were not considered to be significant enough. The occurrence of repeats in many of the virulence proteins of microbial and protozoan pathogens has been reported by Gravekamp et al. (1998), Karlin et al. (2002), Fankhauser et al. (2007) and Ramana and Gupta (2009). None of the public repeat searching tools: *ProtrepeatsDB* and *RepSeq* (Kalita et al., 2006; Depledge et al., 2007) were available online for use. Hence, entries were examined manually for repeats, though the note was taken for natural probability of amino acid repeat occurring for any given sequence. Availability of repeat searching tools/servers would have provided a means of detecting the more complicated mismatch repeats that may be present.

Similarly, there were no notable conserved sequences observed in the alignment of the protein entries generated from MUSCLE. This might have been expected due to a wide range of protein families.

Virulence

The twenty protein entries were used as query on VirulentPred which identifies partial sequence of a protein that could aid virulence according to bacterial models with default settings. The results of these VirulentPred predictions (Table 1) may serve as a form of validation for some of the entries. 13 of the 20 entries queried on the server were declared virulent by all parameters (amino acid composition, dipeptide composition, similarity search and cascade support vector machine algorithms).

According to Garg and Gupta (2008), VirulentPred is highly sensitive even for eukaryotic sequences, but may produce false positives in eukaryotic sequences due to compositional differences.

Although schistosomes are eukaryotic and more highly evolved than bacteria pathogens, certain features may be conserved in virulence proteins. In fact, such conservation is seen in the occurrence of repeats and residues (previous page) in these pathogens. Lysine and serine, two of the most frequent residues in the protein entries (and in eukaryotic virulence proteins) also frequently occur in bacterial virulence proteins. Hence, the VirulentPred results cannot be totally discarded.

Other functional predictions

In the Kyte-Doolittle hydropathy plot, a large number of consecutive negative amino acid residues (20 to 30) are highly indicative of the hydrophobicity of a protein, its ability to be inserted into the internal hydrophobic envi-

ronment of the membrane and its likelihood of being transmembrane. Most of the protein entries possess a significant number of hydrophobic amino acids, with calreticulin having 130 consecutive residues (the highest) and thioredoxin 2 having 14 residues (lowest). Fatty acid binding protein, thioredoxin 1 and 2, and Sm29 were the only entries with less than 20 consecutive residues. These are all evident from ProtScale results generated numerically (verbose format). The algorithm used by ProtScale takes no cognizance of the first 4 amino acids of the protein sequence used as query for such and are usually involved in signal peptide and cleavages. Hence, high number of entries (16 of 20) had strong hydrophobic portions with at least 20 to 30 consecutive negative residues. It has been postulated from previous studies that hydrophobic residues of virulence proteins would aid their integration of membrane, adhesion to host cells or stimulate binding of the proteins to targets in the hosts (Katsir et al., 2008; Quezada et al., 2009; Blanco et al., 2010).

Sites for cleavage of proteins involved in the conventional secretory pathway in cells were identified in 7 of the entries (35%). Such entries have signal sequences and a high D score, and it predicts that the entries are integral to the membrane and non-cytoplasmic. The usage of eukaryotic parameters and truncation of each query sequences to 70 terminal residues (in the signalP queries) increased reliability of the result generated (Bos et al, 2009). Virulence-related outer membrane, integral membrane or transmembrane proteins have been identified in prokaryotic and eukaryotic pathogens (Schulz and Vogt, 1999; Kim et al., 2009).

Associated compounds and drugs

Diverse compounds were found to be associated with different protein entries even among paralogs. As our queries of TDRtargets showed, only 4 of the protein entries including triose phosphate isomerase, 28GST and tyrosinase, had already named or known compounds that could be used to target them. There are still no known compounds to directly target 16 of the protein entries, although 9 of the 16 have known targets for their human orthologs. Hence some key protein factors involved in virulence of schistosomes cannot yet be targeted with any of the synthetic/natural compounds known to humans, at least within the TDRtarget database, a huge database formed by a collaboration of several universities and the WHO TDR drug target network (Crowther et al., 2010).

Ontogenic/stage specific expression

It is pertinent to note that most of the protein entries including tyrosinase, fabp, Sm14, thioredoxin, Tspan-1, cathepsin L, phosphoglycerate kinase, Sm29, calreticulin, 28GST, aldolase and Sm32 have high expression levels in adult schistosomes as results from SchistoDB showed it. Serpin is one exception of the entries (high expression in germball and cercariae). Adult pathogens are highly evolved and would be capable of producing proteins directly involving pathogenesis.

Model search and prediction

Surprisingly, a significant number of the protein entries had no structural data available in the protein data bank (PDB) and MODBASE was relied on for prediction of the structures of most of the entries. 28GST and Sm14 had 3D model data from both databases, 13 entries had model predictions generated from MODBASE. 3 entries: sm23, Sm32 and tspan-1 had no models from both databases. In terms of online availability and accessibility of 3D structural data, research on many proteins directly involved in schistosome pathogenesis may be slow.

Suggested virulence category

The protein entries had specific functions such as evasion of host immune responses, penetration of host barriers, degradation of host protective proteins and establishment in the host, all of which contribute to virulence, the relative ability of parasites to induce pathogenesis. Each of these functions was used to categorize the entries into a suggested virulence category. Hence 4 categories were identified: Proteases, Establishment (uptake of host nutrients, redox homeostasis, etc), proteases and invasion (proteinase inhibitors, host penetration) (Table 1)

Antigenicity

It is worthy of note that all protein entries had at least 5 putative antigenic epitopes with the highest being that of cathepsin L, SmSP1 with 55 putative epitopes. Epitopes or better still, the antigenic determinants are discrete sites on a protein or antigen which B and T lymphocytes recognize. Epitopes are the immunologically active regions in a complex antigen that actually bind to B-cell or T-cell receptors. Such information on epitopes is useful when considering adaptive immunity response to parasites and possible therapeutic targets. Recognition of these epitopes depended on evidence provided by TDR targets v4.0.

Algorithm [Structured English Text]

If a protein name is entered into the query search,
1. [Start] Copy alphabets of a query
2. Compare alphabets of the query with the stored template protein keywords 1 to 20
3. Search for a match
a. There is a match if all the alphabets are the same
b. There is also a match if 3 to 5 alphabets are the same
5. Display the matched protein keyword. If there is no match, display 'no result'
6. Search the annotated protein entry for matched keyword
7. Display the annotation page[End].

8. If additional link search is performed, go to http://schistodb.net/schistodb[End].

Summary, conclusion and recommendation

Studies on molecular aspects of parasitic helminthes can be improved especially in the tropics if a database of key virulence factors which are directly implicated in pathogenesis is developed. This work has laid a foundation for us to develop such a database. It would be useful to the research community at a time when the search for vaccines for several helminth diseases is on the increase. It also provides grounds for further studies related to the significance of proteins involved in virulence of the parasitic helminthes. The database will be made public (depending on funds availability), updated regularly and additional tools for virulence prediction incorporated. It is proposed to expand the database to include other pathogenic helminthes so that users are provided with more possibilities in terms of species coverage.

REFERENCES

Aslam A, Quinn P, McIntosh RS, Shi J, Ghumra A, McKerrow JH, Bunting KA, Dunne DW, Doenhoff MJ, Sherie LM, Ke Z, Richard JP (2008). Proteases from Schistosoma mansoni cercariae cleave IgE at solvent exposed interdomain region. Mol. Immunol. 45(2):567-574.

Bendtsen JD, Nielsen H, von Heijne G, Brunak S (2004). Improved prediction of signal peptides: SignalP 3.0. J. Mol. Biol. 340:783-795.

Berriman M, Haas BJ,LoVerdo PT, Wilson RA, Dillon GP, Cerquiera GC, El Sayed NM (2009). The genome of the blood fluke Schistosoma mansoni. Nature 460:352-358

Bos DH, Mayfield C, Minchella DJ (2009). Analysis of regulatory protease sequences identified through bioinformatic data mining of the Schistosoma mansoni genome. BMC Genomics 10: 488-492.

Boumis G, Angelucci F, Bellelli A, Brunori M, Dimastrogiovanni D, Miele AE (2011). Structural and functional characterization of Schistosoma mansoni Thioredoxin. Protein Sci. 20(6):1069-1076.

Blanco MT, Sacristán B, Lucio L, Blanco J, Pérez-Giraldo C, Gómez-García AC (2010). Cell surface hydrophobicity as an indicator of other virulence factors in Candida albicans. Rev. Iberoam Micol. 27(4):195-199.

Braschi S, Borges WC, Wilson RA (2006). Proteomic analysis of the schistosome tegument and its surface membranes. Mem Inst Oswaldo Cruz. 101(I): 205-212.

Caprona A, Riveaua G, Caprona M, Trottein F (2005). Schistosomes: the road from host–parasite interactions to vaccines in clinical trials. Trends Parasitol. 21(3): 143-149.

Cardoso FC, Macedo GC, Gava E, Kitten GT, Mati VL (2008). Schistosoma mansoni Tegument Protein Sm29 Is Able to Induce a Th1-Type of Immune Response and Protection against Parasite Infection. PLoS Negl Trop Dis. 2(10): e308.

Chalmers IW, McArdle AJ, Coulson RM, Wagner MA, Schmid R, Hirai H, Hoffmann KF (2008). Developmentally regulated expression, alternative splicing and distinct sub-groupings in members of the Schistosoma mansoni venom allergen-like (SmVAL) gene family. BMC Genomics 9:89.

Crowther GJ, Shanmugam D, Carmona SJ, Doyle MA, Hertz-Fowler C, Berriman M, Nwaka S, Ralph SA, Roos DS, Van Voorhis WC, Agüero F (2010). Identification of Attractive Drug Targets in Neglected-Disease Pathogens Using an In Silico Approach. PLoS Negl Trop Dis. 4(8): e804.

Curwen RS, Ashton PD, Sundaralingam S, and Wilson RA (2006). Identification of Novel Proteases and Immunomodulators in the

Secretions of Schistosome Cercariae That Facilitate Host Entry. Mol. Cell. Proteomics 5(5):835-844.

Dalton JP, Clough FA, Jones MK, Brindley PJ (1997). The cysteine proteinases of Schistosoma mansoni cercariae. Parasitology 114: 105-112.

Depledge DP, Lower RP, Smith DF (2007). RepSeq – A database of amino acid repeats present in lower eukaryotic pathogens. BMC Bioinformatics 8:122.

Dvorak J, Mashiyama ST, Braschi S, Sajid M, Knudsen GM, Hansell E, Lim KC, Hsieh I, Bahgat M, Mackenzie B, Medzihradszky KF, Babbitt PC, Caffrey CF and McKerrow JH (2008). Differential use of protease families for invasion by schistosome cercariae. Biochimie 90: 345-358.

Edgar RC (2004). MUSCLE: a multiple sequence alignment method with reduced time and space complexity. BMC Bioinformatics 5:113.

Emanuelsson O, Brunak S, von Heijne G and Nielsen H (2007). Locating proteins in the cell using TargetP, SignalP and related tools. Nat. Protoc. 2:953-971.

Fankhauser N, Nguyen-Ha T, Adler J, Mäse P (2007). Surface antigens and potential virulence factors from parasites detected by comparative genomics of perfect amino acid repeats. Proteome Sci. 5: 20.

Fitzpatrick JM, Hirai YHH, Hoffmann KF (2007). Schistosome egg production is dependent upon the activities of two developmentally regulated tyrosinases. FASEB J. 21: 823-835.

Fumagalli M, Pozzoli U, Cagliani R, Comi GP, Bresolin N, Clerici M, Sironi M (2010). The landscape of human genes involved in the immune response to parasitic worms. BMC Evol. Biol. 10:264.

Garg A, Gupta D (2008). VirulentPred: a SVM based prediction method for virulent proteins in bacterial pathogens. BMC Bioinformatics 9:62.

Gomez C, Ramirez ME, Calixto-Galvez M, Medel O and Rodríguez MA (2010). Regulation of Gene Expression in Protozoa Parasites. J Biomed. Biotechnol. 2010: 726045.

Gravekamp C, Rosner B, Madoff LC (1998). Deletion of repeats in the alpha C protein enhances the pathogenicity of group B streptococci in immune mice. Infect. Immun. 66:4347-4354.

Guillou F, Roger E, Moné Y, Rognon A, Grunau C, Théron A, Mitta G, Coustau C, Gourbal BE (2007). Excretory–secretory proteome of larval Schistosoma mansoni and Echinostoma caproni, two parasites of Biomphalaria glabrata. Mol. Biochem. Parasitol. 155 (1):45-56.

Hansell E, Braschi S, Medzhiradszsky KF, Sajid M, Debnath M (2008). Proteomic Analysis of Skin invasion by blood fluke larvae. PLoS Negl. Trop. Dis. 2(7):e262.

Herve M, Angeli V, Pinzar E, Wintjens R, Faveeuw C, Narumiya S, Capron A (2003). Pivotal roles of the parasite PGD2 synthase and of the host D prostanoid receptor 1 in schistosome immune evasion. Eur. J. Immunol. 33: 2764-2772.

Hogeweg P (2011). The Roots of Bioinformatics in Theoretical Biology. PLoS Comput. Biol. 7(3): e1002021.

Kalita MK, Ramasamy G, Duraisamy S, Chauhan VS and Gupta D (2006). ProtRepeatsDB: a database of amino acid repeats in genomes. BMC Bioinformatics (database) 7:336.

Kane CM, Cervi L, Sun J, McKee AS, Katherine SM, Sagi S, Christopher AH, Edward JP (2004). Helminth Antigens Modulate TLR-Initiated Dendritic Cell Activation. J. Immunol. 173(12):7454-61.

Karlin S, Brocchieri L, Bergman A, Mrazek J, Gentles AJ (2002). Amino acid runs in eukaryotic proteomes, disease associations. Proc. Natl. Acad. Sci. USA 99:333-338.

Katsir LE, Schilmiller AL, Staswick PE, He SY, Howe GA (2008). COI1 is a critical component of a receptor for jasmonate and the bacterial virulence factor coronatine. Proc. Natl. Acad. Sci. 105(19): 7100-7105.

Kim KH, Willger SD, Park SW, Puttikamonkul S, Grahl N (2009). TmpL, a Transmembrane Protein Required for Intracellular Redox Homeostasis and Virulence in a Plant and an Animal Fungal Pathogen. PLoS Pathog 5(11): e1000653.

Lin YL, He S (2006). Sm22.6 antigen is an inhibitor to human thrombin. Mol. Biochem. Parasitol. 147(1):95-100.

Lopez Quezada LA, McKerrow JH (2011). Schistosome serine protease inhibitors: parasite defense or homeostasis. Anais da Academia Brasileira de Ciências (Annals of the Brazilian Academy of Sciences) 83(2): 663-672.

MacDonald AS, Araujo MI, Pearce EJ (2002). Immunology of Parasitic Helminth Infections. Infect. Immun. 70(2):427–433.

Matisz CE, McDougall JJ, Sharkey KA, McKay DM (2011). Helminth Parasites and the Modulation of Joint Inflammation. J. Parasitol. Res. 2011:942616.

Mulder NJ, Apweiler R, Attwood TK, Bairoch A, Bateman A, Binns D, Bork P, Buillard V, Cerutti L (2007). New developments in the InterPro database. Nucleic Acids Res. 35: D224-D228.

Nielsen H, Engelbrecht J, Brunak S and von Heijne G (1997). Identification of prokaryotic and eukaryotic signal peptides and prediction of their cleavage sites. Protein Eng. 10:1-6.

Pieper U, Webb BM, Barkan DT, Schneidman-Duhovny D, Schlessinger A, Braberg H et al (2011). MODBASE, a database of annotated comparative protein structure models and associated resources. Nucleic Acids Res. 39:465-474.

Quezada CM, Hicks SW, Galán JE, Stebbins CE (2009). A family of Salmonella virulence factors functions as a distinct class of autoregulated E3 ubiquitin ligases. Proc. Natl. Acad. Sci. 106(12): 4864-4869.

Rabia I, El-Ahwany E, El-Komy W, Nagy F (2010). Immunomodulation of Hepatic Morbidity in Murine Schistosoma mansoni Using Fatty Acid Binding Protein. J. Am. Sci. 6(7):170-176.

Ramana J, Gupta D (2009). ProtVirDB: a database of protozoan virulent proteins. Bioinformatics 25 (12):1568-1569.

Ramos CR, Figueredo RC, Pertinhez TA, Vilar MM, Nascimento AL et al (2003). Gene structure and M20T polymorphism of the Schistosoma mansoni Sm14 fatty acid-binding protein: structural, functional and immunoprotection analysis. J. Biol. Chem. 278:12745-12751.

Ramos CR, Spisni A, Oyama S Jr, Sforca ML, Ramos HR, Vilar MM et al (2009). Stability Improvement of the fatty acid binding protein Sm14 from S mansoni by Cys rep: Structural and functional characterization of a vaccine candidate. J. Biochim. Biophys. Acta 1794(4):655-662.

Reis EAG, Mauadi Carmo TA, Athanazio R, Reis MG, Harn DA Jr (2008). Schistosoma mansoni triose phosphate isomerase peptide MAP4 is able to trigger naive donor immune response towards a type-1 cytokine profile. Scand. J. Immunol. (Clinical Immunology) 68:169–176.

Sharma M, Khanna S, Bulusu G, Mitra A (2009). Comparative modeling of thioredoxin reductase from Schistosoma mansoni: a multifunctional target for antischistosomal therapy. J. Mol. Graph Model 27(6):665-675.

Schulz GE, Vogt J (1999). The structure of the outer membrane protein OmpX from Escherichia coli reveals possible mechanisms of virulence. Structure 7 (10): 1301–1309.

Sigrist CJA, Cerutti L, De Castro E, Langendijk-Genevaux PS, Bulliard V, Bairoch A, Hulo N (2010). PROSITE, a protein domain database for functional characterization and annotation. Nucleic Acids Res. (Database) 38: 161–166.

Tsai CT, Huang WL, Ho SJ, Shu LS, Ho SY (2009). Virulent-GO: Prediction of Virulent Proteins in Bacterial Pathogens Utilizing Gene Ontology Terms. Int. J. Biol. Life Sci. 5(4):2009

Verjovski-Almeida S, DeMarco R (2008). Current developments on Schistosoma proteomics. Acta Tropica 108:183-185.

World Health Organisation (WHO) Document (2010). Parasitic Diseases-Schistosomiasis. Available at http://who.int/vaccine_research/diseases/soa_parasitic/en/index5.htm l.Accessed 13 July 2011.

Zhou CE, Smith J, Lam M, Zemla A, Dyer MD, Slezak T (2007). MvirDB—a microbial database of protein toxins, virulence factors and antibiotic resistance genes for bio-defence applications. Nucleic Acids Res. (database) 35:391-394.

20

A computational analysis to understand the role of DmsD in the biosynthesis of dimethyl sulfoxide (DMSO) reductase

Nazlee Sharmin

Department of Biological Sciences, University of Alberta, Canada. E-mail: nazlee@ualberta.ca.

The role of DmsD in the biosynthesis of dimethyl sulfoxide (DMSO) reductase is quite controversial. Several studies have indicated its role as 'proof-reading chaperone', which might function to prevent the translocation of misfolded and non-cofactor containing protein. DmsD is also shown to bind to the signal peptide; however, its possible function as a 'guidance factor' for membrane targeting is ruled out by some experimental evidences. In this computational study, the interactions of DmsD with some other proteins were analyzed. The results of the analysis indicate that rather than playing the role of a chaperone directly, DmsD may influence the recruitment of GroEL, MoeB, and DnaK which can function as a chaperone for protein folding. The results of this analysis were also used together with the findings of available literature to generate a hypothetical model, proposing a possible function of DmsD in the biosynthesis of DMSO reductase.

Key words: Dimethyl sulfoxide (DMSO) reductase, DmsD, molecular docking.

INTRODUCTION

Dimethyl sulfoxide (DMSO) reductase is a membrane anchored enzyme in bacteria, which is needed for the anaerobic respiration using DMSO and some other related S-and N-oxides (Chan et al., 2008; Qiu et al., 2008). DMSO is a molybdenum cofactor containing heterotrimeric enzyme consisting of the DmsABC subunits, of which DmsA is the catalytic subunit and DmsB is the electron-transfer subunit (Rajagopalan, 1991). The DmsAB dimer is transported to the cytoplasmic membrane via the Tat system, where it attaches to the membrane-bound subunit DmsC (Chan et al., 2008). The DmsA is found to contain a specific sequence motif (S-R-R-x-F-L-K), known as 'twin-arginine' in its N-terminal leader peptide, which has been reported to be identified by the Tat translocase, leading to the translocation of DmsA across the cytoplasmic membrane in a fully-folded, cofactor-loaded state (Chan et al., 2008; Qiu et al., 2008). The molybdenum cofactor is also shown to be required for this translocation (Yoshida et al., 1991).

Two pathways, known as the Sec and the Tat pathways have been reported in Bacteria for the biosynthesis of cofactor containing proteins. Using the Sec apparatus, the apoprotein and cofactor are transported to the periplasm separately and the cofactor insertion and protein folding occur in the periplasm (Palmer et al., 2003). Tat pathway, on the other hand, is an independent translocation system with an ability to transport fully folded and oligomerized proteins across the cytoplasmic membrane (Qiu et al., 2008; Plamer et al., 2002). The core structure of the system comprises three membrane-associated proteins, TatA, TatB and TatC (Berks et al., 2000; Palmer et al., 2003). The TatBC unit acts as the twin-arginine signal peptide recognition module (Alami et al., 2000), whereas TatA is shown to form a large oligomeric ring-structure, similar to a channel (Palmer et al., 2003).

In the process of the DMSO reductase biosynthesis in bacteria, DmsD has been identified as the most potential candidate for the role of 'proofreading chaperone', which functions is to prevent the translocation of immature, misfolded and non-cofactor containing proteins (Hatzixanthis et al., 2005; Qiu et al., 2008). DmsD has

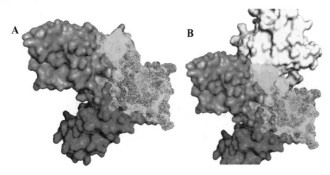

Figure 1. Binding of GroEL subunit (blue), DnaK (magenta) and MoeB (yellow) with DmsD (green). (A) Shows the binding of GroEL and DnaK and (B) shows the complete complex of four proteins. DmsD is shown in mesh format to clarify the binding sites between the proteins. Docking and modeling was done using Auto Dock and Pymol.

been reported to bind with the 'twin arginine' signal peptide of DmsA and also to TatB and TatC (Oresnik et al., 2001), indicating that this protein might have direct role in protein folding, co-factor insertion and also in membrane targeting. However, studies with chimeric proteins have shown that DmsD is not required for the interaction of the DmsA signal peptide with the Tat apparatus (Ray et al., 2003). In their experiment, Ray et al. (2003) showed that in the absence of DmsD, DmsA-GFP fusions were exported with high efficiency, ruling out the possible role of DmsD as guidance factor. Thus, the binding of DmsD to the signal peptide might influence the proper assembly of DmsA and prevent the export of misfolded or pre-folded protein (Ray et al., 2003). However, studies indicate that Tat transport mechanism does not require a correctly folded protein as substrate (Hynds et al., 1998).

The findings of Ray et al. (2003) have indicated towards another important possibility that DmsD might be required for the cofactor insertion in DmsA, similar to its homologus TorD. TorD is shown to stabilize the folding of apoTorA at high temperature and help in acquiring the Mo-cofactor (Genest et al., 2005). However, besides binding to the signal peptide and unlike the DmsD, TorD is found to interact with the mature TorA protein (Pommier et al., 1998). Some studies have also suggested the presence of a secondary binding site in the mature TorA for the binding of TorD (Jack et al., 2004). The interaction between the mature DmsA and the DmsD has not yet been reported.

Besides DmsA and TorBC, some of the key proteins have been identified to interact directly or indirectly with DsmD include elongation factor Ef-Tu, MoeB, GroEL and DnaK (Li et al., 2010). Interaction of the translation elongation factor Ef-Tu with DmsD suggests the possibility that DmsD might approach and bind to the leader peptide immediately after its synthesis, prior to its release from the Ef-Tu (Li et al., 2010). MoeB is considered to be involved with NarJ in some earlier

pathway of nitrate reductase biosynthesis (Schwarz, 2005). Also mutant MoeB is found to affect DmsA maturation (Sambasivarao et al., 2002).

DnaK is well established as an *in vitro* RR-leader binding protein (Oresnik et al., 2001; Graubner et al., 2007). GroEL, in cooperation with DnaK has been shown to play role in the folding of a plant ferredoxin-NADP$^+$ reductase (Dionisi et al., 1998). Furthermore, a recent study has implicated GroEL in an interaction with NapD for the periplasmic nitrate reductase biosynthesis in *Escherichia coli* (Butland et al., 2005). Taken together, these findings suggest that DmsD might work as a 'hub-protein' in the network of interaction and facilitate the folding of DmsA by binding to it and also recruiting GroEL and / or DnaK (Li et al., 2010). In this study, a computational analysis was carried out with a view to predict possible interaction between DmsD and mature DmsA and also to find the involvement of other proteins in DMSO reductase biosynthesis.

MATERIALS AND METHODS

The crystal structure of DmsD from *Salmonella typimurium* (PDB ID: 1S9U) was analyzed using a docking (Auto Dock) and two modeling software (Pymol and Swiss PdbViewer). The homology model was generated for both mature (GI: 119351635) and precursor (GI: 16502128) DmsA from *S. typimurium* from Swiss Model, using 1dmrA as template. In order to visualize the pattern of interaction between DmsD and other proteins, some protein candidates were chosen from various protein-protein interaction studies done *in vitro* and *in silico* using bioinformatics approaches (Kostecki et al., 2010; Li et al., 2010). Although, these studies indicated towards a list of more than 300 candidates from bioinformatic analysis, only four most potential possible proteins were taken here, which include GroEL, DnaK and MoeB. The choice was done on the basis of the previous known function of these proteins.

For molecular docking, the homology model was generated for DnaK (GI: 1389758) of *S. typimurium* using 1q51A as template. 1jw9B was used as a template for modeling MoeB of the same organism (GI: 1256835). In both the cases, Swiss modeler was used. The crystal structure of GroEL was downloaded from Protein databank (PDB ID: 1J4Z).

RESULTS

When protein-protein interaction sites were analyzed using Auto Dock, no possible binding site was found between DmsD and mature DmsA. All the proteins GroEL, DnaK and MoeB were found to bind with DmsD. Moreover, they are found to form a complex (Figure 1). This indicated a possibility that rather than playing the role of a chaperon directly, DmsD may influence the recruitment of GroEL, MoeB and DnaK which function as a chaperone and lead to the folding of DmsA.

To verify this prediction, both the mature and precursor DmsA was docked with the complex and also with the individual molecules. Neither the individual candidate proteins nor the predicted complex showed any

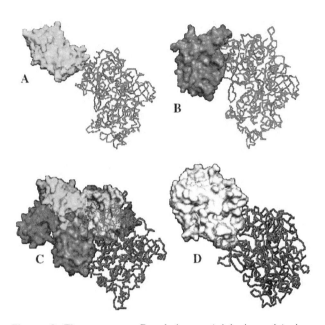

Figure 2. The precursor DmsA (apoprotein) showed to have possible binding sites with DmsD (A), GroEL subunit (B), MoeB (C) and also with the complex of four protein (D). In the protein complex, green is representing DmsD, blue is showing GroEL subunit and yellow and magenta is showing MoeB and DnaK respectively. The apo-protein is shown in red. Docking and modeling was done using Auto Dock and Pymol.

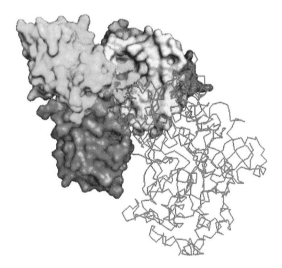

Figure 3. The final predicted protein complex that is assumed to interact with the precursor DmsA (shown in red). In the protein complex, green is representing DmsD, blue is showing GroEL subunit and yellow is showing MoeB. Docking and modeling was done using Auto Dock and Pymol.

interaction with mature DmsA. However, DmsD, GroEL, MoeB and the complex showed interaction with the precursor DmsA (Figure 2). No interaction was found between DnaK and precursor DmsA. This leads to the possibility that DmsD recruits GroEL, MoeB or other molecules before the folding of precursor DmsA and after proper folding; the mature DmsA is released from the complex. The final predicted complex is shown in Figure 3. GroEL is known to play a role in Molybdenum-iron cofactor insertion into the nitrogenase enzyme of

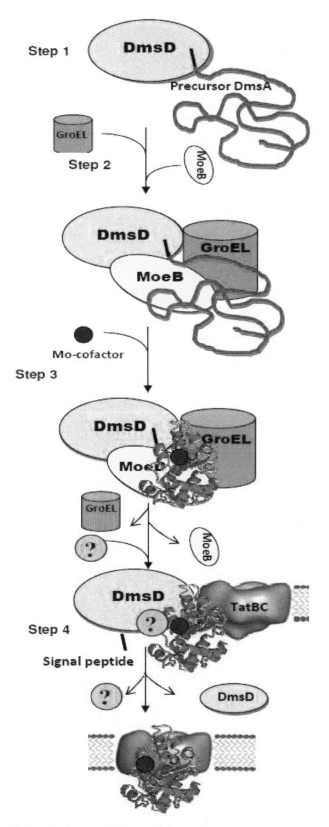

Azobacter vinelandii (Ribbe et al., 2001), which can play the similar role in DMSO biosynthesis as well.

DmsD is found to interact with TatBC complex in *E. coli* (Papish et al., 2003) and it is assumed that TatBC complex initiates a structural change within DmsD that causes the release of the DmsA signal peptide, which then can interact with Tat machinery (Winstone et al., 2006). However the factor that guides the trafficking of DmsA to TatBC is not known and the role of DmsD as a guidance factor is controversial. Thus, it is assumed that some proteins which might be present in this interaction can bind to the mature DmsA or DmsD or both as well as with TatBC complex. Taking all these information together, a hypothetical model is generated explaining the possible role of DmsD in DMSO reductase bio-synthesis (Figure 4). The goal of this model is to use the pieces of information from available literature as well as the computational analysis to generate a complete over view of the scenario. The following steps from Figure 4 explain more succinctly the role of DmsD in DMSO reductase biosynthesis.

Step 1 (Binding of DmsD)

DmsD binds with the signal peptide (shown in black) of the precursor DmsA immediately after its synthesis, prior to its release from Ef-Tu factor.

Step 2 (Binding of GroEL and MoeB)

DmsD influence the recruitment and binding of GroEL and MoeB, forming a complex with the precursor DmsA.

Step 3 (Protein folding and co-factor insertion)

GroEL and MoeB mediate the insertion of Mo-cofactor and guide the proper folding of DmsA. GroEL plays the role of molecular chaperone and the protein folding is done inside the GroEL. GroEL and MoeB are released after this step. DmsD remains bound to the signal peptide.

Step 4 (Interaction with TatBC and release of signal peptide)

DmsD presents the bound DmsA to TatBC complex. This step might have the involvement of an unknown protein, which can bind to the mature DmsA and can act as a guidance factor to guide the binding of the complex with TatBC. The interaction between DmsD, TatBC and mature DmsA cause conformational change in DmsD causing the release signal peptide. DmsD and the unknown protein are also released later in this step.

Figure 4. A hypothetical model showing the possible function of DmsD in the biosynthesis of DMSO reductase. Step 1: (Binding of DmsD); Step 2: (Binding of GroEL and MoeB); Step 3: Protein folding and co-factor insertion; Step 4: (Interaction with TatBC and release of signal peptide).

DISCUSSION

Tat pathway requires a protein to be completely folded and assembled with all subunits and cofactors for its translocation. DmsD is thought to be a regulator of the process, possibly involved in proper folding of DmsA and also to its targeting to membrane bound Tat-complex. However, the exact function of DmsD is controversial and needs further analysis. In this study, a small docking analysis was also carried out which corroborated the involvement of GroEL and MoeB with DmsD for the folding of DmsA. GroEL may play a role in co-factor insertion. Considering all the piece of information from published literature, a hypothetical model was also generated explaining the possible role of DmsD. However, the model indicates the necessity of a guidance factor, which could be DmsD itself or some new protein, which is yet to be discovered. Further studies are needed in this area to end the controversies and to reveal the complete picture of the scenario.

REFERENCES

Alami M, Trescher D, Wu LF, Müller M (2000). Separate analysis of twin-arginine translocation (Tat)-specific membrane binding and translocation in *Escherichia coli*. J. Biol. Chem., 277(23): 20499-20503.

Berks BC, Sargent F, Palmer T (2000). The Tat protein export pathway. Mol. Microbiol., 35(2): 260-274.

Butland G, Peregrín-Alvarez JM, Li J, Yang W, Yang X, Canadien V, Starostine A, Richards D, Beattie B, Krogan N, Davey M, Parkinson J, Greenblatt J, Emili A (2005). Interaction network containing conserved and essential protein complexes in *Escherichia coli*. Nature, 433(7025): 531-537.

Chan CS, Winstone TM, Chang L, Stevens CM, Workentine ML, Li H, Wei Y, Ondrechen MJ, Paetzel M, Turner RJ (2008). Identification of residues in DmsD for twin-arginine leader peptide binding, defined through random and bioinformatics-directed mutagenesis. Biochemistry, 47(9): 2749-2759.

Dionisi HM, Checa SK, Krapp AR, Arakaki AK, Ceccarelli EA, Carrillo N, Viale AM (1998). Cooperation of the DnaK and GroE chaperone systems in the folding pathway of plant ferredoxin-NADP⁺ reductase expressed in *Escherichia coli*. Eur. J. Biochem., 251(3): 7, 24-28.

Graubner W, Schierhorn A, Brüser T (2007). DnaK plays a pivotal role in Tat targeting of CueO and functions beside SlyD as a general Tat signal binding chaperone. J. Biol. Chem., 9; 282(10): 7116-7124.

Hatzixanthis K, Clarke TA, Oubrie A, Richardson DJ, Turner RJ, Sargent F (2005). Signal peptide-chaperone interactions on the twin-arginine protein transport pathway. Proc. Natl. Acad. Sci. USA., 14; 102(24): 8460-8465.

Hynds PJ, Robinson D, Robinson C (1998). The sec-independent twin-arginine translocation system can transport both tightly folded and malfolded proteins across the thylakoid membrane. J. Biol. Chem., 25; 273(52): 34868-34874.

Jack RL, Buchanan G, Dubini A, Hatzixanthis K, Palmer T, Sargent F (2004). Coordinating assembly and export of complex bacterial proteins. EMBO J., 13; 23(20): 3962-3972.

Kostecki JS, Li H, Raymond JT (2010). Visualizing Interactions along the *Escherichia coli* Twin-Arginine Translocation Pathway Using Protein Fragment.

Li H, Chang L, Howell JM, Turner RJ (2010). DmsD, a Tat system specific chaperone, interacts with other general chaperones and proteins involved in the molybdenum cofactor biosynthesis. Biochim. Biophys. Acta. 1804(6): 1301-1309.

Oresnik IJ, Ladner CL, Turner RJ (2001). Identification of a twin-arginine leader-binding protein. Mol. Microbiol., 40(2): 323-331.

Palmer T, Berks BC (2003). Moving folded proteins across the bacterial cell membrane. Microbiology, 149(3): 547-556.

Papish AL, Ladner CL, Turner RJ (2003). The twin-arginine leader-binding protein, DmsD, interacts with the TatB and TatC subunits of the *Escherichia coli* twin-arginine translocase. J. Biol. Chem., 278(35): 32501-32506.

Pommier J, Méjean V, Giordano G, Iobbi-Nivol C (1998). TorD, a cytoplasmic chaperone that interacts with the unfolded trimethylamine N-oxide reductase enzyme (TorA) in *Escherichia coli*. J. Biol. Chem., 273(26): 16615-16620.

Qiu Y, Zhang R, Binkowski TA, Tereshko V, Joachimiak A, Kossiakoff A (2008). The 1.38 A crystal structure of DmsD protein from *Salmonella typhimurium*, a proofreading chaperone on the Tat pathway. Proteins. 71(2): 525-533.

Rajagopalan KV (1991). Novel aspects of the biochemistry of the molybdenum cofactor. Adv. Enzymol. Relat. Areas Mol. Biol., 64: 215-290.

Ray N, Oates J, Turner RJ, Robinson C (2003). DmsD is required for the biogenesis of DMSO reductase in Escherichia coli but not for the interaction of the DmsA signal peptide with the Tat apparatus. FEBS Lett. 534(1-3): 156-160

Ribbe MW, Burgess BK (2010). The chaperone GroEL is required for the final assembly of the molybdenum-iron protein of nitrogenase. Proc. Natl. Acad. Sci. USA., 98(10): 5521-5525.

Sambasivarao D, Turner RJ, Bilous PT, Rothery RA, Shaw G, Weiner JH (2002). Differential effects of a molybdopterin synthase sulfurylase (moeB) mutation on *Escherichia coli* molybdoenzyme maturation. Biochem. Cell Biol., 80(4): 435-443.

Schwarz G (2005). Molybdenum cofactor biosynthesis and deficiency. Cell Mol. Life Sci., 62(23): 2792-2810.

Winstone TL, Workentine ML, Sarfo KJ, Binding AJ, Haslam BD, Turner RJ (2006). Physical nature of signal peptide binding to DmsD. Arch. Biochem. Biophys., 455(1): 89-97.

Yoshida Y, Takai M, Satoh T, Takami S (1991). Molybdenum requirement for translocation of dimethyl sulfoxide reductase to the periplasmic space in a photodenitrifier, Rhodobacter sphaeroides f. sp. denitrificans. J. Bacteriol. 173(11): 3277-3281.

21

Advancement in computational analysis methods of plant antifreeze proteins (AFPs): An application towards classification and gene expression studies of leucine rich repeat (LRR) and ice-recrystallization inhibition domain (IRI) containing AFPs

J. Muthukumaran[1], P. Manivel[1], M. Kannan[1], J. Jeyakanthan[2] and R. Krishna[1*]

[1]Centre for Bioinformatics, School of Life Sciences, Pondicherry University, Puducherry – 605 014, India.
[2]Department of Bioinformatics, Alagappa University, Karaikudi - 630 003, India.

Gene sequence analysis is a key-step for genomic research, which help to understand the genome of species once it has been sequenced. It includes pair-wise, comparative or multiple sequence analysis. The Genome On-Line Database (GOLD) provides information about the number of completed, meta, incomplete and targeted genome projects. The statistics of GOLD show 2942 of completed, 7687 of incomplete, 340 of meta and 440 of targeted genome projects. The Support Vector Machine (SVM) is a widely used technique that analyzes the gene expression or micro array data. In the present study, we performed inter and intra species comparative nucleic acid as well as protein sequence analysis of Leucine Rich Repeat (LRR) and Ice-recrystallization Inhibition (IRI) domain containing plant antifreeze proteins (AFPs), which provide extensive understanding of their sequential characteristics and help in their classification and in production of transgenic constructs to improve the agricultural yields. Here, classification based on their sequential characteristics was made accordingly, the AFPs from *Daucus carota* bearing only LRR domains were placed in Class I group while AFPs with both LRR and IRI domains from *Triticum aestivum, Deschampsia antarctica, Lolium perenne and Hordeum vulgare* were placed in Class II group. In Class II groups, the entries with less than ten occurrences of IRI were placed in a subgroup A, while the other with more than ten incidences of IRI was placed in a subgroup B. Later, the entries in A and B which has single LRR patterns were placed separately under the group A1 and B1, whereas those with more than one occurrence were placed in the groups A2 and B2 respectively. Again, the entries in B1 were reclassified based on the conservation of LRR into C1 and C2 groups respectively. LRR regions were found to be enriched with alpha and beta sheet whereas IRI regions contain coil and sheets. The reported classification scheme and proposed methodology facilitate the identification, annotation and construction of synthetic plant AFPs in near future. Ongoing efforts are directed towards the development of comprehensive database integrated with the prediction server for identification of new class of plant AFPs and their homology in an extensive manner.

Key words: Antifreeze protein, leucine rich repeat, over-wintering plants, comparative sequence analysis, ice-recrystallization inhibition protein.

INTRODUCTION

Increase in the surface temperature of earth caused the significant changes in the global climatic conditions which become evident from the occurrences of unexpected climatic transformations in certain parts of the world.

Variations in the temperature were directly related with agricultural yield of the respective regions and reduce the growth of various economically important crops such as Rice, Wheat, etc. Presence of proteins with antifreeze properties is one sure available natural weapon for treating the effects of cold climatic conditions on growth of various crops (Atici and Nalbantoglu, 2003). AFPs inhibit the growth of ice by occupying the interface between solid ice and liquid crystals and cause the difference in the temperature of melting and freezing point of water, the effect known as thermal hysteresis (TH), and aids in inhibition of thermodynamically favored growth of ice-crystal (Raymond and DeVries, 1977). AFPs also prevent the movement of ice-crystals and obstruct the formation of larger crystals; thereby, they execute the ice-recrystallization inhibition (RI) mechanism (Knight et al., 1984). AFPs are used as additives to enhance the quality and shelf-life of ice-covered food and are also used for low temperature (LT) preservation of cells, tissues and organs for transplant or transfusion in medicine. AFPs can be used as chemical adjuvants for sarcoma cryosurgery (Gage and Baust, 1998) and in the development of transgenic plants with escalating freeze tolerance of crop plants and lengthens the harvest season in winter season (Thomashow, 1998).

The AFPs can be classified into six different types such as Type I (Patel and Graether, 2010), Type I-hyp (Scotter et al., 2006), Type II (Ng and Hew, 1992), Type III (Sonnichsen et al., 1993)], Type IV (Deng et al., 1997), Type V AFPs (Duman, 2001) and Plant AFPs. Of the six different AFPs, the first four AFPs are belonging to fishes and Type V AFP found in insects, which posses greater TH value. The antifreeze activity of plants was first reported in 1992 (Sidebottom et al., 2000). They differ from other AFPs due to low TH (~0.1 to 0.5°C) and high ice RI activity. Plant AFPs have been isolated from various species such as *D. carota, L. perenne, T. aestivum, H. vulgare*, etc. (Kuiper et al., 2001). Upon exposure to freezing conditions, these plants express the proteins conferring protection against the freezing temperatures to protect their cells from damages induced by the growth of ice crystals. These proteins found to have LRR (Meyer et al., 1999) / IRI (Zhang et al., 2010) or both domains to execute the antifreeze activity.

The LRR domain of *D. carota*-AFPs is evolved from the member of Polygalacturonase inhibitor protein (PGIP) family, and it does not show the polygalacturonase inhibiting activity (Zhang et al., 2006) because of the presence of many non conservative basic amino acid residues in the LRR domain, which differentiate the AFP from PGIPs. The AFPs from *D. carota* did not contain IRI

domain, and its LRR domain alone exhibits antifreeze activity (Meyer et al., 1999). The structural skeleton of protein–protein interaction was formed by the conserved amino acid residues of LRR domain, and its specificity was determined by the non-conserved amino acid residues of the same domain (Kobe and Deisenhofer, 1994). In LRR motif, the cysteine residues are postulated to form the disulphide bond, and it plays a significant role in folding and stability of the proteins, particularly in secretory proteins (Sevier and Kaiser, 2002).

Experimental structure of LRR domain containing proteins has a continuous alpha helix in a convex side that is connected to strand forming beta sheets in its concave side by its two loops (Kobe and Deisenhofer, 1994). As with the α-helical regions (convex side) cannot pack as closely as the β- pleated sheet regions (concave side), the β-roll structure will become gradually curved, proportional to the number of LRRs. The individual repeats in LRR domain containing proteins correspond to β-α units, which consist of a short β-strand and the α-helix are similar in size. A single LRR motif does not appear to fold into a defined structure; however several LRRs are essential to form the stable LRR domain. Similar to LRR domain, the IRI domain is also essential for the function of ice-recrystallization inhibition in various plants such as *L. perenne, T. aestivum, H. vulgare* and *D. antarctica*. It consists of ~7-8 amino acid residues with the specific conserved pattern of N-X-V-X-X-G / N-X-V-X-G, and they are rich in aspargine (N), glycine (G), serine (S) and valine (V) residues (Zhang et al., 2010). Although, the LRR domain presents in the AFPs, the main ice-binding region is predicted to be the IRI domain, which contains two ice-binding surfaces. These two ice-binding surfaces are complementary to the prism face of ice-crystal and the highly conserved glycine residues in the IRI domain containing proteins are structurally significant, as they form the turns between the upper and lower β-strand faces of the ice-binding β-roll (Kuiper et al., 2001).

Gene analysis is an important technique in genomic research used to understand the genome of species once it has been sequenced, which includes pair-wise and multiple sequence alignment (Mount, 2004). Epigenetics refer to study of inherited modification in gene function that happens without a change in the nucleic acid sequence for e.g. DNA methylation and chromatin remodeling (Bird, 2007). Various structural and functional studies on fish and insect AFPs have been reported previously. However, the comprehensive computational analysis towards the plant specific AFPs have not been studied so far. In the present study, we analyzed the essential sequence and secondary structural features of LRR and IRI domain containing plant AFPs based on multiple sequence alignment (MSA), phylogenetic analysis, principal coordinate analysis (PCoA) and secondary structure prediction. This has resulted in the identification of sequence and secondary structural

*Corresponding author. E-mail: krishstrucbio@gmail.com, krishna.bic@pondiuni.edu.in. Tel: +91-413-2655580. Fax: +91-413-2655211.

Abbreviations: LRR, Leucine rich repeat; **IRI**: ice-recrystallization inhibition; **PGIP**, polygalacturonase inhibiting protein; **PCoA**, principal coordinate analysis.

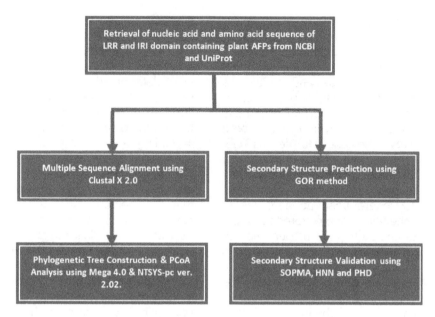

Figure 1. The Flow-Chart representation for the methodology of comparative sequence analysis and secondary structure prediction.

pattern of LRR/IRI domain, which can be used to identify the AFPs and their homology in a newly sequenced plant genome. This analysis could help to classify the plant AFPs based on the sequential characteristics of LRR/IRI patterns. The molecular phylogenetic analysis based classifications are already reported in several studies (Tyagi et al., 2010; Hoegger et al., 2006; Anamika et al., 2008). The present study provides new insight towards the designing of designer AFP with potential industrial and biomedical applications.

MATERIALS AND METHODS

Sequence data collection

The dataset of LRR and IRI domain containing AFPs and their nucleic acid sequences were obtained from UniProt (O'Donovan and Apweiler, 2011) and NCBI (www.ncbi.nlm.nih.gov) databases. The selected AFPs are *D. carota* (AAC62932, AAV66074, CAB69452 and CAB69453), *L. perenne* (ACN38303), *T. aestivum* (ACM61985, ACM61984, Q56B89 and Q56B90), *H. vulgare* (D2CVR1) and *D. antarctica* (ACN38302, ACN38301, ACN38300, ACN38299, ACN38298, ACN38297 and ACN38296). Of these 17 AFPs, four belong with *D. carota*, which contain LRR domain alone; whereas remaining plants contain both LRR and IRI domains. The proposed methodology for comparative sequence analysis and secondary structure prediction is shown in Figure 1.

Multiple sequence alignment and phylogenetic tree construction

MSA was performed for both the nucleic acid and protein sequences of LRR and IRI domain containing AFPs with the help of stand-alone software Clustal X 2.0 (Larkin et al., 2007) using the parameters: Gap Opening-15, Gap Extension-6.66, Delay

Divergent Sequences-30%, Protein Weight Matrix-Gonnet series and DNA Weight Matrix-IUB. The position of the conserved pattern, consensus sequences, and closely related group of selected AFPs were observed from the results of comparative sequence analysis. Based on the results of MSA, the MEGA 4.0 (Molecular Evolutionary Genetic Analysis) (Kumar et al., 2008) was used to construct the un-rooted phylogenetic tree for both nucleic acid and protein sequences, and the evolutionary relationship was inferred using the Neighbor-Joining (NJ) method (Saitou and Nei, 1987). The statistical significance of this method was evaluated by bootstrap analysis with 500 iterative tree constructions.

Principal coordinate analysis

A rectangular binary data matrix was prepared, and all the analysis was carried out by using NTSYS-pc ver. 2.02. (Applied Biostatistic, Exerter Software, Setauket, New York, USA), a program for Numerical Taxonomy System. In order to validate the phylogenetic analysis results, the PCoA of the pair wise genetic distances were also performed using this program.

Secondary structure prediction

The secondary structural elements (helix, sheet and coil) of selected AFPs were predicted using secondary structure prediction server GOR (Sen et al., 2005), and it was validated by SOPMA (Geourjon and Deleage, 1995), HNN (Guermeur et al., 1999) and PHD (Rost, 1996). Moreover, the secondary structural pattern of the LRR and IRI domain present in AFPs were also predicted. The combined sequence and secondary structural patterns would have helped into identify the plant AFPs effectively.

RESULTS AND DISCUSSION

LRR and IRI are two essential ice-binding domains,

which plays an imperative role in ice-recrystallization inhibition mechanism. They are characterized by the conserved sequence pattern of "P-X-X-X-X-X-L-X-X-L-X-X-L-X-L-S-X-N-X-L-X-G-X-I" for LRR (Zhang et al., 2004) and "N-X-V-X-X-G" / "N-X-V-X-G" for IRI domain (Zhang et al., 2010) respectively. Computational analysis of these two domains includes comparative sequence alignment, phylogenetic analysis, PCoA analysis, pattern analysis (nucleic acid and protein sequence) and secondary structure prediction.

Multiple sequence alignment

MSA of both nucleic acid and protein sequences (Figure 2A and B) showed the several conserved regions. MSA results reveal the residues involved in the formation of LRR and IRI domain is conserved in all the sequences, except in the AFPs from *D. carota*, where IRI domain is completely absent. These conserved residues are essential for the mechanism of RI with ice-crystal. The number of conserved and variables sites present in MSA of protein sequences are 61 and 290 respectively. Similarly, the comparative nucleic acid sequence alignment contains 158 conserved and 878 variable sites. The results for the nucleic acid and protein sequence alignment of LRR and IRI domain containing AFPs agreed quite well. The alignment score of AFPs from *D. carota* with others is very low, due to the single-domain sharing property. The AFPs from remaining plant showed the reasonable score (Table 1), because of the conservation of two ice-binding domains. Thus, our results support dividing plant AFPs into two major types: Class I AFP-characterized by the presence of only LRR pattern and Class II AFPs posses both LRR and IRI patterns. The results of MSA are useful to construct the un-rooted phylogenetic tree for both nucleic acid and protein sequences, and it was validated by PCoA analysis.

Phylogenetic analysis for protein sequences

In order to understand the evolutionary relationship of LRR and IRI domain containing AFPs in over-wintering plants, the un-rooted phylogenetic tree was constructed from various plants such as *D. carota*, *D. antarctica*, *L. perenne*, *T. aestivum* and *H. vulgare*. The Jukes – Cantor model was used to compute the phylogenetic tree for nucleic acid sequences (Jukes and Cantor, 1969). We used NJ method to carry out the distance based phylogenetic analysis. The nucleic acid and amino acid data matrix was constructed from inter-species MSA of nucleic acid and protein sequences of selected AFPs. The amino acid data matrix of selected AFPs contains 539 total sites, in which, 61 of conserved, 290 of variable, 241 of parsimony-informative and 49 of singleton sites.

The overall mean distance of seventeen LRR and IRI domain containing AFPs was 0.941. Convergence and divergence are two essential phylogenetic properties, which can be useful to identify the closely as well as distantly related group containing plant AFPs. The pair wise distance matrix (Table 2) was constructed for nucleic acid as well as protein sequences to understand these two properties of selected AFPs. NJ phylogenetic analysis of the selected AFP sequences resulted in the clustering of three major clades (Figures 3A and B), and their details are given below. The first two clades have LRR + IRI pattern containing AFPs (Class II) and third group have only LRR pattern containing AFPs (Class I).

Clade I (*D. antarctica* + *L. perenne* AFPs)

This is strongly supported group, and it composed of numerous sister clades (SC) such as SC1, SC2 and SC3. The amino acid data matrix of this clade consists of 298 total sites, in which, 136 of conserved, 153 of variable, 61 of parsimony-informative and 91 of singleton sites. SC1 has the two Sub Sister Clades (SSC) namely SSC1 (*D. antarctica*: ACN38302 and ACN38298) and SSC2 (*D. antarctica*: ACN38299 and ACN38296). The SC2 (*L. perenne*: ACN38303 and *D. antarctica*: ACN38297) and SC3 (*D. antarctica*: ACN38301 and ACN38300) contains two taxa, which has no further sub-divisions. Homogenous (Same taxa: SC1 and SC3) and heterogeneous SCs (Different taxa: SC2) are also obtained by the above observations. The overall mean distance of this clade was 0.292. The pair wise distance between *L. perenne* – AFP (ACN38303) and *D. antarctica* - AFP (ACN38297) is very low reveals that less divergence has occurred.

Clade II (*T. aestivum* + *H. vulgare* AFPs)

This clade comprised of four AFPs from *T. aestivum* and one protein from *H. vulgare*. The amino acid data matrix of this clade consists of 434 total sites, in which, 163 of conserved, 219 of variable, 12 of parsimony-informative and 108 of singleton sites. The overall mean distance of this clade was 0.289. Three mono-taxa are observed from this clade, and they are ACM61985, ACM61984 and Q56B89. The AFP (D2CVR1) from *H. vulgare* is closely related with the AFP (Q56B90) of *T. aestivum,* which was confirmed by the presence of common LRR pattern "P-S-W-I-G-E-L-D-H-L-C-Y-L-D-L-S-D-N-S-L-V-G-E-V") and good bootstrap value.

Clade III (*D. carota* AFPs)

This is very a smallest clade compared to clade I and II, which comprised of four AFPs from *D. carota*. The amino acid data matrix of this clade consists of 332 total sites, in

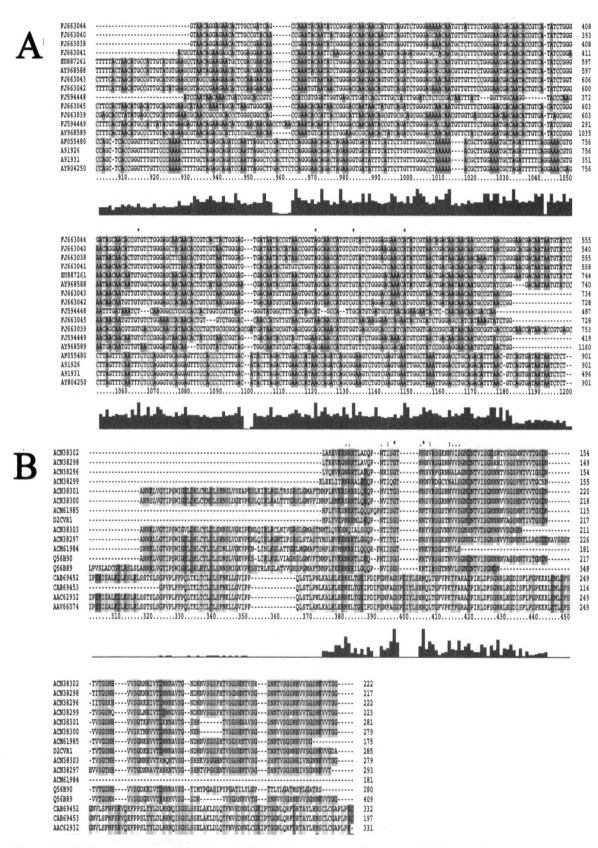

Figure 2. (A) Comparative nucleic acid and (B) Protein sequence alignment of LRR and IRI domain containing antifreeze proteins was performed using ClustalX 2.0. "*" represents single fully conserved residues, ":" represents fully conserved strong groups and periods fully conserved weaker groups are indicated by "."

Table 1. Sequence alignment score of nucleic acid and protein sequences of selected antifreeze proteins computed from Clustal X 2.0. Numerical code indicates accession numbers of nucleic acid and protein sequences of selected antifreeze proteins. 1 = AF055489 (AAC62932), 2 = AY804250 (AAV66074), 3 = A91926 (CAB69452), 4 = A91931 (CAB69453), 5 = FJ594449 (ACM61985), 6 = FJ494448 (ACM61984), 7 = AY968588 (Q56B90), 8 = AY968589 (Q56B89), 9 = FJ663045 (ACN38303), 10 = FJ663044 (ACN38302), 11 = FJ663043 (ACN38301), 12 = FJ663042 (ACN383030), 13 = FJ663041 (ACN38299), 14 = FJ663040 (ACN38298), 15 = FJ663039 (ACN38297), 16 = FJ663038 (ACN38296) and 17 = EU887261 (D2CVR1).

Alignment score table for nucleic acid sequences

	1	2	3	4	5	6	7	8	9	10	11	12	13	14	15	16	17
1	-	98	100	98	03	06	07	02	04	03	05	02	02	05	02	03	04
2	98	-	98	97	03	06	07	02	04	03	05	02	02	05	02	03	04
3	100	98	-	98	03	06	07	02	04	03	05	02	02	05	02	03	04
4	98	97	98	-	05	04	02	03	03	04	03	03	03	04	02	04	02
5	03	03	03	05	-	40	74	56	80	81	55	57	58	56	87	69	87
6	06	06	06	04	40	-	74	36	78	79	39	33	62	37	79	41	79
7	07	07	07	02	74	74	-	40	78	78	73	42	63	39	76	46	75
8	02	02	02	03	56	36	40	-	76	78	79	87	32	85	80	31	81
9	04	04	04	03	80	78	78	76	-	91	78	79	63	78	80	46	80
10	03	03	03	04	81	79	78	78	91	-	78	79	64	79	80	46	80
11	05	05	05	03	55	39	73	79	78	78	-	80	30	80	80	34	81
12	02	02	02	03	57	33	42	87	79	79	80	-	37	86	80	33	81
13	02	02	02	03	58	62	63	32	63	64	30	37	-	32	64	25	61
14	05	05	05	04	56	37	39	85	78	79	80	86	32	-	78	31	80
15	02	02	02	02	87	79	76	80	80	80	80	80	64	78	-	46	92
16	03	03	03	04	69	41	46	31	46	46	34	33	25	31	46	-	45
17	04	04	04	02	87	79	75	81	80	80	81	81	61	80	92	45	-

Alignment score table for protein sequences

	1	2	3	4	5	6	7	8	9	10	11	12	13	14	15	16	17
1	-	98	100	100	14	22	15	06	13	15	09	07	15	11	20	21	13
2	98	-	98	96	14	22	17	06	16	15	09	07	15	11	16	21	17
3	100	98	-	100	14	22	15	06	13	15	09	07	15	11	20	21	13
4	100	96	100	-	10	12	12	03	13	15	05	02	09	05	17	25	13
5	14	14	14	10	-	33	65	58	73	74	52	58	65	55	66	57	85
6	22	22	22	12	33	-	67	44	70	71	44	38	73	44	76	70	75
7	15	17	15	12	65	67	-	63	69	70	65	63	77	63	61	60	69
8	06	06	06	03	58	44	63	-	71	72	72	83	69	81	59	59	76
9	13	16	13	13	73	70	69	71	-	86	69	70	74	70	65	61	72
10	15	15	15	15	74	71	70	72	86	-	72	71	74	72	65	70	73
11	09	09	09	05	52	44	65	72	69	72	-	71	67	74	58	56	75
12	07	07	07	02	58	38	63	83	70	71	71	-	67	82	58	56	75
13	15	15	15	09	65	73	77	69	74	74	67	67	-	68	63	57	71
14	11	11	11	05	55	44	63	81	70	72	74	82	68	-	58	55	75
15	20	16	20	17	66	76	61	59	65	65	58	58	63	58	-	62	78
16	21	21	21	25	57	70	60	59	61	70	56	56	57	55	62	-	65
17	13	17	13	13	85	75	69	76	72	73	75	75	71	75	78	65	-

which, 326 of conserved, six of variable, six of singleton sites where as the parsimony-informative site was not observed in this clade. The overall mean distance of *D. carota* AFPs was 0.016. This clade has the two SCs namely SC1 and SC2. The AFP "AAV66074" exists as mono taxa, which is found in SC1 and SC2, consist of three AFPs, in which, one of the mono-taxa (CAB69452) and two of di-taxa (AAC62932 and CAB69453) respectively. The divergence property was observed between AFPs of *D. carota* with others in the order of

Table 2. Pair wise distance matrix of nucleic acid and protein sequences of selected antifreeze proteins constructed from MEGA. Numerical code indicates accession numbers of nucleic acid and protein sequences of selected antifreeze proteins. 1 = AF055489 (AAC62932), 2 = AY804250 (AAV66074), 3 = A91926 (CAB69452), 4 = A91931 (CAB69453), 5 = FJ594449 (ACM61985), 6 = FJ494448 (ACM61984), 7 = AY968588 (Q56B90), 8 = AY968589 (Q56B89), 9 = FJ663045 (ACN38303), 10 = FJ663044 (ACN38302), 11 = FJ663043 (ACN38301), 12 = FJ663042 (ACN383030), 13 = FJ663041 (ACN38299), 14 = FJ663040 (ACN38298), 15 = FJ663039 (ACN38297), 16 = FJ663038 (ACN38296) and 17 = EU887261 (D2CVR1).

					Pair wise distance matrix for nucleic acid sequences											
	1	2	3	4	5	6	7	8	9	10	11	12	13	14	15	16	17
1	-	0	0	0	1.9	1.9	1.7	1.8	2.2	2.2	2.1	2.0	3.2	1.8	1.8	1.8	1.8
2	0	-	0	0	1.9	1.8	1.6	1.7	2.1	2.1	2.1	1.9	3.0	1.8	1.8	1.8	1.8
3	0	0	-	0	1.9	1.9	1.7	1.8	2.2	2.2	2.1	2.0	3.2	1.8	1.8	1.8	1.8
4	0	0	0	-	1.9	1.9	1.7	1.8	2.2	2.2	2.1	2.0	3.2	1.8	1.8	1.8	1.8
5	1.9	1.9	1.9	1.9	-	1.2	0.4	0.3	0.2	0.2	0.2	0.2	0.7	0.3	0.1	0.3	0.1
6	1.9	1.8	1.9	1.9	1.2	-	1.4	1.1	1.2	1.2	1.1	1.1	1.7	1.2	1.0	1.4	1.0
7	1.7	1.6	1.7	1.7	0.4	1.4	-	0.4	0.3	0.3	0.4	0.4	0.7	0.4	0.3	0.5	0.3
8	1.8	1.7	1.8	1.8	0.3	1.1	0.4	-	0.3	0.2	0.2	0.1	0.6	0.2	0.2	0.4	0.2
9	2.2	2.1	2.2	2.2	0.2	1.2	0.3	0.2	-	0.1	0.3	0.2	0.6	0.3	0.2	0.3	0.2
10	2.2	2.1	2.2	2.2	0.2	1.2	0.3	0.2	0.1	-	0.3	0.2	0.6	0.2	0.2	0.3	0.2
11	2.1	2.1	2.1	2.1	0.2	1.1	0.4	0.2	0.3	0.3	-	0.2	0.7	0.2	0.2	0.4	0.2
12	2.0	1.9	2.0	2.0	0.2	1.1	0.4	0.1	0.2	0.2	0.2	-	0.5	0.2	0.2	0.4	0.2
13	3.2	3.0	3.2	3.2	0.7	1.7	0.7	0.6	0.6	0.6	0.7	0.5	-	0.6	0.7	0.8	0.6
14	1.8	1.8	1.8	1.8	0.3	1.2	0.4	0.2	0.3	0.2	0.2	0.2	0.6	-	0.2	0.4	0.2
15	1.8	1.8	1.8	1.8	0.1	1.0	0.3	0.2	0.2	0.2	0.2	0.2	0.7	0.2	-	0.3	0.1
16	1.8	1.8	1.8	1.8	0.3	1.4	0.5	0.4	0.3	0.3	0.4	0.4	0.8	0.4	0.3	-	0.3
17	1.8	1.8	1.8	1.8	0.1	1.0	0.3	0.2	0.2	0.2	0.2	0.2	0.6	0.2	0.1	0.3	-

					Pair wise distance matrix for amino acid sequences											
	1	2	3	4	5	6	7	8	9	10	11	12	13	14	15	16	17
1	-	0.0	0.0	0.0	1.9	1.7	1.9	1.6	1.7	1.7	1.9	1.9	1.6	1.7	1.6	1.7	1.9
2	0.0	-	0.0	0.0	1.9	1.7	1.9	1.6	1.7	1.7	1.9	1.9	1.6	1.9	1.6	1.7	1.9
3	0.0	0.0	-	0.0	1.9	1.7	1.9	1.6	1.7	1.7	1.9	1.9	1.6	1.7	1.6	1.7	1.9
4	0.0	0.0	0.0	-	1.9	1.7	1.9	1.6	1.7	1.7	1.9	1.9	1.6	1.7	1.6	1.7	1.9
5	1.9	1.9	1.9	1.9	-	0.3	0.4	0.4	0.3	0.3	0.7	0.3	0.3	0.6	0.1	0.4	0.2
6	1.7	1.7	1.7	1.7	0.3	-	0.6	0.4	0.4	0.3	0.6	0.5	0.4	0.5	0.3	0.4	0.4
7	1.9	1.9	1.9	1.9	0.4	0.6	-	0.5	0.5	0.5	0.8	0.4	0.3	0.8	0.5	0.7	0.5
8	1.6	1.6	1.6	1.6	0.4	0.4	0.5	-	0.5	0.4	0.6	0.2	0.3	0.4	0.4	0.6	0.5
9	1.7	1.7	1.7	1.7	0.3	0.4	0.5	0.5	-	0.1	0.8	0.4	0.3	0.6	0.3	0.4	0.3
10	1.7	1.7	1.7	1.7	0.3	0.3	0.5	0.4	0.1	-	0.7	0.4	0.3	0.5	0.3	0.5	0.4
11	1.9	1.9	1.9	1.9	0.7	0.6	0.8	0.6	0.8	0.7	-	0.6	0.7	0.6	0.6	0.8	0.7
12	1.9	1.9	1.9	1.9	0.3	0.5	0.4	0.2	0.4	0.4	0.6	-	0.3	0.4	0.4	0.7	0.4
13	1.6	1.6	1.6	1.6	0.3	0.4	0.3	0.3	0.3	0.3	0.7	0.3	-	0.5	0.3	0.5	0.4
14	1.7	1.9	1.7	1.7	0.6	0.5	0.8	0.4	0.6	0.5	0.6	0.4	0.5	-	0.6	0.8	0.6
15	1.6	1.6	1.6	1.6	0.1	0.3	0.5	0.4	0.3	0.3	0.6	0.4	0.3	0.6	-	0.3	0.1
16	1.7	1.7	1.7	1.7	0.4	0.4	0.7	0.6	0.4	0.5	0.8	0.7	0.5	0.8	0.3	-	0.4
17	1.9	1.9	1.9	1.9	0.2	0.4	0.5	0.5	0.3	0.4	0.7	0.4	0.4	0.6	0.1	0.4	-

D. antarctica > *L. perenne* > *H. vulgare* > *T. aestivum*. Similarly, the AFPs from *D. antarctica*, *L. perenne*, *T. aestivum* and *H. vulgare* posses convergence properties (Lowest pair wise distance) with each other.

The most primitive branch of the molecular phylogenetic tree was, the functional segregation of *D. carota*-AFPs (Clade III) from the remaining AFPs of *T. aestivum*, *L. perenne*, *H. vulgare* and *D. antarctica* (Clade I and II), which was confirmed by the phylogenetic analysis of both nucleic acid and protein sequences. The AFPs from *D. carota* do not have IRI pattern, and it contains only tandemly placed LRR patterns, which is

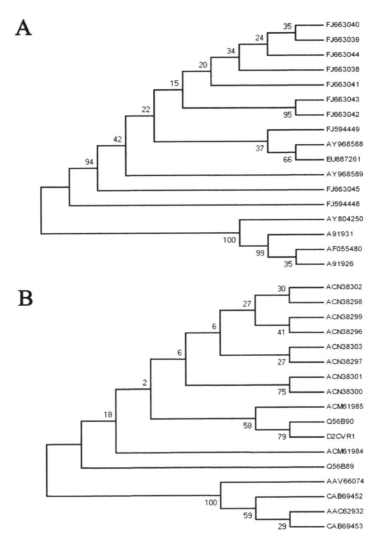

Figure 3. The molecular phylogenetic trees were derived from the NJ analyses of the (A) nucleic acid and (B) protein sequences of selected antifreeze proteins. The Accession number of nucleic acid and protein sequences of selected antifreeze proteins are: *D. carota*: AF055480 (AAC62932), AY804250 (AAV66074), A91926 (CAB69452) and A91931 (CAB69453), *T. aestivum*: FJ594449 (ACM61985), FJ594448 (ACM61984), AY968588 (Q56B90) and AY968589 (Q56B89), *L. perenne*: FJ663045 (ACN38303), *D. antarctica*: FJ663044 (ACN38302), FJ663043 (ACN38301), FJ663042 (ACN38300), FJ663041 (ACN38299), FJ663040 (ACN38298), FJ663039 (ACN38297) and FJ663038 (ACN38296), *H. vulgare*: EU887261 (D2CVR1).

one of the main functional reason for the segregation of *D. carota* AFPs from others.

Phylogenetic analysis for nucleic acid sequences

The nucleic acid data matrix of LRR and IRI domain containing AFPs contains 1333 total sites, in which, 158 of conserved, 878 of variable, 635 of parsimony-informative and 243 of singleton sites. The overall mean distance of nucleic acid sequence of selected AFPs was

1.221. As compared with protein phylogeny, the nucleic acid phylogeny is also showing three clades, which consist of nucleic acid sequences of selected AFPs from various over-wintering plants. In addition, we also observed the functional segregation property of *D. carota* AFPs with others. The similarities between both protein and nucleic acid phylogenetic analysis results showed that, the AFPs of *T. aestivum* and *H. vulgare* are closely related. Similarly, the AFP of *L. perenne* is closely related with *D. antarctica* and *T. aestivum* AFPs, confirmed by the results of both protein and nucleic acid

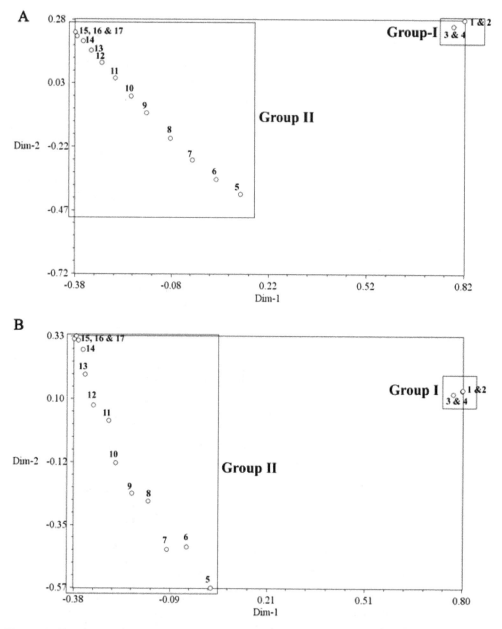

Figure 4. The Principal Coordinate Analysis of (A) nucleic acid and (B) protein sequences of selected antifreeze proteins was performed by NTSYS-pc. Numerical code indicates accession numbers of nucleic acid and protein sequences of selected antifreeze proteins. 1 = AF055480 (AAC62932), 2 = AY804250 (AAV66074), 3 = A91926 (CAB69452), 4 = A91931 (CAB69453), 5 = FJ594449 (ACM61985), 6 = FJ494448 (ACM61984), 7 = AY968588 (Q56B90), 8 = AY968589 (Q56B89), 9 = FJ663045 (ACN38303), 10 = FJ663044 (ACN38302), 11 = FJ663043 (ACN38301), 12 = FJ663042 (ACN38300), 13 = FJ663041 (ACN38299), 14 = FJ663040 (ACN38298), 15 = FJ663039 (ACN38297), 16 = FJ663038 (ACN38296) and 17 = *H. vulgare*: EU887261 (D2CVR1).

phylogenetic analysis.

Principal coordinate analysis

The PCoA is a method for building the orientations using the set of aligned sequences or pair wise genetic distances, which is more informative in highlighting the differences between major taxonomic groups rather than dendrogram representations. In our study, we have performed the PCoA analysis of nucleic acid and protein sequences of plant AFPs to validate the results of phylogenetic analysis. The 2D plot (Figures 4A and 4B) of PCoA is an assorted combination of several AFP data.

The PCoA analysis revealed a pattern, in which the individuals were assigned into two different groups based on the presence of LRR or IRI domains. In this grouping, the individuals from *D. carota* AFPs posses LRR domain alone, which were assigned into the group I. Group II consisted of AFPs from *D. antarctica*, *T. aestivum*, *H. vulgare* and *L. perenne*, which posses both LRR and IRI domains. These two groups were clearly separated from each other.

The *D. carota* AFPs were differed significantly from others due to its functional segregation property, which was validated by the PCoA analysis of nucleic acid as well as protein sequences. The PCoA analysis confirms the homologous nature of AFPs from *T. aestivum* with *H. vulgare*, because these two AFPs (15 and 17) are positioned nearby in Mod3D Plot of NTSYS-pc ver. 2.02. All these findings were consistent with the results of molecular phylogenetic analysis of LRR and IRI domain containing plant AFPs. The results of comparative nucleic acid and protein sequence alignment, phylogenetic analysis and PCoA analysis would support the major classification (Class I and Class II) in plant AFPs and this classification could be extended by in-depth analysis of LRR and IRI sequence patterns.

Secondary structure analysis of conservative and non-conservative portions in LRR and IRI domains

Secondary structural study is necessary to identify the structural classes of these proteins. The secondary structural class of selected AFPs belongs to α+β as experimental structure of LRR domain containing proteins (Kobe and Deisenhofer, 1994). Secondary structure analysis of the conserved and non-conserved portion of LRR and IRI pattern in AFPs would provide a valuable insight towards the identification of new plant AFPs with the addition of their protein sequence patterns.

The conserved portion of LRR repeats in *D. carota*, *T. aestivum* (second LRR repeat), *D. antarctica*, *L. perenne* and *H. vulgare* (second LRR repeat) are rich in coil content rather than helices and sheets, where as the conserved portion of first LRR repeat in *T. aestivum* and *H. vulgare* is rich in helices. The non-conserved part of LRR repeat in all plant AFPs are rich in coil element except *D. antarctica*, because, it contains the equal amount of the coil and helix forming amino acids. The conserved and non-conserved part of LRR repeats in *D. carota* and *L. perenne* do not have helices in their protein secondary structures, whereas all the remaining proteins that we studied contained mixed secondary structural elements.

The secondary structural element "helix" was not observed in any of the conserved and non-conserved portion of IRI patterns in plant AFPs, which contains only coil and sheets. The observed secondary structural LRR

and IRI patterns in selected AFPs are listed in Table 3. The AFPs from *D. carota*, *L. perenne* and *H. vulgare* showing strong secondary structure pattern, whereas, reasonable secondary structure pattern was observed in other two plants such as *T. aestivum* and *D. antarctica*.

Applications

Classification of plant AFPs with reference to the analysis LRR and IRI patterns

All the observed IRI patterns of plant AFPs were arranged in a discontinuous manner, whereas, the LRR patterns were placed in both continuous as well as the discontinuous manner, which is an important difference observed between two domains in terms of arrangement. The summary of protein sequence pattern of the LRR and IRI domain present in the selected AFPs is mentioned in Table 4. The overall classification of plant AFPs is shown in Figure 5. Based on the presence of LRR and IRI patterns, the plant AFPs can be classified into two types namely Class I and Class II.

Class I plant AFPs

The AFPs of *D. carota* belong with Class I AFPs, which is characterized by containing only LRR pattern. The intra-species comparative protein sequence alignment results reveal the AFPs from *D. carota* showing the presence of two conserved LRR patterns. These two LRR patterns were placed tandemly and characterized by the conserved patterns of "P-L-F-F-P-Q-L-T-K-L-T-C-L-D-L-S-F-N-K-L-L-G-V-I" for first LRR repeat and "P-P-Q-L-S-T-L-[PA]-N-L-K-A-L-H-L-E-R-N-E-L-T-G-E-I" for second LRR repeat respectively. These two patterns are encoded by the following triplet series of "CCT-TTA-TTC-TTC-CCT-CAG-CTT-ACG-AAA-CTA-ACT-TGT-TTA-GAC-TTA-TCG-TTT-AAC-AAA-CTT-TTG-GGT-GTA-ATC" for repeat one and "CCT-CCT-CAG-CTT-TCC-ACT-CTT-CCG-AAC-CTT-AAA-GCC-CTG-CAC-TTA-GAA-CGT-AAC-GAA-CTC-ACC-GGT-GAA-ATC" for repeat two in 5' to 3' direction of the +1 reading frame. The substitution was occurred in 16th position of repeat two (TCG => GAA; Serine => Glutamic acid), which convert the original LRR pattern ("CCT-TTA-TTC-TTC-CCT-CAG-CTT-ACG-AAA-CTA-ACT-TGT-TTA-GAC-TTA-TCG-TTT-AAC-AAA-CTT-TTG-GGT-GTA-ATC") into substituted LRR pattern ("CCT-CCT-CAG-CTT-TCC-ACT-CTT-CCG-AAC-CTT-AAA-GCC-CTG-CAC-TTA-GAA-CGT-AAC-GAA-CTC-ACC-GGT-GAA-ATC"). In the molecular phylogenetic tree, the functional segregation property of *D. carota* was aided by the presence of these two tandemly placed LRR patterns and absence of IRI patterns in their protein sequences.

Table 3. Summary of observed protein secondary structure patterns of Leucine Rich Repeat (LRR) and Ice-recrystallization inhibition (IRI) domain containing plant antifreeze proteins.

Plant name	No. of entries	Leucine rich repeat (LRR) domain		Ice-recrystallization inhibition (IRI) domain	
		No. of occurrences	Secondary structural pattern	No. of occurrences	Secondary structural pattern
Class I (LRR pattern alone)					
D. carota	4	2	C-C-C-C-C-C-C-C-C-C-E-E-C-C-C-C-C-C-C-E-E-E-C C-C-C-C-C-C-C-[CH]-H-H-H-H-H-H-H-H-H-C-C-C-E-E-E-C	0	-
Class II – Group A – A1(Both LRR + IRI, IRI < 10, LRR = 1)					
T. aestivum	1	1	C-C-C-C-C-C-C-[CH]-H-H-[HHE]-E-E-C-C-C-[CC]-C-[EE]-[EE]-[EE]-C-[EE]-C	2	C-[EE]-[EE]-E-E-C,C-E-E-E-E-C
Class II – Group A – A2 (Both LRR + IRI, IRI > 10, LRR > = 1)					
T. aestivum	3	2	C-C-C-C-C-C-C-[CH]-H-H-[HHE]-E-E-C-C-C-[CC]-C-[EE]-[EE]-[EE]-C-[EE]-C [CC]-C-[CC]-C-C-C-H-H-H-H-[HHH]-[HH]-H-H-H-H-[HH]-C-[CCC]-C-C-E-E-C	9	C-[EE]-[EE]-E-E-C,C-E-[EE]-[EE]-[EE]-C,C-E-[EE]-[EE]-[EE]-C, C-E-E-E-E-C,C-E-[EE]-E-C,C-[EE]-E-[EEE]-C,C-[EE]-E-[EE]-[EC], C-[EE]-E-[EE]-C and [CC]-[CCE]-[EEE]-[EE]-[EEE]-C
Class II – Group B – B1 – C1 (Both LRR + IRI, IRI > 10, LRR = 1, highly identical)					
L. perenne	1	1	C-C-C-C-C-C-C-C-C-E-E-E-E-C-C-C-C-C-E-E-E-E-C	11	C-E-E-E-C,C-E-E-E-E-C,C-E-E-E-C,C-E-E-E-C,C-E-E-E-E-C,C-E-E-E-E-C,C-E-E-E-C,C-E-E-E-E-C,C-E-E-E-E-C,C-E-E-E-E-C,C-E-E-E-C
Class II – Group B – B1 – C2 (Both LRR + IRI, IRI > 10, LRR = 1, moderately identical)					
D. antarctica	7	1	[CCCC]-[CC]-C-[CC]-[CCCH]-H-H-[HH]-H-[HH]-[HHH]-[HHH]-[HHH]-[HH]-[CC]-[CCCC]-[CCCC]-[CCC]-[CCC]-[EE]-E-[EE]-[EE]-[EC]	12	C-[CCC]-E-E-[EEE]-C,[CC]-C-[EE]-[EEE]-[EE]-C,C-[EE]-E-E-E-C,C-[EEE]-E-E-C, C-C-[CEE]-[EEE]-[EEE]-C,[CE]-[EE]-E-E-C,C-[CCC]-E-[EE]-[EC],[CE]-E-E-E-C,C-[EE]-E-E-C, C-[EE]-E-E-C,C-E-E-E-E-C and C-E-[EE]-E-[EE]-C
Class II – Group B – B2 (Both LRR + IRI, IRI > 10, LRR > = 1)					
H. vulgare	1	2	C-C-C-C-C-C-H-H-H-H-H-H-H-H-H-H-C-C-C-E-E-E-C C-C-C-C-C-C-C-C-H-H-H-H-H-C-C-C-C-C-C-E-E-E-C	12	C-E-E-E-E-C,C-E-E-E-E-C,C-E-E-E-C,C-E-E-E-C,C-E-E-E-C,C-E-E-E-C,C-E-E-E-E-C,C-E-E-E-C,C-E-E-E-C,C-E-E-E-C,C-E-E-E-C and C-E-E-E-C

Class II plant AFPs

The AFPs from *D. antarctica*, *T. aestivum*, *L. perenne* and *H. vulgare* belong to this Class II AFPs, and all these proteins contain both LRR and IRI patterns. Class II classifications could be extended into Group A and Group B on the basis of the occurrence of IRI patterns. The average occurrence of IRI pattern in selected AFPs is nearly ten; hence, we have used this as a criterion for the classification of Class II plant AFPs.

Table 4. Catalog of the observed protein sequence patterns of leucine rich repeat (LRR) and ice-recrystallization inhibition (IRI) domain containing plant antifreeze proteins.

Plant name	No. of entries	Leucine rich repeat (LRR) domain		Ice-recrystallization inhibition (IRI) domain	
		No. of occurrences	Protein sequence pattern	No. of occurrences	Protein sequence pattern
Class I (LRR pattern alone)					
D. carota	4	2	P-L-F-F-P-Q-L-T-K-L-T-C-L-D-L-S-F-N-K-L-L-G-V-I P-P-Q-L-S-T-L-[PA]-N-L-K-A-L-H-L-E-R-N-E-L-T-G-E-I	0	-
Class II – Group A – A1(Both LRR + IRI, IRI < 10, LRR = 1)					
T. aestivum	1	1	P-S-W-I-G-E-L-[DE]-H-L-[HCR]-Y-L-D-L-S-[ND]-N-[SL]-[ML]-[IV]-G-[KE]-V	2	N-[KT]-[VI]-R-S-G,N-T-V-I-S-G
Class II – Group A – A2 (Both LRR + IRI, IRI > 10, LRR > = 1)					
T. aestivum	3	2	P-S-W-I-G-E-L-[DE]-H-L-[HCR]-Y-L-D-L-S-[ND]-N-[SL]-[ML]-[IV]-G-[KE]-V [PL]-I-[PA]-G-A-S-L-A-G-L-[IVA]-[RQ]-L-E-E-L-[FN]-L-[GSA]-S-N-S-F-A	9	N-[KT]-[VI]-R-S-G, N-T-V-I-S-G, N-T-[VI]-[VI]-[ST]-G, N-H-V-V-S-G, N-V-[LV]-S-G, N-[VN]-V-[TAS]-G, N-[VT]-V-[TV]-[EG], N-[VA]-V-[TA]-G and [NT]-[KTN]-[VLT]-[VY]-[TLS]-G
Class II – Group B – B1 – C1 (Both LRR + IRI, IRI > 10, LRR = 1, highly identical)					
L. perenne	1	1	P-S-W-I-G-V-L-D-H-L-C-Y-L-D-L-S-N-N-S-L-V-G-E-I	11	N-T-V-S-G, N-T-V-S-G , N-T-V-S-G, N-T-V-S-G, N-T-V-S-G, N-Y-V-R-S-G, N-N-V-V-S-G , N-T-V-T-S-G, N-H-V-V-T-G, N-K-V-V-T-G and N-V-V-S-G
Class II – Group B – B1 – C2 (Both LRR + IRI, IRI > 10, LRR = 1, moderately identical)					
D. antarctica	7	1	[PLNK]-[KC]-L-[CL]-[WGCL]-L-L-[LQ]-L-[LF]-[SLF]-[AVL]-[LFA]-[LF]-[LF]-[PSHL]-[VAEH]-[ATE]-[SGT]-[ST]-A-[TA]-[SA]-[CS]	12	N-[HNS]-V-R-[SFD]-G, [NY]-N-[VA]-[IVL]-[AS]-G, N-[TI]-V-I-S-G, N-[TIV]-V-S-G,N-T-[VIL]-[TVL]-[TIR]-G, [NK]-[HQ]-V-V-S-G, N-[AKD]-]-V-[TS]-[GR], [NH]-T-V-S-G, N-[TA-]-V-S-G, N-[TV]-V-S-G, N-K-V-V-T-G and N-H-[VI]-V-[ST]-G
Class II – Group B – B2 (Both LRR + IRI, IRI > 10, LRR > = 1)					
H. vulgare	1	2	G-A-S-L-A-G-L-A-W-L-E-E-L-N-L-A-N-N-R-L-V-G-T-I P- S- W- I- G-E-L-D-H-L-Y-Y-L-D-L-S-D-N-S-L-V-G-E-V	12	N-T-V-R-S-G, N-T-V-I-S-G, N-H-V-V-S-G, N-V-V-S-G, N-N-V-A-G, N-T-V-T-G, N-H-V-V-S-G, N-A-V-S-G, N-N-V-S-G, N-T-V-S-G, N-T-V-S-G and N-K-V-V-G

Group A- Plant with less than ten occurrences of IRI pattern

The AFPs from *T. aestivum* contain nine reasonably conserved IRI pattern, in which, the AFP "ACM61984" shares only first two conserved IRI pattern while it lacks others. This Group can also be extended into two sub-groups based on the occurrence of the LRR pattern. Protein with the occurrence of single LRR pattern was placed in A1 group and protein with more than one

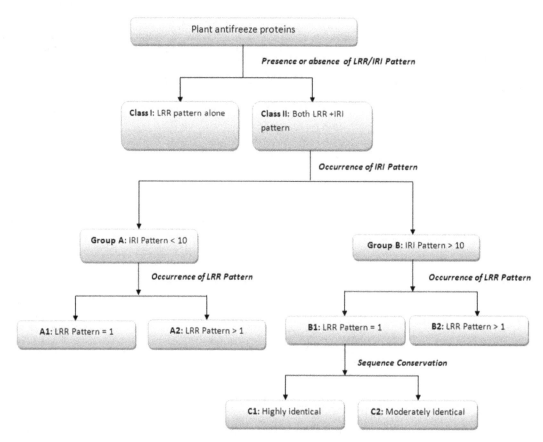

Figure 5. Schematic representation for the classification of antifreeze proteins in over-wintering plants.

occurrence of LRR pattern was placed in A2 group.

A1-Protein with the occurrence of single LRR pattern

One of the AFP in *T. aestivum* "ACM61985" does not have the first LRR repeat due to the deletion of this region. The conserved single LRR pattern in "ACM61985" of *T. aestivum* is "P̲-S-W-I-G-E-L̲-[DE]-H-L̲-[HCR]-Y-L̲-D-L̲-S̲-[ND]-N̲-[SL]-[ML̲]-[IV]-G̲-[KE]-V̲". The amino acid substitution was observed at the 24ᵗʰ position (valine instead of isoleucine) of this repeat in all *T. aestivum* AFPs. The substituted valine residue was encoded by the codon "GTA", which is also conserved in all four AFPs.

A2-Protein with the occurrence of more than one LRR pattern

The three AFPs (ACM61984, Q56B90 and Q56B89) of *T. aestivum* showing the presence of two conserved LRR patterns, which are not placed in tandemly, and they are separated by several amino acid residues such as eight amino acids for ACM61984, 150 amino acids for Q56B89 and 16 amino acids for Q56B90. The two conserved LRR

patterns in *T. aestivum* are "[PL̲]-I-[PA]-G-A-S-L̲-A-G-L̲-[IVA]-[RQ]-L̲-E-E̲-L̲-[FN]-L̲-[GSA]-S̲-N-S̲-F-A̲" and "P̲-S-W-I-G-E-L̲-[DE]-H-L̲-[HCR]-Y-L̲-D-L̲-S̲-[ND]-N̲-[SL]-[ML̲]-[IV]-G̲-[KE]-V̲". The first LRR repeat is moderately conserved due to the high number of insertion/deletion that occurred.

Group B- Plant with more than ten occurrences of IRI pattern

The AFPs of *D. antarctica*, *L. perenne* and *H. vulgare* belong with Group B. *D. antarctica*-AFPs contains 12 conserved IRI patterns, of which, some possess substituted residues. The AFPs of *H. vulgare* and *L. perenne* contain 12 and 11 IRI patterns, which did not contain any substituted residues. This Group can also be further classified into two sub-groups namely B1 and B2, which are based on the occurrence of the LRR pattern.

B1-Protein with the occurrence of single LRR pattern

Based on the sequence conservation of LRR patterns, it has been extended into two groups. Protein with moderately and highly identical LRR pattern was placed under C1 and C2 groups respectively.

C1- Protein with highly identical LRR pattern

The single highly identical LRR pattern "P-S-W-I-G-V-L-D-H-L-C-Y-L-D-L-S-N-N-S-L-V-G-E-I" (Position: 110-133) was observed in AFP of *L. perenne*, which was encoded by "CCA-TCT-TGG-ATT-GGT-GTG-CTT-GAC-CAC-CTT-TGC-TAC-TTG-GAT-CTC-TCA-AAT-AAT-TCA-TTG-GTT-GGT-GAG-ATA" triplets in 5'-3' direction of the +1 reading frame.

C2- Protein with moderately identical LRR pattern

Single moderately identical LRR pattern "[PLNK]-[KC]-L-[CL]-[WGCL]-L-L-[LQ]-L-[LF]-[SLF]-[AVL]-[LFA]-[LF]-[LF]-[PSHL]-[VAEH]-[ATE]-[SGT]-[ST]-A-[TA]-[SA]-[CS]", was observed in AFPs of *D. antarctica* due to the more numbers of INDELS was occurred in their nucleic acid as well as protein sequences.

B2-Protein with the occurrence of more than one LRR pattern

Two nearly identical tandem LRR patterns (Position: 86 – 108 and 109 – 133) were observed in *H. vulgare,* and they are "G-A-S-L-A-G-L-A-W-L-E-E-L-N-L-A-N-N-R-L-V-G-T-I" and "P-S-W-I-G-E-L-D-H-L-Y-Y-L-D-L-S-D-N-S-L-V-G-E-V". These two patterns are encoded by the triplets of "GGA-GCA-TCT-TTG-GCA-GGC-CTC-GCA-TGG-TTG-GAG-GAG-CTC-AAC-CTT-GCC-AAC-AAC-AGA-CTG-GTT-GGC-ACC-ATC" for first LRR repeat and "CCG-TCA-TGG-ATT-GGC-GAG-CTT-GAC-CAC-CTT-TAC-TAC-TTG-GAT-CTT-TCA-GAT-AAT-TCA-TTG-GTT-GGC-GAG-GTA" for second LRR repeat in 5'-3' direction of the +1 reading frame. These two repeats showed three different variations (Two variations for first LRR repeat and one variation for second LRR repeat) at both the nucleic acid as well as amino acid level. Single amino acid substitution was occurred at 1st (CCG => GGA; Proline => Glycine) and 16th (TCA => GCC; Serine => Alanine) position of repeat one and 24th position (ATC => GTA; Isoleucine => Valine) of repeat two. Figures 6 and 7 explain the classification of plant AFPs with reference to the analysis of LRR and IRI patterns.

Recommendation for identification of AFPs in over-wintering plants

Based on our study, we have proposed new methodology (Figure 8) for the identification of plant AFPs. It includes four steps such as (i) Searching with LRR/IRI or both the protein sequence pattern, (ii) Searching with the secondary structural pattern of LRR/IRI or both the domains, (iii) Analysis of non-conservative residues present in the two patterns and (iv) Comparison of given query with existing datasets containing protein sequence of plant AFPs through Local BLAST.

Hints for protein engineering

The mechanism of ice-recrystallization inhibition was guided by the presence of LRR and IRI patterns in protein sequence. The present study provides new insights towards the designing of synthetic construct of plant AFP (Designer plant AFP) with three important properties such as (i) Fusion of LRR and IRI patterns into the single domain, (ii) Increasing the number of LRR and IRI patterns, and (iii) develop the sequence array for continuously arranged LRR and IRI patterns. These three properties would facilitate to increase the ice-recrystallization inhibitory activity, and it will protect the plants from freezing conditions.

Conclusion

Considering the importance of Plant AFPs and to address the unavailability of a detailed classification scheme, we have carried out the comprehensive sequence analysis of Plant AFPs bearing LRR and IRI domains and had presented a novel scheme to classify them based on their pattern, occurrence and conservations. This classification had identified several key features such as the occurrence of two highly conserved and consecutive LRR patterns in the AFPs belonging to the *D. carota*, while it was observed to have a single occurrence in *L.perenne* and *D.antarctica*, with high and moderate conservations respectively. Similar to *D. carota*, AFPs from *H. vulgare* is also observed to have the two nearly identical consecutive LRR patterns but the presence of IRI domain in the latter made it to diverge from the *D.carota*. AFPs from *T. aestivum* also differ from the *H. vulgare* with non consecutive LRR patterns with partial conservation in first one and a high degree of conservation in second one. Similar to *H. vulgare*, the AFPs from *L. perenne*, *T. aestivum* and *D. antarctica* were also found to have both LRR and IRI domains. The presence of both LRR and IRI domains in the former ones made them to be place in a separate Group Class II with respect to AFPs from *D. carota*, which was placed in a group Class I. Similar to LRR patterns, the number, occurrence and conservation of IRI domains were accounted in sub classification of entries placed in the Class II group. In addition to the sequential features of LRR and IRI domains, their secondary structural patterns were also identified and

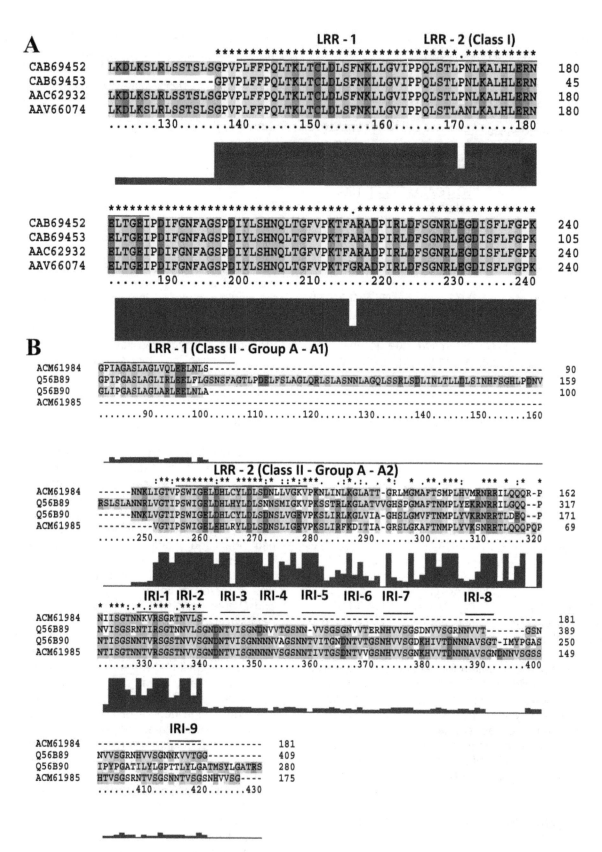

Figure 6. Classification of plant antifreeze proteins with reference to the LRR and IRI patterns (A) Class I (LRR pattern alone), (B) Class II - Group A - A1 and A2 (Both LRR + IRI pattern [Class II] - Occurrence of less than ten IRI pattern [Group A] - Occurrence of single LRR pattern [A1] and Occurrence of more than one LRR pattern [A2].

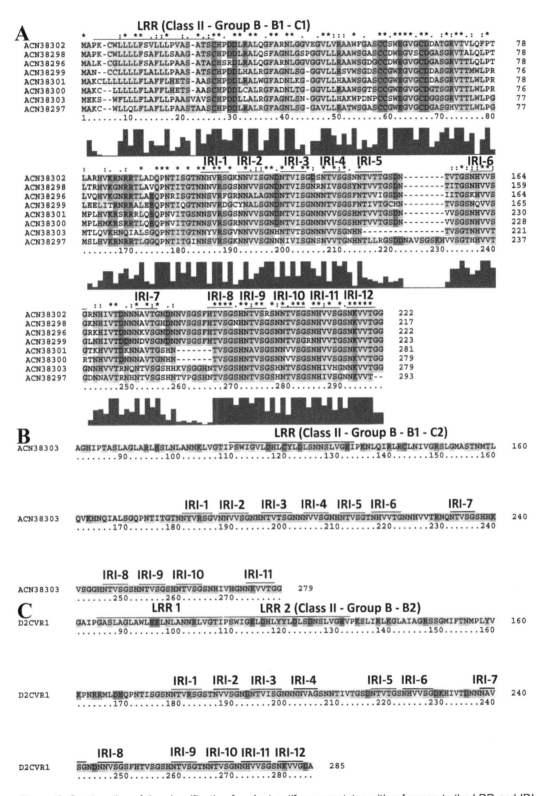

Figure 7. Continuation of the classification for plant antifreeze proteins with reference to the LRR and IRI patterns (A) Class II - Group B - B1 - C1 (Both LRR + IRI pattern [Class II] - Occurrence of more than ten IRI pattern [Group B] - Occurrence of single LRR pattern [B1] - Moderately identical LRR pattern [C1], (B) Class II – Group B – B1 – C2 (Both LRR + IRI pattern [Class II] - Occurrence of more than ten IRI pattern [Group B] - Occurrence of single LRR pattern [B1] - Highly identical LRR pattern [C2]) and (C) Class II - Group B – B2 (Both LRR + IRI pattern [Class II] - Occurrence of more than ten IRI pattern [Group B] – Occurrence of more than one LRR pattern [B2]).

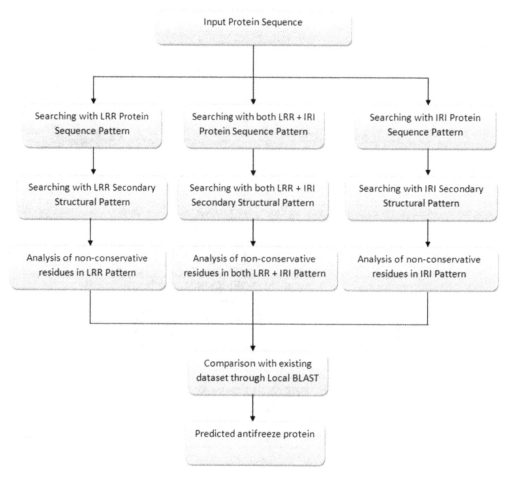

Figure 8. Proposed methodology for the identification of antifreeze proteins in plants.

reported. The observed results might help in the identifi-cation and classification of new plant AFPs in the future. The secondary structural information along with sequential patterns of the identified LRR and IRI can also be employed in the design of synthetic AFPs to account for enhanced RI and TH activities.

ACKNOWLEDGEMENTS

J. Muthukumaran thanks Council for Scientific and Industrial Research (CSIR) for Senior Research Fellowship (SRF). P. Manivel thanks University Grant Commission (UGC), Government of India for providing financial assistance to carry out the research work. M. Kannan thanks UGC for Rajiv Gandhi National Fellowship to pursue his Ph.D degree. R. Krishna thanks Centre of Excellence in Bioinformatics, Pondicherry University funded by Department of Biotechnology and Department of Information technology, Government of India, New Delhi for providing the essential computational resources for carrying out the research work.

REFERENCES

Anamika K, Bhattacharya A, Srinivasan N (2008). Analysis of the protein kinome of Entamoeba histolytica. Proteins, 71: 995-1006.
Atici O, Nalbantoglu B (2003). Antifreeze proteins in higher plants. Phytochemistry, 64: 1187-1196.
Bird A (2007). Perceptions of epigenetics. Nature, 447: 396–398.
Deng G, Andrews DW, Laursen RA (1997). Amino acid sequence of a new type of antifreeze protein, from the longhorn sculpin Myoxocephalus octodecimspinosis. FEBS Lett., 402: 17-20.
Duman JG (2001). Antifreeze and ice nucleator proteins in terrestrial arthropods. Annu. Rev. Physiol., 63: 327–357.
Gage AA, Baust J (1998). Mechanisms of tissue injury in cryosurgery. Cryobiology, 37: 171-186.
Geourjon C, Deleage G (1995). SOPMA: significant improvements in protein secondary structure prediction by consensus prediction from multiple alignments. Comput. Appl. Biosci., 11: 681-684.
Guermeur Y, Geourjon C, Gallinari P, Deleage G (1999). Improved performance in protein secondary structure prediction by inhomogeneous score combination. Bioinformatics, 15:413-421.
Hoegger PJ, Kilaru S, James TY, Thacker JR, Kües U (2006). Phylogenetic comparison and classification of laccase and related multicopper oxidase protein sequences. FEBS J., 273: 2308-2326.
Jukes TH, Cantor CR (1969). Evolution of Protein Molecules, Academic Press, New York, pp. 21–132.
Knight CA, DeVries AL, Oolman LD (1984). Fish antifreeze protein and the freezing and recrystallization of ice. Nature, 308: 295-296.

Kobe B, Deisenhofer J (1994). The leucine-rich repeat: a versatile binding motif. Trends Biochem. Sci., 19: 415-421.

Kuiper MJ, Davies PL, Walker VK (2001). A theoretical model of a plant antifreeze protein from Lolium perenne. Biophys. J., 81: 3560-3565.

Kumar S, Nei M, Dudley J, Tamura K (2008). MEGA: A biologist-centric software for evolutionary analysis of DNA and protein sequences. Brief Bioinformatics, 9: 299-306.

Larkin MA, Blackshields G, Brown NP, Chenna R, McGettigan PA, McWilliam H, Valentin F, Wallace IM, Wilm A, Lopez R, Thompson JD, Gibson TJ, Higgins DG (2007). Clustal W and Clustal X version 2.0. Bioinformatics., 23: 2947-2948.

Meyer K, Keil M, Naldrett MJ (1999). A leucine-rich repeat protein of carrot that exhibits antifreeze activity. FEBS Lett., 447: 171-178.

Mount DW (2004). Bioinformatics: Sequence and Genome Analysis, Second Edition. Cold Spring Harbor Laboratory Press, USA, pp. 1-692.

Ng NF, Hew CL (1992). Structure of an antifreeze polypeptide from the sea raven. Disulfide bonds and similarity to lectin-binding proteins. J. Biol. Chem., 267: 16069-16075.

O'Donovan C, Apweiler R (2011). A Guide to UniProt for Protein Scientists. Methods Mol. Biol., 694: 25-35.

Patel SN, Graether SP (2010). Structures and ice-binding faces of the alanine-rich type I antifreeze proteins. Biochem. Cell. Biol., 88: 223-229.

Raymond JA, DeVries AL (1977). Adsorption inhibition as a mechanism of freezing resistance in polar fishes. Proc. Natl. Acad. Sci. USA., 74: 2589-2593.

Rost B (1996). PHD: predicting one-dimensional protein structure by profile-based neural networks. Methods Enzymol., 266: 525-539.

Saitou N, Nei M (1987). The neighbor-joining method: a new method for reconstructing phylogenetic trees. Mol. Biol. Evol., 4: 406-425.

Scotter AJ, Marshall CB, Graham LA, Gilbert JA, Garnham CP, Davies PL (2006). The basis for hyperactivity of antifreeze proteins. Cryobiol., 53: 229-239.

Sen TZ, Jernigan RL, Garnier J, Kloczkowski A (2005). GOR V server for protein secondary structure prediction. Bioinformatics., 21: 2787-2788.

Sevier CS, Kaiser CA (2002). Formation and transfer of disulphide bonds in living cells. Nat. Rev. Mol. Cell Biol., 3: 836-847.

Sidebottom C, Buckley S, Pudney P, Twigg S, Jarman C, Holt C, Telford J, McArthur A, Worrall D, Hubbard R, Lillford P (2000). Heat-stable antifreeze protein from grass. Nature, 406: 256

Sonnichsen FD, Sykes BD, Chao H, Davies PL (1993). The nonhelical structure of antifreeze protein type III. Sciences, 259: 1154-1157.

Thomashow MF (1998). Role of cold-responsive genes in plant freezing tolerance. Plant Physiol., 118: 1-8.

Tyagi N, Anamika K, Srinivasan N (2010). A framework for classification of prokaryotic protein kinases. PLoS One., 26: e10608.

Zhang C, Fei SZ, Arora R, Hannapel DJ (2010). Ice recrystallization inhibition proteins of perennial ryegrass enhance freezing tolerance. Planta, 232: 155-164.

Zhang DQ, Liu B, Feng DR, He YM, Wang SQ, Wang HB, Wang JF (2004). Significance of conservative asparagine residues in the thermal hysteresis activity of carrot antifreeze protein. Biochem. J., 377: 589-595.

Zhang DQ, Wang HB, Liu B, Feng DR, He YM, Wang JF (2006). Carrot antifreeze protein does not exhibit the polygalacturonase-inhibiting activity of PGIP family. Yi Chuan Xue Bao., 33: 1027-1036.

22

Using the ant colony optimization algorithm in the network inference and parameter estimation of biochemical systems

Philip Christian C. Zuniga

Department of Computer Science, University of the Philippines, Diliman, Quezon City, Philippines.
E-mail: philip_zuniga@yahoo.com.

Developing models that can represent biochemical systems is one of the hallmarks of systems biology. Scientists have been gathering data from actual experiments, but there is a lack in computer models that can be used by scientists in analysing the various biochemical systems more effectively. In this research, we propose to use an ant colony optimization (ACO) algorithm for the network inference and parameter estimation of biochemical systems, particularly S-systems. The ACO has been used for various problems, and with several improvements, it can also be used to solve the problems that we are considering. Since the ACO has discrete and continuous forms, we plan to use each form for the network inference and parameter estimation problems respectively. The results of our work show that the ACO can be effectively used in the formation of model for biochemical systems.

Key words: Biochemical systems, S-systems, ant colony optimization.

INTRODUCTION

The use of biochemical systems theory (BST) has found many applications in metabolic engineering, drug development, etc. Biochemical systems theory is a framework to model and analyze biochemical systems. Since biochemical systems are highly complex and are highly correlated with each other, models used to represent these kinds of systems are usually non-linear. A biochemical system is a system of metabolites/chemical compounds that interact with one another. These interactions can lead to a change in the concentration of each metabolite/compound or even to the formation of new components. One of the main challenges in systems biology is the development of mathematical or computational models that can simulate the effects of the biochemical system on the various components in it.

The GMA and S-systems formulations of BST are non linear differential equations which involves parameters whose values have to be estimated. Unlike linear systems where effective parameter estimation can be used, there is currently no available algorithm which can efficiently handle S-system or GMA-systems. For this work, we concentrate mainly on the use of S-system [del Rosario et al., 2008]. In an S- system formulation, we let

the concentration of metabolites/chemical component at time be represented by: $X_1(t), X_2(t) \dots X_n(t)$ Relationships of the metabolites can be represented as:

$$\dot{X}_i = \alpha_i \prod_{j=1}^{n+m} X_j^{g_{ij}} - \beta_i \prod_{j=1}^{n+m} X_j^{h_{ij}} \tag{1}$$

We replace $X_j(t)$ with X_j with the understanding that X_j is actually a function of time. The parameters α_i and β_i are called rate constants. These parameters represent the rate at which the concentrations of the metabolites/chemical components of the system increases or decreases with respect to time. The parameters g_{ij} and h_{ij} are the kinetic orders and they represent which metabolites are related to other metabolites. Take note that $g_{ij} = 0$ or $h_{ij} = 0$ implies that metabolite or chemical X_j is not related in the production or degradation of X_i. An S-system formulation, like Equation 1 is one of the structures proposed by Voit and

Almeida [2004] in modeling biochemical systems. Each differential equation represents a reaction. Each reaction involves the production or degradation of a metabolite. A system is usually consists of n reactions, each one associated to a metabolite/chemical component that is part of the biochemical system.

The system of differential equations then represents a biochemical system, So, given a biochemical system, our goal is to find an S-system formulation that can represent the system. This problem can be divided into two problems: (1) Network inference problem, and (2) Parameter estimation problem. The network inference problem involves determining which component interacts with another component in the system. This can be considered as a combinatorial optimization problem since the challenge is to find which combination of metabolites is needed in the production and/or degradation of a given chemical component. This is a hard problem since given n metabolites there are $O(2^n)$ possible combinations of metabolites and so a brute force search of all possible combinations is ineffective. Parameter estimation is the problem of determining the actual values of the kinetic and rate constants.

Unlike the network inference problem, parameter estimation is a continuous problem since it involves the estimation of real values. A parameter set consisting of rate constants and kinetic orders represent a unique biochemical system. The problem of determining the model is reduced to a problem of determining which parameters will be plugged in to the model so that it will produce the values of the $X_j's$. This is considered as an inverse problem, because we are given the time series data of the concentrations of the various chemicals involved in the system, and we need to find what kind of model will produce such results. This inverse problem is difficult because we need to estimate a large number of parameters, given only the time series of the concentration of metabolites. In general, given a set of n metabolites, we need to estimate a $2n$ rate constants and $2n(n-1)$ kinetic orders.

Basically, the two problems can be reduced to a minimization problem. We want to find which combination of metabolites/chemical components and parameters will produce the corresponding time series data that will have as small error as possible with the actual time series data. Since these are minimization problems, we will need to define a fitness or cost function. Given a parameter set q, this parameter set is consists of the rate constants and the kinetic constants, we define $\overline{X}_i(q)$ to be the time series data produced by the parameter set. The cost function will be defined as:

$$F(q) = \sum_{i=1}^{n} \frac{(X_i - X_i(q))^2}{X_i}$$

(2)

This cost function (Equation 2) is similar to the one used in [del Rosario et al., 2008].

We propose the use of the ant colony optimization algorithm in solving the network inference and parameter estimation problems.

Ant colony optimization algorithm

It is known that ants have the behavior of leaving a certain kind of chemical called pheromone. This chemical acts as a tool for ants to communicate, so that they will know which paths are being used by the other ants. The more pheromone concentrated in the area means that there were more ants which used the path, and hence it should be a better route for them to find their food. This idea was the one used by Marco Dorigo, in developing a novel optimization algorithm now known as the ant colony optimization algorithm [Dorigo and Caro, 1999; Tsutsui et al., 2005].

There are two basic forms of the ACO. The discrete type is used for combinatorial optimization problems, while the continuous type is used for continuous problem. The basic principle behind the ACO is given by the pseudo code in Figure 1. In the ACO, the solutions are called paths. The first step is to first generate random solutions or paths. Then the cost values of the path will be computed. Then the pheromones will be updated based on the cost of the solutions/path. Then the next time the new generation of solutions will be produced, the production of the solutions will be biased towards the solutions with higher pheromone values.

In some ACO algorithms, pheromone values of previous solutions will be reduced by incorporating an evaporation routine. This is important so that bad solutions will be eliminated thus reducing the search space. The algorithm will terminate once the termination condition is satisfied. Usually, the termination condition is based on the cost value of the best solution.

Discrete ACO

Two things can characterize the discrete ant colony optimization algorithm:

1. The probabilistic transition rule to determine the direction of each of the ants.
2. The pheromone update mechanism.

In solving the traveling salesman problem, the algorithm considers a set of n solutions and performs several iterations until a certain termination condition is reached. For the TSP, a solution to the problem is any random tour that does not pass any city more than once and that terminates at the starting point.

For the first iteration, the probability that a node will be selected is just the same as the other nodes. While

```
1 procedure ACO_MetaHeuristic
2 while (not_termination)
3     generateSolutions()
4     daemonActions()
5     pheromoneUpdate()
6 end while
7 end procedure
```

Figure 1. ACO pseudo code.

making a tour, each ant will leave pheromone trails on its path. The amount of pheromone that will be left on the path will depend on the distance of the path travelled. The shorter the distance, the more the pheromone that will be left, while the longer the distance, the lesser the amount of pheromone that will be dropped.

For the succeeding iterations, the selection of the nodes will depend on the amount of pheromones that were left in the trail. The more pheromone that were left the higher the probability that a certain path will be chosen. The amount of pheromone that will be left on ground will be updated depending on the cost of value of the solution. Consider a general optimization problem where, given a set of discrete choices, the goal is to find the best combination of choices depending on a given cost functions.

Continuous ACO

A similar approach is used for solving continuous optimization problems. We will be adapting the continuous ACO method that was proposed in [Dorigo and Socha, 2007; Tsutsui, 2006]. The objective is to find the parameter set q, that will minimize the cost function (Equation 2). We have to note, that the elements of the q are real numbers. The continuous ACO algorithm solves this problem by first generating a set of m random vectors. These solutions were generated from a Gaussian distribution. The initial means and the variances of the Gaussian distribution are arbitrary.

After the generation of the vectors, the cost of each vector will be computed and the resulting vectors will be sorted based on the cost values. The vector that has the best (lowest) cost value will then be used for the next iteration of algorithm. New solutions will be generated in the next iterations with the elements of the best vector, as the mean of the Gaussian distributions. The process will

be repeated, until a certain threshold value, based on the cost function, is obtained.

METHODOLOGY

Given an initial data set (time courses), the objective is to find a model that produces the given data. The data set will be consists of time courses of the metabolites that are contained in the system that we are modeling. If that data is from a real system, then it is expected that the data set will contain some noise. Hence, data smoothing can first be done to denoise the data. Standard data smoothing techniques can be done on the data [del Rosario et al., 2008].

In the absence of a real system, a system of differential equations can be used to generate an artificial data set. Noise can be added in the artificial data set. After generating the time course, the differential values at the left side of Equation (1) needs to be approximated. These differential values can approximated by:

$$\frac{dx_i}{dt} \approx \frac{X(t_1) - X(t_2)}{t_1 - t_2}$$

(3)

To reduce the computational complexity of solving for the parameters, Voit and Almeida [2004] proposed the use of decoupling. Decoupling is the process where each differential equation is replaced by an algebraic equation. This is done by replacing the left hand side of Equation (1) with Equation (3). After converting the system into an algebraic system, each equation will be treated as an independent equation from the other equations. Network inference and parameter estimation can now be done per equation and not as a system.

We will then use the two-phase ACO for the network inference and parameter estimation of biochemical systems.

Network inference

Given the time courses, the discrete ACO can be used to predict the relationship among the metabolites. We will present in here our algorithm for the network inference problem. This algorithm is based on the ACO for the knapsack problem. We will call this algorithm ACOI. Take note that since the system is decoupled, we

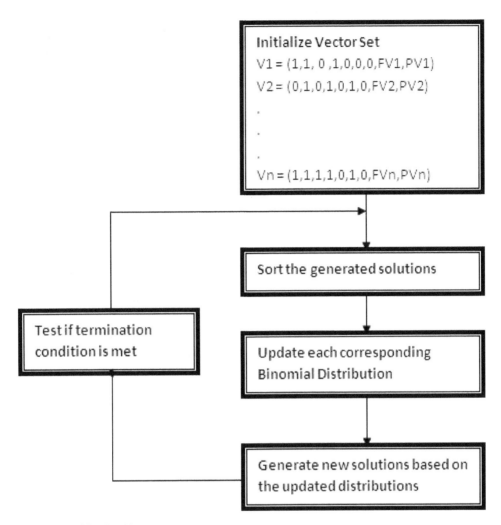

Figure 2. ACOI algorithm.

will be working with each equation separately. Since each equation represents a reaction that yields to the production or degradation of a metabolite, we can associate each equation to a metabolite. We let Y_i to be the metabolite associated to equation/reaction i. A solution vector v for the network inference problem is a $2n + 2$ vector. The first n elements of S are associated to the production of Y_i. If the jth element of the vector is 1, then it means that the jth metabolite is involved in the production of Y_i. If the value is 0, then this means that jth metabolite is not involved in the production of Y_i. The $(n + 1)th$ to $2nth$ elements of S are associated to the degradation of the Y_i. If the $(n + j)th$ element of the vector is 1 then it means that the jth metabolite is involved in the degradation.

Of Y_i. If the value is 0, then this means that jth metabolite is not involved in the degradation of Y_i. The $(2n + 1)th$ element is the cost value (CV) of the solution. This is computed using Equation 2, while the $(2n + 2)th$ element is the pheromone value. The pheromone value, PV is computed as:

$$PV = \frac{1}{CV + 1}$$

Figure 2 shows a flowchart of this revised algorithm:

Initialization

In solving equation i, we will allot a $(2n + 2) \times m$ matrix. We will call this matrix as S. Each column vector of S is a potential solution vector for equation i. Each row K, $k = 1, 2 \ldots 2n$ of S is assigned with a binomial distribution with probability constant p_k. Set $p_k = 0.5$. We used p_k to be initially be equal to 0.5 since we want that there will be an equal probability between getting a 1 (the metabolite is involved in the reaction) or 0 (the metabolite is not involved in the reaction). For each column vector, generate its first $2n$ elements by using the binomial distribution $B(p_k)$. Since $p_k = 0.5$ then it is expected that there is an equal chance of getting a 1 or a 0. The $(2n + 1)th$ element of each column vector is the cost value of the vector, while the $(2n + 2)th$ element is the pheromone value (Equation 3).

178

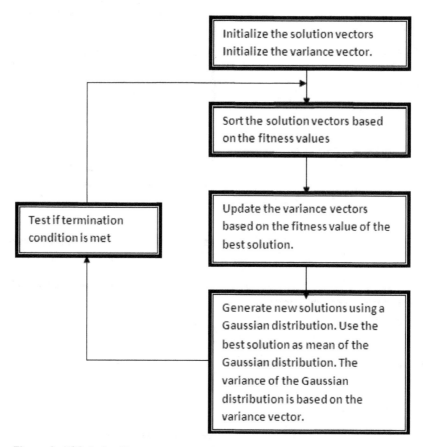

Figure 3. ACO II algorithm.

Sorting of solutions

After generating S , we sort the columns based on the pheromone value of the columns. We then get the upper 10% of the solution. The use of 10% is just an arbitrary choice. These upper 10% serves as the seed for the generation of the next solutions.

Probability update

Each p_k is updated by looking at the kth elements of the seed vectors. If the kth element is 1, then we add an arbitrary value ε to p_k. If the kth element is 0, then we subtract ε from p_k. The update routine is made so that p_k will tend to produce solutions with high pheromone values. We generate new solutions using the updated values of p_k.

Evaporation of pheromones and termination of the ACOI

For each iteration, the stored pheromone values are depreciated using the following equation:

$$PV = \gamma PV$$

where the evaporation constant is γ . This eventually allows the algorithm to delete the combinations with low pheromone value, so

we can save space, and increase the rate of convergence, since we will be searching on a smaller space. We have to remember that γ should not be small enough that it will lead to the immediate termination of the algorithm. Once the cost values of the best solution is less than the threshold, then the algorithm will terminate.

Parameter estimation

We now present our ACO for the parameter estimation problem. We call this algorithm as ACOII. This algorithm is based on the ACO for continuous problems [Dorigo and Socha, 2007; Tsutsui, 2006]. The algorithm is almost similar with ACOI. The main difference is the use of a Gaussian distribution, instead of a binomial distribution. We also put special treatment on the variance that will be used in the Gaussian distribution. Just like in the network inference, the equations will be solved separately. A solution for equation i to the parameter estimation problem is called the parameter set q , where $q = \{\alpha, \beta, g, h\}$. The parameter set is consists of approximations for the kinetic orders and rate constants of equation or reaction i.

Figure 3 shows a flowchart of the ACO for continuous search spaces.

Initiailization

Just like in the network inference problem, we use a matrix, M with size $(2n + 3) \times m$. Each column of M represents a parameter set. The first $2n$ rows represent the kinetic orders, rows $2n + 1$ and $2n + 2$ represent the rate constants. The $(2n + 3)th$ row represents the cost value of the solution. To generate contents, we first use uniform distribution. We assume that the range of the kinetic orders are $(-2, 2)$. while the range of the rate constants are $(-10, 10)$.

Sorting

We then sort the columns of M based on the cost of the solution. The one with the smallest cost will be considered as the best solution and will be represented by vector $\overline{S}$.

Generation of new solutions

We replace the contents of M. For each column vector of M, we generate a corresponding solution vector S. To generate the elements of S, we use a Gaussian distribution $N(s_i, v_i)$. The ith element of S uses a Gaussian distribution with mean, $\overline{S}_i$ and variance v_i. Then we compute for the cost of S. If the cost value of S is lower than the cost value of the corresponding solution vector in M then we replace the vector's contents of S. otherwise, the row vector will stay in M. This enables us to keep the good solutions and remove the bad solutions from M.

Role of the variance

The variance vector plays a very crucial role in the algorithm. The variance vector determines the rate of convergence of the algorithm. A fast depreciating variance vector might make the solutions converge to a local minimum. On the other hand, a slow depreciating variance vector prevents the algorithm from converging to a solution. Traditional continuous ACO algorithms depreciate the variance by either subtracting a constant (linear depreciation) or by multiplying the variance by an arbitrary constant that is less than 1 (exponential depreciation).

A novelty that is introduced in this work is to make the variance dependent on the cost value of the best solution. Currently, thealgorithm imposes a simple direct proportionality relationship between the variance vector and the cost value. If a solution has a higher cost value, then we want the variance to be high too so that ACOII will be able to find other solutions. On the other hand, if a solution has a lower cost value, then we want ACOII to converge immediately, thus requiring a smaller variance. For this purpose, we use a fraction of the cost value of the best solution as the variance of the Gaussian distribution, v_i.

Termination

The algorithm will terminate if the cost value of the best solution is smaller than the threshold value for cost.

Convergence to a local minimum

Converging to a local minimum is a common problem of optimization algorithms. This means that the algorithm has converged to a good solution, but it is not the best solution. This is especially evident if we make our variance vector proportional with the cost

value. A low cost value will mean a low variance vector, but if the solution vector corresponding to the low cost value is not the best solution, then the algorithm will converge to a local minimum.

In order to solve this issue, the researchers introduce a novel innovation to standard ACO algorithms. We will call this as the "jumping ants subroutine". This is a simple innovation to the traditional ACO to help the algorithm find other solutions other than the global minimum.

The jumping ants subroutine works as follows:

1. Set two threshold values, a threshold for the cost value and a threshold for the variance value.
2. If the cost value of the best solution is lower than the threshold for the cost solution, then the algorithm terminates.
3. Since the variance of ACOII constantly depreciates, it will occur that the variance will be less than the variance threshold value. If it is less than the threshold value, but the cost is still higher than the cost threshold, then ACOII will assign the initial value to the variance. This means that the algorithm would look for other solutions.

The graph in Figure 4 illustrates this innovation. It can be seen that the value of the variance already decrease to very small value, but the corresponding cost value is still high. This is a case where the solutions produced by the algorithm will converge to a local minimum. Hence, what ACOII will do is, it will assign a set the variance to its initial value so that the algorithm will be able to find other solutions, and so that the algorithm will not be trapped in a local minimum.

RESULTS AND ANALYSIS

We implemented our algorithm using Matlab 2009, using a 2.2 GHZ computer. We tested two test networks that were proposed in Voit and Almeida [2004]. We used standard networks in our tests. We will be testing the VA04 network given by the following system of differential equations

$$\dot{X}_1 = 20X_3^{-0.8}X_5 - 10X_1^{0.5}$$

$$\dot{X}_2 = 8X_1^{0.5} - 3X_2^{0.75}$$

$$\dot{X}_3 = 3X_2^{0.75} - 5X_2^{0.5}X_3^{0.5}$$

$$\dot{X}_4 = 2X_2^{0.5} - 6X_4^{0.8}$$

$$\dot{X}_5 = 0.9$$

with the following initial values: $X_1 = 5.6$, $X_2 = 3.1$, $X_3 = 2.9$, $X_4 = 3.1$. We also tested the HS96 network given by the following system.

$$\dot{X}_1 = 5X_3X_5^{-1} - 10X_1^2$$

$$\dot{X}_2 = 10X_1^2 - 10X_2^2$$

$$\dot{X}_3 = 10X_2^{-1} - 10X_2^{-1}X_3^2$$

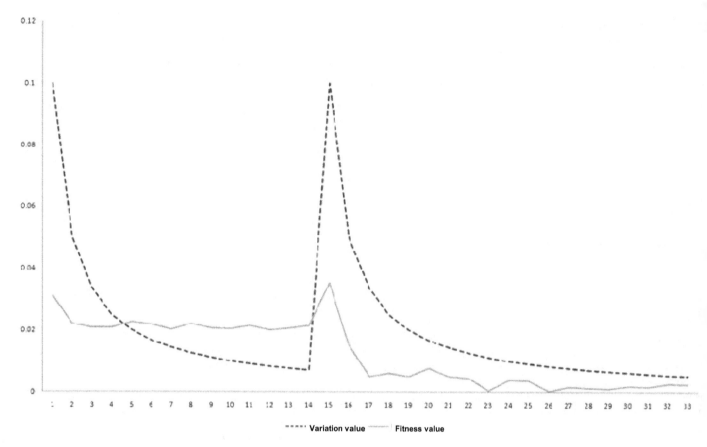

Figure 4. Local minimum.

$$\dot{X_4} = 8X_3{}^2X_5{}^{-1} - 10X_4{}^2$$

$$\dot{X_5} = 10X_4{}^2 - 10X_5$$

with the following initial values: $X_1 = 0.7$, $X_2 = 0.12$, $X_3 = 0.14$, $X_4 = 0.16$ and $X_5 = 0.18$

Network inference results

We first performed network inference on the test networks. The main objective in performing the network inference is to reduce the search space. We do not intend to find the final structure of the system, but rather, we want to reduce the number of metabolites that will be considered for the parameter estimation stage.

The Tables 1 and 2 are the result of the ACOI algorithm for VA04 and HS96. The tables show the number of times a metabolite/component is eliminated after 100 runs. It shows that the metabolites that are eliminated the least number of times are the actual metabolites that are involved in the reaction. The biggest problem in ACOI is when the algorithm eliminates a metabolite that is supposed to be part of the reaction. Once this is done, then the resulting parameter set will be significantly different to the true parameter set.

The results show that the discrete ACO can be used in the network inference problem, but there is still a relatively high rate of error (~10%) where it eliminates metabolites that are supposed to be part of the system.

Accuracy of results

We then tested the accuracy of the resulting time series data. The results in Figure 5 show our results in VA04, while the results of HS96 are shown in Figure 6. The results on both tests have shown that once ACOII terminates, the parameters produced by the algorithm will produce results that are very close to the actual concentration of the metabolites/chemical component. This is expected since termination of ACOII is based on the cost value of the parameters. The graph shows that the cost value after termination is already very small.

We also tested how close the resulting parameter set was with the actual parameter set. Due to the nonlinearity of the differential equations, it is possible that the parameter set producing the actual concentration of metabolites is not unique. Using 100 runs, we counted how many times we hit the correct values of the parameters in both VA04 and HS96. Our results have

Table 1. Network inference for VA04.

	Network inference for VA04									
	Production					Degredation				
	X1	X2	X3	X4	X5	X1	X2	X3	X4	X5
X1	87	62	12	88	3	9	93	45	21	89
X2	12	90	51	41	73	88	11	82	64	39
X3	90	15	89	65	44	43	29	2	3	35
X4	92	19	84	82	82	32	43	49	9	90

Table 2. Network inference for HS96.

	Network Inference for VA04									
	Production					Degredation				
	X1	X2	X3	X4	X5	X1	X2	X3	X4	X5
X1	89	34	10	32	13	6	56	67	98	99
X2	8	89	98	88	71	53	9	43	81	45
X3	19	8	66	91	97	93	9	2	78	88
X4	92	91	3	97	7	94	92	97	14	97
X5	87	65	71	12	65	64	32	21	29	11

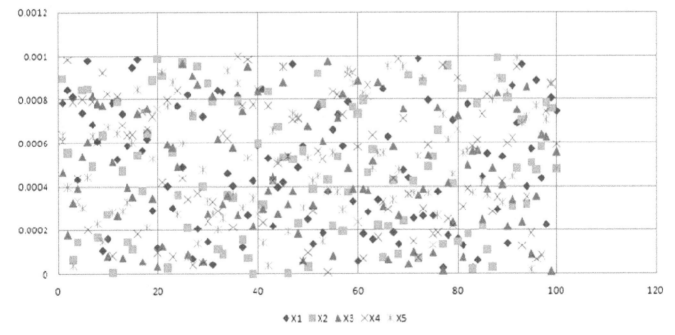

Figure 5. Fitness value results of VA04.

clearly shown that rate constants are more consistent, while the kinetic orders are more vulnerable and have a higher chance of having a different value.

Table 2 shows the percentage of getting the correct parameter values. Since the model depends on the rate constants rather than on kinetic orders, the table shows that the discovery of the rate constants is easier and is more accurate, since the value of the kinetic orders are small. Table 3 shows the % of accurate results that were obtained based on the model, and the original model.

Convergence of solutions

We recorded the number of iterations needed before ACOII terminates. Figures 7 and 8 shows that the

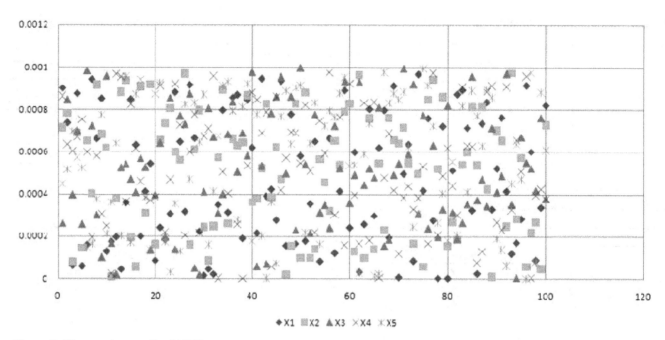

Figure 6. Fitness value results of HS96.

Table 3. Accuracy of parameters.

Parameters	Kinetic orders (%)	Rate constants (%)
VA04	59	83
HS96	67	72

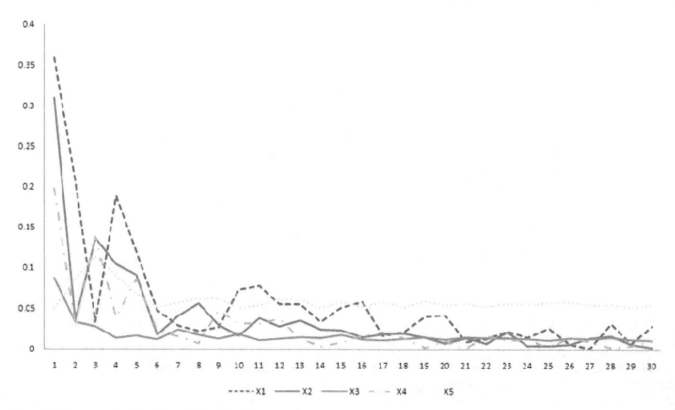

Figure 7. Convergence of solutions (10 ants).

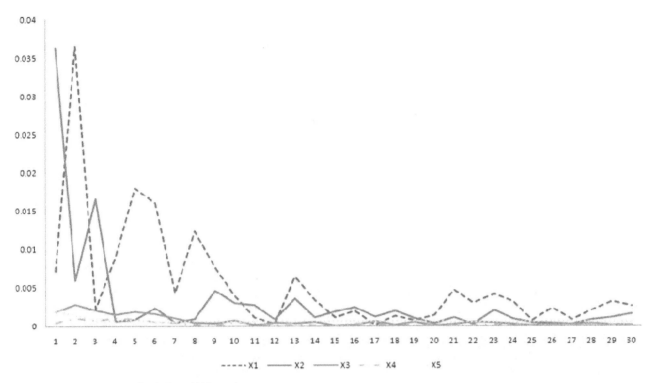

Figure 8. Convergence of solutions (100 ants).

convergence is partly based on the number of ants that were used. We are only presenting our results for VA04, since we obtained the same results as with HS96. We fixed the following parameters:

Cost threshold = 0.0001
Variance threshold = 0.00001

We fixed those two parameters since it is a trivial fact that the smaller the threshold values are, the longer the algorithm will terminate. We varied the number of solution vectors and recorded how many times the solution will fall to a local minimum. Our results have shows that, using more ants will make the solution converge slower (in terms of CPU time), but it approximates the model results closer.

Conclusion

We were able to show that the ant colony optimization algorithm can be used in the modelling biochemical system. The results of the experiments show that the two phase ACO can produce a model that will yield the correct time series data for the concentration of the different metabolites that are involved in the system. We

were able to introduce novel innovations such as a relation between the cost value and the pheromone value, variance depreciation based on the cost value, and the use of the variance threshold and the cost threshold in avoiding converging to local minima.

REFERENCES

Dorigo M, Di Caro G (1999). The Ant Colony Optimization Metaheuristics, New Ideas in Optimization, McGraw-Hill, New York, pp. 11 - 32

Dorigo M, Socha K (2007). An Introduction to Ant Colony Optimization, Approximation Algorithms and Metaheuristics.

Tsutsui S (2006). An Enhanced Aggregation Pheromone System for Real-Parameter Optimization in the ACO Metaphor, ANTS Workshop.

Tsutsui S, Pelikan M, Ghosh A (2005). Performance of Aggregation Pheromone System on Unimodal and Multimodel Problems, Proceedings of IEEE.

Voit EO, Almeida J (2004). Decoupling Dynamical Systems for pathway identification of metabolic profiles, Bioinformatics, Pp. 1670 - 1681

del Rosario R, Echavez M, de Paz M, Zuniga PC, Bargo MC, Arellano C, Pasia JM, Naval P, Voit E, Mendoza E (2008). The MAD Man Benchmarking - User's Guide, Proceedings of the International Conference of Molecular Systems Biology.

23

ATID: Analytical tool for inherited diseases

Hina Iqbal*, Iffat Farzana Anjum and Asif Mir

Department of Bioinformatics and Biotechnology, International Islamic University, Islamabad, Pakistan.

The body of information surrounding molecular and genomic experiments and clinical investigations is rapidly growing. Bioinformatics tools are software programs that are designed for extracting the meaningful information from the mass of molecular biology/biological databases and carry out sequence or structural analysis. Analytical tool for inherited disease (ATID) is a classification database that can hold the complete available information about the inherited diseases. Our designed tool is a set of search programs for the windows platform and is used to perform fast searches for comparison of nucleotide sequences, mutation identification and single nucleotide polymorphism (SNP). Also protein sequences can be searched to find a match against the queried protein sequence. The information comprises their clinical phenotypes, causes and type of disease. Designed software has the ability to classify the disease based on the comparison of given affected individual information (phenotypic and genotypic) with existing information. We analyzed fake data as well as individual's original data on our tool by comparing that with the existing information. That was easy to use and also analyzed results within few seconds. The ATID windows application is designated to solve the problem of extracting the information about the inherited diseases in a fast and simple way. The designed tool can be modified for other diseases as well in future or a single database on the same pattern can be developed comprising of multiple diseases for phenotypic as well as molecular profiling.

Key words: Inherited disease, analytical tool for inherited diseases, bioinformatics, tools.

INTRODUCTION

Inherited genetic variation has a critical but as yet largely characterized role in human disease. Despite the ever-accelerating pace of biomedical research, the root causes of common human disease remain largely unknown, preventative measures are generally inadequate and available treatments are rarely remedial (The international HapMap consortium, 2005). According to the international HapMap consortium, more than a thousand genes for rare, highly heritable "mendalian" disorders have been identified, in which variation in a single gene is both necessary and sufficient to cause disease. Need of the day is to store and to access this huge data, for whom, bioinformatics or computational biology, interdisciplinary fields comprises.

The field of computational biology has seen dramatic growth over the past few years, both in terms of available data, scientific questions and challenges for learning and inference. The rapid pace of discovery in the genomic and proteomic arena requires parallel growth in the field of bioinformatics. Bioinformatics should built databases in a way that facilitates not just the storage of data, but efficient handling and retrieval of information from these databases. This is evident from the fact that modern biology and related sciences are increasingly becoming dependent on this new technology. It is expected that bioinformatics will especially contribute in the future as the leading edge in biomedicine to pharmaceutical companies by expediently yielding a greater quantity of lead drugs for therapy.

The enormous growth of biological data led to the development of several things. First, all these data need to be stored. The second requirement is the need for radical new methods for analyzing these huge databases. Thirdly, powerful hardware is required to carry out the task of analyzing these databases. Development of existing databases as well as the conceptualization and

*Corresponding author. E-mail: hinaiqbaltabassum@gmail.com.

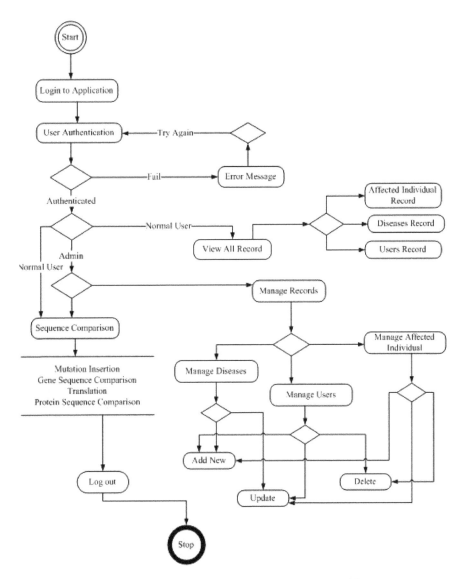

Figure 1. Activity diagram of analytical tool for inherited diseases (ATID).

creation of new types of databases will be critical focal point for the advancement of biological discovery. Analytical tool for inherited diseases (ATID) is a classification database that holds the complete available information about the inherited diseases.

The information comprises their clinical phenotypes, causes, underlying known genes, type of disease, mutation identification and protein comparison. Phenotypic as well as molecular profile of an affected individual can be compared to the existing information and disease can be classified.

MATERIALS AND METHODS

Programming language used for the software was JAVA using the API's of BioJava. And the database used was Microsoft access 2007 that uses the ODBC, JDBC drivers for connectivity.

RESULTS

Design is a meaningful representation of any product/software that is to be built and is the most artistic part of the software development process (Pressman, 2005). ATID design consists of mutation identification, gene sequence comparison and protein sequence comparison. Activity diagram of ATID is given in Figure 1, which describes the work flow behaviour of system and represents the execution state of a mechanism as a sequence of steps grouped sequentially as parallel control flow branches. Hence activity diagram make it easier to understand the design and internal behaviour of ATID. Major modules are gene information, sequence comparisons either gene or protein and affected individual records (Figures 2, 3 and 4). Diseases information can also be added or updated with respect to

GENE INFORMATION

Gene#	Gene Symbol	Gene Function
1	RHO	Visual Transduction Cascade
2	ABCA4	Catabolic Function In The Retina
3	CNGA1	Visual Transduction Cascade
4	PDE6A	Visual Transduction Cascade
5	RPE65	Retinoid Metabolism
6	RP1	Transcription Factor
7	RP2	Protein Folding

Select Any Gene: RHO

Protien Name: Rhodopsin

Chromosome Location: 3q22.1

No. of Mutations: 99

Inheritance Type:)somal Dominant

```
ATGGCAGTTCTCCATGCTGGCCGCCTACATGTTTCTGCTGATCGTGCTGG
GCTTCCCCATCAACTTCCTCACGCTCTACGTCACCGTCCAGCACAAGAAG
CTGCGCACGCCTCTCAACTACATCCTGCTCAACCTAGCCGTGGCTGACCT
CTTCATGGTCCTAGGTGGCTTCACCAGCACCCTCTACACCTCTCTGCATG
GATACTTCGTCTTCGGGCCCACAGGATGCAATTTGGAGGGCTTCTTTGCCA
CCCTGGGCGGTGAAATTGCCCTGTGGTCCTTGGTGGTCCTGGCCATCGA
GCGGTACGTGGTGGTGTGTAAGCCCATGAGCAACTTCCGCTTCGGGGAGA
ACCATGCCATCATGGGCGTTGCCTTCACCTGGGTCATGGCGCTGGCCTG
CGCCGCACCCCCACTCGCCGGCTGGTCCAGGTACATCCCCGAGGGCCT
GCAGTGCTCGTGTGGAATCGACTACTACACGCTCAAGCCGGAGGTCAACA
ACGAGTCTTTTGTCATCTACATGTTCGTGGTCCACTTCACCATCCCCATGAT
TATCATCTTTTTCTGCTATGGGCAGCTCGTCTTCACCGTCAAGGAGGCCGC
TGCCCAGCAGCAGGAGTCAGCCACCACACAGAAGGCAGAGAAGGAGGTCA
CCCGCATGGTCATCATCATGGTCATCGCTTTCCTGATCTGCTGGGTGCCC
TACGCCAGCGTGGCATTCTACATCTTCACCCACCAGGGCTCCAACTTCGG
TCCCATCTTCATGACCATCCCAGCGTTCTTTGCCAAGAGCGCCGCCATCT
ACAACCCTGTCATCTATATCATGATGAACAAGCAGTTCCGGAACTGCATGCT
CACCACCATCTGCTGCGGCAAGAACCCACTGGGTGACGATGAGGCCTCTG
CTACCGTGTCCAAGACGGAGACGAGCCAGGTGGCCCCGGCCTAA
```

Figure 2. Gene selection for detail Information.

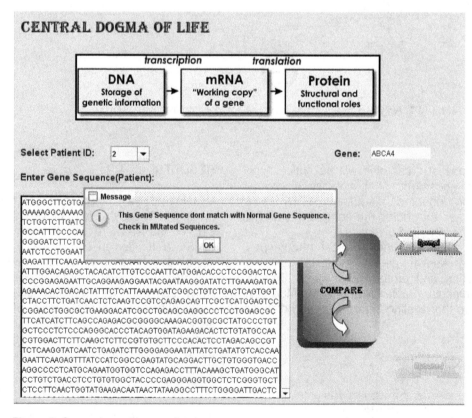

Figure 3. Comparison with normal gene sequence.

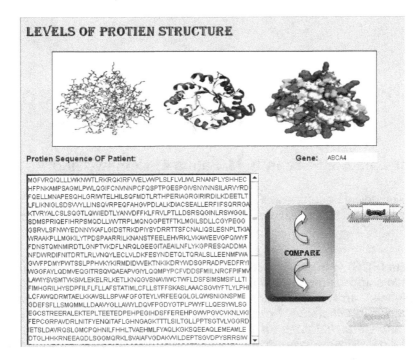

Figure 4. Comparison with mutated gene sequence and conversion into protein sequence.

new discovery or report. It was kept in consideration that testing is to be done at every stage because testing plays a critical role in the success of system.

Analysis to the implementation phase, different testing strategies like black box testing, white box testing, integrated and unit testing are applied to fix the defects and to modify the tool accordingly.

DISCUSSION

Many scientists today complain that it gets increasingly difficult to find useful information in the resulting "data labyrinth". This may largely be due to the fact that the information gets more and more scattered over an increasingly number of heterogeneous resources (Altschul et al, 1990) and as the things become complicated, system become a dilemma. The ATID windows application is designated to solve the problem of extracting the information about the inherited diseases in a fast and simple way. An application with proper "graphical user interface" provides no switching from one program to another is required as it is sequential software. No as such training is required for its practise. All the data is united at a single place.

The designed tool can be modified for other diseases as well in future or a single database on the same pattern can be developed comprising of multiple diseases for phenotypic as well as molecular profiling.

ACKNOWLEDGMENTS

We thank our parents, teachers especially our supervisor for his kind supervision, our institute on providing us space to perform this work and our friends for their moral support.

REFERENCES

The international HapMap Consortium (2005). "Haplotype map of the human genome" Nature, 437; 1299-1320.
Pressmen RS (2005). Software Engineering: A Practitioner's Approach. McGraw-Hill Inc., New York, p. 860.
Altschul SF, Gish W, Miller W, Myers EW, Lipman DJ (1990). Basic local alignment search tool. J. Mol. Biol., 215: 403-410.
BioJava:http://www.biojava.org/download/bj16/bin/biojava.jar.

24

Model-based parameter estimation applied on electrocardiogram signal

A. Moustafa Bani-Hasan [1]*, M. Fatma El-Hefnawi[2] and M. Yasser Kadah[1]

[1]Biomedical Department, Faculty of Engineering, Cairo University, Egypt.
[2]Electronic Research Institute to National Authority for Remote Sensing and Space Science, Egypt.

An Electrocardiogram (ECG) feature extraction system was developed based on the calculation of the poles employing Pade's approximation techniques. Pade's approximation was applied on five different classes of ECG signals' arrhythmia. Each signal was represented as a rational function of two polynomials of unknown coefficients. Poles were calculated for this rational function for each ECG signals' arrhythmia and were evaluated for a large number of signal windows for each arrhythmia. The ECG signals of lead II (ML II) were taken from MIT-BIH database for five different types. These were the ventricular couplet, ventricular tachycardia, ventricular bigeminy, and ventricular fibrillation and the normal. ECG signal was divided into multiple windows, where the poles were calculated for each window, and was compared with the poles computed from the different arrhythmias. This novel method can be extended to any number of arrhythmias. Different classification techniques were tried using neural networks, K nearest neighbor, linear discriminate analysis and multi-class support vector machine.

Key words: Arrhythmias analysis, electrocardiogram, feature extraction, statistical classifiers.

INTRODUCTION

Cardiovascular diseases are the main cause of death globally, where more people die annually from cardiovascular diseases compared to other causes. Approximately 17.5 million people died from cardiovascular diseases in 2005, representing at least 30% of all global deaths according to the World Health Organization report. By 2015, almost 20 million people will die from cardiovascular diseases. The electrocardiogram (ECG) signal is one of the most important tools in clinical practice to assess the cardiac status of patients. This signal represents the potential difference between two points on the body surface, versus time, Rajendra et al. (2007). Extracting the features from this signal has been found very helpful in explaining and identifying various cardiac arrhythmias.

This could be difficult, when the size of the data of the ECG is huge and the existence of different noise types may be contained in the ECG signals. Furthermore, manual analysis is considered time consuming and is prone to errors; hence arises the importance of automatic

recognition of the extraction of the features ECG signals.

Many tools and algorithms have been proposed to extract feature from ECG signals such as, total least squares based Prony modeling algorithm (Chen, 2000) Chaos theory (Owis et al., 2001), autoregressive and multivariate autoregressive models (Dingfei et al., 2002; 2007), heartbeat interval and ECG morphology (Chazal et al., 2004), wavelet transform (Inan et al., 2006), and multiple signal classification algorithm (Ahmad et al., 2008). Most of the aforementioned techniques, involve significant amounts of computation and processing time for features extraction and classification. Another disadvantage is the small number of arrhythmias that can be classified to two or three arrhythmias. Therefore, there is a need for a new technique to classify a larger number of arrhythmias. In addition, the proposed technique can be amenable to real time implementation so it can be used in intensive care units or ECG signal collected.

The objective of the present work is to apply Pade's approximation technique to represent the ECG signal as a rational function of two polynomials of unknown coefficients in order to classify cardiac arrhythmias based on the calculation of poles. These poles of the ECG signal can be used as a signature and a useful feature for

*Corresponding author. E-mail: arabony2004@hotmail.com.

signal discrimination and identification.

MATERIALS AND METHODS

The proposed method for heartbeat classification schema consists of three stages: the preprocessing stage, the feature extraction stage, and the classification stage. First, the ECG signals were pre-processed by filtering it to remove the baseline wander, the power line interference, and the high frequency noise, hence enhancing the signal quality, and omitting the equipment and the environmental effects. Next Pade's approximation technique was applied to model ECG signals, where the poles calculated were used as feature set. Finally, different classifier models were employed to evaluate the proposed method.

The ECG signal may be affected by the different noise types, the baseline wander, the artifact, and the power line interference. Generally, the presence of several noise sources in the signal may corrupt the ECG signal, and make the feature extraction and classification less accurate. To minimize the negative effects of the noise, a Butterworth Band Pass Filter was designed to perform noise reduction. The cutoff frequencies of the band pass filter were selected to be from 0.5 to 40 Hz.

Pade introduced a technique for modelling sampled data as a rational function of two polynomials, Liao et al. (1992), Monsoon et al. (1996), Fatma (1996), Jozef et al. (2001), Van Assche et al. (2006). This method has been applied to various areas, notably electromagnetic scattering, antenna problems signal processing, and radar target identification, Berni (1975).

Let $f(t)$ represent the ECG signal for a certain time interval T and is sampled at D sampling points. Hence it can be written as a rational function of two polynomials $P_n(t)$, $Q_m(t)$ as follows:

$$f(t) \cong \frac{P_n(t_i)}{Q_m(t_i)} \cong \sum_{\alpha=0}^{n} a_\alpha t_i^\alpha \Big/ \sum_{\beta=0}^{m} b_\beta t_i^\beta \qquad (1)$$

Where a, b are the unknown coefficients to be determined. Equation (1) can be written in the following form,

$$f(t).\sum_{\beta=0}^{m} b_\beta t^\beta = \sum_{\alpha=0}^{n} a_\alpha t^\alpha \qquad (2)$$

Where b_0 can be taken equal one for linear predictor constrain. Thus, Equation (2) can be rewritten as,

$$f(t) = \sum_{\alpha=0}^{n} a_\alpha t^\alpha - \sum_{\beta=1}^{m} f(t) b_\beta t^\beta \qquad (3)$$

Equation (3) has $n+m+1$ unknowns (a's, b's). Those unknown coefficients can be calculated using Gauss Jordan method if $D = n+m+1$, or using the least squares method if $D > n+m+1$. Finally, the denominator polynomial m zeros are calculated, which are the poles P_β of the ECG signal $f(t)$, defined by the real and imaginary pars as follows:

$$P_\beta = \varphi_\beta + j\omega_\beta \quad , \beta = 1,2,3,...,m \qquad (4)$$

Where $\omega_\beta = 2\pi f_\beta$, and f_β are the β resonance complex frequency or its inverse is the β pole of the ECG signal's window interval T, Fatma (1996).

The proposed algorithm for heartbeat classification schema was tested on the MIT-BIH Arrhythmia database (www.physionet.org). The data set used for this work comprises five different types including normal, ventricular couplet, ventricular tachycardia, ventricular bigeminy, and ventricular fibrillation. Each type is represented by 64 different patients signal having duration of three seconds long, they are taken from lead number two (MLII). The signal duration can be divided into multiple windows each of 3 s, then the process of calculation the poles P_β or f_β is applied on each window consecutively.

In order to investigate the validity of the proposed method, four classifiers model are employed. Neural networks, K nearest neighbor, linear discriminate analysis and multi-class support vector machine. All classifier models are designed trained and tested using the poles sets extracted from ECG signals (43 for training and 21 for testing). All features sets are divided into independent training and testing sets using n-fold cross validation method. This scheme randomly divides the available data into n approximately equal size and mutually exclusive folds. For an n-fold cross validation run, the classifiers are trained with a different n fold used each time as the testing set, while the other n-1 folds are used for the training data. In this study three fold cross validation are employed.

A feed forward Multilayer Perceptron (MLP) neural network with three layers is implemented, input layer, hidden layer, and output layer. The number of neurons selected at input layer is equal to the number of poles and the accompanied complex frequencies. The neurons at the output layer are selected according to the number of classes. One step secant back propagations training function is used to update the weight. The Tan-Sigmoid function is used as the transfer function in the first and second layers, and pure line function is used in the output layer. An error-correction rule is used to adjust the synaptic weights; where the error is the difference between the target and actual network output.

The distance function applied for K nearest neighbor technique is the Euclidean distance to match the test examples with training examples and for different values of k where k is taken to be 1, 3 and 5. One versus the rest MC-SVM technique with linear training algorithm is employed in this work.

Following the guidelines proposed by the Association for the Advancement of Medical Instrumentation, AAMI (1987), three benchmark parameters were used to assess the algorithm performance: accuracy, specificity, sensitivity defined in the followings Equations (5-7) and is tabulated in Table 1.

$$Accuracy = \frac{(TN + TP)}{\Sigma} \qquad (5)$$

$$Sensitivity = \frac{TP}{TP + FN} \qquad (6)$$

$$Specificity = \frac{TN}{TN + FP} \qquad (7)$$

Where, TP, TN, FP, and FN stand for true positives, true negatives, false positives, and false negatives respectively.

True positives represent abnormal beats classified in their respective classes whereas true negative represents normal beats classified as normal. False positives represent normal beats classified as abnormal and false negatives represent abnormal beats classified

Table 1. The performance measures used in this study.

		Algorithm label					
		nr	**vc**	**vt**	**vb**	**vf**	**sum**
Reference label	NR	NRnr	NRvc	NRvt	NRvb	NRvf	ΣNR
	VC	VCnr	VCvc	VCvt	VCvb	VCvf	ΣVC
	VT	VTnr	VTvc	VTvt	VTb	VTvf	ΣVT
	VB	VBnr	VBvc	VBvt	VBvb	VBvf	ΣVB
	VF	VFnr	VFvc	VBvt	VFvb	VFvf	ΣVF
							Σ

$TN = NRnr$, $TP = VCvc + VTvt + VBvb + VFvf$; $FP = NRvc + NRvt + NRvb + NRvf$; $FN = VCnr + VTnr + VBnr + VFnr$. NR: normal rhythm. VC: ventricular couplet. VT: ventricular tachycardia. VB: ventricular bigeminy. VF: ventricular fibrillation

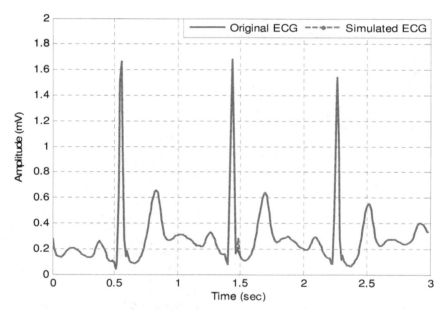

Figure 1. A patient ECG (blue line) and simulated ECG (red line) with normal rhythm using Pade's approximation technique.

beats classified as normal.

RESULTS AND DISCUSSION

Initially, ECG signals are filtered using a Butterworth band pass filter with cutoff frequencies of 0.5 to 40 Hz to reduce the noise. Then, Pade's approximation technique is employed for all the filtered ECG signals to extract the poles. A reconstruction of all these ECG signals using the previous calculated poles, complex natural frequency resonances, proves the exactness of the method employed. This is shown in Figures 1. Both the original filtered ECG signal and the constructed ECG signal from Pade's approximation technique coincide on each other.

Application of various classifier models to test those features is the final stage of the proposed schema. The Artificial Neural Network and K nearest neighbor gave the best results, where the accuracy and specificity and sensitivity reached to 100%. The accuracy for multi-class support vector machine and linear discriminate analysis reaches to 98.10%, where two signals are classified incorrectly. But, the specificity and sensitivity for multi-class support vector machine is reached to 100% and reached for linear discriminate analysis to 99.05%. This mean, the multi-class support vector machine is better than linear discriminate analysis to classify normal beat as normal.

Table 2 shows a comparison between the proposed technique with other method introduced by Owis et al (2001) and Kafieh et al. (2007). Owis et al. (2001) developed a feature extraction technique using the correlation dimension and the largest Lyapunov exponent, to model the chaotic nature of five different classes of ECG signals. Kafieh et al. (2007) presented a method to

Table 2. Comparison between presented and other techniques.

Feature extraction technique	Classifier model	Specificity (%)	Sensitivity (%)
Owis et al. (2001)	K nearest neighbor	40.63	80.45
Kefieh et al. (2007)	Learning vector quantization	88	98
Proposed Method	Neural network	100	100

Kafieh et al. (2007) presented a method to discriminate the ECG rhythms using their roots location in auto regressive (AR) model. It can be seen from Table 2, the author presented method achieves higher specificity and sensitivity than other techniques. On other hand, three seconds of data were necessary to discriminate the rhythms in the proposed method by Owis et al. (2001). Although two seconds can be implemented to apply the proposed method and even less in this study, three seconds were used to compare with Owis et al. (2001).

Heartbeat classification schema based on poles of the ECG signal windows using Pade's approximation technique is presented. Also, neural network and K nearest neighbor gave more accuracy than other techniques to classify the ECG heartbeats based on the calculated poles extracted. The experimental results show the ability and the efficiency of this proposed schema for detecting the poles and identifying the ECG signal features with high accuracy.

REFERENCES

Ahmad R, Naghsh-Nilchi A, Mohammadi RK (2008). "Cardiac Arrhythmias Classification Method Based on MUSIC, Morphological Descriptors, and Neural Network." EURASIP J. Adv. Signal Process., 202: 25-34.

Berni AJ (1975). "Target identification by natural resonance estimation", IEEE Trans. Aerosp. Electron. Syst., 11(2):147-154.

Chazal P de, O'Dwyer M, Reilly RB (2004). "Automatic Classification of Heartbeats Using ECG Morphology and Heartbeat Interval Features." IEEE Trans. Biomed. Eng., 51(7): 1196-1206.

Dingfei G, Narayanan S, Shankar MK (2002). "Cardiac arrhythmia classification using autoregressive modeling." Biomed. Eng. Online, 1(5): 1585–1588.

Dingfei G, Bei-Ping HOU, Xin-Jian X (2007). "Study of Feature Extraction Based on Autoregressive Modeling in ECG Automatic Diagnosis." ACTA Automation Sinica, 33 (5): 462-466.

Fatma ME (1996). "Frequency perturbation for a circular array of coupled cylindrical dipole antenna." Microw. Opt. Technol. Lett., 12(1): 36-40.

Inan OT, Giovangrandi L, Kovacs GTA (2006). "Robust neural-network-based classification of premature ventricular contractions using wavelet transform and timing interval features." IEEE Trans. Biomed. Eng., 53(12):2507-2515.

Jozef B, Margarita K (2001). "Approximation by Rational Functions." Measur. Sci. Rev., 1:1.

Kafieh R, Mehri A, Amirfattahi R (2007). "Detection of ventricular Arrhythmias using roots location in AR-modelling." Int. Conference Commun. Signal Process., pp. 1-4.

Liao SP, Fang DG, Li XG (1992). "Target feature extraction of frequency domain data with optimal rational approximation." Antennas Propag. Soc. Int. Symp., 1: 242-245, 18-25.

MIT-BIH Arrhythmia Database, www.physionet.org.

Monsoon HH (1996). "Statistical Digital Signal Processing and Modeling", New York, USA: Wiley, ISBN-0-471-59431-8, pp.133-138.

Owis M, Abou-Zied A, Youssef AB, Kadah Y (2001). "Robust feature extraction from ECG signals based on nonlinear dynamical modeling." 23rd Annual International Conference IEEE Eng. Med. Biol. Soc. (EMBC'01), 2: 1585-1588.

Rajendra AU, Jasjit SS, Jos AES, Krishnan SM (2007). "Advances in Cardiac Signal Processing." Springer Berlin Heidelberg New York, ISBN-13 978-3-540-36674-4, pp. 1-53.

Recommended Practice for Testing and Reporting Performance Results of Ventricular Arrhythmia Detection Algorithms (AAMI ECAR-1987). Arlington, VA: Association for the Advancement of Medical Instrumentation (AAMI). Tech. Rep., pp. 1-16.

Chen SW (2000). "Two-stage discrimination of cardiac arrhythmias using a total least squares-based prony modeling algorithm." IEEE Trans. Biomed. Eng., 47: 1317-1326.

Van Assche W (2006). "Padé and Hermite–Padé approximation and orthogonality." Surv. Approximation Theory, 2: 61-91.

25

MLH1 gene: An *in silico* analysis

Amitha Joy*, Jubil, C. A, Syama, P. S and Rohini Menon

Department of Biotechnology, Sahrdaya college of Engineering and Technology, Kodakara-680684, Thrissur, India.

The MLH1 gene responsible for colon cancer has been examined to identify functional consequences of single-nucleotide polymorphisms (SNPs). 16 SNPs have been identified in the MLH1 gene in which all are found to be nonsynonymous. Non synymous SNPs are relevant in many of the human inherited diseases since they change the aminoacid sequence of the protein. 56% of the identified nsSNPs have been reported as damaging. In the analysis of SNPs using SIFT, UTRscan, FastSNP and PolyPhen-2, it was recognized that rs41295284 and rs35001569 were responsible for the alteration in levels of expression. It has been concluded that among all SNPs of MLH1 gene, the mutation in rs41295284 and rs35001569 have the most significant effect on functional variation.

Key words: Single nucleotide polymorphism, non-synonymous, colon cancer.

INTRODUCTION

A single nucleotide polymorphism (SNP) is a source variance in a genome. A SNP is a single base mutation in DNA. SNPs are the most simple form and most common source of genetic polymorphism in the human genome (90% of all human DNA polymorphisms (Smith, 2002). A SNP in a coding region may have two different effects on the resulting protein: Synonymous, the substitution causes no amino acid change to the protein it produces; non-synonymous, the substitution results in an alteration of the encoded amino acid. One half of all coding sequence SNPs result in non-synonymous codon changes (Smith, 2002). A non-synonymous single nucleotide polymorphism (nsSNP) occurring in a coding gene may cause an amino acid substitution in the corresponding protein product, thus affecting the phenotype of the host organism. Non-synonymous variants constitute more than 50% of the mutations known to be involved in human inherited diseases (Kumar et al., 2009).

Familial colorectal cancer (CRC) is a major public health problem by virtue of its relatively high frequency. Hereditary non-polyposis colorectal cancer (HNPCC), also called Lynch syndrome, accounts for approximately 5-8% of all CRC patients. Among these, 3% are mutation positive that is, caused by germline mutations in the DNA mismatch repair genes that have so far been implicated (*MLH1*,

MSH2, *MSH6*, *PMS1*, and *PMS2*) (Henry and Albert, 1999).

MLH1, MSH2 and MSH6 genes play an important role in repairing mistakes made in DNA replication in colon cancer [9]. In the present study, the role of the SNPs of MutL homolog 1 (MLH1) in disease mutations is discussed. MLH1 is a human gene located on the short (p) arm of chromosome 3 and base pair from 37,034,840 to base pair 37,092,336 and cytogenetic location: 3p21.3. Its Locus ID (NCBI) is 4292. This gene was identified as a locus frequently mutated in hereditary non polyposis colon cancer (HNPCC) (US National Library of Medicine).

Computational techniques have been used to characterize the polymorphs and predict their involvement in the disease by studying all mutations of MLH1 gene with their variation in individuals (Namboori et al., 2011). Single-nucleotide polymorphisms (SNPs) can be prioritized and classified according to their functional impact based on prediction using bioinformatics and computational tools. The present study analysed the MLH1gene mutations using the tools Sorting intolerant from tolerant (SIFT), PolyPhen-2, functional analysis and selection tool for single nucleotide polymorphisms (FASTSNP) and UTRscan.

MATERIALS AND METHODS

SIFT

SIFT is a sequence homology-based tool that sorts intolerant from

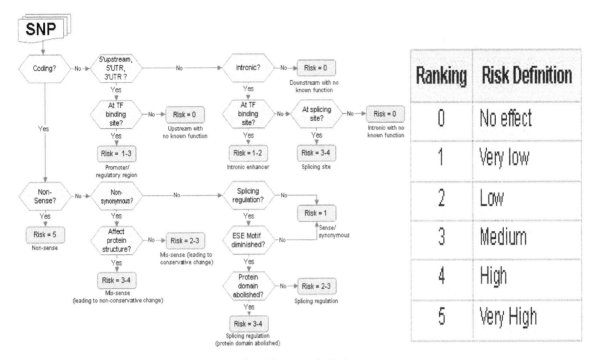

Figure 1. SNP prioritization based on the predicted functional effects.

tolerant amino acid substitutions and predicts whether an amino acid substitution in a protein will have a phenotypic effect (http://sift-dna.org). SIFT is based on the premise that protein evolution is correlated with protein function. Positions important for function should be conserved in an alignment of the protein family, whereas unimportant positions should appear diverse in an alignment (Kumar et al., 2009; Pauline and Henikoff, 2002; Pauline and Henikoff, 2001; Pauline and Henikoff, 2003; Pauline and Henikoff, 2006). The algorithm makes an in-depth search of the protein repositories to find the tolerance of each deviation from the conserved pattern (Namboori et al., 2011). This probability factor helps us to predict the effect of the deviation, that is whether it is deleterious or not. The cutoff value of tolerance has been fixed as 0.05. Hence, if the value is more than or equal to 0.05, the corresponding deviation can be treated as tolerating, while the tolerance value less than 0.05 predicts the change to be harmful.

A library of MLH1 sequences were prepared by providing the NCBI database of SNP by applying appropriate limits like homo-sapiens, chromosome 3, cited in Pubmed, etc. The corresponding rsids of the obtained result were compiled. SIFT analysis of the selected rsids were done using the online software. The SIFT program works on the hypothesis that most of the conserved regions of amino acids are retained in normal protein molecules. The observed changes in these positions may lead to malfunctioning of the protein molecules, and in most cases, deviations are likely to be deleterious (Namboori et al., 2011).

FastSNP server

FastSNP is a web server that allows users to efficiently identify the SNPs most likely to have functional effects (http://fastsnp.ibms.sinica.edu.tw). FastSNP prioritizes SNPs according to 12 phenotypic risks and putative functional effects, such as changes to the transcriptional level, pre-mRNA splicing, protein structure, etc (Hsiang-Yu et al., 2006). The SNP prioritization result is based on the predicted functional effects and their estimated risk

proposed by Tabor et al. (2002) as shown in the flowchart (Figure 1).

UTRscan server

UTRscan is a pattern matcher which searches protein or nucleotide (DNA, RNA, tRNA) sequences in order to find UTR motifs (http://itbtools.ba.itb.cnr.it/utrscan). It is able to find, in a given sequence, motifs that characterize 3'UTR and 5'UTR sequences. Such motifs are defined in the UTRSite Database, a collection of functional sequence patterns located in the 5'- or 3'-UTR sequences. The UTRsite entries describe the various regulatory elements present in UTR regions and whose functional role has been established on experimental basis. Each UTRsite entry is constucted on the basis of information reported in the literature and revised by scientists experimentally working on the functional characterization of the relevant UTR regulatory element (UTRdb and UTRsite, 2010; UTRdb and UTRsite, 2005; UTRdb and UTRsite, 2000).

PolyPhen-2

Functional activity of protein was also investigated with the tool PolyPhen-2, which works on structure and multiple alignments with homologous proteins (http://genetics.bwh.harvard.edu/pph2/). The same SNPs were used for this characterization. PolyPhen-2 makes use of a set of features consisting of Dictionary of Secondary Structure in Proteins database to extract secondary structure, "solvent accessible surface area" and "phi–psi" dihedral angle. The calculated parameters include "normed accessible surface area" change in accessible surface propensity resulting from the substitution, change in residue side chain volume, region of the phi–psi map from the Ramachandran plot, and normalized B factor (temperature factor) for the residue (Namboori et al., 2011). With all these parameters, the algorithm computes the "position-specific independent count" (PSIC) score of each SNP. The PSIC score

Table 1. SIFT analysis of the SNPs.

SNP	Amino acid change	Prediction	Score
rs41295282	S93G	Damaging	0.02
rs1295280	G22A	Damaging	0
rs28930073	D132H	Damaging	0
rs11541859	E89Q	Damaging	0.01
rs63750549	G638*	Damaging	0.02
rs63750540	K461*	Tolerated	0.3
rs41295284	L607H	Damaging	0
rs35831931	V716M	Tolerated	0.09
rs35338630	H264D	Tolerated	0.1
rs35045067	Y646C	Damaging	0
rs35001569	K618E	Damaging	0
rs34213726	K443Q	Tolerated	0.53
rs2020873	H718Y	Damaging	0
rs2020872	I32V	Tolerated	0.32
rs1800149	L729V	Tolerated	0.13
rs1799977	I219V	Tolerated	0.27

Table 2. UTRScan analysis of the SNPs

SNP	Number of signal matches	Regulatory element
rs41295284	5	IRES, ADH_DRE, uORF, MBE, PAS.
rs35001569	4	ADH_DRE, uORF, MBE, PAS.
rs35831931	3	IRES, K-BOX, uORF.
rs28930073	3	BRD-BOX, uORF, MBE.
rs2020873	3	IRES, K-BOX, uORF.
rs63750540	2	uORF, MBE.
rs11541859	2	IRES, uORF.
rs1799977	2	uORF, MBE.
rs63750549	1	uORF.
rs41295282	1	uORF.
rs35338630	1	uORF.
rs35045067	1	uORF.
rs2020872	1	uORF.
rs34285587	0	–
rs34213726	0	–
rs1800149	0	–

IRES, internal ribosome entry site (IRES),;ADH_DRE , alcohol dehydrogenase 3'UTR downregulation control element (ADH_DRE); uORF, Upstream Open Reading Frame (uORF); MBE, Musashi binding element (MBE);PAS, polyadenylation Signal (PAS); BRD-BOX, Brd-Box (Brd); K, BOX - K-Box (KB).

differences between the variations due to different SNPs have been calculated. As this difference increases, the possibility of functional impact on the variation increases. If the PSIC score difference is ≥0.9, the variation can be treated as probably damaging.

RESULTS AND DISCUSSION

The computational analysis of MLH1 gene using the tools SIFT, UTRscan, FastSNP and Polyphen2 led to the following conclusions. SIFT analysis predicted 9 out of 16

mutations as damaging as shown in Table 1. The SNPs rs41295284 and rs35001569 with score 0 for both the mutations, correlated with the results of other analysis. In the rsid rs41295284, amino acid leucine was mutated to histidine at 607th position and in rs35001569 amino acid lysine was mutated to glutamic acid at 618th position. Table 2 shows functional significance analysis using UTRscan which predicted the rsid rs41295284 and rs35001569 as damaging since they contained the regulatory elements: internal ribosome entry site, alcoho

Table 3. FastSNP analysis of the SNPs.

SNP	Possible functional effects for the top ranking	Lower risk	Upper risk
rs2020873	Missense (non-conservative)	3	4
rs35338630	splicing site	3	4
rs63750540	Nonsense	5	5
rs41295282	Missense (conservative)	2	3
rs1799977	Missense (conservative); Splicing regulation	2	3
rs1800149	Missense (conservative); Splicing regulation	2	3
rs2020872	Promoter/regulatory region	1	3
rs11541859	Missense (conservative); Splicing regulation	2	3
rs28930073	Missense (conservative); Splicing regulation	2	3
rs34213726	Missense (conservative)	2	3
rs34285587	Missense (conservative); Splicing regulation	2	3
rs35001569	Missense (conservative); Splicing regulation	2	3
rs35045067	Missense (conservative); Splicing regulation	2	3
rs35831931	Missense (conservative); Splicing regulation	2	3
rs41295284	Missense (conservative); Splicing regulation	2	3
rs63750549	Nonsense	5	5

Table 4. Polyphen2 analysis of SNPs.

SNP	Mutation effect	Score
rs2020873	Probably damaging	0.973
rs41295282	benign	0.019
rs28930073	Probably damaging	1
rs41295284	Probably damaging	1
rs35831931	Probably damaging	0.973
rs35045067	Probably damaging	1
rs34213726	benign	0.022
rs2020872	benign	0.012
rs1800149	benign	0.00

dehydrogenase 3'UTR downregulation, Upstream open reading frame (uORF), Musashi binding element (MBE) and polyadenylation Signal (PAS). Various studies have shown that the transcriptional regulation is biologically important and the alteration in the transcriptional components leads to disease.

FastSNP results predicted the rsids rs41295284 and rs35001569 as medium risk ranking ones as shown in Table 3. Further, Table 4 shows the polyphen2 analysis which predicted only nine results among which was the rsid rs41295284 as 'probably damaging one' with score 1. The mutations observed in nsSNP are of three types, missense, nonsense, and frameshift. Besides the coding regions, SNPs may also be found in mRNA untranslated regions (UTRs) and promoter regions, which may affect the gene expression, transcription factor binding, sequence of RNA which is noncoding, and gene splicing (Namboori et al., 2011).

Conclusion

Hence the combined approach using SIFT, UTRscan, FastSNP and PolyPhen2 predicts that the mutation rs41295284 and rs35001569 are the most deleterious among the mutations for MLH1 gene causing colon cancer characterized by the mutation amino acid leucine to histidine. The recognition of these SNPs as deleterious ones provides insight into cancer biology and presents as anticancer therapeutic targets and diagnostic markers.

Since the missense mutations are nucleotide substitutions that change an amino acid in a protein, the deleterious effects of these mutations are commonly attributed to their impact on primary amino acid sequence and protein structure.

REFERENCES

Henry TL, Albert C (1999). Genetic susceptibility to non-polyposis colorectal cancer. J. Med. Genet. 36:801–818.
Hsiang-Yu Y, Jen-Jie C, Wen-Hsien T, Chia-Hung L, Chuan-Kun L, Yi-Jung L, Hui-Hung W, Adam Y, Yuan-Tsong C, Chun-Nan H (2006). FASTSNP: an always up-to-date and extendable service for SNP function analysis and prioritization. Nucleic Acids Res. 34:635-641.
Kumar P, Henikoff S, Pauline C (2009). Predicting the effects of coding non-synonymous variants on protein function using the SIFT algorithm, Nat. Protoc. 4:8-9.
Kumar P, Henikoff S, Pauline C (2009). Predicting the effects of coding non-synonymous variants on protein function using the SIFT algorithm. Nat. Protoc. 4:1073-81.
Pauline C, Henikoff S (2002). Accounting for Human Polymorphisms Predicted to Affect Protein Function. Genome Res. 12:436-446.
Pauline C, Henikoff S (2001). Predicting Deleterious Amino Acid Substitutions. Genome Res. 11:863-874.
Pauline C, Henikoff S (2003). SIFT: predicting amino acid changes that affect protein function. Nucleic Acids Res. 131:3812-3814.
Pauline C, Henikoff S (2006). Predicting the Effects of Amino Acid Substitutions on Protein Function. Annu. Rev. Genomics Hum Genet.

7:61-80.

Namboori PK, Vineeth KV, Rohith V, Hassan I, Lekshmi S, Akhila S, Nidheesh M (2011). The ApoE gene of Alzheimer's disease (AD). Funct. Integr. Genomics 11:519–522.

Smith K (2002). Genetic Polymorphism and SNPs Genotyping, Haplotype Assembly Problem Haplotype Map. Functional Genomics and Proteomics

Tabor HK, Risch NJ, Myers RM (2002). Candidate-gene approaches for studying complex genetic traits: practical considerations. Nat. Rev. Genet. 3(5):391-397

UTRdb, UTRsite (2010). A collection of sequences and regulator motifs of the untranslated regions of eukaryotic mRNAs. Nuclei Acids Res., 38:75-80.

UTRdb, UTRsite (2005). A collection of sequences and regulator motifs of the untranslated regions of eukaryotic mRNAs. Nuclei Acids Res., 33:141-146.

UTRdb, UTRsite (2000). Specialized databases of sequences an functional elements of 5' and 3' untranslated regions of eukaryoti mRNAs. Nucleic Acids Res., 28: 193-196.

26

Computational sequence analysis and *in silico* modeling of a stripe rust resistance protein encoded by wheat *TaHSC70* gene

Zarrin Basharat

Microbiology and Biotechnology Research Lab, Department of Environmental Sciences, Fatima Jinnah Women University, 46000, Pakistan.

TaHSC70 gene of *Triticum* sp. is an associate of the heat shock protein family and plays a significant role in stress-related and defense responses educed by contagion with stripe rust fungus through a Jasmonic acid dependent signal transduction pathway. Hence, understanding molecular structure and function of the protein coded by this gene is of paramount importance for plant biologists working on stripe rust. The present study was aimed at sequence and *in silico* structural analysis of Hsp70 protein coded by this gene, through comparative modeling approach. Validation of the overall folds and structure, errors over localized regions and stereo chemical parameters was carried out using PDBSum server. Structure was a monomer with seven sheets, 1 β-α-βunit, 12 hairpins, 13β-bulges, 29 strands, 21 helices, 16 helix-helix interacs, 44 β-turns and 1 Y-turn. Two major domains were detected belonging to Hsp70 family while neural network analysis revealed protein to be highly phosphorylated at serine and threonine residues.

Key words: *TaHSC70*, Hsp70, Stripe rust, homology modelling, wheat.

INTRODUCTION

Stress impacts plants negatively and hinders proper activity. Stress protective roles in plants are played by Hsp70 family, which are induced in response to potential detrimental simulations (Efeoglu et al., 2009). TaHSC70 demonstrates a decisive role in protecting plant cells against heat stress (Guo et al., 2014). Heat stress is one of the reasons behind pollen sterility, drying of stigmatic fluid/shrivelled seeds in wheat, pseudo-seed setting and empty endosperm pockets. The defence mechanisms of wheat to cope up with these conditions consists of heat responsive miRNAs, signalling molecules, transcription factors and stress associated proteins like heat shock proteins (HSPs), antioxidant enzymes etc (Kumar and Rai, 2014). *TaHSC70* gene (70-kDa heat-shock cognate) is a constitutively expressed Hsp70 family member (Duan et al., 2011; Usman et al., 2014) in wheat. Furthurmore, it is involved in protein-protein interactions, assisting the folding of de novo synthesized polypeptides and the import/translocation of precursor proteins (Feng et al., 2013; Wang et al., 2014). Heat shock proteins (HSPs) exist in nearly all living organisms (Feng et al., 2013). The major Hsps vary in molecular weights and are synthesized in eukaryotes belonging to six structurally distinct classes: Hsp100,Hsp90, Hsp70, Hsp60 (or chaperonins), ~17-30 kDa small Hsps and ~8-5 kDa ubiquitin (Safdar et al., 2012). Hsp70 family chaperones are considered to be the most highly conserved heat shock proteins (Jego et al., 2013). In plants, many Hsp70 proteins have been identified in different species (Daugaard et al., 2007). The Arabidopsis genome contains at least 18 genes encoding members of the Hsp70 family, Rice genome contains 32 (Sarkar et al., 2012), while, around 12 Hsp70 members have been found in the spinach genome (Guy and Li, 1998). The Hsp70 in wheat was reported by Duan et al. (2011) in expression profile analysis of the Arabidopsis and spinach. HSP70 has been observed to be increased in thermotolerant wheat variety so it is anticipated that HSP70 modulates the thermotolerance level of wheat (*Triticum aestivum*) pollen under heat stress (Kumar and Rai, 2014). This reveals that the over expression of Hsp70 genes correlates positively with the acquisition of thermo tolerance. HSPs are expressed in response to environmental stress conditions such as heat, cold and drought, as well as to chemical and other stresses (Daugaard et al., 2007) and results in enhanced tolerance to salt, water and high-temperature stress in plants (Alvim et al., 2001). However, the cellular mechanisms of Hsp70 function under stress conditions are not fully understood.

3D structure and conserved domain analysis can shed light on the function of a protein. The 3D structure of the wheat heat shock protein has not been modeled previously. Modeling is ground principally on alignment of query protein to the target (known structure or template). Prediction method may entail fold assignment, target–template alignment, model building followed by model evaluation (Marti-Renom et al., 2000). Comparative modeling approach has been utilized in this study to predict the three-dimensional structure of a given protein sequence (target) harnessing the bioinformatics tools. Functional analysis has also been attempted using a battery of computational tools and webservers.

MATERIALS AND METHODS

The 690 amino acid protein sequence encoded by the gene TaHSC70 with Accession ACT65562 was retrieved from the NCBI database.

Sequence analysis

Physiochemical properties of the protein were computed by ProtParam tool (http://web.expasy.org/protparam/). The parameters computed by ProtParam included the molecular weight, theoretical pI, instability index, aliphatic index, and grand average of hydropath icity (GRAVY). Subcellular localization of any protein aids understanding protein function. Prediction of subcellular localization of protein was carried out by CELLO v.2.5 (http://cello.life.nctu.edu.tw/). Phosphorylation profile analysis was

carried out using Netphos 2.0 server (http://www.cbs.dtu.dk/services/NetPhos/).

Structure analysis

Blast (Altschul et al., 1990) search was performed with this query sequence against the Protein Data Bank (Berman et al., 2000). Query and template protein sequence were aligned using BioEdit program. Modeller (Fiser and Sali, 2003) was used to build a protein model using automated approach to comparative protein structure modeling by satisfaction of spatial restraints (Sali and Blundell, 1993; Eswar et al., 2008). The structure was energy minimized by SwissPDB viewer (Guex and Peitsch, 1997) using GROMOS96 force field and rendered in PYMOL (Delano, 2002). PDBSum analysis for secondary structure analysis was followed by PROCHECK (Laskowski et al., 1998) verification of the model by checking stereo chemical quality. Ramachandran plot (Ramachandran et al., 1963; Morris et al., 1992) was generated and the quality of the structure was computed in terms of percentage of residues in favourable regions, percentage of non Proline, glycine residues etc. ERRAT webserver (Colovos and Yeates, 1993) was also used to access quality of structure.

RESULTS AND DISCUSSION

Availability of plethora of quality tools and webservers has enabled computational biologists to perform reliable analysis of protein sequence and structure. The present study was aimed at sequence analysis and homology modeling of the wheat Hsp70 protein to shed light on its function.

Sequence analysis

Swiss protParam tool revealed the protein to be of ~73.5 KDa with theoretical pI value of 5.01. Total number of negatively charged residues (Asp + Glu) were 99 while total number of positively charged residues (Arg + Lys) were 82. The instability index was computed to be 29.0, classifying the protein as stable. Aliphatic index was found to be 86.33 while Grand average of hydropathicity (GRAVY) index was calculated as -0.272 demonstrating amino acid to be of soluble protein. CELLO results showed that the wheat Hsp70 protein is localized in the chloroplast. This is suggestive of the fact that chloroplast is the major site of function for wheat Hsp70 and the protein may be associated with the thermostability of chloroplast membranes. This can be allied to a study conducted by Bhadula and colleagues demonstrating association of 45 kD Hsps with heat stability of chloroplast membranes in a drought and heat resistant maize line (Bhadula et al., 2001).

Two major domains were detected in the sequence HSPA9-Ssq1-like_NBD (residues: 51-427) and PLN03184 (residue: 21-688). HSPA9-Ssq1-like_NBD or nucleotide-binding domain of HSPA9 belongs to the heat shock protein 70 (Hsp70) family of chaperones that contribute to protein folding and assembly and degrada-

Table 1. Phosphorylation profile of analysed Hsp70 protein using neural network approach. Specific residue positions in the query protein are shown to be phosphorylated based on a significant score. *S* refers to phosphorylation on serine residue and *T* refers to phosphorylation on threonine residue.

Position	Context	Score	Prediction	Position	Context	Score	Prediction
6	ATFTSQVSA	0.043	.	3	--MATFTSQ	0.014	.
9	TSQVSAMAG	0.686	*S*	5	MATFTSQVS	0.145	.
15	MAGASPSCS	0.901	*S*	50	AMRVTCEKV	0.569	*T*
17	GASPSCSLF	0.012	.	61	IDLGTTNSA	0.051	.
19	SPSCSLFVS	0.038	.	62	DLGTTNSAV	0.115	.
23	SLFVSRRRP	0.414	.	75	GGKPTVITN	0.020	.
64	GTTNSAVAA	0.005	.	78	PTVITNAEG	0.173	.
88	RTTPSVVAY	0.035	.	85	EGQRTTPSV	0.206	.
118	NTFFSVKRF	0.939	*S*	86	GQRTTPSVV	0.982	*T*
138	AKQVSYNVV	0.068	.	93	VVAYTKGGE	0.251	.
166	AEEISAQVL	0.013	.	115	NPENTFFSV	0.745	*T*
178	VDDASKFLN	0.057	.	186	NDKITKAVV	0.071	.
199	YFNDSQRTA	0.793	*S*	191	KAVVTVPAY	0.058	.
226	PTAASLAYG	0.023	.	202	DSQRTATKD	0.212	.
252	TFDVSVLEV	0.423	.	204	QRTATKDAG	0.699	*T*
265	FEVLSTSGD	0.145	.	223	INEPTAASL	0.035	.
267	VLSTSGDTH	0.321	.	238	KNNETILVF	0.030	.
287	DWLASTFKN	0.024	.	248	LGGGTFDVS	0.215	.
319	KMELSTLTQ	0.026	.	266	EVLSTSGDT	0.560	*T*
327	QANISLPFI	0.093	.	270	TSGDTHLGG	0.076	.
346	EATLSRAKF	0.226	.	288	WLASTFKND	0.579	*T*
355	EELCSDLID	0.007	.	308	LQRLTEAAE	0.284	.
375	DAKLSVSNL	0.984	*S*	320	MELSTLTQA	0.056	.
377	KLSVSNLDE	0.959	*S*	322	LSTLTQANI	0.020	.
388	LVGGSTRIP	0.314	.	332	LPFITATAD	0.028	.
417	DEVVSLGAA	0.520	*S*	334	FITATADGP	0.110	.
443	VTPLSIGLE	0.264	.	344	HIEATLSRA	0.496	.
466	TLPTSKSEV	0.995	*S*	363	DRLKTPVNN	0.943	*T*
468	PTSKSEVFS	0.171	.	389	VGGSTRIPA	0.248	.
472	SEVFSTAAD	0.480	.	397	AVQETVRKI	0.429	.
480	DGQTSVEIN	0.959	*S*	402	VRKITGKDP	0.940	*T*
498	RDNKSLGSF	0.503	*S*	409	DPNVTVNPD	0.183	.
501	KSLGSFRLD	0.077	.	440	LLDVTPLSI	0.013	.
530	NGILSVAAV	0.040	.	448	IGLETLGGV	0.306	.
550	ITGASTLPK	0.291	.	454	GGVMTKIIP	0.172	.

tion of incompetent proteins. Typically, Hsp70s have a nucleotide-binding domain (NBD) which hosts nucleotide and a substrate-binding domain (SBD) which increases rate of ATP-hydrolysis. NBD site (17 residues), nucleotide exchange factor (NEF) co-chaperone interaction site (19 residues) for regulation of HSP70 and SBD interface (11 residues) existing on the conserved domain HSPA-9-Ssq1-like-NB were detected on the query protein.

Protein phosphorylation is a type of post-translational modification which can turn a protein on and off, thus modifying its function and activity. Phosphorylation generally occurs on serine, threonine, tyrosine and histidine residues in eukaryotic proteins. Artificial neural networks have been extensively used in biological sequence analysis (Wu, 1997; Blom et al., 1999) for phosphorylation analysis. Regions of wheat Hsp70 sequence showed extensive phosphorylation on serine and threonine residues (Table 1) while no phosphorylation capability of tyrosine residues was predicted. This result is in accordance with the study conducted by May and Soll (2000) that chloroplast-destined precursor proteins are phosphorylated on serine or threonine residues. This finding can be further validated

Table 1. Contd.

Position	Context	Score	Prediction	Position	Context	Score	Prediction
586	NQADSVVYQ	0.861	*S*	461	IPRNTTLPT	0.968	*T*
625	IAGGSTQNM	0.062	.	462	PRNTTLPTS	0.285	.
652	YNQTSAGGA	0.459	.	465	TTLPTSKSE	0.572	*T*
658	GGAGSTDAE	0.174	.	473	EVFSTAADG	0.083	.
669	PGAGSTSSG	0.884	*S*	479	ADGQTSVEI	0.504	*T*
671	AGSTSSGKG	0.859	*S*	538	VDKGTGKKQ	0.305	.
672	GSTSSGKGP	0.833	*S*	545	KQDITITGA	0.061	.
689	DFTDSN---	0.016	.	547	DITITGAST	0.125	.
				551	TGASTLPKD	0.216	.
				580	DAIDTKNQA	0.863	*T*
				591	VVYQTEKQL	0.856	*T*
				626	AGGSTQNMK	0.067	.
				631	QNMKTAMEA	0.208	.
				651	MYNQTSAGG	0.090	.
				659	GAGSTDAET	0.593	*T*
				663	TDAETEPGA	0.092	.
				670	GAGSTSSGK	0.434	.
				687	DADFTDSN-	0.043	.

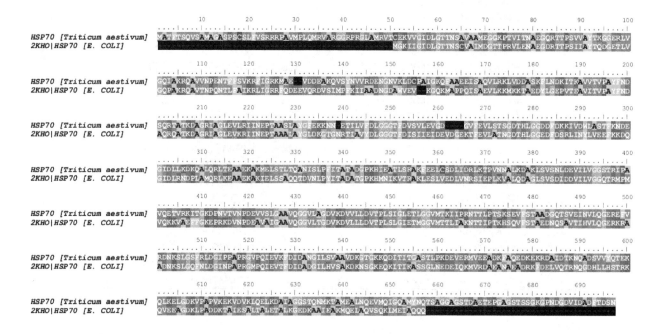

Figure 1. Aligned sequences of query and target protein visualized in BioEdit.

in the Lab and also tested for glycosylation that can further deepen our insight of the post translational modifications associated with wheat Hsp70.

Structure analysis

Homology modeling has gained popularity due to increas-

ing accuracy of the predictions using computational tools. For homology modelling, the suitable template structure selected was based X-ray structure of *E-coli* HSP70 protein (PDB ID:2KHO) (Bertelsen et al., 2009), having 55% identity with the query sequence and an E value of zero. Sequence was aligned to observe the residue conservation (Figure 1). Then, MODELLER was used to generate 3D structure. Predicted structure was a

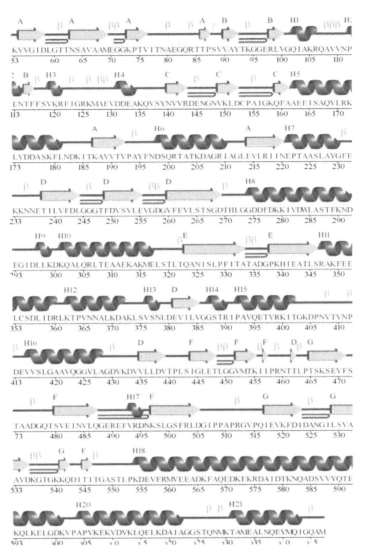

Figure 2. Secondary structure analysis of wheat Hsp70 protein. Helices (🔵🔵) labelled by H1, H2..., strands (➡️) by their sheets A,B... motifs by β,γ turn and (═══) for beta hairpin.

monomer with molpdf score of 3662.76880, DOPE score value of -60344.10156 and a GA341 score of 1.00000. Protein consisted of 7 sheets, 1 beta alpha beta unit, 12 hairpins, 13 beta bulges, 29 strands, 21 helices, 16 helix-helix interacs, 44 beta turns and 1 gamma turn (Figure 2). Total number of bonds were 5216 while number of atoms were 5157. Structure validation of the predicted structures was done by feeding the predicting structure into the ERRAT protein verification server. The overall quality factor obtained was 74.671. The comparative peaks of DOPE scores of both template and model obtained from Modeller output demonstrate that there is no defect in the loop regions in the residues. So in the present case the loop refinement method was not required for the model (Figure 3). The validation of the model was carried out using Ramachandran plot calcula-

tions computed with the PROCHECK program. The Φ and Ψ distributions of the Ramachandran plots of non-Glycine, non-Proline residues are summarized in Figure 4. Altogether 99.2% of the residues were in favoured and allowed regions.

The overall G-factor used was computed as -0.1 which is good as compared to the typical value of -0.4. This is an initial attempt in modelling the structure of wheat Hsp70 and understanding its function. It is believed that this work has practical significance as it provides a foundation to not only the structure but also post translational modification of this protein. Post translational modification analysis can be further expanded to obtain new insights into the underpinnings of conformational changes in not only the cellular environment but also the chaperone itself. Structure can be utilized for interaction study with

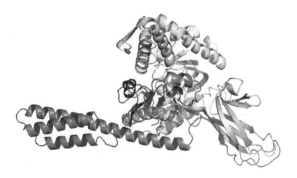

Figure 3. 3D structure of wheat Hsp70 protein visualized in PYMOL.

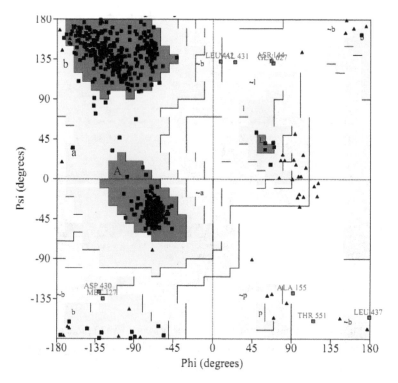

Figure 4. Ramachandran plot showing 94.0% residues in most favoured regions, 4.5% in additional allowed regions, 0.7% in generously allowed regions and only 0.8% in disallowed regions.

co-factors or other proteins/peptides in the cell to shed light on communication mechanism between chaperone and wheat cellular components under stress.

Conclusion

The wheat heat shock protein is one of the most important protein which provides the natural resistance against the stress due to stripe rust fungus. In the present work, sequence analysis has been conducted to shed light on post translational modification of Hsp70 domains associated with this protein and 3D structure study of the

protein. Computational study conducted can serve as a baseline source of information and can be further validated in the lab.

The validated protein model proposed in this study may be used further to dock with possible co-factors or relevant protein interactors to understand the potential mechanism of anti-stress and defense properties of this protein.

Conflict of interests

The authors did not declare any conflict of interest.

REFERENCES

Altschul SF, Gish W, Miller W, Myers EW, Lipman DJ (1990). Basic local alignment search tool. J. Mol. Biol. 215 (3):403-410.

Alvim FC (2001). Enhanced accumulation of BiP in transgenic plants confers tolerance to water stress. Plant Physiol. 126:1042-1054.

Berman HM, Westbrook J, Feng Z, Gilliland G, Bhat TN, Weissig H, Shindyalov IN, Bourne PE (2000). The Protein Data Bank. Nucleic Acids Res. 28 (1):235-242.

Bhadula SK, Elthon TE, Habben JE, Helentjaris TG, Jiao S, Ristic Z (2001). Heat-stress induced synthesis of chloroplast protein synthesis elongation factor (EF-Tu) in a heat-tolerant maize line. Planta 212(3):359-366.

Blom N, Gammeltoft S, Brunak S (1999). Sequence and structure-based prediction of eukaryotic protein phosphorylation sites. J. Mo. Biol. 294(5):1351-1362.

Colovos C, Yeates TO (1993). Verification of protein structures: patterns of nonbonded atomic interactions. Protein Sci. 2(9):1511-1519.

Daugaard M, Rohde M, Jäättelä M (2007). The heat shock protein 70 family: Highly homologous proteins with overlapping and distinct functions. FEBS Lett. 581(19):3702-3710.

Duan YH, Guo J, Ding K, Wang SJ, Zhang H, Dai XW, Chen YY, Govers F, Huang LL, Kang ZS (2011). Characterization of a wheat HSP70 gene and its expression in response to stripe rust infection and abiotic stresses. Mol. Biol. Rep. 38(1):301-307.

Efeoğlu B, Ekmekci Y, Cicek N (2009). Physiological responses of three maize cultivars to drought stress and recovery. S. Afr. J. Bot. 75(1):34-42.

Eswar N, Eramian D, Webb B, Shen M, Sali A (2008). Protein structure modelling with MODELLER. Methods. J Mol Biol. 426:145-159.

Feng PM, Chen W, Lin H, Chou KC. (2013). iHSP-PseRAAAC: Identifying the heat shock protein families using pseudo reduced amino acid alphabet composition. Anal. Biochem. 442(1):118-125.

Fiser A, Sali A (2003). Modeller: generation and refinement of homology-based protein structure models. Methods Enzymol. 374:461-491.

Guex N, Peitsch MC (1997). SWISS-MODEL and the Swiss-Pdb Viewer: an environment for comparative protein modeling. Electrophoresis 18(15):2714-2723.

Guo M, Zhai YF, Lu JP, Chai L, Chai WG, Gong ZH, Lu MH. (2014). Characterization of CaHsp70-1, a Pepper Heat-Shock Protein Gene in Response to Heat Stress and Some Regulation Exogenous Substances in Capsicum annuum L. Int. J. Mol. Sci. 15(11):19741-19759.

Guy CL, Li QB (1998). The organization and evolution of thenspinach stress 70 molecular chaperone gene family. Plant Cell. 10:539-556.

Jego G, Hazoumé A, Seigneuric R, Garrido C. (2013). Targeting heat shock proteins in cancer. Cancer Lett. 332(2): 275-285.

Kumar RR, Rai RD (2014). Can Wheat Beat the Heat: Understanding the Mechanism of Thermotolerance in Wheat (Triticum aestivum L.). Cereal Res. Commun. 42(1):1-18.

Laskowski RA, MacArthur MW, Moss DS, Thornton JM (1993). PROCHECK: A program to check the stereochemical quality of protein structures. J. Appl. Crystallogr. 26:283-291.

Martí-Renom MA, Stuart AC, Fiser A, Sánchez R, Melo F, Šali A (2000). Comparative protein structure modeling of genes and genomes. Annu. Rev. Biophys. Biomol. Struct. 29(1): 291-325.

May T, Soll J (2000). 14-3-3 proteins form a guidance complex with chloroplast precursor proteins in plants. Plant Cell Online 12(1):53-63.

Morris AL, MacArthur MW, Hutchinson EG, Thornton JM (1992). Stereochemical quality of protein structure coordinates. Proteins 12 (4): 345-364.

Ramachandran GN, Ramakrishnan C, Sasisekharan V (1963). Stereochemistry of polypeptide chain configurations. J. Mol. Biol. 7:95-99.

Safdar W, Majeed H, Ali B, Naveed I (2012). Molecular evolution and diversity of small heat shock proteins genes in plants. Pak. J. Bot. 44:211-218.

Sali A, Blundell TL (1993). Comparative protein modelling by satisfaction of spatial restraints. J. Mol. Biol. 234 (3): 779–815.

Sarkar NK, Kundnani P, Grover A (2013). Functional analysis of Hsp70 superfamily proteins of rice (Oryza sativa). Cell Stress Chaperones 18(4):427-437.

Usman MG, Rafii MY, Ismail MR, Malek MA, Latif MA, Oladosu Y (2014). Heat Shock Proteins: Functions And Response Against Heat Stress In Plants. Int. J. Sci. Technol. Res. 3(11):204-218.

Wang X, Gou M, Bu H, Zhang S, Wang G (2014). Proteomic analysis of Arabidopsis constitutive expresser of pathogenesis-related gene1 (Cpr30/cpr1-2) mutant. Plant Omics J. 7(3): 142-151.

27

Three dimensional modelling of beta endorphin and its interaction with three opioid receptors

Swathi Aluri* and Ramana Terli

Department of Biotechnology, College of Science and Technology, Andhra University, Visakhapatnam - 530003, Andhra Pradesh, India.

Beta endorphin is a neurotransmitter and is involved in functions like enhancement of immune system, deceleration of cancer cell growth and induction of euphoria and relaxation. It is an opioid like neuropeptide synthesized in neurons of hypothalamus and pituitary gland. The study of its structure and its interaction with opioid receptors can throw light on its neuropsychopharmacology. Protein data bank does not contain the structural information of beta endorphin and mu opioid receptor. Hence, in the present study, we aimed at predicting their three dimensional structures. Owing to homologues with low sequence identity and unsatisfactory results from threading methods, we resorted to *ab initio* modelling. Quark algorithm was used for beta endorphin structure prediction. The structure of mu opioid receptor was modelled by I TASSER simulations. The quality of the protein models were evaluated with PROCHECK server. Functionally important regions in beta endorphin were located using ConSurf web server. Docking studies were performed on beta endorphin with three opioid receptors mu, kappa and gamma to anticipate residues important for binding.

Key words: *Ab initio* modelling, homology, docking, beta endorphin, opioid receptors, threading, QUARK, PROCHECK, AUTODOCK, template, binding sites.

INTRODUCTION

Beta endorphin was discovered by Li and Chung (1976) from camel pituitary glands. In *Homo sapiens,* it comprises of 31 amino acids. It is processed from 267 amino acids long proopiomelanocortin protein. Beta endorphin synthesized in pituitary gland is released into blood and that synthesized in hypothalamus is transuded into spinal cord and brain. Owing to blood brain barrier, beta endorphin released into blood cannot enter brain in sizeable quantities. It is produced in vertebrates during excitement, pain, orgasm and exercise. Beta endorphin stimulates the release of growth hormone, ACTH, prolactin and antidiuretic hormone and inhibits the release of thyrotropin, luteinizing hormone and follicle stimulating hormone (Chrétien et al., 1981). Major function of beta endorphin, however, is regulation of pain. Pain receptors in the skin sense the pain and send the pain impulse to the thalamus via spinal cord and then to sensory and motor cortices. The pain receptors broadcast pain by releasing a transmitter called substance P. Substance P is a neurotransmitter found in neurons at both sides of dorsal horns of spinal cord. It causes other neurons to fire in response to pain impulse. The dorsal horns also contain endorphin containing neurons. Endorphins are released from these neurons

---
*Corresponding author. E-mail: swathialuri@yahoo.com.

Abbreviations: ACTH, Adrenocorticotropic hormone; **CASP,** critical assessment of techniques for protein structure prediction; **GRAMM,** global range molecular matching; **JCSG,** joint centre for structural genomics; **NCBI,** National Centre for Biotechnology Information; **PDB,** protein data bank; **PSI Blast,** position specific iterated blast; **RMS,** root mean square distance.

synapse between two pain transmitting neurons and inhibit the release of substance P thereby sending fewer pain impulses to brain (Dalayeun et al., 1993).

Its function is mediated by its interaction with opioid receptors. There are three subtypes of opioid receptors – mu, gamma and kappa. Naloxone is a competitive antagonist to mu opioid receptor. Beta endorphin has highest affinity for mu 1 opioid receptor and least affinity for kappa 1 opioid receptor. The order of its affinity for opioid receptors is: mu 1 > mu 2 > delta > kappa 1. Docking studies were performed on beta endorphin with three opioid receptors mu, kappa and gamma to anticipate residues important for binding (Janecka et al., 2004).

METHODOLOGY

The protein sequences of beta endorphin and mu opioid receptor were obtained from protein knowledgebase (UniprotKB) (Bairoch et al., 2004). The NCBI Blast (Altschul et al., 1990) server was used to find structural templates for beta endorphin and mu opioid receptor. PSI Blast was carried out against Protein Data Bank (PDB) (Bernstein et al., 1977). Suitable templates could not be found for modelling beta endorphin and mu opioid receptor. Protein threading methods did not provide reliable results as well. Hence, we resorted to *ab initio* modelling.

QUARK algorithm (http://zhanglab.ccmb.med.umich.edu/QUARK/) was used to predict the three dimensional structures of beta endorphin. I -Tasser simulations (Ambrish et al., 2010) deduced the structure of mu opioid receptor. I – Tasser and QUARK servers were ranked number 1 and number 2 respectively in CASP 9 experiments. Models predicted using QUARK algorithm and I – Tasser simulations were submitted to JCSG server for structure validation. Evaluation reports were generated from PROCHECK (Laskowski et al., 1993). It performs assessment of various parameters of the models such as bond length, bond angle, residue by residue properties, main chain properties, side chain properties, RMS distance from planarity and distorted geometry plots (Morris et al., 1992). ConSurf web server was used to predict functionally important regions of beta endorphin (Glaser et al., 2003). This automated web server calculates the degree of conservation of amino acids among close sequence homologues of the query protein. These conservation patches are envisaged onto the molecular surface of proteins to expose the patches of highly conserved residues. Highly conserved residues are often crucial for biological functions.

The structures of the other two opioid receptors – kappa and delta were obtained from PDB (Protein Data Bank). The molecular interaction studies of beta endorphin with three opioid receptors were performed using AutoDock tools. AutoDock software consists of two programs – autodock and autogrid. Autodock program docks ligand molecule onto a set of grids outlining the target molecule or protein. These grids are calculated by autogrid program (Morris et al., 1998).

RESULTS AND DISCUSSION

Beta endorphin modelling

Sequence analysis

The protein sequence of beta endorphin was obtained from protein knowledgebase (UniprotKB) (*Homo sapiens* beta endorphin protein sequence (Length – 31 amino acids)).

YGGFMTSEKSQTPLVTLFKNAIIKNAYKKGE

Proopiomelanocortin protein in *Homo sapiens* (POMC ID – P01189) is cleaved at 237th residue to yield beta endorphin.

Ab initio modelling

Ab initio protein structure prediction method is based on thermodynamic hypothesis which states that for native structure of protein the free energy achieves the global minimum. Hence, in this method, all the energetics involved in protein folding is modelled and the structure with lowest free energy is found. Though it is computationally intensive, it is a very good approach for protein modelling.

We used QUARK algorithm for beta endorphin structure prediction. In this method, models are built under the focal point of atomic level knowledge based force field. Replica Exchange Monte Carlo simulation is used to build protein models from small fragments. In Critical Assessment of Structure Prediction (CASP) 9 experiment, QUARK is ranked number 1 in Free Modelling section. Ten models were predicted by QUARK server. The most accurate model was model (a) (Figure 1)

Structure validation

Verification and evaluation was performed by PROCHECK server. 96% of the residues were in favourable region of Ramachandran plot and other parameters in PROCHECK were also in allowed ranges. Hence, the quality of the predicted model is good (Figure 2).

Analysis of important residues in beta endorphin theoretical model

ConSurf server predicted high conservation scores for residues tyr1, gly3, phe4, met5, pro13, leu14, thr16, leu17, phe18, asn20, ala21, ile 22, lys24, lys28, lys29. High scores assigned to these residues are indicative of evolutionary conservation and their functional significance (Figure 3).

Mu opioid receptor modelling

Sequence analysis

The UniprotKB entry for human mu opioid receptor

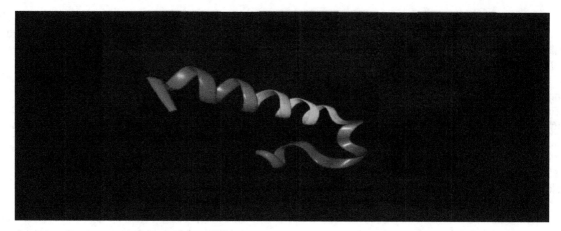

Figure 1. Theoretical model of beta endorphin. *Ab initio* modelling was performed by QUARK. The images were generated using PYMOL (http://www.pymol.org).

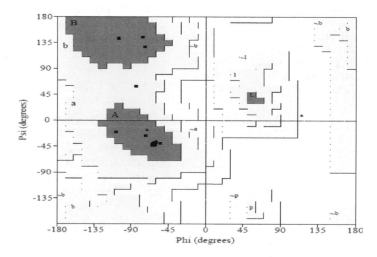

Figure 2. Ramachandran plot for theoretical model of beta endorphin.

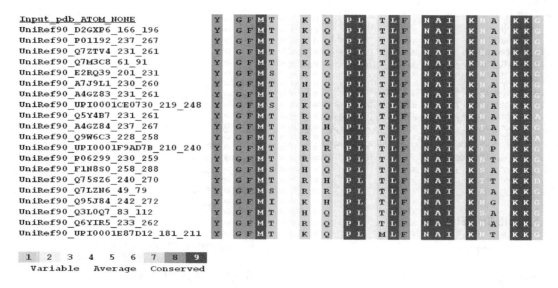

Figure 3. ConSurf analysis: The amino acids of beta endorphin are coloured in range from turquoise to maroon based on conservation grades.

```
>sp|P35372|OPRM_HUMAN Mu-type opioid receptor OS=Homo sapiens GN=OPRM1 PE=1 SV=2
MDSSAAPTNASNCTDALAYSSCSPAPSPGSWVNLSHLDGNLSDPCGPNRTDLGGRDSLCP
PTGSPSMITAITIMALYSIVCVVGLFGNFLVMYVIVRYTKMKTATNIYIFNLALADALAT
STLPFQSVNYLMGTWPFGTILCKIVISIDYYNMFTSIFTLCTMSVDRYIAVCHPVKALDF
RTPRNAKIINVCNWILSSAIGLPVMFMATTKYRQGSIDCTLTFSHPTWYWENLLKICVFI
FAFIMPVLIITVCYGLMILRLKSVRMLSGSKEKDRNLRRITRMVLVVVAVFIVCWTPIHI
YVIIKALVTIPETTFQTVSWHFCIALGYTNSCLNPVLYAFLDENFKRCFREFCIPTSSNI
EQQNSTRIRQNTRDHPSTANTVDRTNHQLENLEAETAPLP
```

Figure 4. *Homo sapiens* mu opioid receptor sequence.

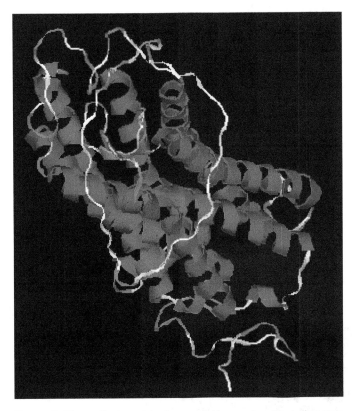

Figure 5. Theoretical model of mu opioid receptor. Modelling was performed by I TASSER.

(P35372) is used for modelling. The protein is *Homo sapiens* in origin and is 400 amino acids long (Figure 4).

Ab initio modelling

We used I-TASSER server for modelling mu opioid receptor structure. The server generates the structure from a query protein sequence in three steps. In the first step, it tries to find possible templates for the query protein using LOMETS (Local Meta Threading Server). The fragments expunged from different PDB templates are assembled into full length models by replica exchange Monte Carlo simulations in the second step. Gaps created by unaligned regions are built by *ab initio* modelling. The low free energy state models are

determined by an algorithm, SPICKER, through gathering simulation decoys. In the third step, SPICKER cluster steroids are used as starting material for performing fragment assembly simulation. This simulation is performed to remove steric clashes and improve the global topology of cluster centroids. The lowest energy structures are selected from clustered decoys obtained from second simulation. The final atomic models are built from these selected structures using REMO which optimizes hydrogen bonding network. Five energy minimized models resulted from I TASSER simulations and first model was found to be the best (Figure 5).

Structure validation

PROCHECK analysis showed that only 4 out of 400 residues of mu opioid receptor were in disallowed region. 2.2% of the residues were in generously allowed region, 38% of the residues were in additionally allowed regions and 86.1% of the residues were in most favoured regions. Hence the quality of the predicted model is considered satisfactory (Figure 6).

Docking studies: Interaction of beta endorphin with three opioid receptors

We report first study of interaction of beta endorphin with three opioid receptors. Earlier, interaction of opioid receptors with ligands JOM6, JOM13 and MP16, respectively, were studied by Irina D Pogozheva et al. (2005). The docking studies of beta endorphin with three opioid receptors were performed to determine the important beta endorphin residues involved in interaction. Docking studies were performed with AutoDock tools. Structures of beta endorphin and mu opioid receptor were modelled in the present study. The structures of the other two opioid receptors were obtained from PDB (Protein Data Bank). Hydrogen bonds and hydrophobic interactions between beta endorphin and opioid receptors were studied using LigPlot (Wallace et al., 1995). The docking studies showed that the residues Tyr 1, Gly 2, Gly 3, Gln 11, Thr 12, Pro 13, Leu 14, and Val 15 of beta endorphin interacted with mu opioid receptor (Figure 7). Lys 9, Gln 11, Thr 12, Pro 13, Leu 14, Val 15, Phe 18,

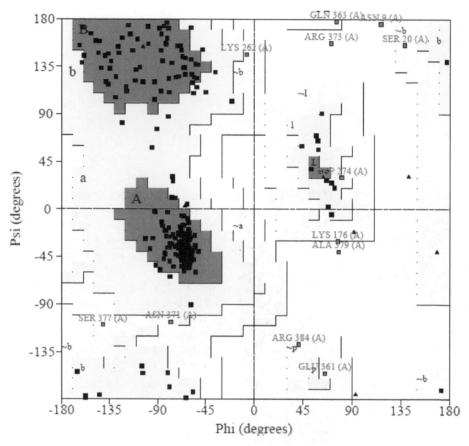

Figure 6. Ramachandran plot for theoretical model of mu opioid receptor.

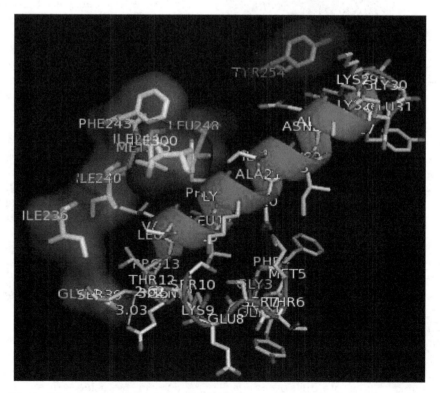

Figure 7. Interaction between beta endorphin and mu opioid receptor after docking.

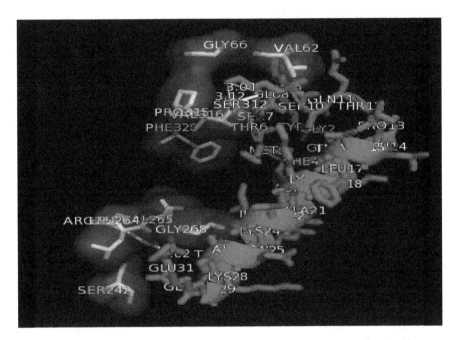

Figure 8. Interaction between beta endorphin and delta opioid receptor after docking.

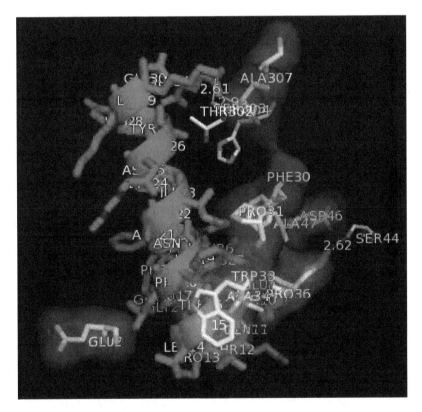

Figure 9. Interaction between beta endorphin and kappa opioid receptor after docking.

Lys 19 and Lys 29 residues of beta endorphin were found to be important for its binding to delta opioid receptor (Figure 8). With kappa opioid receptor, Tyr 1, Gly 2, Gly 3, Phe 4, Thr 6, Lys 9, Phe 18, Ile 22, Ala 26, Tyr 27, Lys 29 and Glu 31 residues of beta endorphin were involved in interaction (Figure 9). ConSurf server predicted

Table 1. The amino acid residues involved in interaction between beta endorphin and three opioid receptor types.

Complex	Residues of beta endorphin involved in interaction
Beta endorphin and mu opioid receptor	Tyr 1, Gly 2, Gly 3, Gln 11, Thr 12, Pro 13, Leu 14, Val 15
Beta endorphin and delta opioid receptor	Lys 9, Gln 11, Thr 12, Pro 13, Leu 14, Val 15, Phe 18, Lys 19, Lys 29
Beta endorphin and kappa opioid receptor	Tyr 1, Gly 2, Gly 3, Phe 4, Thr 6, Lys 9, Phe 18, Ile 22, Ala 26, Tyr 27, Lys 29, Glu 31

Table 2. The amino acid residues involved in interaction between beta endorphin and three opioid receptor types.

Complex	Residues of opioid receptor involved in interaction
Beta endorphin and mu opioid receptor	Thr 69, Leu 76, Pro 297, Tyr 301, Thr 313, Ser 319, His 321, Phe 322, Cys 323, Ala 325, Leu 326
Beta endorphin and delta opioid receptor	Leu 55, Tyr 56, Val 59, Val 62, Arg 244, Leu 245, Ser 247, Val 265, Val 272, Leu 306, Ala 309, Ser 312, Leu 313, Val 316
Beta endorphin and kappa opioid receptor	Glu 2, Ser 3, Pro 4, Ile 5, Gln 6, Glu 35, Pro 36, Ser 44, Asp 46, Ala 47, Glu 50, Thr 302, Ser 303, His 304

residues Tyr1, Gly3, Phe4, Met5, Pro13, Leu14, Thr16, Leu17, Phe18, Asn20, Ala21, Ile 22, Lys24, Lys28, and Lys29 to be evolutionarily conserved (Tables 1 and 2). ConSurf results are found to be in concurrence with the results of docking studies performed between beta endorphin and three opioid receptors. Gln 11 residue of beta endorphin was involved in interaction with mu opioid receptor and delta opioid receptor. Lys 9, Phe 18 and Lys 29 residues of beta endorphin were found to be involved in binding with both delta and kappa opioid receptor. ConSurf predicted high conservation scores for Gln 11, Lys 9, Phe 18 and Lys 29 residues of beta endorphin.

Conclusion

Our work on *ab initio* modelling of beta endorphin and mu opioid receptor was helpful in inferring the binding pattern of these proteins. The docking results and ConSurf analysis results were in agreement with each other manifesting the pivotal residues. Thus, the present work provides valuable insight for future studies into the role of beta endorphin in biological processes.

ACKNOWLEDGEMENT

The authors acknowledge the facilities provided by the Department of Biotechnology, Andhra University, Visakhapatnam, 530003, India.

REFERENCES

Altschul SF, Gish W, Miller W, Myers EW, Lipman DJ (1990). Basic local alignment search tool. J. Mol. Biol. 215:403 [PMID:2231712].

Ambrish R, Alper K, Yang (2010). I-TASSER: a unified platform for automated protein structure and function prediction. Nature Protoc. 5:725-738 PMID:20360767.

Bairoch A, Boeckmann B, Ferro S, Gasteiger E (2004). Swiss Prot: juggling between evolution and stability. Brief Bioinform. 5:39 [PMID: 15153305].

Bernstein FC, Koetzle TF, Williams GJ, Meyer EE Jr, Brice MD, Rodgers JR, Kennard O, Shimanouchi T, Tasumi M (1977). The Protein Data Bank: A Computer-based Archival File For Macromolecular Structures J. Mol. Biol. 112:535. http://zhanglab.ccmb.med.umich.edu/QUARK/

Chrétien M, Seidah NG, Scherrer H (1981). Endorphins: Structure, roles and biogenesis. Can. J. Physiol. Pharmacol. 59(5):413-431. PMID:6263434.

Dalayeun JF, Norès JM, Bergal S (1993). Physiology of beta endorphins. A close up view and a review of the literature. Biomed. Pharmacother. 47(8):311-320. PMID: 7520295.

Glaser F, Pupko T, Paz I, Bell RE, Bechor D, Martz E, Ben-Tal N (2003). ConSurf: identification of functional regions in proteins by surface-mapping of phylogenetic information. Bioinformatics 19:163 [PMID:12499312].

Janecka A, Fichna J, Janecki T (2004). Opioid receptors and their ligands. Curr. Top. Med. Chem. 4(1):1-17. PMID:14754373.

Laskowski RA; MacArthur MW; Moss DS; Thornton JM (1993). PROCHECK: a program to check the stereochemical quality of protein structures. J. Appl. Cryst. 26:283 [doi:10.1107/S0021889892009944].

Li CH, Chung D (1976). Isolation and structure of an untriakontapeptide with opiate activity from camel pituitary glands. PNAS 73(4):1145-1148. PMID 1063395.

Morris AL, MacArthur MW, Hutchinson EG, Thornton JM (1992). Stereochemical quality of protein structure coordinates. Proteins 12:345. [PMID:1579569].

Morris GM, Goodsell DS, Halliday RS, Huey R, Hart WE, Belew RK, Olson AJ (1998). Automated Docking Using a Lamarckian Genetic Algorithm and an Empirical Binding Free Energy Function. J Comput. Chem. 19:1639-1662.

Pogozheva ID, Przydzial MJ, Mosberg HI. 2005 Homology Modeling of Opioid Receptor-Ligand Complexes Using Experimental Constraints AAPS J. 07(02):E434-E448. DOI:10.1208/aapsj070243.

Wallace AC, Roman A Laskowski, Janet M Thornton (1995). LIGPLOT A program to generate schematic diagrams of protein-ligand interactions. Protein Eng. 8(2):127-134. doi:10.1093/protein/8.2.127 http://www.pymol.org

Permissions

The contributors of this book come from diverse backgrounds, making this book a truly international effort. This book will bring forth new frontiers with its revolutionizing research information and detailed analysis of the nascent developments around the world.

We would like to thank all the contributing authors for lending their expertise to make the book truly unique. They have played a crucial role in the development of this book. Without their invaluable contributions this book wouldn't have been possible. They have made vital efforts to compile up to date information on the varied aspects of this subject to make this book a valuable addition to the collection of many professionals and students.

This book was conceptualized with the vision of imparting up-to-date information and advanced data in this field. To ensure the same, a matchless editorial board was set up. Every individual on the board went through rigorous rounds of assessment to prove their worth. After which they invested a large part of their time researching and compiling the most relevant data for our readers.

The editorial board has been involved in producing this book since its inception. They have spent rigorous hours researching and exploring the diverse topics which have resulted in the successful publishing of this book. They have passed on their knowledge of decades through this book. To expedite this challenging task, the publisher supported the team at every step. A small team of assistant editors was also appointed to further simplify the editing procedure and attain best results for the readers.

Apart from the editorial board, the designing team has also invested a significant amount of their time in understanding the subject and creating the most relevant covers. They scrutinized every image to scout for the most suitable representation of the subject and create an appropriate cover for the book.

The publishing team has been an ardent support to the editorial, designing and production team. Their endless efforts to recruit the best for this project, has resulted in the accomplishment of this book. They are a veteran in the field of academics and their pool of knowledge is as vast as their experience in printing. Their expertise and guidance has proved useful at every step. Their uncompromising quality standards have made this book an exceptional effort. Their encouragement from time to time has been an inspiration for everyone.

The publisher and the editorial board hope that this book will prove to be a valuable piece of knowledge for researchers, students, practitioners and scholars across the globe.

List of Contributors

James Lindesay
Computational Physics Laboratory, Department of Physics and Astronomy, Haward University, Washington, DC, 20059 U.S

Tshela E Mason
National Human Genome Center, Haward University, Washington, DC, 20060, U.S

William Hercules
Computational Physics Laboratory, Department of Physics and Astronomy, Haward University, Washington, DC, 20059 U.S

Georgia M Dunston
National Human Genome Center, Haward University, Washington, DC, 20060, U.S
Department of Microbiology, Haward University, Washington, DC, 20059, U.S

Masood ur Rehman Kayani
Department of Biosciences,COMSATS Institute of Information Technology,Bio-Physics Block, Chak Shahzad Campus,Islamabad-44000, Pakistan

Umair Shahzad Alam
Department of Biosciences,COMSATS Institute of Information Technology,Bio-Physics Block, Chak Shahzad Campus,Islamabad-44000, Pakistan

Farida Anjum
Department of Biosciences,COMSATS Institute of Information Technology,Bio-Physics Block, Chak Shahzad Campus,Islamabad-44000, Pakistan

Asif Mir
Department of Biosciences,COMSATS Institute of Information Technology,Bio-Physics Block, Chak Shahzad Campus,Islamabad-44000, Pakistan

Koichi Itoh
The Institute for Theoretical Molecular Biology, 21-13, Rokurokuso-cho, Ashiya, Hyogo, Japan 659-0011

Samina Bilal
Department of Biosciences, Comsats Institute of Information Technology, Bio-Physics Block, Chak Shahzad Campus, Islamabad-44000, Pakistan

Hina Iqbal
Department of Biosciences, Comsats Institute of Information Technology, Bio-Physics Block, Chak Shahzad Campus, Islamabad-44000, Pakistan

Farida Anjum
Pakistan Council for Science and Technology, Islamabad-44000, Pakistan

Asif Mir
Department of Biosciences, Comsats Institute of Information Technology, Bio-Physics Block, Chak Shahzad Campus, Islamabad-44000, Pakistan

Guangli Cao
School of Biology and Basic Medical Science, Medical college of Soochow University, Suzhou, 215123, China
National Engineering Laboratory for Modern Silk, Soochow University, Suzhou, 215123, China

Renyu Xue
School of Biology and Basic Medical Science, Medical college of Soochow University, Suzhou, 215123, China
National Engineering Laboratory for Modern Silk, Soochow University, Suzhou, 215123, China

Yuexiong Zhu
School of Biology and Basic Medical Science, Medical college of Soochow University, Suzhou, 215123, China

Yuhong Wei
School of Biology and Basic Medical Science, Medical college of Soochow University, Suzhou, 215123, China

Chengliang Gong
School of Biology and Basic Medical Science, Medical college of Soochow University, Suzhou, 215123, China
National Engineering Laboratory for Modern Silk, Soochow University, Suzhou, 215123, China

Dlnya A. Mohammed
College of Science, University of Sulaimani, Sulaimani 964, Iraq

Dana Sabir Khder
College of Science, University of Sulaimani, Sulaimani 964, Iraq

Guillaume Koum
Laboratoire D'Informatique, de Mathématiques et de Simulation des Systèmes- ENSP. B. P. 8390, Yaoundé, Cameroun

Augustin Yekel
Laboratoire D'Informatique, de Mathématiques et de Simulation des Systèmes- ENSP. B. P. 8390, Yaoundé, Cameroun

Bernabé Batchakui
Laboratoire D'Informatique, de Mathématiques et de Simulation des Systèmes- ENSP. B. P. 8390, Yaoundé, Cameroun

Josiane Etang
Organisation de Coordination pour la lutte contre les Endémies en Afrique Centrale B. P. 288, Yaoundé, Cameroun

Parul Johri
Department of Biotechnology and Bioinformatics, Dr. D. Y. Patil University, Navi Mumbai, India

Sagar Nagare
Department of Biotechnology and Bioinformatics, Dr. D. Y. Patil University, Navi Mumbai, India

Kakumani Venkateswara Swamy
Bioinformatics Facility, Department Biochemistry, Sri Krishnadevaraya University, Anantapur, Andhra Pradesh, India

Chitta Suresh Kumar
Bioinformatics Facility, Department Biochemistry, Sri Krishnadevaraya University, Anantapur, Andhra Pradesh, India

Salam Pradeep Singh
Bioinformatics Infrastructure Facility, Department of Molecular Biology and Biotechnology, School of Science and Technology Tezpur University, Tezpur 784028, Assam, India

B. K. Konwar
Bioinformatics Infrastructure Facility, Department of Molecular Biology and Biotechnology, School of Science and Technology Tezpur University, Tezpur 784028, Assam, India

Yong Poh Yu
Department of Electrical Engineering, University of Malaya, 50603 Lembah Pantai, Kuala Lumpur, Malaysia

Rosli Omar
Department of Electrical Engineering, University of Malaya, 50603 Lembah Pantai, Kuala Lumpur, Malaysia

Rhett D. Harrison
Xishuangbanna Tropical Botanical Garden, Menglun, Mengla, 666303, Yunnan, China

Mohan Kumar Sammathuria
Malaysia Meteorological Department, Jalan Sultan, 46667 Petaling Jaya, Malaysia

Abdul Rahim Nik
Forest Research Institute, 52110 Kepong, Selangor, Malaysia

Sriram Kannan
Graduate Studies, Molecular Mechanism of Disease, NCMLS, Radboud University, K603, Erasmuslaan17, 6525GE, Nijmegen, Netherlands

Mathilde Pellerin
Université de Lyon, Université Lyon 1, Centre de Génétique et de Physiologie Moléculaire et Cellulaire (CGPHIMC), CNRS UMR5534, F-69622 Lyon, France
Statlife, Espace Maurice Tubiana, 39 rue Camille Desmoulins, 94805 VILLEJUIF, France

Olivier Gandrillon
Université de Lyon, Université Lyon 1, Centre de Génétique et de Physiologie Moléculaire et Cellulaire (CGPHIMC), CNRS UMR5534, F-69622 Lyon, France

James Lindesay
Computational Physics Laboratory, Howard University, Washington, DC, 20060, U.S. 2National Human Genome Center, Howard University, Washington, DC, 20060, U.S

Tshela E. Mason
National Human Genome Center, Howard University, Washington, DC, 20060, U.S

Luisel Ricks-Santi
Cancer Center, Howard University, Washington, DC, 20060, U.S. 4Department of Microbiology, Howard University, Washington, DC, 20060, U.S

William Hercules
Computational Physics Laboratory, Howard University, Washington, DC, 20060, U.S. 2National Human Genome Center, Howard University, Washington, DC, 20060, U.S

Philip Kurian
Computational Physics Laboratory, Howard University, Washington, DC, 20060, U.S. 2National Human Genome Center, Howard University, Washington, DC, 20060, U.S

Georgia M Dunston
National Human Genome Center, Howard University, Washington, DC, 20060, U.S
Department of Microbiology, Howard University, Washington, DC, 20060, U.S

K. Shyamala
Department of Bioinformatics, Stella Maris College, 17, Cathedral Road, Chennai – 600 086, India

A. Suhasini Cherine
Department of Bioinformatics, Stella Maris College, 17, Cathedral Road, Chennai – 600 086, India

E. Nandha Devi
Department of Bioinformatics, Stella Maris College, 17, Cathedral Road, Chennai – 600 086, India

Deepa Gaauthem
Department of Bioinformatics, Stella Maris College, 17, Cathedral Road, Chennai – 600 086, India

P. Senthilraja
Department of Zoology, Annamalai University, Annamalai Nagar, Chidambaram-608002, TN, India

Sunil Kumar Sahu
CAS in Marine Biology, Faculty of Marine Sciences, Annamalai University, Parangipettai-608502, TN, India

K. Kathiresan
CAS in Marine Biology, Faculty of Marine Sciences, Annamalai University, Parangipettai-608502, TN, India

Partha Sarathi Sengupta
Chemistry department, Vivekananda Mahavidyalaya, Burdwan, India, 713103

Snehasis Banerjee
Darjeeling Government College India, Darjeeling, 734101, India

Ashish Kumar Ghosh
Central Institute of Mining and Fuel Research Institute, Dhanbad, India 828108

P. S. Solanki
Birla Institute of Scientific Research, Jaipur, India

M. Krishna Mohan
Birla Institute of Scientific Research, Jaipur, India

P. Ghosh
Birla Institute of Scientific Research, Jaipur, India

S. L. Kothari
Department of Botany, University of Rajasthan, Jaipur, India

K. W. Chang
Department of Leisure and Recreation Studies, Aletheia University, Tainan, 721, Taiwan, Republic of China

Adewale S. Adebayo
Cell Biology and Genetics Unit, Department of Zoology, University of Ibadan, Oyo State, Nigeria

Chiaka I. Anumudu
Cellular Parasitology Programme, Department of Zoology, University of Ibadan, Oyo State, Nigeria

Nazlee Sharmin
Department of Biological Sciences, University of Alberta, Canada

J. Muthukumaran
Centre for Bioinformatics, School of Life Sciences, Pondicherry University, Puducherry – 605 014, India

P. Manivel
Centre for Bioinformatics, School of Life Sciences, Pondicherry University, Puducherry – 605 014, India

M. Kannan
Centre for Bioinformatics, School of Life Sciences, Pondicherry University, Puducherry – 605 014, India

J. Jeyakanthan
Department of Bioinformatics, Alagappa University, Karaikudi - 630 003, India

R. Krishna
Centre for Bioinformatics, School of Life Sciences, Pondicherry University, Puducherry – 605 014, India

Philip Christian C. Zuniga
Department of Computer Science, University of the Philippines, Diliman, Quezon City, Philippines

Hina Iqbal
Department of Bioinformatics and Biotechnology, International Islamic University, Islamabad, Pakistan

Iffat Farzana Anjum
Department of Bioinformatics and Biotechnology, International Islamic University, Islamabad, Pakistan

Asif Mir
Department of Bioinformatics and Biotechnology, International Islamic University, Islamabad, Pakistan

A. Moustafa Bani-Hasan
Biomedical Department, Faculty of Engineering, Cairo University, Egypt

M. Fatma El-Hefnawi
Electronic Research Institute to National Authority for Remote Sensing and Space Science, Egypt

M. Yasser Kadah
Biomedical Department, Faculty of Engineering, Cairo University, Egypt

Amitha Joy
Department of Biotechnology, Sahrdaya college of Engineering and Technology, Kodakara-680684, Thrissur, India

C. A Jubil
Department of Biotechnology, Sahrdaya college of Engineering and Technology, Kodakara-680684, Thrissur, India

P. S Syama
Department of Biotechnology, Sahrdaya college of Engineering and Technology, Kodakara-680684, Thrissur, India

Rohini Menon
Department of Biotechnology, Sahrdaya college of Engineering and Technology, Kodakara-680684, Thrissur, India

Zarrin Basharat
Microbiology and Biotechnology Research Lab, Department of Environmental Sciences, Fatima Jinnah Women University, 46000, Pakistan

Swathi Aluri
Department of Biotechnology, College of Science and Technology, Andhra University, Visakhapatnam - 530003, Andhra Pradesh, India

Ramana Terli
Department of Biotechnology, College of Science and Technology, Andhra University, Visakhapatnam - 530003, Andhra Pradesh, India

Printed in the USA
CPSIA information can be obtained
at www.ICGtesting.com
JSHW052022301024
72690JS00004B/140